CROSS-CULTURAL
AND
INTERCULTURAL
COMMUNICATION

CROSS-CULTURAL
AND
INTERCULTURAL
COMMUNICATION

William B. Gudykunst

California State University, Fullerton

EDITOR

SAGE Publications
International Educational and Professional Publisher
Thousand Oaks ▪ London ▪ New Delhi

For information:

Sage Publications, Inc.
2455 Teller Road
Thousand Oaks, California 91320
E-mail: order@sagepub.com

Sage Publications Ltd.
6 Bonhill Street
London EC2A 4PU
United Kingdom

Sage Publications India Pvt. Ltd.
B-42, Panchsheel Enclave
Post Box 4109
New Delhi 110 017 India

Printed in the United States of America

Library of Congress Cataloging-in-Publication Data

Cross-cultural and intercultural communication / editor, William B. Gudykunst.
    p. cm.
Includes bibliographical references and index.
ISBN 0-7619-2900-2 (Paper)
1. Intercultural communication. I. Gudykunst, William B.
P94.6.C76 2003
302.2—dc21
                          2003005273

03 04 05 06 10 9 8 7 6 5 4 3 2 1

Acquiring Editor:	Todd R. Armstrong
Editorial Assistant:	Veronica K. Novak
Production Editor:	Sanford Robinson
Typesetter:	Christina Hill
Indexer:	Molly Hall
Cover Designer:	Michelle Lee

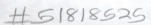

Contents

PART II: INTERCULTURAL COMMUNICATION

Foreword

This volume comprises Parts I and II of the second edition of the *Handbook of International and Intercultural Communication*. The chapters in this volume contain state-of-the-art summaries of research and theory in cross-cultural communication (Part I) and intercultural communication (Part II). These parts of the *Handbook* are being published in paperback form, separate from the parts of the *Handbook* on international and development communication, to make them available for use in upper-division and graduate classes in intercultural communication.

Intercultural communication generally involves face-to-face communication between people from different national cultures, but the term also is used frequently to include all aspects of the study of culture and communication. One major area of research within the broad rubric *intercultural communication* is cross-cultural communication (i.e., the comparison of face-to-face communication across cultures; for example, comparing speech convergence in initial interactions in Japan and the United States). The study of cross-cultural communication grew out of cultural anthropological studies of communication processes in different cultures (e.g., Edward T. Hall's work

published in books such as *The Silent Language, The Hidden Dimension,* and *Beyond Culture*).

Most cross-cultural communication research tends to be comparative. A related area of research that falls under this rubric is cultural communication, which focuses on the role of communication in the creation and negotiation of shared identities (e.g., cultural identities). Research on cultural communication tends to focus on understanding communication within one culture from the insiders' points of view, but there has been comparative research published on cultural communication. Understanding cross-cultural communication is a prerequisite to understanding intercultural communication.

As indicated earlier, research on intercultural communication generally focuses on communication between people from different national cultures (e.g., studying speech convergence when Japanese and U.S. Americans communicate). Some researchers, however, use broad definitions of "culture" and include studies of communication between people from different ethnic/racial groups, able-bodied/disabled communication, intergenerational communication, and other areas of research under the heading of intercultural communication. I view these areas of research, including intercultural communication, as "types" of intergroup communication (i.e., communication between members of different social groups). Because of space limitations and the focus of the other parts of the *Handbook* not included here (international and development communication), the focus of the second edition of the *Handbook of International and Intercultural Communication* was intercultural, not intergroup, communication.

Intercultural communication is a relatively new area of research in the communication discipline. Often, the origins of the term "intercultural communication" are traced to Edward T. Hall's book *The Silent Language,* published in 1959. It was not until the 1970s, however, that courses in intercultural communication began to be offered in universities and texts in the area were published. It was also during the 1970s that intercultural communication divisions were formed in the major professional associations (e.g., Speech [now National] Communication Association, International Communication Association). The *International and Intercultural Communication Annual* was established in 1974 under the editorship of Fred Casmir, and *The International Journal of Intercultural Relations* (which includes a large number of articles on intercultural communication) was established by Dan Landis in 1977.

One way to judge the development of intercultural communication as a field of inquiry is by looking at theories in the area. Probably the first theory in the area was Young Yun Kim's integrative theory of intercultural adaptation, which was published in *Human Communication Research* in 1977. The first edited volume on intercultural communication theory was Volume VII of the *International and Intercultural Communication Annual,* edited by William B. Gudykunst in

1983 (published under the title *Intercultural Communication Theory* by Sage). Since that time, Volumes XII (edited by Young Yun Kim and William B. Gudykunst in 1988; published under the title *Theories in Intercultural Communication* by Sage) and XIX (edited by Richard L. Wiseman in 1995; published under the title *Intercultural Communication Theory* by Sage) of the *Annual* also have focused on theory.

The original volume of the *Annual* (1983) focusing on theory contained mainly discussions of theoretical perspectives (e.g., rules, constructivism, systems, linguistics, phenomenology) for the study of intercultural communication and only a couple of formal theories. The most recent volume (1995) contains a large number of theories from a wide variety of theoretical perspectives. Today, there are well-established theories (e.g., theories that have been tested and gone through several revisions) in intercultural communication supported by extensive lines of research from numerous theoretical perspectives (updated versions of many of these theories will be included in *Theorizing About Culture and Communication* [tentative title], edited by William B. Gudykunst and to be published by Sage in 2004). Some of these theories are extensions of theories from other areas of communication research (e.g., interpersonal communication), but most were developed specifically to describe or explain specific aspects of intercultural communication.

The state of theory and research in intercultural communication has made tremendous progress since the 1970s and the 1980s. Taken together, the chapters in this volume provide a summary of the state of our knowledge about cross-cultural and intercultural communication. As indicated earlier, the volume is divided into two parts: cross-cultural communication (Part I) and intercultural communication (Part II). Each part of this volume begins with an introduction to the part, then there is a chapter on theory, and each part ends with a chapter on research issues. In between the theory and research chapters are chapters containing reviews of the major substantive areas of research. I overview the chapters in the introductions to each part. I also provide cross-references to other recent publications that are related directly to the chapters in this volume, as well as references for material not included in this volume in the introductions to each part.

This volume would not have been possible without the contributions of the authors. I want to thank them for doing excellent work in a timely fashion and for staying within the space limitations imposed upon them. I also want to thank Margaret Seawell and Todd Armstrong, the communication editors at Sage, for supporting the publication of the *Handbook* in paperback form.

Bill Gudykunst
Laguna Beach, CA

PART I

Cross-Cultural Communication

Introduction

William B. Gudykunst

The purpose of this part is to examine how communication varies across cultures. I draw a distinction between cross-cultural and intercultural aspects of communication. Cross-cultural involves comparisons of communication across cultures (Note: I include cultural communication, emic analyses of communication within cultures, with cross-cultural in the *volume*). Intercultural communication involves communication between people from different cultures. Most authors use this conceptualization in Parts I and II. This part focuses on cross-cultural communication, and Part II focuses on intercultural communication.

It was difficult to decide what to include in this section. One reason for this is that the boundary between cross-cultural communication and cross-cultural psychology is not always clear, and some psychological processes

(e.g., perception) clearly are part of the communication process. In recent years, the second edition of the *Handbook of Cross-Cultural Psychology* was published (Berry, Dasen, & Saraswathi, 1997; Berry, Poortinga, & Pandey, 1997; Berry, Segall, & Kâgitçibasi, 1997), and the *Handbook of Culture and Psychology* (Matsumoto, in 2001b) was published recently. Many of the chapters in these volumes are related directly to the study of communication across cultures (e.g., Mohanty & Perregaux, 1997; Russell, Deregowski, & Kinnear, 1997; Schliemann, Carraher, & Ceci, 1997).

Another reason it was difficult to decide what to include in this section has to do with the close connection between ethnicity and communication. Research comparing communication across ethnic groups within cultures could be included under the rubric of cross-cultural communication. Given space limitations and the fact that two recent volumes address the issues of communication across ethnic groups (e.g., Gudykunst, 2001; Johnson, 1999), I decided not to include a chapter on ethnicity in this section.

This part is divided into chapters based on the major processes involved in communication. Not all of the processes could be included, given the space limitations. Influence processes, for example, are not included. There is, however, a recent book in this area (Wosinska, Cialdini, Barrett, & Reykowski, 2000). Smith (2001) also reviews social influence from a cultural perspective. Gender issues are not examined, but Best and Williams (2001) provide an excellent review of this area of research. Perception processes also are not included in this section. Russell et al. (1997), however, provide a review of this topic.

The first chapter is Gudykunst and Lee's review of cross-cultural communication theories. They begin by looking at how culture can be treated as a theoretical variable. Gudykunst and Lee contend that dimensions of cultural variability (e.g., individualism-collectivism) can be used to make theoretical predictions at the cultural level. They also point out, however, that individual-level factors that mediate the influence of dimensions of cultural variability on communication (e.g., self construals) must be taken into consideration. Gudykunst and Lee examine how theoretical predictions can be made based on individualism-collectivism (see also Kâgitçibasi, 1997; Triandis, 2001) and Hofstede's (1991, 2001) dimensions of cultural variability. They also summarize the major theories that explain specific aspects of communication across cultures. Gudykunst and Lee conclude by providing criteria for evaluating cross-cultural communication theories.

The second chapter is Philipsen's analysis of cultural communication. Cultural communi-

nication generally looks at the influence of communication or, more specifically, the role of communication in the creation and negotiation of shared identities. Philipsen isolates two principles of cultural communication and examines research related to these principles. The first principle is: "Every communal conversation bears traces of culturally distinctive means and meaning of communicative conduct." The second principle is: "Communication is a heuristic and performative resource for performing the cultural function in the lives of individuals and communities." Spencer-Oatey's (2000) volume on discourse process across cultures and Kim's (2001) review of indigenous psychologies complement Philipsen's analysis.

The third chapter is Lim's analysis of language and verbal communication. He begins by reviewing the Sapir-Whorf hypothesis. Following this, he examines how verbal communication varies across cultures. Lim concludes by looking at the possibility of language universals. There are several recent major reviews related to issues in Lim's chapter. Mohanty and Perregaux (1997), for example, examine research on language acquisition across culture. Kim (1999) summarizes motivations for verbal communication across cultures. As mentioned earlier, Wosinska et al. (2000) and Smith (2001) examine influence processes across cultures, and Spencer-Oatey's (2000) volume contains studies of discourse processes across cultures.

The fourth chapter is Andersen, Hecht, Hoobler, and Smallwood's review of nonverbal communication across cultures. This chapter is an update of Andersen and Hecht's chapter from the first edition of the *Handbook*. Andersen et al. review the major theoretical dimensions that can be used to explain nonverbal communication across cultures (i.e., immediacy, individualism, gender, power distance, uncertainty avoidance, low and high context; these dimensions also are discussed in Chapter 2). They summarize research that is theoretically consistent with these dimensions.

The fifth chapter is Matsumoto, Franklin, Choi, Rogers, and Tatani's analysis of emotions across cultures. Matsumoto et al. review research on perceptions of emotions and expression of emotions across cultures with particular emphasis on studies of the expression of emotion in the face. They provide a table that summarizes the methods and findings for studies in this area. Matsumoto et al. also summarize research that can be explained using the dimensions of cultural variability discussed in Chapter 2. Mesquita, Frijda, and Scherer (1997) provide another review in this area that complements Matsumoto et al.'s. Matsumoto (2001a) provides a historical review of this area of research and provides suggestions for future research.

The sixth chapter is Stephan and Stephan's review of social cognition and affect across cultures. They begin by presenting a model that can be used to explain the role of cognition and affect in behavior. Stephan and Stephan examine the major cognitions relevant to intercultural communication such as ethnocentrism, stereotyping, cognitive biases, and social identities. They also look at the role of affect in intercultural communication focusing on intergroup anxiety, affective responses to injustice, prejudice, and moods. They conclude by looking at how the influence of ethnocentrism, stereotypes, cognitive biases, cultural differences, and social identities can be reduced in intercultural communication. Semin and Zwier (1997) and Kashima (2001) also provide reviews of social cognition across cultures that complement Stephan and Stephan's analysis.

The seventh chapter is Ting-Toomey and Oetzel's analysis of theory and research on face-negotiation and conflict management across cultures. The material in this chapter draws on Ting-Toomey's face-negotiation

theory but includes other lines of research and theory as well. They summarize how dimensions of cultural variability and self construals influence face, facework, and conflict styles. Ting-Toomey and Oetzel (2001) expand upon the material in their chapter and also look at intercultural conflict management. Kim and Leung's (2000) review of conflict management and Earley's (1997) analysis of face complement Ting-Toomey and Oetzel's chapter. Leung and Stephan (2001) review research on distributive, procedural, and retributive justice and perceptions of injustice across cultures. This research provides a background for understanding conflict management across cultures.

The final chapter is Gudykunst's analysis of the issues facing individuals doing theory-based cross-cultural communication research. Gudykunst focuses on methodological issues that need to be taken into consideration to conduct cross-cultural research to test cross-cultural communication theories. The issues examined include making theoretical predictions, designing cross-cultural research, isolating effects to be studied, establishing equivalence, developing derived etic measures, and establishing reliability/validity of measures. He concludes by isolating major problems with recent research that hinders adequately testing cross-cultural theories. The problems isolated include the cultures studied (e.g., a focus on Asian cultures), using only one dimension of cultural variability, the numbers of cultures studied (e.g., four are needed to test one dimension of cultural variability), representativeness of respondents, and methods of data analysis.

Taken together, the chapters in this section provide an extensive summary of what we know about cross-cultural variations in communication. All of the authors provide plausible suggestions for future cross-cultural research in the areas of their reviews. I hope readers will use these chapters as resources for constructing new cross-cultural theories and for conducting cross-cultural research.

REFERENCES

Berry, J. W., Dasen, P. R., & Saraswathi, T. S. (Eds.). (1997). *Handbook of cross-cultural psychology: Vol. 2. Basic processes and human development* (2nd ed.). Boston: Allyn & Bacon.

Berry, J. W., Poortinga, Y. H., & Pandey, J. (Eds.). (1997). *Handbook of cross-cultural psychology: Vol. 1. Theory and method* (2nd ed.). Boston: Allyn & Bacon.

Berry, J. W., Segall, M. H., & Kâgitçibasi, Ç. (Eds.). (1997). *Handbook of cross-cultural psychology: Vol. 3. Social behavior and applications* (2nd ed.). Boston: Allyn & Bacon.

Best, D., & Williams, J. (2001). Gender and culture. In D. Matsumoto (Ed.), *Handbook of culture and psychology* (pp. 195-219). New York: Oxford University Press.

Earley, P. C. (1997). *Face, harmony, and social structure.* New York: Oxford University Press.

Gudykunst, W. B. (2001). *Asian American ethnicity and communication.* Thousand Oaks, CA: Sage.

Hofstede, G. (1991). *Cultures and organizations: Software of the mind.* London: McGraw-Hill.

Hofstede, G. (2001). *Culture's consequences* (2nd ed.). Thousand Oaks, CA: Sage.

Johnson, F. (1999). *Speaking culturally: Language diversity in the United States.* Thousand Oaks, CA: Sage.

Kâgitçibasi, Ç. (1997). Individualism and collectivism. In J. W. Berry, M. H. Segall, & Ç. Kâgitçibasi (Eds.), *Handbook of cross-cultural psychology: Vol. 3. Social behavior and applications* (2nd ed., pp. 1-50). Boston: Allyn & Bacon.

Kashima, Y. (2001). Culture and social cognition. In D. Matsumoto (Ed.), *Handbook of culture and psychology* (pp. 325-360). New York: Oxford University Press.

Kim, M. S. (1999). Cross-cultural perspectives on motivations of verbal communication. In M. Roloff (Ed.), *Communication yearbook 22* (pp. 51-90). Thousand Oaks, CA: Sage.

Kim, M. S., & Leung, T. (2000). A multicultural view of conflict management styles. In M. Roloff (Ed.), *Communication yearbook 23* (pp. 227-270). Thousand Oaks, CA: Sage.

Kim, U. (2001). Culture, science, and indigenous psychologies. In D. Matsumoto (Ed.), *Handbook of culture and psychology* (pp. 51-75). New York: Oxford University Press.

Leung, K., & Stephan, W. (2001). Social justice from a cultural perspective. In D. Matsumoto (Ed.), *Handbook of culture and psychology* (pp. 375-410). New York: Oxford University Press.

Matsumoto, D. (2001a). Culture and emotion. In D. Matsumoto (Ed.), *Handbook of culture and psychology.* New York: Oxford University Press.

Matsumoto, D. (Ed.). (2001b). *Handbook of culture and psychology* (pp. 171-194). New York: Oxford University Press.

Mesquita, B., Frijda, N., & Scherer, K. (1997). Culture and emotion. In J. W. Berry, P. R. Dasen, & T. S. Saraswathi (Eds.), *Handbook of cross-cultural psychology: Vol. 2. Basic processes and human development* (2nd ed., pp. 255-298). Boston: Allyn & Bacon.

Mohanty, A., & Perregaux, C. (1997). Language acquisition and bilingualism. In J. W. Berry, P. R. Dasen, & T. S. Saraswathi (Eds.), *Handbook of cross-cultural psychology: Vol. 2. Basic processes and human development* (2nd ed., pp. 217-254). Boston: Allyn & Bacon.

Russell, P., Deregowski, J., & Kinnear, P. (1997). Perception and aesthetics. In J. W. Berry, P. R. Dasen, & T. S. Saraswathi (Eds.), *Handbook of cross-cultural psychology: Vol. 2. Basic processes and human development* (2nd ed., pp. 107-141). Boston: Allyn & Bacon.

Schliemann, A., Carraher, D., & Ceci, S. (1997). Everyday cognition. In J. W. Berry, P. R. Dasen, & T. S. Saraswathi (Eds.), *Handbook of cross-cultural psychology: Vol. 2. Basic processes and human development* (2nd ed., pp. 177-216). Boston: Allyn & Bacon.

Semin, G., & Zwier, S. (1997). Social cognition. In J. W. Berry, M. H. Segall, & Ç. Kâgitçibasi (Eds.), *Handbook of cross-cultural psychology: Vol. 3. Social behavior and applications* (2nd ed., pp. 51-76). Boston: Allyn & Bacon.

Smith, P. (2001). Cross-cultural studies of social influence. In D. Matsumoto (Ed.), *Handbook of culture and psychology* (pp. 361-374). New York: Oxford University Press.

Spencer-Oatey, H. (Ed.). (2000). *Culturally speaking*. London: Continuum.

Ting-Toomey, S., & Oetzel, J. (2001). *Managing intercultural conflicts effectively*. Thousand Oaks, CA: Sage.

Triandis, H. C. (2001). Individualism and collectivism. In D. Matsumoto (Ed.), *Handbook of culture and psychology* (pp. 35-50). New York: Oxford University Press.

Wosinska, W., Cialdini, R. B., Barrett, D. W., & Reykowski, J. (Eds.). (2000). *The practice of social influence in multiple cultures*. Hillsdale, NJ: Lawrence Erlbaum.

1

Cross-Cultural Communication Theories

WILLIAM B. GUDYKUNST
California State University, Fullerton

CARMEN M. LEE
University of California, Santa Barbara

There are several approaches to incorporating culture into communication theories. First, culture can be viewed as part of the communication process in theories (e.g., Applegate & Sypher, 1983, 1988, view culture as part of constructivist theory; Cronen, Chen, & Pearce, 1988, view culture as part of coordinated management of meaning theory). Second, communication can be viewed as creating culture (see the discussion of cultural communication by Philipsen, Chapter 3 in this volume). Third, theories designed in one culture can be generalized to other cultures (e.g., Gudykunst & Nishida, 2001), or culture can be treated as a boundary condition for propositions within theories. Fourth, theories can be generated to explain communication between people from different cultures

(see Gudykunst, Chapter 10 in this volume). Fifth, theories can be designed to explain how communication varies across cultures.[1] This is the approach to theory examined in this chapter.

We begin by explaining how culture can be treated as a theoretical construct in theories of communication. One way to accomplish this is to focus on dimensions of cultural variability. Second, we examine individualism-collectivism, the dimension of cultural variability that is used most widely to explain how communication varies across cultures. Third, we present other dimensions of cultural variability that can be used to explain how communication varies across cultures (i.e., Hofstede's, 1980, 1991, 2001, dimensions of cultural variability). Fourth, we

AUTHORS' NOTE: Portions of this chapter are adapted from Gudykunst's earlier writings on cultural variability in communication (e.g., W. B. Gudykunst, *Bridging Differences*, 3rd ed., Sage, 1998).

summarize current theories designed to explain cultural variability in specific aspects of communication (e.g., face-negotiation theory, conversational constraints theory). Finally, we conclude by isolating criteria for evaluating cross-cultural theories of communication.

TREATING CULTURE THEORETICALLY IN CROSS-CULTURAL RESEARCH

Over the years, culture has been conceptualized in many ways. Herskovits (1955), for example, views culture as everything that is human made. Geertz (1973), in contrast, sees culture as a system of meanings (see Shore, 1996; Sperber, 1996, for recent cognitive views of culture). Hall (1959) equates culture with communication: "Culture is communication and communication is culture" (p. 169). We find Keesing's (1974) definition useful because it is compatible with all of the approaches to integrating culture with communication theory isolated earlier:

> Culture, conceived as a system of competence shared in its broad design and deeper principles, and varying between individuals in its specificities, is then not all of what an individual knows and thinks and feels about his [or her] world. It is his [or her] theory of what his [or her] fellows know, believe, and mean, his [or her] theory of the code being followed, the game being played, in the society into which he [or she] was born. . . . It is this theory to which a native actor [or actress] refers in interpreting the unfamiliar or the ambiguous, in interacting with strangers (or supernaturals), and in other settings peripheral to the familiarity of mundane everyday life space; and with which he [or she] creates the stage on which the games of life are played. . . . But note that the actor's [or actress's] "theory"

of his [or her] culture, like his [or her] theory of his [or her] language, may be in large measure unconscious. Actors [or actresses] follow rules of which they are not consciously aware, and assume a world to be "out there" that they have in fact created with culturally shaped and shaded patterns of mind. We can recognize that not every individual shares precisely the same theory of the cultural code, that not every individual knows all the sectors of the culture . . . even though no one native actor [or actress] knows all the culture, and each has a variant version of the code. Culture in this view is ordered not simply as a collection of symbols fitted together by the analyst but as a system of knowledge, shaped and constrained by the way the human brain acquires, organizes, and processes information and creates "internal models of reality." (p. 89)

The implicit theories of culture individuals use obviously vary across cultures.

For cross-cultural research to be theoretically based, we need a way to explain the similarities and differences in the implicit theories of the games being played across cultures. Incorporating culture in communication theory requires a way to treat culture as a theoretical variable. Foschi and Hales (1979) point out that when culture is treated as a theoretical variable "culture x and culture y serve to operationally define a characteristic *a,* which the two cultures exhibit to different degrees" (p. 246). There are dimensions on which cultures can be different or similar that can be used to explain communication across cultures (e.g., Hofstede's, 1980, dimensions of cultural variability; Kluckhohn & Strodtbeck's, 1961, value orientations; Parsons & Shils's, 1951, pattern variables). These dimensions describe selected aspects of individuals' implicit theories of the games played in their cultures.

Communication is unique within each culture, and at the same time, there are systematic similarities and differences across cultures. The similarities and differences can be explained and predicted theoretically using dimensions of cultural variability (e.g., individualism-collectivism). In individualistic cultures, for example, individuals take precedence over groups; in collectivistic cultures, groups take precedence over individuals (Triandis, 1988). There are systematic variations in communication that can be explained by individualism-collectivism. To illustrate, members of individualistic cultures emphasize person-based information to predict others' communication, and members of collectivistic cultures emphasize group-based information to predict others' communication (Gudykunst & Nishida, 1986a).

There are general patterns of communication that are consistent with individualism-collectivism, but individualism-collectivism is manifested in unique ways in each culture. In the Japanese culture, for example, collectivism involves a focus on contextualism (Hamaguchi, 1980). The concepts of *wa* ("harmony"), *amae* ("dependency"), and *enryo* ("reserve," "restraint") also are critical to understanding Japanese collectivism (Gudykunst & Nishida, 1994). Other collectivistic cultures emphasize different cultural constructs as part of their collectivistic tendencies. Understanding communication in any culture, therefore, requires culture-general information (i.e., where the culture falls on the various dimensions of cultural variability) and culture-specific information (i.e., the specific cultural constructs associated with the dimensions of cultural variability).

INDIVIDUALISM-COLLECTIVISM

Individualism-collectivism is the major dimension of cultural variability used to explain differences and similarities in communication across cultures. Individualism-collectivism exists at the cultural level (e.g., cultural norms/rules) and the individual level (e.g., individual values). We begin with cultural-level individualism-collectivism.

Cultural-Level Individualism-Collectivism

Individuals' goals are emphasized more than groups' goals in individualistic cultures. Groups' goals, in contrast, take precedence over individuals' goals in collectivistic cultures. In individualistic cultures, "people are supposed to look after themselves and their immediate family only," and in collectivistic cultures, "people belong to ingroups or collectivities which are supposed to look after them in exchange for loyalty" (Hofstede & Bond, 1984, p. 419).

Importance of ingroups. Triandis (1988, 1995, in press) argues that the relative importance of ingroups is the major factor that differentiates individualistic and collectivistic cultures (see also Gudykunst & Bond, 1997; Kâgitçibasi, 1997). Ingroups are groups that are important to their members and groups for which individuals will make sacrifices (Triandis, 1988). Members of individualistic cultures have many specific ingroups (e.g., families, religions, social clubs, professions, to name only a few) that might influence their behavior in any particular social situation. Because there are many ingroups, specific ingroups exert relatively little influence on individuals' behavior. Members of collectivistic cultures have only a few general ingroups (e.g., work groups, universities, families, to name the major ingroups that influence behavior in Asian collectivistic cultures) that influence their behavior across situations. Members of individualistic cultures tend to be universalistic and apply the same value standards to everyone. Members of collectivistic cultures, in contrast, tend to be particularistic and apply different value standards for members of their ingroups and members of outgroups (Gudykunst & Ting-Toomey, 1988).

Ingroups may be the same in individualistic and collectivistic cultures, but their spheres of influence are different. The spheres of ingroups' influence in individualistic cultures is very specific (e.g., ingroups affect behavior in very specific circumstances). The spheres of ingroups' influence in collectivistic cultures is general (e.g., ingroups affect behavior in many different aspects of individuals' lives). In the individualistic culture of the United States, for example, the universities individuals attend tend to influence their behavior only when the individuals are at their universities or at alumni events. In collectivistic cultures such as Japan and Korea, in contrast, the universities individuals attend tend to influence their behavior throughout their adult lives, including situations that do not directly involve their universities.

Ingroups have different rank orders of importance in collectivistic cultures; some, for example, put families ahead of all other ingroups, and others put their companies ahead of other ingroups (Triandis, 1988). To illustrate, the company often is considered the primary ingroup in Japan (Nakane, 1970), but the family tends to be the primary ingroup in other Asian and Latin collectivistic cultures, and the community is the primary ingroup throughout Africa.

Individualism-collectivism affects communication through its influence on cultural norms and rules related to group identities and the differentiation between members of ingroups and outgroups. Cultures tend to be predominantly either individualistic or collectivistic, but both tendencies exist in all cultures. Parsons and Shils (1951), for example, suggest that a self-orientation involves the

"pursuit of private interests" (p. 60), and a collectivity orientation involves the "pursuit of the common interests of the collectivity" (p. 60). They claim that the same behavior can be simultaneously self- and collectivity oriented. To illustrate this position, Parsons and Shils point to department heads in organizations whose actions may be aimed toward their own welfare, their departments' welfare, their firms' welfare, and even their societies' welfare at the same time.

Self-ingroup relationships in collectivistic cultures. In most writing on collectivism, the self-ingroup relationship is portrayed one way. U. Kim (1994) argues, however, that there are three types of self-ingroup relationships that can be isolated: undifferentiated, relational, and coexistence.

The undifferentiated facet of collectivism "is defined by firm and explicit group boundaries, coupled with undifferentiated self-group boundaries" (U. Kim, 1994, p. 33). U. Kim contends that most discussions of collectivism (e.g., Triandis, 1995) and Markus and Kitayama's (1991) notion of interdependent self construals (see below) are based on this type of collectivism. The preceding discussion of collectivism in this chapter is based on this view.

The relational facet of collectivism "is depicted by porous boundaries between ingroup members that allow thoughts, ideas, and emotions to flow freely. It focuses on the relationship shared by in-group members" (U. Kim, 1994, p. 34). The qualities of this type of collectivism have been discussed in terms of *amae* ("dependence") in Japan and *chong* ("affection") in Korea.

The coexistence facet of collectivism separates the public self and private self (U. Kim, 1994). The public self is "enmeshed with collectivist values" (e.g., ingroup solidarity, family loyalty) and "coexists with the private self, which maintains individualist values" (e.g., personal striving) (U. Kim, 1994, p. 36). This relates to the notion of *tatemae* ("conventions") and *honne* ("true intentions") in Japan.

As indicated earlier, U. Kim (1994) argues that most analyses of collectivism focus on the undifferentiated facet of collectivism. U. Kim contends that the relational and coexistence facets of collectivism are used in Southeast Asian cultures. The relational facet is used in the Mexican culture, traditional African cultures, and Pacific Island cultures. The coexistence facet is used in the Bedouin Arab culture and Moroccan culture. Yuki and Brewer's (1999) research suggests that the undifferentiated facet of collectivism is used in the United States more than in Japan. They report that the relational facet of collectivism is used in Japan.

Horizontal versus vertical cultures. Triandis (1995) argues that individualistic and collectivistic cultures can differ whether relations among individuals in the culture are horizontal or vertical. Individuals are not expected to stand out from other members of their ingroups in horizontal cultures. In horizontal cultures, individuals tend to see themselves as the same as others, and there is an emphasis on valuing equality. Individuals are expected to stand out from other members of their ingroups in vertical cultures. In vertical cultures, individuals tend to see themselves as different from others, and equality is not valued highly.

In horizontal, collectivistic cultures, high value is placed on equality, but little value is placed on freedom (Triandis, 1995). In Japan, for example, there is a saying, "The nail that sticks out gets hammered down," which illustrates that members of the culture are not expected to stand out from other ingroup members. In vertical, collectivistic cultures (e.g., the Philippines, Korea), individuals are expected to fit into their ingroups and, at the same time, are allowed or expected to stand out from their ingroups. Individuals in

vertical, collectivistic cultures do not value equality or freedom. In vertical, individualistic cultures (e.g., United States), individuals are expected to act as individuals and try to stand out from others. Individuals in these culture place a low value on equality and a high value on freedom. In horizontal, individualistic cultures (e.g., Sweden, Norway), individuals are expected to act as individuals but, at the same time, not stand out from others. People in these cultures place a high value on equality and freedom.

Is distinctiveness universal? Brewer (1991) argues that individuals have needs for inclusion in social groups as well as distinctiveness from others. Optimal distinctiveness occurs at the point of equilibrium between the two needs, and this involves moderate distinctiveness. Brewer points out that "being highly individuated leaves one vulnerable to isolation. . . . However, total deindividuation provides no basis for comparative appraisal and self-definition" (p. 478). Brewer and Pickett (1999) suggest that inclusion and differentiation are "universal human motives," not cultural values (p. 85).

Vignoles, Chryssochoou, and Breakwell (2000) argue that distinctiveness and similarity play important roles in the construction of identities across cultures. They conclude that

the distinctiveness principle has a fundamental role in establishing meaning in identity, which does not appear to be specific to individualistic cultures. . . . Distinctiveness can be achieved in terms of position, difference, or separateness. These constructs coexist within cultures and individuals, but they will be emphasized differently according to culture and context, and they have different implications for identity processes and behavior. (p. 350)

There is, however, a need to test these conclusions in a variety of contexts and cultures.

Cultural individualism-collectivism and communication. There have been numerous studies using cultural individualism-collectivism to predict various aspects of communication.[2] Members of collectivistic cultures, for example, are more concerned with avoiding hurting others' feelings and not imposing on others than are members of individualistic cultures (M. S. Kim, 1994). Members of individualistic cultures are more concerned with clarity in conversations and view clarity as necessary for effective communication more than members of collectivistic cultures (M. S. Kim, 1994; Kim & Wilson, 1994). Members of individualistic cultures perceive direct requests as the most effective strategies to accomplish their goals, and members of collectivistic cultures perceive direct requests as the least effective strategies (Kim & Wilson, 1994).

Gudykunst and Nishida (1986b) report that Japanese perceive ingroup relationships (e.g., classmate) as more intimate than outgroup relationships (e.g., strangers), but there is no significant difference in perceived intimacy for U.S. Americans. Gudykunst, Yoon, and Nishida (1987) note that the greater the degree of collectivism in cultures (Japan, Korea, United States), the greater the difference in the intimacy of communication, the synchronization of communication, and the difficulty of communication in ingroup and outgroup relationships. Gudykunst, Gao, Schmidt, et al. (1992) find that there is a main effect for group membership (ingroup vs. outgroup) for uncertainty reduction processes (e.g., self-disclosure, uncertainty reduction) in Japan and Hong Kong, but not in the United States and Australia. These findings support Triandis's (1995) argument that there is a greater distinction between ingroups and outgroups in collectivistic cultures than in individualistic cultures.

Summary. Individualism and collectivism exist in all cultures.[3] One tendency, however, tends to predominate in each culture. Cultures that tend to be mainly individualistic include the United States, Canada, Australia, New Zealand, and northern Europe. Cultures that tend to be mainly collectivistic include African, Arab, Asian, Latin, and southern European cultures.

Individualism-collectivism is used widely to explain communication across cultures. Frequently, researchers use individualism-collectivism but do not develop clear rationales as to why this dimension of cultural variability is linked to the variables being studied. These researchers appear to assume that if there is difference in communication expected between the United States and a culture in Asia, for example, it is due to individualism-collectivism. This is not necessarily the case. Individualism-collectivism must be linked to cultural norms and rules regarding self-ingroup relationships. Furthermore, the facet of collectivism (i.e., undifferentiated, relational, coexistence) should be specified.

Individual Factors That Mediate the Influence of Cultural Individualism-Collectivism on Individuals' Communication

Cultural individualism-collectivism influences communication in a culture through the cultural norms and rules associated with the major cultural tendency (e.g., the United States tends to have individualistic norms/rules, Asian cultures tend to have collectivistic norms/rules). In addition to cultural norms/rules, individualism-collectivism also influences the ways individuals are socialized in their cultures. Individuals in a culture generally are socialized in ways consistent with the cultural-level tendencies, but some individuals

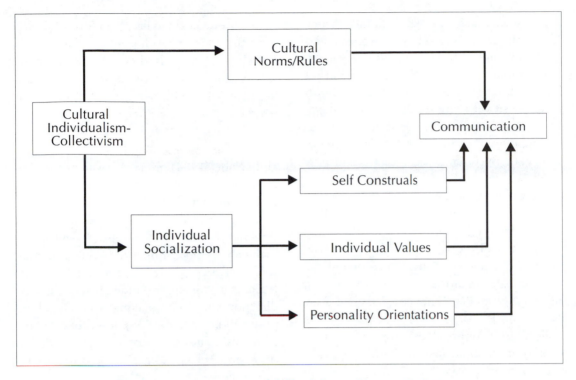

Figure 1.1. The Influence of Individualism and Collectivism on Communication
SOURCE: Gudykunst (1998). Used with permission.

in every culture learn different tendencies (e.g., most individuals in the United States learn mainly individualistic tendencies, but some learn mainly collectivistic tendencies). Cultural individualism-collectivism, therefore, indirectly influences communication through the characteristics individuals learn when they are socialized.

At least three individual characteristics mediate the influence of cultural individualism-collectivism on individuals' communication: their personalities, their individual values, and their self construals. These individual-level characteristics are related to cultural-level individualism-collectivism and can be used to explain variability in communication within cultures. Figure 1.1 schematically illustrates how the influence of cultural individualism-

collectivism on communication is mediated by individual-level factors. Similar figures can be constructed for the other dimensions of cultural variability and the individual-level factors that mediate their effects.

Individuals' communication can be influenced by their personalities, their values, or their self construals. Researchers and theorists must decide which of the three individual-level factors mediate the influence of cultural-level individualism-collectivism with respect to the specific communication variables they are explaining. Some variables may be affected by one and only one individual-level mediator; others may be influenced by more than one mediator. Researchers and theorists should make clear arguments for the specific mediator(s) being used.

Personality orientations. Triandis, Leung, Villareal, and Clack (1985) propose idiocentrism and allocentrism as personality orientations related to individualism and collectivism, respectively.[4] Allocentrism is associated positively with social support and negatively with alienation and anomie (e.g., feelings of normlessness) in the United States. Idiocentrism, in contrast, is associated positively with an emphasis on achievement and perceived loneliness in the United States.

Idiocentric individuals in individualistic cultures see it as natural to "do their own thing" and disregard the needs of their ingroups, and allocentric individuals in individualistic cultures are concerned about their ingroups (Triandis, Bontempo, Villareal, Asai, & Lucca, 1988). Allocentric individuals in collectivistic cultures "feel positive about accepting ingroup norms and do not even raise the question of whether or not to accept them," and idiocentric individuals in collectivistic cultures "feel ambivalent and even bitter about acceptance of ingroup norms" (Triandis et al., 1988, p. 325).

Yamaguchi (1994) suggests that collectivism at the individual level involves giving priority to the collective self over the private self, especially when the two are in conflict. He reports that the more collectivistic Japanese are, the more sensitive they are to others' rejection, the more their affiliative tendencies, and the less they want to be unique. Yamaguchi, Kuhlman, and Sugimori (1995) find these associations hold in Korea and the United States.

Gudykunst, Gao, Nishida, et al. (1992) report that the more idiocentric U.S. Americans are, the less sensitive they are to others' behavior. The more idiocentric Japanese are, the less sensitive they are to others' behavior, the less they pay attention to others' status characteristics, and the less concern they have for behaving in appropriate ways.

Gudykunst, Gao, and Franklyn-Stokes (1996) note that the more idiocentric Chinese and British are, the less they pay attention to others' status characteristics and the less they are concerned with behaving in appropriate ways.

Individual values. Ball-Rokeach, Rokeach, and Grube (1984) argue that values serve as the major component of individuals' personalities and that values help individuals maintain and enhance their self-esteem. Feather (1995) reports that the type of values individuals hold influences the valences (positiveness/negativeness) they attach to different behaviors (e.g., if individuals value self-direction they view making decisions alone positively). Feather (1990) points out that individuals' values influence the way they define situations, but values are not tied to specific situations.

Schwartz (1992) isolates 11 individual value domains.[5] Value domains specify the structure of values and consist of specific values. Schwartz argues that value domains can serve individualistic, collectivistic, or mixed interests. Stimulation, hedonism, power, achievement, and self-direction serve individual interests; tradition, conformity, and benevolence serve collective interests; and security, universalism, and spirituality serve mixed interests.

Schwartz (1990) contends that individualistic and collectivistic values do not necessarily conflict. Individuals can hold both individualistic and collectivistic tendencies, but one tends to predominate. In the mainstream U.S. culture, for example, there are collective tendencies and some subcultures tend to be collectivistic, but most people hold individualistic values. Matsumoto, Weissman, Preston, Brown, and Kupperbusch (1997) use a value approach to assess individualism-collectivism at the individual level (they use one factor, rather than two).

Gudykunst, Matsumoto, et al. (1996) use individual-level individualistic and collectivistic values to predict communication styles. Individualistic values positively predict the use of a dramatic communication style, the use of feelings to guide behavior, and openness and preciseness in communication. Collectivistic values, in contrast, positively predict the tendency to use indirect communication and being interpersonally sensitive.

Self construals. Triandis (1989) argues that cultural variations in individualism-collectivism are linked directly to the ways members of cultures conceive of themselves. Markus and Kitayama (1991, 1998; see also Fiske, Kitayama, Markus, & Nisbett, 1998) contend that people use two different construals of the self: independent and interdependent self construals.[6] Emphasizing independent self construals *predominates* in individualistic cultures, and emphasizing interdependent self construals *predominates* in collectivistic cultures (Gudykunst, Matsumoto, et al., 1996; Singelis & Brown, 1995).[7]

Endorsing the independent self construal involves viewing the self as a unique, independent entity. Geertz (1975), for example, describes the self "as a bounded, unique, more or less integrated motivational and cognitive universe, a dynamic center of awareness, emotion, judgment, and action organized into a distinctive whole and set contrastively both against other such wholes and against a social and natural background" (p. 48). Individualists' cultural "goal of independence requires construing oneself as an individual whose behavior is organized and made meaningful primarily by reference to one's own internal repertoire of thoughts, feelings, and action, rather than by reference to the thoughts,

feelings, and actions of others" (Markus & Kitayama, 1991, p. 226).

The important tasks for individuals emphasizing independent self construals are to be unique, strive for their own goals, express themselves, and be direct (e.g., "say what you mean"; Markus & Kitayama, 1991). The self-esteem of individuals who emphasize independent self construals is based on their abilities to express themselves and their abilities to validate their internal attributes (Markus & Kitayama, 1991).

Markus and Kitayama (1991) point out that "experiencing interdependence entails seeing oneself as part of an encompassing social relationship and recognizing that one's behavior is determined, contingent on, and, to a large extent, organized by what the actor [or actress] perceives to be the thoughts, feelings, and actions of *others* in the relationship" (p. 227). The self-in-relation to specific others guides behavior in specific social situations. Depending on the situation, different aspects of the interdependent self construal guide individuals' behavior. If the behavior is taking place at home, the family interdependent self construal guides behavior; if the behavior is taking place on the job, the coworker interdependent self construal guides behavior.

The important tasks for individuals emphasizing interdependent self construals are to fit in with their ingroups, act in an appropriate fashion, promote their ingroups' goals, occupy their proper places, be indirect, and read other people's minds (Markus & Kitayama, 1991). Markus and Kitayama also point out that "giving in is not a sign of weakness, rather it reflects tolerance, self-control, flexibility, and maturity" (p. 229). The self-esteem of individuals who emphasize interdependent self construals is based on individuals' abilities to adjust to others and their abilities to maintain harmony in social contexts (Markus & Kitayama, 1991).

Self construals are linked to various aspects of communication.[8] Kim, Sharkey, and Singelis (1994), for example, report that using interdependent self construals is associated with concern for others' feelings, and using independent self construals is associated with concern for clarity in conversations. Singelis and Brown (1995) observe that using interdependent self construals is related to using high-context communication (see below).

Gudykunst, Matsumoto, et al. (1996) note that using independent self construals positively predicts the use of dramatic communication, the use of feelings to guide behavior, openness, and preciseness in communication. Gudykunst et al. also report that using interdependent self construals is associated with using indirect communication and being sensitive to others. Their data suggest that self construals are better predictors of communication styles than cultural-level individualism-collectivism or individual-level individualistic and collectivistic values.

Gardner, Gabriel, and Lee (1999) argue that situations prime individuals to think or behave in individualistic or collectivistic ways. They had respondents in the United States and Hong Kong read a story about a trip to a city and circle either collective pronouns (e.g., "we," "they"; the interdependent prime) or independent pronouns (e.g., "I," "me"; the independent prime). The self construal that was primed by circling pronouns influenced the values the respondents endorsed (e.g., respondents in the independent prime condition in both cultures endorsed individualistic values more than those in the interdependent prime in both cultures, and vice versa). This research suggests that situational factors influence the self construals individuals activate.

Everyone has both independent and interdependent self construals, but they tend to use one to guide their behavior more than the other.[9] The critical issue is which self construal predominates to influence individuals' behavior, and which self construal guides their behavior in particular situations.

There are five theoretical issues regarding self construals that need clarification. First, there is a question about the number of aspects of the self that exist. Markus and Kitayama (1991) isolate two: independent and interdependent self construals. Kashima et al. (1995) and Kashima and Hardie (2000), in contrast, propose three aspects of self construals: (1) individual self, (2) relational self, and (3) collective self. Obviously, the number of aspects of the self is critical to the development of cross-cultural theories that include self construals as individual-level mediators of cultural individualism-collectivism.[10]

The second area where theoretical clarification is needed is whether aspects of the self are independent of each other or whether they interact to form self construal "types." Markus and Kitayama (1991) discuss independent and interdependent self construals as though they are independent of each other, and most researchers use this conceptualization. This conceptualization suggests that individuals have both self construals, and one of them guides communication in specific situations. This view is consistent with identity theories that suggest that individuals' behavior is guided by one identity at a time (e.g., Turner, 1987).

Some researchers treat self construals as though they interact to form types. Singelis (1994), for example, uses Berry's (1980) typology of acculturation to isolate four self construal types: (1) bicultural (strong independent, strong interdependent), (2) Western (strong independent, weak interdependent), (3) traditional (weak independent, strong interdependent), and (4) culturally alienated (weak independent, weak interdependent).[11] Ting-Toomey and Kurogi (1998) use self construal types in the most recent version of face-negotiation theory. Whether types exist is an empirical question. If self construals interact to form types, then there will be statistical interactions between the independent and interdependent self construals when they are dichotomized into weak versus strong. If there is no statistical interaction, the types do not exist. The existence of types should not be assumed; it should be tested empirically.[12]

The third issue that needs theoretical clarification regarding self construals is whether they are situation, context, or relationship specific or general (i.e., have similar effects across situations, contexts, or relationships). Markus and Kitayama's (1991) conceptualization suggests that the interdependent self construal is based on specific ingroups. If this is the case, self construals, especially interdependent self construals, should be viewed as situation specific because individuals tend to have one ingroup guiding their behavior in specific situations (e.g., individuals have self construals vis-à-vis the family that guide their behavior when the family is relevant). To date, virtually all theoretical discussions of self construals focus on general self construals (but see Gardner et al., 1999). Gudykunst, Matsumoto, et al. (1996), however, suggest that they should be conceptualized and measured as situation specific.

The fourth issue regarding self construals, independence of self construals, is related to the issue of types, but it is separate. For purpose of illustration only, we *assume* that two self construals exist. If there are independent and interdependent self construals, theoretically they should be orthogonal to each other (e.g., independent of each other) and not mirror images of each other. The independent self construal is *not* the opposite of the interdependent self construal. The independent self construal should *not* correlate positively with one communication variable and the interdependent self construal correlate

negatively with the same communication variable. Independent and interdependent self construals should be related to different variables. There have been many studies where the independent self construal positively predicts a variable and the interdependent self construal negatively predicts the same variable. This is theoretically problematic in our view.

The fifth issue regarding self construals is whether researchers should expect respondents in individualistic cultures to be higher on measures of the independent self construal than respondents in collectivistic cultures, and for respondents in collectivistic cultures to be higher on measures of interdependent self construals than respondents in individualistic cultures. On the surface, these appear to be reasonable expectations. This is not, however, the case. Any sample drawn from a culture may or may not be representative of the cultural tendencies. College student samples, especially in cultures where only a small percentage of the population goes to college, frequently are not representative of their cultures. Similarly, college student samples where the students are living away from home for the first time may not be representative of their cultures, especially in collectivistic cultures. There are numerous studies that have found that the samples are consistent with the cultural tendencies, and there are numerous studies that have found that the samples are not consistent with the cultural tendencies. When the samples are not representative of the cultures, it is imperative that it be taken into consideration in data analysis for cultural-level hypotheses (see Gudykunst, Chapter 9 in this volume).

The five issues raised here are not minor issues. Positions on each of these issues must be taken when cross-cultural theories are constructed incorporating self construals. They also are empirical issues that must be tested in future research.

Low- and High-Context Communication

Individualism-collectivism provides an explanatory framework for understanding cultural similarities and differences in self-ingroup communication. Gudykunst and Ting-Toomey (1988) argue that low-context communication predominates in individualistic and high-context communication predominates in collectivistic cultures.

Hall (1976) differentiates between low- and high-context communication. High-context communication occurs when "most of the information is either in the physical context or internalized in the person, while very little is in the coded, explicit, transmitted part of the message" (Hall, 1976, p. 79). Low-context communication, in contrast, occurs when "the mass of information is vested in the explicit code" (p. 70).

Low- and high-context communication is used in all cultures. One form, however, tends to predominate. Members of individualistic cultures tend to use low-context communication and communicate in a direct fashion. Members of collectivistic cultures, in contrast, tend to use high-context messages when maintaining ingroup harmony is important and communicate in an indirect fashion (Gudykunst & Ting-Toomey, 1988).

Members of individualistic cultures who use low-context communication often assume that indirect communication is ineffective. This, however, is not necessarily the case. High-context communication can be effective or ineffective like low-context communication. Most high-context communication is effective. The effectiveness comes from listeners knowing how to interpret speakers' indirect messages in specific contexts.

Many studies of cultural individualism-collectivism have examined some aspect of low- and high-context communication (e.g.,

Gudykunst, Matsumoto, et al., 1996; M. S. Kim, 1994; Singelis & Brown, 1995). Similarly, many of the studies that have looked at the effect of self construals on communication also have used low- and high-context communication (e.g., Kim et al., 1996; Kim et al., 1994).

HOFSTEDE'S DIMENSIONS OF CULTURAL VARIABILITY

Hofstede (1980, 1983, 1991, 2001) empirically derives four dimensions of cultural variability. The first dimension isolated in his study, individualism, already has been discussed. The other three dimensions are uncertainty avoidance, power distance, and masculinity-femininity.[13] As with individualism-collectivism, there are cultural-level and individual-level manifestations of the three dimensions. The cultural-level effects of the three dimensions of cultural variability influence communication through cultural norms and rules.

Uncertainty Avoidance

Uncertainty avoidance deals with the degree to which members of a culture try to avoid uncertainty. We begin with cultural-level uncertainty avoidance.

Cultural uncertainty avoidance. Members of high uncertainty avoidance cultures have a lower tolerance "for uncertainty and ambiguity, which expresses itself in higher levels of anxiety and energy release, greater need for formal rules and absolute truth, and less tolerance for people or groups with deviant ideas or behavior" than members of low uncertainty avoidance cultures (Hofstede, 1979, p. 395). Members of low uncertainty avoidance cultures have lower stress levels and weaker superegos, and they accept dissent and taking risks more than members of high uncertainty avoidance cultures.

High uncertainty avoidance cultures tend to have clear norms and rules to guide behavior for virtually all situations. Norms and rules in low uncertainty avoidance cultures are not as clear-cut and rigid as those in high uncertainty avoidance cultures. In high uncertainty avoidance cultures, aggressive behavior is acceptable, but individuals prefer to contain aggression by avoiding conflict and competition (Hofstede, 1980). There also is a strong desire for consensus in high uncertainty avoidance cultures, and deviant behavior is not acceptable. Hofstede (1991) points out that uncertainty avoidance should not be equated with risk avoidance. Individuals in

> uncertainty avoiding cultures shun ambiguous situations. People in such cultures look for a structure in their organizations, institutions, and relationships which makes events clearly interpretable and predictable. Paradoxically, they are often prepared to engage in risky behavior to reduce ambiguities, like starting a fight with a potential opponent rather than sitting back and waiting. (p. 116)

Hofstede contends that members of high uncertainty avoidance cultures believe that "what is different, is dangerous" (p. 119), and members of low uncertainty avoidance cultures believe that "what is different, is curious" (p. 119).

High and low uncertainty avoidance exists in all cultures, but one tends to predominate. Cultures that tend to be mainly high in uncertainty avoidance include Japan, Mexico, Greece, France, Chile, Belgium, Argentina, and Egypt. Cultures that tend to be mainly low in uncertainty avoidance include Canada, Denmark, India, Jamaica, Sweden, and the United States.

Individual-level uncertainty avoidance. One individual-level factor that mediates the influence of cultural uncertainty avoidance on communication is the uncertainty-certainty orientation (Gudykunst, 1995).

> There are many people who simply are not interested in finding out information about themselves or the world, who do not conduct causal searches, who could not care less about comparing themselves with others, and who "don't give a hoot" for resolving discrepancies or inconsistencies about the self. Indeed, such people (we call them certainty oriented) will go out of their way not to perform activities such as these (we call people who *do* go out of their way to do such things uncertainty oriented). (Sorrentino & Short, 1986, pp. 379-380)

Uncertainty-oriented individuals are interested in reducing uncertainty, and certainty-oriented individuals try to avoid looking at uncertainty when it is present.

A certainty orientation at the individual level predominates in high uncertainty avoidance cultures. An uncertainty orientation, in contrast, predominates in low uncertainty avoidance cultures.

Power Distance

Power distance is "the extent to which the less powerful members of institutions and organizations accept that power is distributed unequally" (Hofstede & Bond, 1984, p. 419). We begin with cultural-level power distance.

Cultural power distance. Members of high power distance cultures accept power as part of society (e.g., superiors consider their subordinates to be different from themselves and vice versa). Members of high power distance cultures see power as a basic fact in society, and they stress coercive or referent power. Members of low power distance cultures, in contrast, believe power should be used only when it is legitimate and prefer expert or legitimate power.

In summarizing the differences between cultures low in power distance and cultures high in power distance, Hofstede (1991) points out that

> in small power distance countries there is limited dependence of subordinates on bosses, and a preference for consultation, that is, *interdependence* between boss and subordinate. The emotional distance between them is relatively small: subordinates will quite readily approach and contradict their bosses. In large power distance countries there is considerable dependence of subordinates on bosses. Subordinates respond by either *preferring* such dependence (in the form of autocratic or paternalistic boss), or rejecting it entirely, which in psychology is known as *counterdependence*: that is dependence, but with a negative sign. (p. 27)

The power distance dimension focuses on the relationships between people of different statuses (e.g., superiors and subordinates in organization).

Low and high power distance exists in all cultures, but one tends to predominate. Cultures that tend to be mainly high in power distance include Egypt, Ethiopia, Ghana, India, Malaysia, Nigeria, Panama, Saudi Arabia, and Venezuela. Cultures that tend to be mainly low in power distance include Australia, Canada, Denmark, Germany, Ireland, New Zealand, Sweden, and the United States.

Individual-level power distance. One individual-level factor that mediates the influence of cultural power distance on communication

is egalitarianism (Gudykunst, 1995). Egalitarianism involves viewing others as equals.

High egalitarianism predominates in low power distance cultures. Low egalitarianism, in contrast, predominates in high power distance cultures.

Earley and Erez (1997) provide an alternative individual-level view of power distance. They provide a measure based on Hofstede's (1980) description of cultural-level power distance.

Masculinity-Femininity

Masculinity-femininity focuses on gender issues at the cultural and individual levels. We begin with cultural-level masculinity-femininity.

Cultural masculinity-femininity. The major differentiation between masculine and feminine cultures is how gender roles are distributed in a culture.

> *Masculinity* pertains to societies in which social gender roles are clearly distinct (i.e., men are supposed to be assertive, tough, and focused on material success whereas women are supposed to be more modest, tender, and concerned with the quality of life); *femininity* pertains to societies in which social gender roles overlap (i.e., both men and women are supposed to be modest, tender, and concerned with the quality of life). (Hofstede, 1991, pp. 82-83)

Members of cultures high in masculinity value performance, ambition, things, power, and assertiveness (Hofstede, 1980). Members of cultures high in femininity value quality of life, service, caring for others, and being nurturing.

Hofstede (1998) points out that in masculine cultures, women are assigned the role of being tender and taking care of relationships. In feminine cultures, in contrast, both men and women are allowed to engage in these behaviors. In masculine cultures, fathers are expected to deal with facts with the children and mothers should deal with feelings with children. Both parents engage in both behaviors in feminine cultures. In masculine cultures, employees "live in order to work," and in feminine cultures, employees "work in order to live" (p. 16). Masculine cultures focus on ego enhancement, and feminine cultures focus on relationship enhancement, regardless of group ties.

Masculinity and femininity exist in all cultures, but one tends to predominate. Cultures that tend to be mainly masculine include Arab cultures, Austria, Germany, Italy, Japan, Mexico, New Zealand, Switzerland, and Venezuela. Cultures that tend to be mainly feminine include Chile, Costa Rica, Denmark, eastern Africa, Finland, the Netherlands, Portugal, and Sweden (the United States is below the median).

Individual-level masculinity-femininity. One individual-level factor that mediates the influence of cultural masculinity-femininity on communication is psychological sex roles (Gudykunst, 1995). Individuals have masculine gender identities if they exhibit high degrees of stereotypical masculine traits and behaviors (e.g., aggressive, competitive, dominant) and low degrees of stereotypical feminine traits and behaviors (e.g., compassionate, sensitive, warm) (Bem, 1974). Individuals have feminine gender identities if they exhibit high degrees of stereotypical feminine traits and behaviors and low degrees of stereotypical masculine traits and behaviors. Individuals have androgynous gender identities if they exhibit high degrees of stereotypical masculine and feminine traits and behaviors. Individuals have undifferentiated gender identities if they exhibit low degrees of stereotypical masculine and feminine traits and behaviors.[14]

Traditional-gender-oriented individuals (highly masculine men, highly feminine women) tend to organize and recall information about others on the basis of their genders (Bem, 1993). Also, traditional-gender-oriented individuals tend to follow cultural definitions of appropriate behavior. To illustrate, "conventionally masculine men [are] independent but not nurturant, and conventionally feminine women [are] nurturant but not independent" in the U.S. mainstream culture (Bem, 1993, p. 157). Androgyny predominates in feminine cultures, and high masculinity and high femininity predominate in masculine cultures. Best and Williams (1997, in press) review research on gender roles across cultures.

Confucianism

Hofstede (1980) isolates the four dimensions of cultural variability discussed so far. These dimensions, however, may have a Western bias because of the methods used in collecting Hofstede's data.

The Chinese Culture Connection (1987) looked at Hofstede's conclusions using a methodology with a Chinese bias.[15] They isolate four dimensions of cultural variability: Confucian dynamism (e.g., "ordering relationships by status and observing this order," "having a sense of shame"), integration (e.g., "harmony with others," "solidarity with others"), human-heartedness (e.g., "patience," "courtesy," "kindness"), and moral discipline (e.g., "having few desires," "moderation"). Three of these dimensions correlate with dimensions in Hofstede's study: integration correlates with individualism, moral discipline correlates with power distance, and human-heartedness correlates with masculinity-femininity. The only dimension in the Chinese Culture Connection's study that does not correlate with one of Hofstede's dimensions is Confucian dynamism.

The Confucian dynamism dimension involves eight values. Four values are associated positively with the dimension: ordering relationships, thrift, persistence, and having a sense of shame; four are associated negatively with the dimension: protecting one's face, personal steadiness, respect for tradition, and reciprocation. The Chinese Culture Connection (1987) argues that the four positively loaded items reflect a hierarchical dynamism present in Chinese society, and the four negatively loaded items reflect "checks and distractions" to this dynamism.[16]

THEORIES OF CULTURAL VARIABILITY IN COMMUNICATION

Various theorists have attempted to explain cross-cultural differences in communication using cultural-level and/or individual-level dimensions. These theories include face-negotiation theory (FNT; Ting-Toomey, 1988; Ting-Toomey & Kurogi, 1998), conversational constraints theory (CCT; Kim, 1993, 1995), expectancy violations theory (EVT; Burgoon, 1992, 1995), anxiety/uncertainty management theory (AUM theory; Gudykunst, 1995), and communication accommodation theory (CAT; Giles, Mulac, Bradac, & Johnson, 1987). AUM and CAT are theories of intergroup communication that include cross-cultural variability. Only the cross-cultural variability portion of these theories is discussed here. The intergroup portion of these theories is discussed in Gudykunst's "Intercultural Communication Theories" chapter in this volume.

Face-Negotiation Theory

Cultural norms and values influence and shape how members of cultures manage face and how they manage conflict situations. Originally a theory focusing on conflict (Ting-

Toomey, 1985), FNT has been expanded to integrate cultural-level dimensions and individual-level attributes to explain face concerns, conflict styles, and facework behaviors (e.g., Ting-Toomey, 1988; Ting-Toomey & Kurogi, 1998; see also Ting-Toomey & Oetzel, Chapter 8 in this volume).

Ting-Toomey (1985) argues that conflict is a face-negotiation process whereby individuals engaged in conflict have their situated identities or "faces" threatened or questioned (Ting-Toomey, 1988). Face is "a claimed sense of favorable social self-worth that a person wants others to have of her or him" (Ting-Toomey & Kurogi, 1998, p. 187). Although only mentioned briefly in the 1988 version of the theory, the concept of face is an integral part of the most recent version of the theory (Ting-Toomey & Kurogi, 1998).

The current version of FNT (Ting-Toomey & Kurogi, 1998) includes 32 propositions (20 propositions are based on dimensions of cultural variability, and 12 propositions are based on individual-level mediators of cultural variability). Ting-Toomey and Kurogi (1998) argue that members of collectivistic cultures use other-oriented face-saving strategies and use other-face approval-enhancement interaction strategies more than members of individualistic cultures. Conversely, members of individualistic cultures use more self-oriented face-saving strategies and use self-face approval-seeking interaction strategies more than members of collectivistic cultures.

Members of low power distance cultures defend and assert their personal rights more than members of high power distance cultures. Members of high power distance cultures, in contrast, perform their ascribed duties responsibly more than members of low power distance cultures. Members of low power distance cultures tend to minimize the respect-deference distance via information-based interactions more than members of high power distance cultures. Members of high power distance cultures are concerned with vertical facework interactions (e.g., they maximize the respect-deference distance via formal interaction) more than members of low power distance cultures.

Ting-Toomey and Kurogi (1998) contend that members of collectivistic cultures use relational, process-oriented conflict strategies more than members of individualistic cultures. Members of individualistic cultures, in contrast, tend to use more substantive, outcome-oriented conflict strategies than members of collectivistic cultures. High-status members of high power distance cultures tend to use verbally indirect facework strategies (e.g., indirect questioning and relational pressuring) more than low-status members of high power distance cultures. High-status members of low power distance cultures tend to use verbally direct strategies (e.g., criticism, reprimands) more than high-status members of high power distance cultures.

Ting-Toomey and Kurogi (1998) also link individual-level mediators of the dimensions of cultural variability to face behaviors and conflict styles. Emphasizing self-face leads to using dominating/competing conflict styles and substantive conflict resolution modes. Emphasizing other-face leads to using avoiding/obliging conflict styles and relational conflict resolution modes.

Ting-Toomey and Kurogi (1998) use the type model of self construals, rather than treating self construals as independent of each other. Independent self construal types tend to use dominating/competing conflict styles and substantive conflict resolution modes. Interdependent self construal types tend to use avoiding/obliging conflict styles and relational conflict resolution modes. Biconstrual types (high on both self construals) use substantive and relational conflict resolution modes, and ambivalent types (low on both self construals) tend not to use either.

Conversational Constraints Theory

Conversations are goal directed and require coordination between communicators in CCT (Kim, 1995). Individuals pursue a wide variety of interaction goals such as gaining compliance, seeking information, or altering relationships. In the pursuit of these goals, individuals generate messages while adhering to a variety of constraints, either personal or cultural. Conversational constraints influence the manner in which messages are constructed and individuals' conversational styles (Kim, 1993).

Kim (1993) isolates two types of conversational constraints: social relational and task oriented. Social-relational constraints emphasize concern for others that focus on avoiding hurting hearers' feelings and minimizing imposition on hearers. Embedded in this constraint is the notion that individuals may take into account how their projected actions may affect targets' (hearers') feelings when they plan to achieve interaction goals. Communicative acts may threaten others to the extent that the acts impose on others' autonomy. The task-oriented constraint emphasizes a concern for clarity (e.g., the degree to which the intentions of messages are communicated explicitly) (Kim, 1995).

Kim (1993) explains cross-cultural differences in the selection of communicative strategies. There are six propositions in the theory. Kim (1993) posits that collectivism influences the importance members of cultures place on relational concerns in conversations. The emphasis on relational concerns centers on face. Members of collectivistic cultures view face-supporting behavior (e.g., avoiding hurting the hearers' feelings, minimizing imposition, and avoiding negative evaluation by the hearer) as more important than members of collectivistic cultures when pursuing goals (P1). Members of collectivistic cultures have higher thresholds for face support and select strategies that maximize face support more than members of individualistic cultures (P2, P3). Members of individualistic cultures, in contrast, view clarity as more important than members of collectivistic cultures when pursuing goals (P4). Members of individualistic cultures have higher thresholds and maximize concern for clarity more than members of collectivistic cultures (P5, P6).

At the individual level, Kim (1995) uses self construals to explain variability in conversational constraints. There are 11 propositions in this theory. Individuals who emphasize interdependent self construals have the desire to avoid the loss of face and to be accepted by ingroup members. Individuals who emphasize independent self construals tend to be pointed, direct, clear, unambiguous, and concise in their choice of verbal tactics.

Kim (1995) argues that individuals who activate interdependent self construals view not hurting hearers' feelings and minimizing impositions on hearers in the pursuit of their goals as more important than individuals who activate independent self construals (P1, P2).[17] Individuals who activate independent self construals view clarity as more important in pursuing goals than individuals who activate interdependent self construals (P3). Individuals who activate both self construals are concerned with relational and clarity constraints (P4). Individuals who do not activate either self construal do not view clarity and relational constraints as important (P5).

In addition to self construals, Kim (1995) uses need for approval, need for dominance, and gender roles to explain conversational constraints. The more individuals need approval, the more important they view being concerned with hearers' feelings and minimizing impositions on hearers (P6, P7). The more individuals need to be dominant, the more importance they place on clarity (P8). The more masculine individuals' psychological sex roles, the more importance they place on

clarity (P9). The more feminine individuals' psychological sex roles, the more importance they place on not hurting hearers' feelings and not imposing on hearers (P10, P11).

Kim (1993, 1995) links both dimensions of cultural variability and individual-level factors that mediate the effects of dimensions of cultural variability to the same communication processes. There is research supporting the cultural-level (e.g., M. S. Kim, 1994) and the individual-level (e.g., Kim et al., 1994) predictions, as well as comparisons of the effect of the two levels (e.g., Kim et al., 1996).

Expectancy Violations Theory

Every culture has guidelines for human conduct that provide expectations for how others will behave (Burgoon, 1978). EVT frames interpersonal communication within the context of the expectations held by individuals and how individuals respond to violations of those expectations. Initially designed to deal with nonverbal proxemic violations (Burgoon, 1978), EVT has been used to understand cross-cultural variations in communication and intercultural interactions (Burgoon, 1992, 1995; Gudykunst & Ting-Toomey, 1988).[18]

Communication expectancies are patterns of verbal and nonverbal behavior that are anticipated (Burgoon & Walther, 1990). Expectancies are based on social norms and rules as well as individual-specific patterns of typical behavior (Burgoon, 1995). Individual deviation in expected behavior causes arousal or alertness in others. Whether or not deviant behavior is interpreted as positive or negative depends on communicators' valences. Communicators' valences refer to characteristics of individuals (e.g., how attractive and familiar they are perceived to be). Once violations have occurred, factors such as the communicators (e.g., salient features of individuals such as personalities, social skills), the relationships (e.g., the degree of familiarity, attraction, similarity between interaction partners), and the contexts (e.g., environmental constraints, situations) are taken into consideration in evaluating expectation violations. Burgoon (1995) argues that "the communicator's positive or negative characteristics are posited to moderate how violations are interpreted and evaluated" (p. 201).

Burgoon (1992) contends that the "content" of each culture's expectancies vary along dimensions of cultural variability.[19] Specifically, members of collectivistic cultures expect greater verbal indirectness, politeness, and nonimmediacy than members of individualistic cultures.

Uncertainty avoidance is linked to expectancies to the extent that communication behavior is regulated by rules and social norms (Burgoon, 1995). Low uncertainty avoidance cultures have fewer rules and norms regulating behavior than high uncertainty avoidance cultures. Members of high uncertainty avoidance cultures tend to be more intolerant of deviant behavior than are members of low uncertainty avoidance cultures.

Power distance influences how violations of high status and low status are interpreted (Burgoon, 1995). A violation (e.g., nonverbal proxemic violation) by a high-status person in a high power distance culture, for example, would be perceived as a violation of ascribed role behavior, and such an action would inevitably produce stress and anxiety, a negative outcome.

Anxiety/Uncertainty Management Theory

AUM theory focuses on effective interpersonal and intergroup communication (e.g., Gudykunst, 1995) and incorporates cross-cultural variability in anxiety/uncertainty management processes. The basic contention of the theory is that effective communication emerges from mindfully managing uncertainty and anxiety. Other factors (e.g., social identities, attitudes) that vary across cultures influence the amount of uncertainty and anxiety that individuals experience. Our focus here is on the cross-cultural variability portion of the theory. Gudykunst summarizes the intergroup part of the theory in the "Intercultural Communication Theories" chapter in this volume.

Gudykunst (1995) links individualism-collectivism to numerous variables related to the self and ingroup (e.g., self and self-concept, social and personal identities, self-monitoring, social categorization). Generally, he argues that members of individualistic cultures need to sustain their independent self construals, allow personal identities to influence their behavior, and self-monitor more with strangers than do members of collectivistic cultures. Similarly, he suggests that members of collectivistic cultures use interdependent self construals to guide their behavior, allow social identities to influence their behavior, and are concerned with social appropriateness when interacting with strangers more than are members of individualistic cultures.

Gudykunst (1995) also links uncertainty avoidance to numerous variables (e.g., reactions to strangers, social categorization, and situational processes). Generally, he argues that members of high uncertainty avoidance cultures tend to display rigidity of attitudes toward strangers, indicate an inability to tolerate ambiguity when interacting with strangers, have negative expectations regarding strangers' behavior, and view the situation in which interaction with strangers occurs as formal more than members of low uncertainty avoidance cultures. Power distance also is linked to AUM processes. Members of high power distance cultures are less able to complexly process information about strangers and less able to display cooperative behavior with strangers than are members of low power distance cultures.

Masculinity-femininity also is linked to numerous variables in AUM theory (e.g., self and self-concept, motivation, reactions to strangers, and social categorization). To illustrate, Gudykunst (1995) argues that members of highly masculine cultures demonstrate lower interdependence between themselves and strangers than do members of highly feminine cultures.

Communication Accommodation Theory

CAT is concerned with understanding interactions between people of different groups by assessing the language, nonverbal behavior, and paralanguage individuals use (Gallois, Giles, Jones, Cargile, & Ota, 1995). Individuals signal their attitudes (e.g., like or dislike) toward each other through different strategies (e.g., convergence or moving toward speakers, divergence or moving away from speakers, and maintenance or not attempting to move toward or away from speakers). The intergroup aspects of this theory are examined in Gudykunst's "Intercultural Communication Theories" chapter in this volume. Our focus here is on how cross-cultural variability is incorporated in the theory (see Williams et al., 1997, for a cross-cultural study based on CAT).

CAT incorporates the influence of individualism and collectivism on accommodation processes. Gallois et al. (1995) contend that individualism and collectivism can be instrumental in what strategies of accommodation people adopt. In individualistic cultures, verbal communication tends to be personal and individuals tend to converge toward others more than do members of collectivistic cultures.

Members of individualistic cultures tend to react to convergence from outgroup members

in a positive manner, and reciprocally converge toward outgroup members (Gallois et al., 1995). Members of collectivistic cultures, in contrast, use a verbal contextual style (e.g., a style that emphasizes role relationships) more than members of individualistic cultures. This style tends to result in politeness strategies being used and formal language being used with outgroup members.

Members of collectivistic cultures who perceive hard group boundaries tend to react negatively toward outgroup members who attempt to converge communicatively more than do members of individualistic cultures (Gallois et al., 1995). Moreover, members of collectivistic cultures diverge if they perceive the convergence as overstepping ingroup boundaries more than do members of individualistic cultures.

CRITERIA FOR EVALUATING THEORIES OF CULTURAL VARIABILITY IN COMMUNICATION

There are generally acceptable criteria for evaluating social science theories (e.g., logical consistency, explanatory power, parsimony). When we evaluate cross-cultural theories of communication, additional criteria also must be taken into consideration.

First, it is important that cross-cultural theories of communication incorporate more than one dimension of cultural variability. One dimension probably is not adequate to explain specific communication behavior.[20] To explain communication with strangers (e.g., members of outgroups), for example, at least individualism-collectivism and uncertainty avoidance are needed (see Gudykunst, Nishida, Morisaki, & Ogawa, 1999). In evaluating cross-cultural theories, we must assess whether theorists oversimplified their explanations if they use only one dimension of cultural variability.

Second, cross-cultural theories must directly link the dimensions of cultural variability being used to specific cultural norms and rules that influence the communication behavior being explained. Dimensions of cultural variability influence cultural norms and rules directly. The influence of the dimensions of cultural variability on communication behavior is mediated through members of cultures following these cultural norms and rules. It, therefore, is important that this linkage be spelled out explicitly in cross-cultural theories.

Third, communication behavior linked to individual-level factors that mediate the dimensions of cultural variability (e.g., self construals) should not be related to cultural norms or rules. The individual-level factors such as self construals explain variability in communication within cultures, not communication guided by cultural norms or rules. Communication styles, for example, are not guided by cultural norms and rules, they are a function of individual-level factors (e.g., self construals).

Given the different influences of the dimensions of cultural variability and the individual-level factors that mediate their effects on communication, both levels of analysis generally should not be linked to the same variables. To illustrate, communication apprehension is explained either by dimensions of cultural variability or individual-level factors that mediate their effects (e.g., self construals), not both. If both levels of analysis are linked to the same communication behaviors and these behaviors are guided by cultural norms/rules, then the individual-level mediators will be indicators of how likely members of cultures are to follow the cultural norms/rules.

To conclude, we have made tremendous progress in recent years in theoretically explaining similarities and differences in communication across cultures. There is, nevertheless, a need for more theories linking specific communication processes to dimensions of cultural variability and individual-level factors that mediate their effects. Both cultural-level and individual-level phenomena need to be incorporated into the same theories and taken into consideration when conducting cross-cultural research (see Gudykunst, Chapter 9 in this volume). Given the state of cross-cultural theorizing, it is unacceptable to generate hypotheses based on regional variations such as Western versus Eastern cultures, or to conduct atheoretical cross-cultural research.

NOTES

1. These approaches to integrating culture with communication theory are not necessarily incompatible. It is possible, for example, to integrate cultural communication and the approach we use in this chapter. The integration tends not to occur because the theorists have different objectives.

2. Only a few representative studies are cited here. See Ting-Toomey and Oetzel's chapter in this volume for a review of research on the effects of individualism-collectivism on face-negotiation and conflict styles. See Andersen et al.'s chapter in this volume for nonverbal differences in communication based on individualism-collectivism.

3. Some theorists suggest that cultures are either individualistic *or* collectivistic (e.g., Hofstede, 1980). We agree with other theorists (e.g., Kluckhohn & Strodtbeck, 1961; Parsons & Shils, 1951) who argue that both tendencies exist in all cultures.

4. Hui (1988) uses a similar approach. He isolates individualism-collectivism at the individual level in five relationships: spouse, parent, kin, neighbor, and friend.

5. Schwartz argues that individual-level and cultural-level values are different. See Schwartz (1994) for a discussion of cultural-level values. See also Smith and Schwartz (1997) for a discussion of culture and values.

28

6. There are researchers who argue that there are at least three components to the self. Kashima et al. (1995), for example, argue that there is the individual self, relational self, and the collective self.

7. Matsumoto (1999) reviews research using measures of self construals and concludes that the evidence challenges the validity of Markus and Kitayama's framework. Matsumoto's conclusions are based, at least in part, on an implicit assumption that the respondents in these studies were representative of the cultural syndromes (i.e., cultural individualism-collectivism) being studied. This may not be the case. College students simply may not be representative of the general cultural tendencies, especially in Asian cultures. Matsumoto, Kudoh, and Takeuchi (1996, Study 2), for example, report that college students are more collectivistic with respect to strangers than are working adults (mean age = 39), but working adults are more collectivistic with respect to their families than are college students. The same problem exists with Takano and Osaka's (1997, 1999) review of studies that have assessed individual-level individualism-collectivism in Japan and the United States. They suggest that the "common view" that Japan is more collectivistic than the United States may be incorrect. This does not make sense to us. The college student respondents in these studies can explain the findings. Clearly, more research that compares working adults and college students is needed. We believe that studies need to assess self construals in relation to the specific ingroup defining interdependence.

8. Only representative studies are cited here. See Ting-Toomey and Oetzel's chapter in this volume for other studies.

9. Matsumoto et al. (1997) use a value and behavior approach and find that individualism-collectivism at the individual level is unidimensional. Their measure is relationship specific.

10. Gudykunst, Nishida, and Moriguchi (1999) collected data to compare general and ingroup-specific versions of self construals, and general and ingroup-specific versions of Kashima and Hardie's (2000) individual, relational, and collective aspects of the self scales.

11. Obviously, there is a problem using these labels when referring to European Americans.

12. Most researchers using types of self construals simply assume they exist and do not test whether they exist.

13. As indicated earlier, there are other conceptualizations of dimensions of cultural variability (e.g., Kluckhohn & Strodtbeck's, 1961, value orientations; Parsons & Shils's, 1951, pattern variables). We focus on Hofstede's for two reasons. First, there are data on which to base positioning a large number of cultures on Hofstede's dimensions. Second, Hofstede's dimensions are used in specific theories discussed in this chapter and in the vast majority of research conducted.

14. See Best and Williams (1997, in press) for discussions of gender roles across cultures.

15. The Chinese Culture Connection is a group of researchers organized by Michael Bond at the Chinese University of Hong Kong.

16. For a discussion of specific aspects of Confucianism in Asian cultures, see Gudykunst (2001).

17. Kim does not complete the comparison, we do.

18. Expectancy violations theory has been incorporated into interpersonal adaptation theory (Burgoon, Stern, & Dillman, 1995).

19. Burgoon draws on Gudykunst and Ting-Toomey's (1988) discussion of cultural differences in expectation violations. What Burgoon proposes is not a cross-cultural theory per se, but rather cultural variability in a theory developed in the United States.

20. There may, of course, be exceptions when only one dimension is needed, but these are exceptions and not the rule.

REFERENCES

Applegate, J., & Sypher, H. (1983). A constructivist outline. In W. B. Gudykunst (Ed.), *Intercultural communication theory* (pp. 63-78). Beverly Hills, CA: Sage.

Applegate, J., & Sypher, H. (1988). A constructivist theory of communication and culture. In Y. Y. Kim & W. B. Gudykunst (Eds.), *Theories in intercultural communication* (pp. 41-65). Newbury Park, CA: Sage.

Ball-Rokeach, S., Rokeach, M., & Grube, J. (1984). *The great American values test*. New York: Free Press.

Bem, S. (1974). The measurement of psychological androgyny. *Journal of Consulting and Clinical Psychology, 42,* 155-162.

Bem, S. (1993). *The lens of gender*. New Haven, CT: Yale University Press.

Berry, J. (1980). Acculturation as varieties of adaptation. In A. Padilla (Ed.), *Acculturation theory* (pp. 9-25). Washington, DC: Westview.

Best, D., & Williams, J. (1997). Sex, gender, and culture. In J. W. Berry, M. H. Segall, & Ç. Kâgitçibasi (Eds.), *Handbook of cross-cultural psychology: Vol. 3. Social behavior and applications* (2nd ed., pp. 163-212). Boston: Allyn & Bacon.

Best, D., & Williams, J. (in press). Gender and culture. In D. Matsumoto (Ed.), *Handbook of culture and psychology*. New York: Oxford University Press.

Brewer, M. B. (1991). The social self: On being the same and different at the same time. *Personality and Social Psychology Bulletin, 17,* 475-482.

Brewer, M. B., & Pickett, C. (1999). Distinctiveness motives as a source of the social self. In T. Tyler, R. Kramer, & O. John (Eds.), *The psychology of the social self* (pp. 71-87). Hillsdale, NJ: Lawrence Erlbaum.

Burgoon, J. K. (1978). A communication model of personal space violations. *Human Communication Research, 4,* 129-142.

Burgoon, J. K. (1992). Applying a comparative approach to nonverbal expectancy violation theory. In J. Blumler, K. Rosengren, & J. McLeod (Eds.), *Comparatively speaking* (pp. 53-69). Newbury Park, CA: Sage.

Burgoon, J. K. (1995). Cross-cultural and intercultural applications of expectancy violations theory. In R. L. Wiseman (Ed.), *Intercultural communication theory* (pp. 194-214). Thousand Oaks, CA: Sage.

Burgoon, J. K., Stern, L., & Dillman, D. (1995). *Interpersonal adaptation*. New York: Cambridge University Press.

Burgoon, J. K., & Walther, J. (1990). Nonverbal expectancies and the evaluative consequences of violations. *Human Communication Research, 17,* 232-265.

Chinese Culture Connection. (1987). Chinese values and the search for culture-free dimensions of culture. *Journal of Cross-Cultural Psychology, 18,* 143-164.

Cronen, V., Chen, V., & Pearce, W. B. (1988). Coordinated management of meaning. In Y. Y. Kim & W. B. Gudykunst (Eds.), *Theories in intercultural communication* (pp. 66-98). Newbury Park, CA: Sage.

Earley, P. C., & Erez, M. (1997). *The transplanted executive*. New York: Oxford University Press.

Feather, N. (1990). Bridging the gap between values and action. In E. Higgins & R. Sorrentino (Eds.), *Handbook of motivation and cognition* (Vol. 2, pp. 151-192). New York: Guilford.

Feather, N. (1995). Values, valences, and choices. *Journal of Personality and Social Psychology, 68,* 1135-1151.

Fiske, A., Kitayama, S., Markus, H., & Nisbett, R. (1998). The cultural matrix of social psychology. In D. Gilbert, S. Fiske, & G. Lindzey (Eds.), *Handbook of social psychology* (4th ed., Vol. 2, pp. 915-981). New York: McGraw-Hill.

Foschi, M., & Hales, W. (1979). The theoretical role of cross-cultural comparisons in experimental social psychology. In L. Eckensberger, W. Lonner, & Y. Poortinga (Eds.), *Cross-cultural contributions to psychology* (pp. 244-254). Amsterdam: Swets & Zeitlinger.

Gallois, C., Giles, H., Jones, E., Cargile, A. C., & Ota, H. (1995). Accommodating intercultural encounters: Elaborations and extensions. In R. L. Wiseman (Ed.), *Intercultural communication theory* (pp. 115-147). Thousand Oaks, CA: Sage.

Gardner, W., Gabriel, S., & Lee, A. (1999). "I" value freedom but "we" value relationships. Self construals priming mirrors cultural differences in judgment. *Psychological Science, 10,* 321-326.

Geertz, C. (1973). *The interpretation of cultures*. New York: Basic Books.

Geertz, C. (1975). On the nature of anthropological understanding. *American Scientist, 63,* 47-53.

Giles, H., Mulac, A., Bradac, J., & Johnson, P. (1987). Speech accommodation theory: The next decade and beyond. In M. McLaughlin

(Ed.), *Communication yearbook 10* (pp. 13-48). Newbury Park, CA: Sage.

Gudykunst, W. B. (1995). Anxiety/uncertainty management (AUM) theory: Current status. In R. L. Wiseman (Ed.), *Intercultural communication theory* (pp. 8-58). Thousand Oaks, CA: Sage.

Gudykunst, W. B. (1998). *Bridging differences* (3rd ed.). Thousand Oaks, CA: Sage.

Gudykunst, W. B. (2001). *Asian American ethnicity and communication.* Thousand Oaks, CA: Sage.

Gudykunst, W. B., & Bond, M. H. (1997). Intergroup relations. In J. W. Berry, M. H. Segall, & Ç. Kâgitçibasi (Eds.), *Handbook of cross-cultural psychology: Vol. 3. Social behavior and applications* (2nd ed., pp. 119-161). Boston: Allyn & Bacon.

Gudykunst, W. B., Gao, G., & Franklyn-Stokes, A. (1996). Self-monitoring and concern for social appropriateness in China and England. In J. Pandey, D. Sinha, & D. Bhawuk (Eds.), *Asian contributions to cross-cultural psychology* (pp. 255-267). New Delhi: Sage.

Gudykunst, W. B., Gao, G., Nishida, T., Nadamitsu, Y., & Sakai, J. (1992). Self-monitoring in Japan and the United States. In S. Iwawaki, Y. Kashima, & K. Leung (Eds.), *Innovations in cross-cultural psychology* (pp. 185-198). Lisse, the Netherlands: Swets & Zeitlinger.

Gudykunst, W. B., Gao, G., Schmidt, K., Nishida, T., Bond, M., Leung, K., Wang, G., & Barraclough, R. (1992). The influence of individualism-collectivism on communication in ingroup and outgroup relationships. *Journal of Cross-Cultural Psychology, 23,* 196-213.

Gudykunst, W. B., Matsumoto, Y., Ting-Toomey, S., Nishida, T., Kim, K. S., & Heyman, S. (1996). The influence of cultural individualism-collectivism, self construals, and individual values on communication styles across cultures. *Human Communication Research, 22,* 510-543.

Gudykunst, W. B., & Nishida, T. (1986a). Attributional confidence in low- and high-context cultures. *Human Communication Research, 12,* 525-549.

Gudykunst, W. B., & Nishida, T. (1986b). The influence of cultural variability on perceptions of communication associated with relationship terms. *Human Communication Research, 13,* 147-166.

Gudykunst, W. B., & Nishida, T. (1994). *Bridging Japanese/North American differences.* Thousand Oaks, CA: Sage.

Gudykunst, W. B., & Nishida, T. (2001). Anxiety, uncertainty, and perceived effectiveness of communication across relationships and cultures. *International Journal of Intercultural Relations, 25,* 55-72.

Gudykunst, W. B., Nishida, T., & Moriguchi, K. (1999). [Survey of self perceptions and communication in Japan and the United States]. Unreported data. California State University, Fullerton/Nihon University, Mishima.

Gudykunst, W. B., Nishida, T., Morisaki, S., & Ogawa, N. (1999). The influence of students' personal and social identities on their perceptions of interpersonal and intergroup encounters in Japan and the United States. *Japanese Journal of Social Psychology, 15,* 47-58. (In English)

Gudykunst, W. B., & Ting-Toomey, S. (with Chua, E.) (1988). *Culture and interpersonal communication.* Newbury Park, CA: Sage.

Gudykunst, W. B., Yoon, Y.-C., & Nishida, T. (1987). The influence of individualism-collectivism on perceptions of communication in ingroup-outgroup relationships. *Communication Monographs, 54,* 295-306.

Hall, E. T. (1959). *The silent language.* New York: Doubleday.

Hall, E. T. (1976). *Beyond culture.* Garden City, NY: Doubleday/Anchor.

Hamaguchi, E. (1980). *Nihonjin no rentaiteki jiritsusei: Kanjinshugi to kojinshugi* [Japanese connected autonomy: Contextualism and individualism]. *Gendai no Esupuri* [Contemporary Spirit], *160,* 127-143.

Herskovits, M. (1955). *Cultural anthropology.* New York: Knopf.

Hofstede, G. (1979). Value systems in forty countries. In L. Eckensberger, W. Lonner, & Y. Poortinga (Eds.), *Cross-cultural contributions to psychology* (pp. 389-407). Amsterdam: Swets and Zeitlinger.

Hofstede, G. (1980). *Culture's consequences: International differences in work-related values.* Beverly Hills, CA: Sage.

Hofstede, G. (1983). Dimensions of national cultures in fifty countries and three regions. In J. Deregowski, S. Dziurawiec, & R. Annis (Eds.), *Expiscations in cross-cultural psychology* (pp. 335-355). Lisse, the Netherlands: Swets & Zeitlinger.

Hofstede, G. (1991). *Cultures and organizations: Software of the mind.* London: McGraw-Hill.

Hofstede, G. (Ed.). (1998). *Masculinity and femininity.* Thousand Oaks, CA: Sage.

Hofstede, G. (2001). *Culture's consequences* (2nd ed.). Thousand Oaks, CA: Sage.

Hofstede, G., & Bond, M. (1984). Hofstede's culture dimensions. *Journal of Cross-Cultural Psychology, 15,* 417-433.

Hui, C. H. (1988). Measurement of individualism-collectivism. *Journal of Research in Personality, 22,* 17-36.

Kâgitçibasi, Ç. (1997). Individualism and collectivism. In J. W. Berry, M. H. Segall, & Ç. Kâgitçibasi (Eds.), *Handbook of cross-cultural psychology: Vol. 3. Social behavior and applications* (2nd ed., pp. 1-50). Boston: Allyn & Bacon.

Kashima, E., & Hardie, E. (2000). The development and validation of the relational, individual, collective self aspects (RIC) scale. *Asian Journal of Social Psychology, 3,* 19-48.

Kashima, Y., Yamaguchi, S., Kim, U., Choi, S.-C., Gelfand, M., & Yuki, M. (1995). Culture, gender, and self. *Journal of Personality and Social Psychology, 69,* 925-937.

Keesing, R. (1974). Theories of culture. *Annual Review of Anthropology, 3,* 73-97.

Kim, M. S. (1993). Culture-based interactive constraints in explaining intercultural strategic competence. In R. L. Wiseman & J. Koester (Eds.), *Intercultural communication competence* (pp. 132-150). Newbury Park, CA: Sage.

Kim, M. S. (1994). Cross-cultural comparisons of the perceived importance of conversational constraints. *Human Communication Research, 21,* 128-151.

Kim, M. S. (1995). Toward a theory of conversational constraints: Focusing on individual-level dimensions of culture. In R. L. Wiseman (Ed.), *Intercultural communication theory* (pp. 148-169). Thousand Oaks, CA: Sage.

Kim, M. S., Hunter, J. E., Miyahara, A., Horvath, A., Bresnahan, M., & Yoon, H. (1996). Individual vs. culture level dimensions of individualism and collectivism: Effects on preferred conversational styles. *Communication Monographs, 63,* 29-49.

Kim, M. S., Sharkey, W. F., & Singelis, T. M. (1994). The relationship between individual's self-construals and perceived importance of interactive constraints. *International Journal of Intercultural Relations, 18,* 117-140.

Kim, M. S., & Wilson, S. (1994). A cross-cultural comparison of implicit theories of requesting. *Communication Monographs, 61,* 210-235.

Kim, U. (1994). Individualism and collectivism: Conceptual clarification and elaboration. In U. Kim, H. Triandis, Ç. Kâgitçibasi, S.-C. Choi, & G. Yoon (Eds.), *Individualism and collectivism: Theory, method, and applications* (pp. 19-40). Thousand Oaks, CA: Sage.

Kluckhohn, F., & Strodtbeck, R. (1961). *Variations in value orientations.* New York: Row, Peterson.

Markus, H. R., & Kitayama, S. (1991). Culture and the self: Implications for cognition, emotion, and motivation. *Psychological Review, 98,* 224-253.

Markus, H., & Kitayama, S. (1998). The cultural psychology of personality. *Journal of Cross-Cultural Psychology, 29,* 63-87.

Matsumoto, D. (1999). Culture and self: An empirical assessment of Markus and Kitayama's theory of independent and interdependent self construals. *Asian Journal of Social Psychology, 2,* 289-310.

Matsumoto, D., Kudoh, T., & Takeuchi, S. (1996). Changing patterns of individualism and collectivism in the United States and Japan. *Culture and Psychology, 2,* 77-107.

Matsumoto, D., Weissman, M., Preston, K., Brown, B., & Kupperbusch, C. (1997). Context-specific measurement of individualism-collectivism on the individual level. *Journal of Cross-Cultural Psychology, 28,* 743-767.

Nakane, C. (1970). *Japanese society.* Berkeley: University of California Press.

Parsons, T., & Shils, E. (1951). *Toward a general theory of action.* Cambridge, MA: Harvard University Press.

Schwartz, S. (1990). Individualism-collectivism. *Journal of Cross-Cultural Psychology, 21,* 139-157.

Schwartz, S. (1992). Universals in the content and structure of values. In M. Zanna (Ed.), *Advances in experimental social psychology* (Vol. 25, pp. 1-65). New York: Academic Press.

Schwartz, S. (1994). Beyond individualism/collectivism: New cultural dimensions of values. In U. Kim, H. Triandis, Ç. Kâgitçibasi, S.-C. Choi, & G. Yoon (Eds.), *Individualism and collectivism: Theory, method, and applications* (pp. 85-119). Thousand Oaks, CA: Sage.

Shore, B. (1996). *Culture in mind: Culture and the problem of meaning.* New York: Oxford University Press.

Singelis, T. (1994). The measurement of independent and interdependent self construals. *Personality and Social Psychology Bulletin, 20,* 580-591.

Singelis, T., & Brown, W. (1995). Culture, self, and collectivistic communication. *Human Communication Research, 21,* 354-389.

Smith, P., & Schwartz, S. (1997). Values. In J. W. Berry, M. H. Segall, & Ç. Kâgitçibasi (Eds.), *Handbook of cross-cultural psychology: Vol. 3. Social behavior and applications* (2nd ed., pp. 77-118). Boston: Allyn & Bacon.

Sorrentino, R., & Short, J. (1986). Uncertainty orientation, motivation, and cognition. In R. Sorrentino & E. Higgins (Eds.), *Handbook of motivation and cognition* (pp. 379-403). New York: Guilford.

Sperber, D. (1996). *Explaining culture: A naturalistic approach.* Oxford, UK: Basil Blackwell.

Takano, Y., & Osaka, E. (1997). *"Nihonjin no shiyudan shiyugi" to "Amerijajin no kojin shiyugi": Tsuusetsu no saikento* ["Japanese collectivism" and "American individualism": Reexamining the dominant view]. *Shinri Gakukenkyu* [Japanese Journal of Psychology], *10,* 312-327.

Takano, Y., & Osaka, E. (1999). An unsupported common view: Comparing Japan and the U.S. on individualism/collectivism. *Asian Journal of Social Psychology, 2,* 311-341.

Ting-Toomey, S. (1985). Toward a theory of conflict and culture. In W. B. Gudykunst, L. Stewart, & S. Ting-Toomey (Eds.), *Communication, culture, and organizational processes* (pp. 71-86). Beverly Hills, CA: Sage.

Ting-Toomey, S. (1988). Intercultural conflict styles: A face-negotiation theory. In Y. Y. Kim & W. B. Gudykunst (Eds.), *Theories in intercultural communication* (pp. 213-238). Newbury Park, CA: Sage.

Ting-Toomey, S., & Kurogi, A. (1998). Facework competence in intercultural conflict: An updated face-negotiation theory. *International Journal of Intercultural Relations, 22,* 187-225.

Triandis, H. C. (1988). Collectivism vs. individualism: A reconceptualization of a basic concept in cross-cultural psychology. In G. Verma & C. Bagley (Eds.), *Cross-cultural studies of personality, attitudes and cognition* (pp. 60-95). London: Macmillan.

Triandis, H. C. (1989). The self and social behavior in differing cultural contexts. *Psychological Review, 96,* 506-517.

Triandis, H. C. (1995). *Individualism & collectivism.* Boulder, CO: Westview.

Triandis, H. C. (in press). Individualism and collectivism. In D. Matsumoto (Ed.), *Handbook of culture and psychology.* New York: Oxford University Press.

Triandis, H. C., Bontempo, R., Villareal, M., Asai, M., & Lucca, N. (1988). Individualism-collectivism: Cross-cultural studies on self-ingroup relationships. *Journal of Personality and Social Psychology, 54,* 323-338.

Triandis, H. C., Leung, K., Villareal, M., & Clack, F. (1985). Allocentric versus idiocentric tendencies. *Journal of Research in Personality, 19,* 395-415.

Turner, R. (1987). Articulating self and social structure. In K. Yardley & T. Honess (Eds.), *Self and society* (pp. 119-132). Chichester, UK: Wiley.

Vignoles, V., Chryssochoou, X., & Breakwell, G. (2000). The distinctiveness principle. *Personality and Social Psychology Review, 4,* 337-354.

Williams, A., Ota, H., Giles, H., Pierson, H. D., Gallois, C., Ng, S., Lim, T., Ryan, E. B., Somera, L., Maher, J., Cai, D., & Harwood, J. (1997). Young people's beliefs about intergenerational communication: An initial cross-cultural comparison. *Communication Research, 24,* 370-393.

Yamaguchi, S. (1994). Collectivism among the Japanese: A perspective from the self. In U. Kim, H. Triandis, Ç. Kâgitçibasi, S.-C. Choi, & G. Yoon (Eds.), *Individualism and collectivism: Theory, method, and applications* (pp. 175-188). Thousand Oaks, CA: Sage.

Yamaguchi, S., Kuhlman, D., & Sugimori, S. (1995). Personality correlates of allocentric tendencies in individualistic and collectivistic cultures. *Journal of Cross-Cultural Psychology, 26,* 658-672.

Yuki, M., & Brewer, M. B. (1999, August). *Japanese collectivism versus American collectivism: A comparison of group-loyalty across cultures.* Paper presented at the Asian Social Psychology Association conference, Taipei.

2

Cultural Communication

GERRY PHILIPSEN
University of Washington

Cultural communication is a complex human practice that encompasses two interrelated aspects of social life. The first aspect is culturally distinctive ways of communicating—the use of particular means and meanings of communication that can be found in particular times, places, and social milieus. In this sense, cultural communication is communicative conduct that is infused with the particulars of cultures. The second aspect is the role of communication in performing the cultural, or communal, function—the workings of communication in constituting the communal life of a community and in providing individuals the opportunity to participate in, identify with, and negotiate that life. In this sense, cultural communication is the work that people do in coming to terms with the communicative demands of their life-worlds. In this chapter, I examine cultural communication in both of these aspects and in terms of their interrelation.

THE TERM *CULTURAL COMMUNICATION*

When people use the term *cultural communication,* what do they mean? I begin with a consideration of three early, undefined uses of the term, and then turn to a later, programmatic use of it, to provide a basis for establishing a working definition of cultural communication that is grounded in the way the term has been used in extant scholarship.

An early use of cultural communication in anthropology suggests a reference to communication as a process through which cultural difference is expressed and constructed. Schwartz (1980) used the title *Socialization as Cultural Communication: Development of a Theme in the Work of Margaret Mead* for an edited collection of works by the anthropologist Margaret Mead. Hanson (1982) makes a similar use of the term in his edited volume of essays dedicated to the memory of Gregory Bateson, *Studies in Symbolism and Cultural*

35

Communication. The theme that both of these collections develop is that humans grow up not to be just any human, or universal human, but rather, through a process of communication, become socialized into a particularly cultured version of a human being. Schwartz and Hanson, and by implication Mead and Bateson, think of cultural communication in terms of differences in conduct across societies and of the mediating role of communication in socializing individuals into a particular cultural way of being.

In "The Problem of Speech Genres," first published in Russia in 1953, the Russian literary scholar Bakhtin (1953/1986) used an expression that was later translated as "cultural communication." In that essay, Bakhtin refers to "highly developed and organized cultural communication (primarily written)," "complex cultural communication," "complexly organized cultural communication (scientific and artistic)," and "cultural communication." He juxtaposes "cultural communication" in apparent contrast to "active speech communication" and to "various primary (simple) genres that have taken form in unmediated communication." He also integrates secondary and primary genres into one inter-animating system of communicative practices. In this usage, cultural communication refers to those speech genres of a society that manifest its public, relatively permanent, widely distributed forms and ways of communicating, but ways and forms that are interdependent with the everyday speech habits of individuals in that society.

Writing in the field of communication studies, in an essay about communication systems Cushman and Craig (1976) articulated the basic functions, typical structures, and typical processes of cultural, social-organizational, and interpersonal communication systems. For cultural communication systems, Cushman and Craig proposed that

"consensus about institutions" is the basic function. The basic structures of cultural communication are, to Cushman and Craig, networks (nation, culture, class, subculture, region, community, and family) and codes (language, dialect, and accent). Typical processes are diffusion, especially via mass media, and customs and rituals. In this usage, cultural communication refers to a process of activity in which individuals in a society act so as to produce and regulate shared understandings about social life that will serve as a warrant for shared meaning and coordinated activity among the members of that society.

Each of these early uses of cultural communication emphasizes a particular aspect of cultural communication, but they all have two features in common as well. First, each is concerned with the distinctiveness of communication in particular societies and cultures. Second, each treats communication as a site and resource for establishing, sustaining, and negotiating a community's sense of identity and an individual's sense of membership in and identification with a community.

The three early uses of cultural communication mentioned above can be seen, in retrospect, as having set the stage for an explicit formulation of cultural communication as a programmatic enterprise in the field of communication. Cultural communication, as a named field of study, was proposed by Philipsen in an essay titled "The Prospect for Cultural Communication," which was first circulated in 1981 but not published until 1987. Prior to its eventual publication, the 1981 formulation of cultural communication was acknowledged as a programmatic enterprise by Carbaugh (1985), Cushman and Cahn (1985), Eastman (1985), Hiemstra (1983), Katriel (1986), and Ting-Toomey (1984). Subsequent references to the program proposed by Philipsen include Baxter (1993), Braithwaite (1990b), Carbaugh (1988a, 1988b,

1995), Carbaugh, Gibson, and Milburn (1997), Collier and Thomas (1988), Dissanayake (1989), Griffin (1997), Hall (1994), Hecht, Collier, and Ribeau (1993), Katriel (1991), Miyahira (1999), Ruud (1995), and Sequeira (1993, 1994). Carbaugh's (1990b) article and (1990a) edited volume, *Cultural Communication and Intercultural Contact*, use the expression in a way that is consistent with the earlier formulation.

At the time of the writing of "The Prospect for Cultural Communication" (Philipsen, 1981, 1987), there were in the communication studies discipline several important lines of research and pedagogy that treated communication from a cultural standpoint. "The ethnography of communication" was a call for and realization of a program of descriptive-comparative study of cultural ways of speaking (see Hymes, 1962; Philipsen, 1975; Murray, 1993). "Intercultural communication" emphasized the study of misunderstandings between people who use different cultures from each other (Condon & Yousef, 1975; Leeds-Hurwitz, 1990; Samovar & Porter, 1972). The study of "cultural communication systems" emphasized the role of communication as a practical resource in facilitating consensus about institutions among members within social groups (Cushman & Craig, 1976). Communication and critical "cultural studies" (Hall, 1980) treated communicative practices as a site and resource for the expression and maintenance of cultural domination by some people over others, thus problematizing the consensus model of cultural communication systems explicated by Cushman and Craig. By 1981, all of these had been conceived and had been developed into full-blown areas of study, each with its own assumptions, literatures, and commitments.

Philipsen (1981, 1987) proposed cultural communication as a distinctive approach to the study of culturally situated communication, one that is related and indebted to, but distinctive from, such approaches as cultural communication systems, intercultural communication, critical studies of communication and culture, and the ethnography of communication. Drawing from these other traditions, cultural communication, as proposed by Philipsen, brought together two important strands of earlier research on culture and communication. These two strands are (1) differences across groups in terms of communicative practices and (2) the role of communication as a resource in managing discursively the individual-communal dialectic. Woven together, these strands constitute the fabric of cultural communication as an academic enterprise, and it is to that fabric that I now turn.

TWO PRINCIPLES OF CULTURAL COMMUNICATION

In this section of the chapter, I present and develop two principles of cultural communication. For each of these, I state and elaborate the principle. Then, for each principle I acknowledge key texts from which it is in part drawn and point to some of the empirical evidence that cultural communication researchers have produced that bear on it.

Principle 1: Every communal conversation bears traces of culturally distinctive means and meanings of communicative conduct.

A *communal conversation* is a historically situated, ongoing communicative process in which participants in the life of a social world construct, express, and negotiate the terms on which they conduct their lives together. In *The Philosophy of Literary Form*, Kenneth Burke (1941) describes such a process:

Imagine that you enter a parlor. You come late. When you arrive, others have long preceded you, and they are engaged in a heated discussion, a discussion too heated for them to pause and tell you exactly what it is about. In fact, the discussion had already begun long before any of them got there, so that no one present is qualified to retrace for you all the steps that had gone before. You listen for a while, until you decide that you have caught the tenor of the argument; then you put in your oar. Someone answers; you answer him; another comes to your defense; another aligns himself against you, to either the embarrassment or gratification of your opponent, depending upon the quality of your ally's assistance. However, the discussion is interminable. The hour grows late, you must depart. And you do depart, with the discussion still vigorously in progress. (pp. 110-111)

Burke's description of a "discussion" has several features that apply to what I am calling a communal conversation. First, it is an ongoing communicative event—in this case a discussion—with a past ("others have long preceded you"), present ("they are engaged in . . . discussion"), and future ("the discussion is interminable"). Second, the discussion is situated physically—this one is in "a parlor." Third, the discussion precedes and outlives its momentary participants ("others have long preceded you," "you . . . depart, with the discussion still . . . in progress"). Finally, individuals figure out the nature of the discussion and then insinuate themselves into it ("you listen for a while" and when "you have caught the tenor of the argument . . . then you put in your oar").

The discussion that Burke describes is an ongoing communicative event, is physically situated, transcends its momentary participants, provides an opportunity for individuals to learn to participate in it, and has a dynamic potential. In these ways, it is much like any communal conversation. But his characteriza-

tion also has many local particulars written into it. It is a *particular type* of communicative event, a discussion, and if discussions might be found everywhere, in all times and places, not every community has a word for "discussion" and not every community has discussions precisely like the one Burke imagines. Such ongoing communicative events are held in *various places* across various societies, not always in parlors. They are, for example, conducted around the stove in a general store (Bauman, 1972), on the street or street corner (Philipsen, 1976), in an office or office building (Carbaugh, 1988a; Hiemstra, 1983), in electronic space (Wick, 1997), and so forth. The discussion has a *particular tone*—described here in terms of heat. Some societies, historical and contemporary, do indeed have "heated" (Burke's word) discussions and have a vocabulary for talking about "heat" in speech. Such a historical society is 17th-century New England, where everyday discourse was filled with many common expressions for heated speech (St. George, 1984), and the Chamula use many terms and expressions to designate the speech of "people whose hearts are heated" (Gossen, 1974). Two reports by French observers of contemporary American discussion comment on how cool American discussions seem in contrast to similar communicative events in France (Carroll, 1988; Varenne, 1977). Although there might be heated discussions in every communal conversation, they vary in terms of how heated they are, how frequent they are, how they are judged because of their heat, and how many types of heated speech there might be. Finally, Burke's discussion is characterized by a *particular discursive structure,* with one person speaking, another responding with an objection, another then responding to the objection; it is not ever or everywhere thus (Reisman, 1974).

The members of every group or community partake of a communal conversation. This is a universal aspect of human experience. But each particular communal conversation has traces of a distinctive culture; that is, it is infused with local particulars of setting (parlor vs. corner), genre (discussion vs. small talk), tone (heated vs. cool), structure (sequential vs. contrapuntal participation), and so forth. When Burke, inevitably, infuses cultural particulars into the hypothetical discussion he describes, he describes it as something very particular—very cultured. Although his portrait of a communal conversation is infused with cultural particulars, it is, at the same time, a portrait that is true of all communicative events—that is, all communal conversations bear traces of local, particular means and meanings. The particulars vary; that there are particulars is a constant.

A communal conversation is always conducted in and through particular means of communication, and these means have particular meanings for the people who use and experience them. *Means* refer to particular languages, dialects, styles, routines, organizing principles, interpretive conventions, ways of speaking, and genres of communication. The *meanings* of these means refer to the significance that people experience in relation to them, that is, what they take them to be and whether they judge them to be appropriate, intelligible, efficacious, pleasing, and so forth. The culturally distinctive resources for communicative conduct that appear in a communal conversation consist of the particular communicative means and meanings, or the particular configuration of means and meanings, which can be found in it.

Wherever people construct, express, and negotiate the terms on which they conduct their lives together, there will be traces of means of communication, and of their meanings to those who produce and experience them, that are particular to that setting, era, or milieus. Therefore, to come to know the possibilities for participation in a given commu-

nal conversation requires learning the answer to two questions. First, what, here and now, are the particular means with which the particular conversation is conducted? The answer encompasses languages, dialects, styles, gestures, speech genres, communicative routines, principles for interpreting and evaluating communicative conduct, and the like. Second, what, in this particular here and now, do these means mean to those who use and experience them? What, for example, does it mean, in the context of a particular communal conversation, for someone to use one or another language, to perform a particular communicative act, to enact a particular episodic sequence, and the like?

An early seminal statement about the cultural distinctiveness of communicative conduct is found in Hymes (1962), a treatise that sets forth key assumptions and a call for fieldwork pertaining to culturally distinctive communication in various speech communities. This was followed by a restatement of the original program, a modification of the initial descriptive framework that had been proposed, and a review of preliminary fieldwork that had been produced, or discovered, to illustrate and help refine the framework (Hymes, 1972). Hymes's development of the ethnography of communication as a programmatic enterprise, and his reviews of fieldwork studies that provided empirical materials in which to ground the development, painted a picture of substantial difference in communicative means, meanings, and conduct not only across but also within social communities (Hymes, 1962, 1972, 1977). They also painted a picture of such means, meanings, and conduct as subject to negotiation and change within communities (in this regard, see, especially, Hymes, 1977).

Initially, Hymes (1962, 1972) worked with a body of fieldwork data that bear only indirectly on cultural distinctiveness in communication. But his calls for basic fieldwork directed to cross-cultural studies of communication, first sounded in 1962 (Hymes, 1962), had by 1986 yielded some 250 separate publications that document culturally distinctive patterns of communicative conduct (Philipsen & Carbaugh, 1986). By 1993, the ethnography of communication had been established as an "elite interdisciplinary scientific field" (Murray, 1993), whose literature documented considerable variation across speech communities in the ways people talked about, conceptualized, practiced, and experienced communication.

Building on the work of the ethnography of communication, Philipsen (1989a) presents the axiom of cultural particularity and arrays a wide range of ethnographic research that supports the axiom. The central claim of the axiom of cultural particularity is that the efficacious resources for creating shared meaning and motivating coordinated action vary across social groups. The support arrayed for this axiom consists of a series of ethnographic studies that, following Hymes's original proposal, provides evidence for cultural particularity, rather than universality, in terms of such communicative phenomena as speech acts (Rosaldo, 1982), the self concept as a generative mechanism in communicative conduct (Philipsen, 1975), facework rules (Katriel, 1986), and rules of conversational sequencing (Reisman, 1974).

Philipsen (1992, 1997) draws from a program of ethnographic fieldwork in multiple societies so as to formulate speech codes theory, that is, a theory of culturally distinctive codes of communicative conduct. See, for empirical works that have particularly influenced the development of the theory, ethnographies by Carbaugh (1988a), Fitch (1991), Katriel (1986), Katriel and Philipsen (1981), and Philipsen (1975, 1976, 1986) and the comparative review by Carbaugh (1989) of a wide range of ethnographies. Speech codes theory, building on the extant literature, posits that

the distinctive communicative record of a communal conversation can be interpreted as implicating a distinctive code (or, as in Philipsen, 1992, codes) of communication. In this sense, a speech code refers to a historically enacted, socially constructed system of terms, meanings, premises, and rules pertaining to communicative conduct.

A speech code, the theory posits, implicates a distinctive way of answering the following questions: What is a person, and how is personhood efficaciously and properly enacted communicatively? What is an ideal state of sociation, and how do people efficaciously and properly link themselves into such states through communicative conduct? What are efficacious and proper means of communication, and what meanings are expressed in and through their situated use? Thus, to say, from this perspective, that every communal conversation bears traces of distinctive means of communicative conduct and distinctive meanings associated with their use is to say that every communal conversation is its own world of personal possibility, social morality, and strategic efficacy. This is a principal theoretical conclusion of cultural communication research.

Scholars working in the cultural communication tradition have now produced a substantial body of empirical fieldwork that examines in depth a culturally distinctive communicative practice in a particular society. These include such studies, cited chronologically, as the following:

- Philipsen (1975, 1976, 1986, 1992; Katriel & Philipsen, 1981): "Teamsterville" and "Nacirema" ways of communicating, ways found within a single society, the former reporting an indigenous system of rules and terms for communicative conduct that manifest a code of honor, the latter reporting an indigenous code that configures historically distinctive meanings that are mapped by such words as *communication, self, relationship,* and *work*

- Hiemstra (1983): a code of meanings pertaining to communication technologies used in an American office

- Katriel (1986): Israeli "speaking dugri," a culturally distinctive way of communicating whereby speakers simultaneously express themselves to others in a confrontational way and affirm a widely appreciated social code of assertiveness, sincerity, and naturalness

- Carbaugh (1988a): talk, on an American television talk show, about communication in the intimate aspects of the speakers' lives, talk that implicates a code of "communication" that privileges the individual over the social

- Fitch (1991): Colombian terms for addressing others in face-to-face interaction, with an emphasis on multiple meanings and terms that configure culturally distinctive senses of Spanish *madre* (mother)

- Sequeira (1993, 1994): personal address, speaking in tongues, and performance of healing rituals, in an American church, that at once express, for the participants who enact them, a personal faith and a code of communal identification

- Hecht et al. (1993): African American communication patterns and their meanings to those who produce them

- Braithwaite (1990b): rituals, myths, and social dramas, in the communal talk of American veterans of the Vietnam War

- Carbaugh (1996): American ways of expressing one's culturally distinctive sense of "self" and attendant ideological expressions

- Fong (1998): Chinese immigrant responses to Euro-American compliments and the social code implicated therein

- Miyahira (1999): Japanese and American presentations of self in a bilingual English classroom, with attention to ritualized expressions of a code of personhood

- Covarrubias (1999): pronouns of personal address (*tu* and *usted*) and the ethic of cooperativeness that they implicate, in a Mexican business organization

- Coutu (2000): oppositional codes in justificatory political discourse in American discussions of the Vietnam War

- Carbaugh (2000): Blackfeet (Native Americans in Montana, United States) communicative practices for experiencing self in relation to nature

- Winchatz (in press): pronouns of personal address (*du* and *Sie*) in German daily interactions, and the culturally distinctive dimensions of social meaning they express for those who produce and experience them in context

Each of the studies cited above draws from the communal conversation of a different society. Taken together, they represent research conducted in several languages, including English, Hebrew, Spanish (including a Colombian and a Mexican variety), Japanese, and German. They differ in terms of the specific communicative and cultural phenomena with which they deal. These include, as examples: ways of presenting oneself in social situations, rules for participating in communicative events, the enactment of everyday speech genres, rules and meanings pertaining to personal address, and meta-communicative terms and premises (i.e., culturally distinctive terminology pertaining to communicative conduct).

For all their differences in terms of what phenomena were focused on and in terms of the distinctiveness across societies of communicative practices found, there are substantial similarities in approach in all of these studies. First, all of them were based on the descriptive framework of the ethnography of communication model. Second, all of them examined particular means of communication and the particular meanings these means have for the participants in some particular communal conversation. Third, all of them go beyond describing a communicative practice in terms of behavioral enactment and meaning to show the culturally distinctive model of an ideal person, social relations, and strategic action implicated in the local practice.

In addition to studies done in one particular society, several cultural communication researchers have reviewed ethnographic studies from multiple societies, based on multiple languages, with an eye to differences across societies in the way particular communicative practices are enacted. In all of the following, a common methodological approach was used. Ethnographies were selected for comparative study that (1) employ a common descriptive-comparative framework (that of the ethnography of communication; Hymes 1962, 1972), (2) represent a range of communities and languages, and (3) focus on a similar particular aspect of communication. In each study, the separate ethnographies were then juxtaposed to each other so as to search for comparisons and contrasts in terms of how a particular communicative phenomenon does or does not occur across distinctive communal conversations.

Studies using this comparative approach have found substantial differences, across societies, in terms of the particular cultural elements that are infused into such communicative acts or practices as

- The use of indirection in speech acts (Katriel, 1986)

- Indigenous terms used to refer to communicative acts and ways of communicating (Carbaugh, 1989)

- Local ways of expressing one's sense of identification with a local code or community and for presenting oneself as a member of a community (Philipsen, 1989b)

- Indigenous terms and associated practices pertaining to gossip (Goldsmith, 1989/1990)

- Rules for whether to speak or remain silent in a given social situation (Braithwaite, 1990a)

- Cultural forms for providing social support (Katriel, 1993)

- Rules for responding to compliments (Fong, 1994)

- Rules for the giving of advice in interpersonal contexts (Goldsmith & Fitch, 1997)

- Expressions of power in interpersonal relationships (Fitch, 1998)

These comparative studies show considerable variation across societies, in terms of how culture is manifested in a wide range of communicative activities.

It is important to emphasize not only what is said in this explication of Principle 1 but also what is not said. In saying that every communal conversation bears traces of a distinctive culture is to say that everywhere there are particulars in the means and meanings of communicative conduct. It is not to say that there are no universal features of communicative conduct, that is, ways of communicating that transcend particular times, places, and milieus. The empirical record suggests that, indeed, there are universals in communicative conduct. Two types of universals that have received empirical support are (1) ways that people produce and interpret nonverbal expressions of emotion (Ekman & Keltner, 1999) and (2) ways that conversations are structured, in terms of some of the details of how persons are referred to and in how turns are managed in conversation (Hopper & Chen, 1996; Moerman, 1988). These appear to be consequential findings, in and of themselves, and further consequential in that they suggest, by implication, the possibility and probability of universals in communicative conduct. The point of Principle 1 is that one of the transcultural facts of communicative conduct is that there is much in communicative conduct that is culturally distinctive.

Principle 2: Communication is a heuristic and performative resource for performing the cultural function in the lives of individuals and communities.

The cultural, or communal, function is concerned with what a group or individual has settled, or is trying to settle, as to how individuals are to live as members of a community. From the standpoint of the community as a whole, the cultural function consists of establishing, sustaining, and negotiating a communal sense of what its principles and standards are for conducting the communal conversation. These are principles and standards of who may communicate to or with whom, about what, through which means, and toward what ends. From the standpoint of an individual, the cultural function consists of establishing, sustaining, and negotiating how the individual can, will, or should, personally, come to terms with the communal sense of communicative conduct. This involves whether and how individuals participate in, and thereby identify and align with, a given communal conversation.

It is in communicative conduct that the locally distinctive agreements and understandings about communication are displayed for observers of and participants in a communal conversation. It is through observing the conversation that its prospective participants learn the ways that people act, and respond to communicative actions, in that conversation. Thus, the terms of a communal conversation—the means (and the meanings of those means) that constitute it—are displayed in the conversation itself. This is the sense in which communication is *heuristic*— it is a resource in and through which the infant or the newcomer can learn about the distinctive local means and meanings of communication.

Communication is also a *performative* resource. It is a means in and through which an individual not only can learn about the communal conversation but can participate in it as well. As Burke (1941) put it, "You listen for a while, until you decide that you have caught the tenor of the argument; then you put in your oar" (p. 10). The listening until you decide that you have caught the tenor is a heuristic use of the communication that constitutes, at any given moment, a communal conversation; the putting in of your oar is a performative act in which an individual acts in and toward the conversation. Treating communication as a performative act draws attention to human purposes, to the individual capacity for artful and strategic conduct in coming to terms with the codes of a given lifeworld.

The ethnography of communication had focused attention on the speech community as a site for studying communicative conduct, on the multiple functions that communicative conduct can serve in the life of a community, and on the diversity of communicative means across and within communities (Hymes, 1962, 1972, 1974, 1977). This emphasis on diverse functional possibilities created an opportunity to think about what I am calling the cultural function. Although Hymes did not formulate a cultural function of communicative conduct, he hinted at it in his treatment of two previous lines of thinking. One is Malinowski's (1935) idea of phatic communion, the use of language in creating contact, a tie of pure interpersonal union, independent of any referential content (Hymes, 1972, p. 40). The second is Mead's (1937) proposal, and reference to suggestive cases, that a sense of communal participation and identification is accomplished with different communicative means and meanings in different societies. Drawing on these resources, Hymes (1972) left the way open for an eventual formulation of the cultural function.

The work of the anthropologist Victor Turner (1980) is also an important resource in developing the idea of the cultural function of communication, as it is formulated here. Turner focused on communicative forms in the cultural work of a community and in the cultural work of individuals within a community. His formulation of such forms as myth, ritual, and social drama, as processual enactments in the life of a community, provided the basis for proposing communicative conduct as a site of cultural work and as a resource for doing that work. It is in and through the creative use of such forms that, first, the communal life of a community is enacted, and thus, second, those who experience a particular communal conversation can learn what is being said about the possibilities and proprieties of communication as social action in that community. The use of such forms, third, provides the individual with resources for communicative performance. In Turner's scheme, it is in and through the use of such forms that the individual can do three things. One of these is to enact an identity vis-à-vis the community, as through participation in a ritual. Another is to appropriate and to display some variation on the communal story, through monitoring myths and telling, in communal terms, one's own story. A third is to monitor and engage critically with the communal moral system through taking a part in the social dramas, what Burke called the "dramas of living," of the community.

Building on both Hymes and Turner, Philipsen (1981, 1987) proposed an explicit theoretical formulation of cultural communication. That proposal can be summarized in three parts. First, cultural communication is that communicative conduct that performs the cultural function. Second, communication is a performative resource in doing the cultural work of communities and individuals.

Third, the cultural function is performed, communicatively, in distinctive ways across different communal conversations.

Philipsen's (1981, 1987) formulation of cultural communication called for fieldwork studies that focused on communication in the performance of the cultural function. By 1989, it was possible to review a body of work that had responded to that call. Philipsen (1989b) reviews studies of four different communal conversations: (1) that of a workingclass neighborhood in Chicago, Illinois (Philipsen, 1975, 1976, 1986), (2) a generalized U.S. conversation that is carried out at the public level (on televised talk shows) and at the interpersonal level in face-to-face interaction (Carbaugh, 1988b; Katriel & Philipsen, 1981), (3) that of Israeli Sabras (Katriel, 1986), and (4) that of a small community in Bond, Kentucky (Ray, 1987). For each of these communal conversations, there were found distinctive communicative routines and episodic sequences in and through which participants experienced a subjective sense of social identity and community membership. Furthermore, each of these distinctive ways of performing the cultural function also implicates a distinctive communal sense of the nature of persons, society, and communicative action.

Following the early studies of communication in the performance of the cultural function, a large body of studies was published in which distinctive cultural ways of performing the cultural function and different cultural outlooks on persons, society, and communicative action were documented. These include, among others, the following:

- Studies of rituals as episodic sequences in and through which a local code is implicated and individuals enact a sense of communal membership: Braithwaite (1990b), Carbaugh (1993), Fitch (1991), Katriel (1991), Katriel and Philipsen (1981), Philipsen (1992,

1997), Sequeira (1993), and Schely-Newman (1999)

- Studies of stories, myths, and narratives as forms in which communal identities are displayed, appropriated, and deployed in expressions of personal identity: Braithwaite (1990b), Hiemstra (1983), Katriel (1986), Philipsen (1992, particularly chaps. 4 and 5), and Schely-Newman (1999)

- Studies of social dramas as a processual form in and through which the rules for communicative conduct in a communal conversation are exposed, tested, and negotiated: Baxter (1993), Braithwaite (1990b), Carbaugh (1996), Katriel (1986), Philipsen (1975, 1986, 2000), and Ruud (1995, 2000)

- Studies of the use of indigenous meta-communicative vocabularies as resources for communal identification and alignment, and expression of division and tension: Carbaugh (1989, 2000), Coutu (2000), Eastman (1985), Huspek (1993), Katriel and Philipsen (1981), and Katriel (1991, 1993)

Although the initial formulation of the descriptive-theoretic framework for cultural communication (Philipsen, 1981, 1987, 1992) provided specific ways that diversity, difference, and dynamism are manifested in a community's communicative life, much of the early work in this tradition emphasized identification and alignment with a single community and a dominant code. Recently, however, several cultural communication researchers have applied the framework in ways and to situations that foreground diversity, even division, within a particular communal conversation. Furthermore, recently several cultural communication scholars have focused on communicative situations in which the focus is the contact of distinctive codes in interaction. For example, Carbaugh's (1990a) volume addresses *cultural* communication and *inter*cultural contact. Philipsen (1992, particularly chap. 6) shows the dialectical re-

lation of two codes operative in the communicative conduct of one society. Huspek (1993, 2000) opens the way for a treatment of dueling or opposing codes. Such work has, at once, demonstrated the robustness of the basic impetus of the initial formulation but has also led to its expansion. Such studies include the following:

- Carbaugh (1993) shows how a specific series of televised confrontations between Russians and Americans reveals the use of two communicative codes, Russian and American, codes that differentially treat the nature of the individual, social relations, and strategic action. This shows, in a powerful way, how the framework can be used to create an understanding of cross-cultural communication that is truly cross-code communication (see also Lindsley, 1999).

- Huspek and Kendall (1993) show workers in a lumberyard consciously using meta-communicative vocabularies as a strategic resource to position themselves in opposition to a dominant organizational and societal code of communicative conduct.

- Baxter (1993), Coutu (2000), and Ruud (1995, 2000) apply the framework in such a way as to produce pictures of communal conversations in which the use of divergent (Huspek, 1993, would say "dueling") codes manifests discursive tension as a central fact of those conversations.

- Schely-Newman (1999) shows communication as a performative activity through which individuals not only adapt to the communal conversation but also act so as to remake that conversation.

- Philipsen (2000) shows how speakers who challenge the dominant practices of a communal conversation can demonstrate that such practices are incompatible with a larger social code and thus serve to undermine the legitimacy of those practices.

Cases such as those described above have prompted an elaboration and reformulation of the cultural communication framework. Philipsen (1998) proposes that every person's life task, and it is a task that must be performed and renewed throughout one's life, is to come to terms with the communal conversations of one's life-worlds. Performing that task can include (1) fashioning and expressing a cultural identity, (2) communicating across cultural codes, (3) appropriating and integrating from among the multiple cultural identities that are available to oneself, and (4) critically evaluating, or endeavoring to undermine, a given culture. Coming to terms with a communal conversation is the performance of such tasks as these.

Each of the four tasks mentioned above varies in terms of the communicative demands placed on the individual and in terms of the communicative competencies linked to performance of the task. The first situation, fashioning and expressing a cultural identity, requires locating action chains, scenarios, and scripts that are at the center of a communal conversation and with which the individual's story can be identified. The second situation, communicating across codes, requires locating differences in interpretation and evaluation in the discourses indigenous to other communal conversations and then negotiating bases of meaning and action that transcend the codes drawn from different conversations. The third situation, appropriating and integrating from among the multiple cultural identities that are available to and have existential significance for oneself, requires learning to think through paradoxes and reconcile elements of disparate discourses into an integrative whole (Orbe, 1998, is an important resource here). Finally, critically evaluating requires that one locate contradictions between theory and practice of a code, locate internal contradictions in a dominant code, and

articulate a new image of good that has rhetorical power in a particular community.

Philipsen (1998) presents a systematic framework for investigating cultural communication in the various situations described above—learning a single cultural code, communicating across codes, integrating diverse codes within one life, and critically undermining a dominant code. That framework posits underlying mechanisms that characterize each of the four situations as well as rhetorical devices that interlocutors deploy in working through the demands of those situations. This new framework, like that proposed in Philipsen (1981, 1987), was inspired by and grounded in cases produced by cultural communication researchers. Likewise, it was formulated so as to be open to revision based on new cases, a methodological strategy that has informed the ethnography of communication since its inception (Hymes, 1962, 1972).

CONCLUSION

In this chapter, I have discussed cultural communication, first, by interpreting what the term *cultural communication* means. I have proposed that cultural communication refers to that communicative conduct that is infused with cultural particulars of the means and meanings of communicative conduct. Furthermore, I have proposed that cultural communication refers to the activity in and through which a community and the people that comprise it construct, enact, and negotiate a communal sense of communicative conduct. Thus, the term refers to a structural aspect of all communicative conduct—it is infused with cultural particulars. And it refers to a functional aspect of communicative conduct—it is a resource through which communities and the individuals that comprise them come to terms with their cultures.

During the past 20 years, a considerable body of research has been produced that documents the distinctiveness of communicative conduct across distinctive times, places, and milieus. Thus, the research provides substantial support for Principle 1: Every communal conversation bears traces of culturally distinctive means and meanings of communicative conduct.

Although the research conducted under the name of cultural communication does not argue against universals in communicative conduct, it does provide substantial evidence of the universality of cultural particulars. These particulars can be observed at two levels. One is the particular communicative means that are deployed in a particular milieu—in short, distinctive ways of communicating. The second level is the meanings of those means to those who use and experience them. The empirical record documents considerable variety across and within communal conversations in what those means are and in what significance they have for those who partake of them. The record is based on studies conducted in several parts of the world and on studies done in several languages.

The research record shows that the diverse ways of communicating that have been observed and reported by cultural communication researchers have an important common characteristic. That common characteristic is that the communicative details of each particular communal conversation implicate preferred ways of being a person, a model of the ideal society, and a theory of the role of communication in linking persons in social relations.

Given the distinctiveness, across and within communal conversations, of the codes of communication that people use, and given the social ideologies implicated in those codes, it should be no surprise that communicative conduct is an arena for learning about and performing the communal function in particular

societies. The research record documents (a) great variety in the communicative forms used to perform the cultural function and (b) great variety in the ways that individuals use communication as a strategic resource in performing the cultural function. Such research provides substantial illustration and elaboration of Principle 2: Communication is a heuristic and performative resource for performing the cultural function in the lives of individuals and communities.

Current theoretical work is directed to encompassing cultural communication research generated in all four of these contexts, and others, to produce a systematic, comprehensive framework of culture in communication and communication in the process of learning, sustaining, negotiating, and transforming cultures.

Cultural communication, as a complex human practice, has been formulated here by defining it and by developing two related principles that elaborate and constitute that formulation. There is a substantial record of research that supports, illustrates, and elaborates this formulation. The record of research in cultural communication is one that is marked by new discoveries in ways of communicating and in performing the cultural function, and thus it is anticipated that there are many new discoveries to be anticipated in the years to come.

REFERENCES

Bakhtin, M. (1986). *Speech genres and other late essays* (V. W. McGee, Trans.). Austin: University of Texas Press. (Original work published 1953)

Bauman, R. (1972). The La Have Island general store: Sociability and verbal art in a Nova Scotia community. *Journal of American Folklore, 85,* 330-343.

Baxter, L. (1993). "Talking things through" and "putting it in writing": Two codes of communication in an academic institution. *Journal of Applied Communication Research, 21,* 313-326.

Braithwaite, C. (1990a). Communicative silence: A crosscultural study of Basso's hypothesis. In D. Carbaugh (Ed.), *Cultural communication and intercultural contact* (pp. 321-327). Hillsdale, NJ: Lawrence Erlbaum.

Braithwaite, C. (1990b). Cultural communication among Vietnam veterans: Ritual, myth and social drama. In R. Morris & P. Ehrenhaus (Eds.), *The cultural legacy of Vietnam* (pp. 145-170). Norwood, NJ: Lawrence Erlbaum.

Burke, K. (1941). *The philosophy of literary form.* New York: Random House.

Carbaugh, D. (1985). Cultural communication and organizing. *International and Intercultural Communication Annual, 9,* 30-47.

Carbaugh, D. (1988a). Cultural terms and tensions in the speech at a television station. *Western Journal of Speech Communication, 52,* 216-237.

Carbaugh, D. (1988b). *Talking American: Cultural discourses on* Donahue. Norwood, NJ: Ablex.

Carbaugh, D. (1989). Fifty terms for talk: A cross-cultural study. *International and Intercultural Communication Annual, 13,* 93-120.

Carbaugh, D. (Ed.). (1990a). *Cultural communication and intercultural contact.* Hillsdale, NJ: Lawrence Erlbaum.

Carbaugh, D. (1990b). Toward a perspective on cultural communication and intercultural contact. *Semiotica, 80,* 15-35.

Carbaugh, D. (1993). "Soul" and "self": Soviet and American cultures in conversation. *Quarterly Journal of Speech, 79,* 182-200.

Carbaugh, D. (1995). The ethnographic communication theory of Philipsen and associates. In D. Cushman & B. Kovacic (Eds.), *Watershed research traditions in human communication theory* (pp. 269-298). Albany: State University of New York Press.

Carbaugh, D. (1996). *Situating selves: The communication of social identities in American scenes.* Albany: State University of New York Press.

Carbaugh, D. (2000). "Just listen": "Listening" and landscape among the Blackfeet. *Western Journal of Communication, 63,* 250-270.

Carbaugh, D., Gibson, T., & Milburn, T. (1997). A view of communication and culture: Scenes in an ethnic cultural center at a private college. In B. Kovacic (Ed.), *Emerging theories of human communication* (pp. 1-24). Albany: State University of New York Press.

Carroll, R. (1988). *Cultural misunderstandings: The French-American experience* (C. Volk, Trans.). Chicago: University of Chicago Press.

Collier, M., & Thomas, M. (1998). Cultural identity: An interpretive perspective. *International and Intercultural Communication Annual, 12,* 99-120.

Condon, J., & Yousef, F. (1975). *An introduction to intercultural communication.* Indianapolis, IN: Bobbs-Merrill.

Coutu, L. (2000). Communication codes of rationality and spirituality in the discourse of and about Robert S. McNamara's *In retrospect. Research on Language and Social Interaction, 33,* 179-212.

Covarrubias, P. (1999). *Pronominally speaking: Mexican enactments of* tu *and* usted *as interpersonal components of organizational networks of cooperation.* Doctoral dissertation, University of Washington, Seattle.

Cushman, D., & Cahn, D. (1985). *Communication in interpersonal relationships.* Albany: State University of New York Press.

Cushman, D., & Craig, R. (1976). Communication systems: Interpersonal implications. In G. Miller (Ed.), *Explorations in interpersonal communication* (pp. 37-58). Beverly Hills, CA: Sage.

Dissanayake, W. (1990). Intercultural communication as a focus of research: A programmatic note. In S. King (Ed.), *Human communication as a field of study: Selected contemporary views* (pp. 105-112). Albany: State University of New York Press.

Eastman, C. (1983). Establishing social identity through language use. *Journal of Language and Social Psychology, 4,* 1-20.

Ekman, P., & Keltner, D. (1999). Universal facial expressions of emotion: An old controversy and new findings. In U. Segerstrale & P. Molnar (Eds.), *Nonverbal communication: Where nature meets culture* (pp. 27-46). Mahwah, NJ: Lawrence Erlbaum.

Fitch, K. (1991). The interplay of linguistic universals and cultural knowledge in personal address: Colombian *madre* terms. *Communication Monographs, 58,* 254-272.

Fitch, K. (1998). *Speaking relationally: Culture, communication, and interpersonal communication.* New York: Guilford.

Fong, M. **(1994).** *Chinese immigrants' interpretations of their intercultural compliment interactions with European Americans.* Doctoral dissertation, University of Washington, Seattle.

Fong, M. (1998). Chinese immigrants' perceptions of semantic dimensions of direct/indirect communication in intercultural compliment interactions with North Americans. *Howard Journal of Communications, 9,* 245-262.

Goldsmith, D. (1989/1990). Gossip from the native's point of view: A comparative analysis. *Research on Language and Social Interaction, 23,* 163-194.

Goldsmith, D., & Fitch, K. (1997). The normative context of advice as social support. *Human Communication Research, 23,* 454-476.

Gossen, G. (1974). *Chamulas in the world of the sun: Time and space in a Maya oral tradition.* Cambridge: Harvard University Press.

Griffin, E. (1997). Speech codes theory (the ethnography of communication) of Gerry Philipsen. In *A first look at communication theory* (pp. 432-443). New York: McGrawHill.

Hall, B. (1991). An elaboration of the structural possibilities for engaging in alignment episodes. *Communication Monographs, 58,* 79-100.

Hall, B. (1994). Understanding intercultural conflict through an analysis of kernel images and rhetorical visions. *International Journal of Conflict Management, 5,* 63-87.

Hall, S. (1980). Encoding/decoding. In S. Hall, D. Hobson, A. Lowe, & Paul Willis (Eds.), *Culture, media, language: Working papers in cultural studies, 1972-1979* (pp. 128-138). London: Hutchinson.

Hanson, A. (Ed.). (1982). *Studies in symbolism and cultural communication* (Publications in Anthropology No. 14). Lawrence: University of Kansas.

Hecht, M., Collier, M., & Ribeau, S. (1993). *African American communication: Ethnic identity and cultural interpretation.* Newbury Park, CA: Sage.

Hiemstra, G. (1983). You say you want a revolution? "Information technology" in organizations. In R. Bostrom (Ed.), *Communication yearbook 7* (pp. 802-827). Beverly Hills, CA: Sage.

Hopper, R., & Chen, C. (1996). Languages, cultures, relationships: Telephone openings in Taiwan. *Research on Language and Social Interaction, 29,* 291-313.

Huspek, M. (1993). Dueling structures: The theory of resistance in discourse. *Communication Theory, 3,* 1-25.

Huspek, M. (2000). Oppositional codes: The case of the Penitentiary of New Mexico riot. *Journal of Applied Communication Research, 28,* 144-163.

Huspek, M., & Kendall, K. (1993). On withholding voice: An analysis of the political vocabulary of a "nonpolitical" speech community. *Quarterly Journal of Speech, 77,* 1-19.

Hymes, D. (1962). The ethnography of speaking. In T. Gladwin & W. Sturtevant (Eds.), *Anthropology and human behavior* (pp. 13-53). Washington, DC: Anthropological Society of Washington.

Hymes, D. (1972). Models of the interaction of language and social life. In J. Gumperz & D. Hymes (Eds.), *Directions in sociolinguistics: The ethnography of communication* (pp. 35-71). New York: Holt, Rinehart & Winston.

Hymes, D. (1974). Ways of speaking. In R. Bauman & J. Sherzer (Eds.), *Explorations in the ethnography of speaking* (pp. 433-451). London: Cambridge University Press.

Hymes, D. (1977). Qualitative/quantitative research methodologies in education: A linguistic perspective. *Anthropology and Education Quarterly, 8,* 165-176.

Katriel, T. (1986). *Talking straight: Dugri speech in Israeli Sabra culture.* Cambridge, UK: Cambridge University Press.

Katriel, T. (1991). *Communal webs: Communication and culture in contemporary Israel.* Albany: State University of New York Press.

Katriel, T. (1993). Lefargen: A study in Israeli semantics of social relations. *Research on Language and Social Interaction, 26,* 31-54.

Katriel, T., & Philipsen, G. (1981). "What we need is communication": "Communication" as a cultural category in some American speech. *Communication Monographs, 48,* 301-317.

Leeds-Hurwitz, W. (1990). Notes on the history of intercultural communication: The Foreign Service Institute and the mandate for intercultural training. *Quarterly Journal of Speech, 76,* 262-281.

Lindsley, S. (1999). Communication and "the Mexican way": Stability and trust as core symbols in maquiladoras. *Western Journal of Communication, 63,* 1-31.

Malinowksi, B. (1935). *Coral gardens and their magic* (Vol. 2). London: Allen and Unwin.

Mead, M. (1937). Public opinion mechanisms among primitive peoples. *Public Opinion Quarterly, 1,* 5-16.

Miyahira, K. (1999). Plotting a course of action: Ritual coordination of intercultural directive-response sequence in team-taught English classes. *Speech Communication Education, 2,* 151-172.

Moerman, M. (1988). *Talking culture: Ethnography and conversation analysis.* Philadelphia: University of Pennsylvania Press.

Murray, S. (1993). *Theory groups and the study of language in North America: A social history.* Amsterdam: John Benjamins.

Orbe, M. (1998). *Constructing co-cultural theory: An explication of culture, power, and communication.* Thousand Oaks, CA: Sage.

Philipsen, G. (1975). Speaking "like a man" in Teamsterville: Culture patterns of role enactment in an urban neighborhood. *Quarterly Journal of Speech, 61,* 13-22.

Philipsen, G. (1976). Places for speaking in Teamsterville. *Quarterly Journal of Speech, 62,* 15-25.

Philipsen, G. (1981). *The prospect for cultural communication.* Unpublished manuscript, East-West Center, Honolulu, HI.

Philipsen, G. (1986). Mayor Daley's council speech: A cultural analysis. *Quarterly Journal of Speech, 72,* 247-260.

Philipsen, G. (1987). The prospect for cultural communication. In D. Kincaid (Ed.), *Communication theory from Eastern and Western perspectives* (pp. 245-254). San Diego, CA: Academic Press.

Philipsen, G. (1989a). An ethnographic approach to communication studies. In B. Dervin (Ed.), *Paradigm dialogues: Research exemplars* (pp. 258-268). Newbury Park, CA: Sage.

Philipsen, G. (1989b). Speaking as a communal resource in four cultures. *International and Intercultural Communication Annual, 13,* 79-92.

Philipsen, G. (1992). *Speaking culturally: Explorations in social communication.* Albany: State University of New York Press.

Philipsen, G. (1997). A theory of speech codes. In G. Philipsen & T. Albrecht (Eds.), *Developing communication theories* (pp. 119-156). Albany: State University of New York Press.

Philipsen, G. (November, 1998). *Coming to terms with cultures.* Paper presented at the annual convention of the National Communication Association, New York.

Philipsen, G. (2000). Permission to speak the discourse of difference: A case study." *Research on Language and Social Interaction, 33,* 213-234.

Philipsen, G., & Carbaugh, D. (1986). A bibliography of fieldwork in the ethnography of communication. *Language in Society, 15,* 387-397.

Ray, G. (1987). An ethnography of nonverbal communication in an Appalachian community. *Research on Language and Social Interaction, 21,* 171-188.

Reisman, K. (1974). Contrapuntal conversations in an Antiguan village. In R. Bauman & J. Sherzer (Eds.), *Explorations in the ethnography of speaking* (pp. 110-124). London: Cambridge University Press.

Rosaldo, M. (1982). The things we do with words: Ilongot speech acts and speech act theory in philosophy. *Language in Society, 11,* 203-237.

Ruud, G. (1995). The symbolic construction of organizational identities and community in a regional symphony. *Communication Studies, 46,* 201-221.

Ruud, G. (2000). The symphony: Organizational discourse and the symbolic tensions between artistic and business ideologies. *Journal of Applied Communication Research, 28,* 117-143.

Samovar, L., & Porter, R. (Eds.). (1972). *Intercultural communication: A reader.* Belmont, CA: Wadsworth.

Schely-Newman, E. (1999). Competence and ideology in performance: Language games, identity and Israeli bureaucracy in personal narrative. *Text and Performance Quarterly, 18,* 96-113.

Schwartz, T. (Ed.). (1980). *Socialization as cultural communication: Development of a theme in the work of Margaret Mead.* Berkeley: University of California Press.

Sequeira, D. (1993). Personal address as negotiated meaning in an American church community. *Research on Language and Social Interaction, 26,* 259-285.

Sequeira, D. (1994). Gifts of tongues and healing: The performance of charismatic renewal. *Text and Performance Quarterly, 14,* 126-143.

St. George, R. (1984). "Heated" speech and literacy in seventeenth-century New England. In D. Hall & D. Allen (Eds.), *Seventeenth-century New England* (pp. 275-322). Boston: Colonial Society of Massachusetts.

Ting-Toomey, S. (1984). Qualitative research: An overview. *International and Intercultural Communication Annual, 8,* 169-184.

Turner, V. (1980). Social dramas and stories about them. *Critical Inquiry, 6,* 141-168.

Varenne, H. (1977). *Americans together: Structured diversity in a Midwestern town.* New York: Teachers College Press.

Wick, N. (1997). *Speech community in the virtual world: The case of one listserv.* Doctoral dissertation, University of Washington, Seattle.

Winchatz, M. (in press). Social meanings in German interactions: An ethnographic analysis of the second-person pronoun *Sie. Research on Language and Social Interaction, 34.*

3

Language and Verbal Communication Across Cultures

TAE-SEOP LIM
Kwangwoon University, Seoul

> The Lord said, "If as one people speaking the same language they
> have begun to do this, then nothing they plan to do will be impossible for them.
> Come, let us go down and confuse their language so they will not understand each other."
>
> —*Genesis 11:6-7*

Different cultures have different systems of meaning (i.e., languages), which confuses people from different cultures and makes it difficult, if not impossible, for them to understand each other. People, however, did not give in to the unfriendly intention of the Lord and have tenaciously tried to decode different languages into their own language. Unfortunately, these attempts have not been very successful. In the 1950s, the U.S. government tried to develop systems for machine translation of Russian and other languages, leading to the conclusion that "the only reliable, and ultimately the fastest translator is a human being deeply conversant not only with the language but with the subject as well" (Hall, 1976, p. 75). Later, the computer industry took over the task, and by the end of the 20th century several seemingly efficient automatic translation programs were put on the software market. No language researchers, however, will believe that the earlier conclusion drawn from the unsuccessful government project was premature. This software can translate most words and grammatical structures, but not the exact sense or the thought behind the words.

Hall (1976) attributed the problems of mechanical translation to the *context,* which does not appear in the message but in some cases is more important than the message itself. Because the proportion that the context occupies in a given message is widely different from language to language, and because the way in which people use the context in understanding the message is different from culture to culture, translation requires more than the knowledge of equivalent terms and grammatical structures between two languages. The whole idea of the message, expressed in the context as well as the text, must be understood first, and then translated into the matching idea in the other language. To do so, one has to have deep understandings of both cultures and both languages (Hall, 1976).

Hall's criticism of mechanical translation is deeply rooted in linguistic relativism. Yet it is not as harsh as the criticism that can be expected from a typical linguistic relativist. Had Whorf lived long enough to witness the endeavor to develop mechanical translation systems, he must have criticized it as a futile effort. Because ideas are confined in linguistic forms, following Whorf (1956), it is often impossible to express the idea of one language in another language.

Different from Hall and Whorf, there are a number of researchers who believe that languages share more similarities than differences. The sky is the sky and a table is a table, no matter how different cultures call them. With a better understanding of the universal features of language, following this perspective, people will eventually enjoy the benefits of mechanical translation systems.

In this chapter, a body of literature on the relationships between language and culture will be reviewed. First, two opposing perspectives on language and thought, linguistic relativism and universalism, will be examined. Second, a synthetic view on which most studies on language are based will be discussed. Third, the similarities and differences in language use across cultures will be reviewed in

detail. Finally, the cross-cultural validity of some universal theories of language use will be discussed.

LINGUISTIC RELATIVISM AND UNIVERSALISM

"Linguistic relativity" has become a common phrase since Whorf (1956) used it to crystallize the fundamental incommensurability between different languages. However, the observation that language, thought, and culture are closely tied together can be lineally traced through Sapir to Boas, and to Humboldt (1903-1936, Vol. 7, p. 60), who proposed that each language has its own worldview and that "the whole of language mediates between human beings and the internal and external nature that affects them." Boas (1911/1966) observed that languages delineate underlying classifications of experience, that various languages classify experience differently, and that such classifications need not rise to conscious awareness (Lucy, 1992). Boas was mainly interested in the way in which languages reflect the thought or psychology of their speakers. In later years, however, he also considered the possibility that linguistic categories might impose themselves on the thoughts of their speakers (Lucy, 1992).

Sapir (1924/1949) developed a much stronger claim on the relationship between language and thought. He maintained that language is a guide to "social reality" by powerfully conditioning all our thinking about social problems and processes. In other words, human beings do not live in the objective world alone, "but are very much at the mercy of the particular language which has become the medium of expression for their society (Sapir, 1924/1949, p. 162).

Whorf (1956) built on Sapir and claimed that "automatic, involuntary patterns of language" (p. 221), which are not the same for all languages but specific for each language, constitute the formalized side of language, or its "grammar." Then, he proceeded to propose the "linguistic relativity principle":

> which means, in informal terms, that users of markedly different grammars are pointed by their grammars toward different types of observations and different evaluations of externally similar acts of observation, and hence are not equivalent as observers but must arrive at somewhat different views of the world. (p. 221)

Whorf (1956) went further to claim that "the forms of a person's thoughts are controlled by inexorable laws of pattern of which he is unconscious. These patterns are the unperceived intricate systematizations of his own language shown readily enough by a candid comparison and contrast with other languages, especially those of a different linguistic family" (p. 252). In simpler terms, language could to some extent determine the nature of our thinking.

To demonstrate his formulation, linguistic determinism, Whorf (1956) compared the Hopi and English languages and showed the correspondences between the meaning structures and specific modes of thinking. Whorf argued, for example, that the two languages have different ways of encoding *time,* which leads speakers of these languages to different orientations toward temporal notions. The English language treats *time* in the same grammatical frame used for ordinary object nouns, which leads its speakers to treat *time* as an object that has a substance and is countable just like other tangible objects. On the contrary, the Hopi language, although it has words for temporal cycles, does not formally structure the abstract notion of *time* in grammar. The Hopi, therefore, do not treat *time* as an object but a recurrent event.

Whorf's proposition has evoked intense interests from various disciplines, but it has not led to a commensurate volume and quality of empirical research. Although a number of studies attempted to test the proposition, most of them failed to prove anything significant. Lucy (1996), who made a thorough review of the empirical studies on Whorf's proposition, concluded that "a mere handful of studies actually addressed the linguistic relativity principle directly and nearly all are conceptually flawed in very fundamental ways" (p. 37). Common defects, following Lucy, include working within a single language, privileging the categories of one language or culture in comparative studies, dealing with a relatively marginal aspect of language, and failing to provide direct evidence regarding individual cognition.

With the rise of the cognitive sciences in the second half of the 20th century, Whorf's proposition seemed to be discarded as a wild imagination. Pinker (1994) maintained "the discussions that assume that language determines thought carry on only by a collective suspension of disbelief" (p. 58). To cognitive scientists, mind is "inbuilt" capacities that have universal properties. Thinking, in other words, is built in an inner language that is structurally the same for all human beings and is not related to the facts of linguistic diversity (Fodor, 1983).

Wason and Johnson-Laird (1977) claimed that "there is no evidence for the strong version of the hypothesis—that language imposes upon its speakers a particular way of thinking about the world" (p. 411). The effort to disprove Whorf's proposition empirically, however, did not seem to be successful. Several psycholinguistic studies showed that some lexical terms, particularly basic color terms, could be universal (Berlin & Kay, 1969; Heider, 1972; Kay & McDaniel, 1978; Lucy & Shweder, 1979; Newman, 1954). These studies, however, were critically flawed. They, firmly based on the reality of the Western society, compared basic color terms of a few exotic languages with those of Western languages, mainly English. This approach inevitably leads to the conclusion that basic color terms are universal. It precludes any alternative finding, because "radically different languages will tend to look deficient by comparison with our own to the extent that much of their descriptive vocabulary is eliminated from consideration" (Lucy, 1996, p. 47).

A more critical problem of these studies is that they shifted away from the sort of grammatical data central to Whorf's work and focused on lexical items (Lucy, 1996). This shift gave rise to a number of unfair assessments of Whorf's proposition. Rosch (1977), for example, criticizes that "for the vocabulary of the language, in and of its self, to be a molder of thought, lexical dissections and categorizations of nature would have to be almost accidentally formed, rather as though some Johnny Appleseed had scattered named categories capriciously over the earth" (p. 519). Ferroluzzi (1992) reported, "Only a tiny minority of figurative expressions create problems for cross-cultural understanding and in only about 2% of the verses rhyme or double meaning seems to inspire what is said" and, then, claimed that even the weak version of the linguistic determinism has to be qualified (p. 391).

Those who attempted to undermine directly the credibility of Whorf's evidence (i.e., the Hopi concept of time) also unfairly shifted the focus of Whorf's argument (Keesing, 1994; Malotki, 1983; Wierzbicka, 1996). Malotki (1983), who examined the concept of time in the Hopi language, concluded that Whorf's claim about Hopi time conception, "being radically different from ours, does not hold" (p. 530). Whorf's (1956) claim here refers to the statement that "the Hopi language is seen to contain no words, grammatical

forms, constructions or expressions that refer directly to what we call 'time,' or to past, or future, or to enduring or lasting" (p. 57). What Whorf claims here is not that the Hopi language does not have terms expressing cyclical events but that it has no such terms that directly correspond to "time," "past," "future," "enduring," or "lasting." What Whorf emphasized was not these "exoticized" (Keesing, 1994) lexical differences but the ways in which different languages frame their worldviews in different grammatical forms.

Linguistic relativism and universalism seem to have irreconcilable differences. They are nevertheless very "compatible, as long as one subscribes to the distinction between atomic and molecular levels of semantic representation" (Gumperz & Levinson, 1996). On an atomic level (i.e., on the lexical level), semantic representations are drawn from a universal language of thought, whereas on the molecular level (i.e., on the grammatical level), there are language-specific combinations of universal atomic primitives, which may have specific conceptual effects on the users.

FUNCTIONAL RELATIVITY

At the center of the controversy between linguistic relativism and universalism are not cross-cultural linguistic differences but the cognitive effects of language. Unlike linguistic relativists or Boasian linguists, several other groups of researchers such as ethnographers (Gumperz, 1982; Gumperz & Hymes, 1972; Hymes, 1974), sociolinguists (Bernstein, 1971; Labov, 1975), and anthropologists (Hall, 1976) do not regard cognition as a central concern, yet brought about significant advancements of understanding the relationships between language and culture. These researchers focus on the functional features of language use, that is, the ways in which different cultural or social groups develop particular uses of language to accomplish certain communicative goals.

The Ethnography of Speaking

The ethnography of speaking assumes that speech is calculated (Sanders, 1987) and that speakers are purposefully applying linguistic codes toward social ends in culturally defined situations (Palmer, 1996). Philipsen (1992) argued that every distinctive culture has a distinctive speech code that implicates a culturally distinctive psychology, sociology, and rhetoric. Competent speakers, therefore, should be able to not only produce appropriate sentences but also use language pragmatically in specific social and cultural contexts (Hymes, 1971). The implication of this view is that to understand people's use of language, one must come to understand "how it is culturally shaped and constituted" (Philipsen, 1992, p. 7). The ethnography of speaking is purported to come to the understanding of such shapings and then systematically report such understandings.

Rather than presenting an explanatory theory, Hymes (1972) advocated a "descriptive theory" aimed at producing a general outline of the contexts and components of ways of speaking (Philipsen, 1992). The job of an ethnographer of speaking is to observe and identify distinctive ways of language use in a particular speech community (see also Philipsen, this volume). This descriptive approach tends to encourage ethnographers to focus on one specific aspect of language use of one particular cultural group at a given time. And, more often than not, ethnographers study nonmainstream speech events or communities such as black street talk (Abrahams, 1989), Indian time (Philips, 1989), and the truck driver community (Philipsen, 1992). This approach over years has produced a significant amount of research on various languages and cultures

around the world including the Native South American discourse (Sherzer & Urban, 1986), the Papua New Guinean language and discourse (Brison, 1992; Schieffelin, 1990), pragmatics and cultures of African languages (Dahl, 1995; Hayward & Lewis, 1996; Huttar & Gregerson, 1985), ritual speech in Indonesia (Kuipers, 1998), and the power semantics in Pohnpei, Micronesia (Keating, 1998). These studies showed that languages are closely tied to the values and ideologies of their users, and syntactic structures and lexical items inevitably reflect the idiosyncratic experiences of the speech communities. Thus, what is needed to understand the ways in which a cultural group communicates is not the anglocentric global perspective but the specific local perspective.

Several studies done by sociolinguists and anthropological linguists are also considered ethnographic research (e.g., the power and solidarity semantics of the Indo-European pronominal system by Brown & Gilman, 1960; systematic cultural shapings of male and female language by Keenan, 1974, Sherzer, 1987; subtlety of modes of indirection in making requests by Ervin-Tripp, 1976; the addressing system of North American English by Ervin-Tripp, 1974). Although the majority of ethnographic research deals with one particular language and culture, a few exceptions attempt to apply this approach to intercultural pragmatics. Davis and Henze (1998) propose ways in which issues in intercultural pragmatics can be approached from an ethnographic perspective, and then provide two illustrative analyses: second-language education and intercultural communication in the workplace. Clyne (1994) observes and analyzes verbal interactions among speakers who migrated to Australia as adults and whose first language is a language other than English. Most noticeably, the edited volume by Knapp, Enninger, and Knapp-Potthoff (1987) contains a dozen studies on a variety of intercultural settings including the contact between German and Turkish, the negotiation between French and Dutch, and the multilingual Singapore society. Given a rapid growth of intercultural contacts and the increasing number of problems caused by unmindful intercultural communication, these studies, employing a variety of approaches, attempt to identify the factors influencing communication between people from different cultural backgrounds. Lack of knowledge on the other's culture (not on the other's language), ethnocentric attributions, stereotypes, sociopolitical problems, and unwarranted beliefs of universality are proposed to be some of the major factors causing intercultural miscommunications.

Language and Context

Bernstein (1971), while examining children's language, learned that different classes within a single-language community use different types of language. Children from middle-class families used what he called the elaborated code, whereas children from lower-working-class families used the restricted code. The elaborated code makes use of accurate and sophisticated grammatical structures, uses a wide range of adjectives and adverbs, and manifests a relatively large vocabulary. It is context-free; it requires no shared assumptions and takes very little for granted. The speaker's intention, therefore, is explicit and verbally elaborate. Speech depends little on extraverbal channels. In contrast, the restricted code employs short, grammatically simple, and often incomplete sentences of poor syntactic structure; is rigid and limited in the use of adjectives and adverbs; and manifests a small vocabulary. It is context-bound; it requires many shared experiences and takes a great deal for granted. The speaker's intention is implicit

and unelaborated, and speech shows high dependency on extraverbal channels.

Bernstein (1971, 1972) argued that because schools adopt the elaborated code as the standard language, the users of the restricted code, the working-class children, have obvious disadvantages. Although Bernstein never intended to imply that the working-class children were linguistically deficient, his emphasis on their disadvantage at school led his critics (e.g., Edwards, 1987; Labov, 1972a, 1972b; Rosen, 1972) to charge him with disgracing the language of the powerless.

Bernstein (1971, 1972) relates codes to not only classes but also family types: *positional* and *person oriented*. In a positional family, members are seen as the occupant of the position in the family hierarchy, whereas in a person-oriented family, members are seen as equal individuals and judged by their individual qualities. In a positional family, the communication system is closed. What one is allowed to say and how one is allowed to say it are largely dependent on the position one is occupying in the family. Meanings, therefore, are realized in a reduced range of alternatives. In a person-oriented family, the communication system is open; that is, all family members are allowed to communicate freely. In this system, therefore, meanings are realized in a variety of ways.

In different family types, parents use different modes of control toward their children (Bernstein, 1971). In a positional family, parents use imperative modes of control that do not make use of any appeals but simply give orders, or at best positional appeals, which, based on stereotypical social norms, ask children to pursue the obligation that the occupant of the position must fulfill. Parents in a person-oriented family, in contrast, use personal appeals that are rational and personalized and require sophisticated skills of persuasion.

Children in person-oriented families grow up hearing a variety of messages that are delivered in well-elaborated manners and realize that they also have to elaborate to get their meanings across. These children, therefore, acquire the elaborated code. On the contrary, children who are raised in positional families neither experience enough elaborated messages nor realize the necessity to elaborate their meanings. Thus, these children end up acquiring only the restricted code.

Bernstein's explanation of children's code acquisition is deterministic in nature. However, his explanation of why different types of families use different codes opens up the possibility to look into the functional aspect of codes. Bernstein (1971, 1972) argues that members of a positional family share a strong sense of social identity with some loss of personal autonomy, which fosters high solidarity, shared identifications, shared expectations, and common assumptions. Within these families, elaboration is not only unnecessary but also disruptive. Positional orientation also leads to the belief that meanings are particular; that is, meanings are closely tied to the context and would only be fully understood by others if they had access to the context. Thus, members of a positional family do not bother to elaborate their meanings to an outsider. In contrast, members of a person-oriented family pursue personal autonomy even at the expense of social identity, which fosters high independence, separate identities, and minimum amount of shared expectations and common assumptions. Because of low sharedness in these families, speakers are forced to elaborate their meanings and make them both explicit and specific. Personal orientation also leads to the belief that meanings are universal; that is, anyone can understand the message if it is well elaborated. Thus, members of a person-oriented family tend to use elaborated codes to outsiders as well. In short, the restricted code manifests the communal and particularistic ideologies, whereas the elaborated code reflects the individualistic and universal ideologies.

Hall (1976) expands Bernstein's (1971) perspective to a theory of context. Hall argues that the code, the context, and the meaning are mutually nondetachable; that is, understanding the context is crucial to understanding the message. However, the proportion that the context occupies in the communication varies.

> A high-context communication or message is one in which most of the information is either in the physical context or internalized in the person, while very little is in the coded, explicit, transmitted part of the message. A low-context communication is just the opposite; i.e., the mass of the information is vested in the explicit code. (Hall, 1976, p. 79)

Hall (1976) states the linguistic features of high-context and low-context messages are the same as what Bernstein "terms restricted and elaborated codes" (p. 80).

Hall applies the theory of context to the explanation of cultural differences in language use. He argued that we can place different cultures on a continuum of the context dependency of communication. Roughly, Eastern societies manifest high-context cultures, and Western societies, low-context cultures. Hall does not make specific efforts to explain why context dependency is different across cultures. However, Bernstein's distinction between positional and person oriented can shed light on this question: The East is more positional, and the West is more person oriented.

Most empirical research on language use across cultures seems to adopt functional relativism rather than linguistic relativism. Functional relativism assumes that the particular form taken by the grammatical system of language is closely related to the social and personal needs that language is required to serve

(Halliday, 1973, 1978). Forms of language not only reflect people's social position and the circumstance but also express their view of the way society is organized, and of their own position within the social network. In other words, the forms of language encode a socially constructed representation of the world. Because different cultures have different environments, values, beliefs, and attitudes, their languages tend to be different from each other. This perspective seemingly reverses the direction of causality of Whorf's proposition. Functional relativism, although it assumes that the linguistic forms are the product of necessity, believes that once the linguistic forms are systematized, they influence the thought patterns of the users. Below, I will discuss major cultural differences in language use that are reported by empirical studies adopting the functional relativity perspective.

DIFFERENCES IN LANGUAGE USE ACROSS CULTURES

Values on Speech

Zen Buddhists may be the most enthusiastic supporters and the worst critics of linguistic determinism. They realize that language confines people's capability of thinking, limiting the imagination and imposing biases, and therefore, they try to meditate without language and communicate beyond language. The emergence of Zen Buddhism is not surprising, when we consider how little faith Eastern cultures place in words. The West has developed a rich tradition of speech, subscribing to the principle of the universality of meanings. The East, however, has firmly believed that meanings are particular, which has given rise to the belief that a total understanding requires mental unification with the other person. The belief of oneness, or a perfect

harmony, became a tenet for all major East Asian religions including Taoism, Buddhism, and Confucianism (Yum, 1988).

The Western culture of words and the Eastern culture of harmony are well illustrated in their respective explanations of the creation of the universe. A book in the New Testament describes the process as "In the beginning was *the Word*, and the Word was with God, and the Word was God. He was with God in the beginning. Through him all things were made; without him nothing was made that has been made." (John 1:1-e). On the contrary, Lao-Tze describes the process as "Tao bears *the One (the whole)*, the One bears the Two (Yin [Femaleness] and Yang [Maleness]), the Two bears the Three (Yin, Yang, and Human), and the Three bears the world" (Tao De Jing, 42). Lao-Tze taught to stay away from words, saying, "To become the way the Nature intended you to be, you should speak rarely" (Tao De Jing, 23) and "Who understands does not preach; Who preaches does not understand; Reserve your judgments and words; Smooth differences and forgive disagreements; Dull your wit and simplify your purpose" (Tao De Jing, 58).

Confucius demystifies Lao-Tze's teachings and applies them to real-life communication. His teachings on verbal communication, therefore, are no more liberal than those of Lao-Tze. He taught that "fancy words and embellished styles do not bear virtues" and "words more often than not cause troubles." Prudent speech is always encouraged: "If a gentleman is frivolous, he will lose the respect of his inferiors" (Waley, 1938, p. 85). Even today, these religious teachings are deeply rooted in the minds of Asians (Gudykunst & Kim, 1984). By Western standards, therefore, Asians are very reticent (Kang & Pearce, 1983).

Roughly at the same time when Lao-Tze and Confucius preached the futility of verbalization in the East, Socrates, Plato, and Aristotle taught the importance of reasoning and logical persuasion on the other side of the world.

> This rhetorical tradition reflects in a profound way the Western cultural pattern of logical, rational, and analytic thinking. A primary function of speech in this tradition is to express one's ideas and thoughts as clearly, logically, and persuasively as possible, so the speaker can be fully recognized for his or her individuality in influencing others. (Gudykunst & Kim, 1984, p. 140)

In Asian cultures, however, rhetoric has been "too important to be severed from its religio-philosophical context" (Oliver, 1971, p. 11).

The Asian attitude toward speech and rhetoric is characteristically a holistic one; that is, the words are only part of, and are inseparable from, the total communication context, which includes the personal characters of the parties involved and the nature of the interpersonal relationships between them (Gudykunst & Kim, 1984). Korean voters, for example, do not tend to be significantly influenced by televised political debates. In many cases, including the 1994 mayoral election in Seoul, pre-debate favorites gained even more grounds after relatively poor performances at the debates. Koreans, like other East Asians, believe that speech aimed at social integration and harmony, rather than at the well-being of a specific speaker, naturally tends to lack arguments and logicality (Gudykunst & Kim, 1984). Thus, the lack of rhetorical competence (i.e., stuttering and hesitation, and irrationality and emotionality) manifested by their favorite candidates was believed to reflect their sincere and trustworthy character (Lim, 1997). Lee and Boster (1992) compared the effects of speech rate between Korea and the United States. Rapid delivery can be used as an effective means of enhancing one's

credibility in the United States, and this principle can be generalized to Korean female speakers. On the other hand, slow delivery is more effective in increasing the credibility of Korean male speakers.

Silence in the West is often considered a pause, empty space, absence of sound, or blank in communication (Hasegawa & Gudykunst, 1998). When silence prolongs, conversationalists become uneasy. In Asia, however, silence is valued rather than feared (Morsbach, 1976; Oliver, 1971). Two friends can sit side-by-side for hours not talking to each other. A subordinate may remain silent for the entire period of a superior's preaching. Smutkupt and Barna (1976) observe the significance of silence in Thailand as a sign of respect, agreement, or disagreement and as a beautiful form of speech. European culture places a great premium not only on knowing but also on saying what one knows (Wierzbicka, 1991). Asian culture, though it values knowledge, discourages verbalizing knowledge. If what one said is truthful, the verbalization constitutes a violation of the modesty principle; if not, a manifestation of ignorance. In either case, the person ends up losing face. There is a saying in Korea that "silence guarantees you a second place," which means silence is preferred to improper words.

However, silence is not always valued in Asia. It is preferred to verbalization only when the latter poses a threat to the face of self or the other such as in disagreement, challenge, talking back to superiors, interrupting the other's speech, breaking peace by initiating a conversation, and speaking out one's knowledge. When a response or active participation is expected by the other person, keeping silent is rather considered impolite or uncooperative. Hasegawa and Gudykunst (1998) report that Japanese viewed silence very negative in some situations. Particularly when communicating with a stranger, silence is considered more negative than it is in America.

Languages Styles and Code-Choice

"The cardinal devotion of the Asian mind to the related concepts of unity and harmony" (Oliver, 1971, p. 10) gave rise to two crucial linguistic characteristics: status-markedness and group-orientedness. Goldstein and Tamura (1975), after a lengthy comparison between Japanese and American English, concluded that Japanese focuses much more sharply on two elements, status and group, than does American English.

That Asians are more concerned with status than are Westerners and that the concerns are always manifested in their messages is nothing new. The crucial point Goldstein and Tamura (1975) are making, however, is that the Japanese language itself has a rich system of marking status. Whereas Indo-European languages use some isolated linguistic devices, such as pronouns (Brown & Gilman, 1960), address terms (Ervin-Tripp, 1974), and more or less imposing speech acts (Brown & Levinson, 1987), to mark status differences, Japanese (and Korean as well) manifests the differences in the whole system of language. Koreans distinguish five different styles of language in terms of formality: formal one-down, informal one-down, one-across, formal one-up, and informal one-up, in order of the respect manifested. Different styles have different sets of inflectional endings, address terms, pronouns, lexical items, honorific prefixes and suffixes, particles, and so on.

In Western societies, of the two essential dimensions of interpersonal relationships (i.e., intimacy [or social distance] and power [or status] difference) the former has more influences on code-choices since the historic egalitarian movement (Brown & Gilman, 1960). In Asia, however, status difference overrules

social distance (Hijirida & Sohn, 1986). Whenever one speaks to a superior or an elder, one has to employ honorifics no matter how close they may be. The informal one-down style in the Korean language is especially used toward intimate superiors. The formal one-up style is used toward inferiors who have already established respectable degrees of status.

Asians often distinguish between the private code, language used when no third parties are present, and the public code, language used in presence of others. In Japan, the parents or grandparents, when speaking to one another in the presence of children, mostly use the same kinship terms used by the children to respect the other's status (Goldstein & Tamura, 1975). In Korea, to address adults by name in the presence of their inferiors (e.g., children, subordinates, students) is considered an attempt, such as by use of an insult or humor, to ignore the status of the addressee.

Traditionally in Asia, age has been one of the most important elements of status. In Korea, a difference of even one or two years in age creates a difference in status. Within the sibling group, age differences are well respected in Japanese and Korean families. Although older siblings call the younger by name, younger siblings address the older by kinship terms such as "older brother" or "older sister" (Goldstein & Tamura, 1975). Age differences outside family are also well respected. A child may call an older girl by the term meaning "older sister," a young woman by the term meaning "aunt," an old woman by the term meaning "grandmother." A mother speaking to her child in American English about an older girl across the street may address her as "that girl" or by name. In Japanese, on the other hand, the term used is in direct relationship to the age of the child being spoken to, that is, "that older sister" or "older sister Hiroko."

Japanese are keenly concerned with group identities when they make code-choices. In American English, the self never becomes reunited with the other except through the pronoun form *we* and its variants; Japanese linguistic structure, on the other hand, locks the individual and group and separates both from the outside (Goldstein & Tamura, 1975). British norms also prioritize separateness and clear boundaries in relationships, individuality, and autonomy (Tamura & Lau, 1992). Japanese, on the other hand, are seen as parts of the embedded interconnectedness of relationships, which is manifested in the language.

Children learn gradually to conceive of their family as a linguistic unit, identical with themselves. Although they make various status distinctions within the family and use various degrees of polite forms in speaking to their own family members, they gradually learn to use the same plain (and later also humble) forms in talking to outsiders that they would use for themselves (Goldstein & Tamura, 1975). This distinction also applies to other groups (e.g., class, school, and business groups). American English associates individual to individual by name and nonreciprocal pronoun usage. Although loyalty to certain groups, of course, exists and various vocabulary, insignia, and other trappings bind the individual to his or her group, linguistic structure does not, on the whole.

The emphasis on group identities in Japanese and Korean goes beyond identifying with ingroup members. Their languages manifest careful considerations not to separate the other from self. In English, one cannot carry on a conversation without pronouns, and one feels uncomfortable speaking when the name of the hearer has been forgotten (Goldstein & Tamura, 1975). English speakers need to confirm constantly the individual identity of the other person. In Japanese and Korean, the confirmation of individual identities is avoided throughout the conversation by minimizing the use of *you, I,* and each other's name. They can speak perfectly well with minimal reliance on pronouns (when the subject of a sentence is a pronoun, it is usually omitted) and are quite comfortable even if they cannot remember the other's name (Goldstein & Tamura, 1975).

Other studies comparing collectivist and individualist cultures reported results that are consistent with what was found in Far East Asia. Kashima and Kashima (1998), examining the use of first- and second-person singular pronouns (e.g., *I* and *you*) across 39 languages spoken in 71 cultures, found that cultures with "pronoun-drop languages" tended to be less individualistic than those with "non-pronoun-drop languages."

Speech Acts

Although the observation that communication is a process where no clear-cut beginning or end exists was made by Western scholars (e.g., Miller & Steinberg, 1975), those who seem to be really conscious of this fact are Asians. In Asia, particularly in East Asia, global goals precede local goals, relationships precede actions, styles precede contents, and characters precede arguments. In other words, accomplishing the current task or performing the intended speech act successfully by elaborating the informational content and reasoning with evidence is not as important as maintaining the relationship by following culturally mandated styles or establishing one's character by showing good deeds. "Asians tend to be concerned more with the overall emotional quality of the interaction than with the meaning of particular words or sentences" (Gudykunst & Kim, 1984, p. 142). They believe that in the long run their relationships—

not their words—will help accomplish their communication goals.

Emphasis of global goals over local goals in Asian communication leads them to be less assertive and less expressive. First, Asians, compared to Westerners, are very low in self-assertiveness. Barnlund (1975) reported that Japanese is more regulated than white English, which, in turn, is more regulated than black English (Kochman, 1981). Particularly between ingroups, Asians tend to suppress confrontations or expression of negative verbal messages. "Courtesy often takes precedence over truthfulness" (Gudykunst & Kim, 1984, p. 142), which leads Asians to give an agreeable and pleasant answer to a question when a literal, factual answer might be unpleasant or embarrassing (Hall & Whyte, 1960). The Japanese culture is called a "culture of consideration" (Suzuki, 1986) in which people always try not to cause trouble for others and not to hurt their feelings, which leads Japanese to be circumspect and reserved (Lebra, 1976). A similar tendency was reported of Thai culture. In Thailand, doubts are rarely verbalized, especially when one is communicating with elders and persons of higher status (Smutkupt & Barna, 1976).

Second, Asians often suppress expression of their emotions. Being emotional in Asian culture is believed to reflect a lack of self-control, which is a sign of a frivolous nature. Asians will say *good* instead of *fantastic* and *not very good* instead of *terrible*. "Even when expressing strong personal affection, a style of hesitancy and indirectness is commonly preferred. Asians can even be suspicious of the genuineness of direct verbal expressions of love and respect. Excessive verbal praise or compliments sometimes are received with feelings of embarrassment" (Gudykunst & Kim, 1984, p. 142).

On the contrary, Arabic cultures, although high-context in communication, tend to be overly expressive. The Arabic language abounds with grammatical features of assertion and exaggeration: Some common-ending words are designed to emphasize the meaning, the doubling of the sounds of some consonants creates stronger effects, and the repetition of pronouns and words increases assertiveness (Gudykunst & Kim, 1984; Suleiman, 1973). In addition, Arabs use stylistic and rhetorical devices, such as metaphors, similes, and long arrays of adjectives, to accomplish even stronger exaggerations (Suleiman, 1973). Seemingly, it is a paradox that the over-assertiveness and over-expressiveness of Arabic communication create as ambiguous a message as the under-assertiveness and under-expressiveness of Asian communication. However, over-ssertiveness and over-expressiveness reflect the tendency of the Arabic culture to emphasize affect over accuracy, image over meaning, and form over function (Zaharna, 1995). Asians realize the same preferences in opposite ways.

Italian culture, Slavic cultures, Jewish culture, and American black culture are also very expressive. These cultures value "uninhibited emotional expression" whether the feelings are good or bad (Wierzbicka, 1991).

Low assertiveness and expressiveness of Asians inevitably lead to high ambiguity of their messages. Even without these tendencies, some Asian languages have grammatical structures that cultivate ambiguity. In the Japanese and the Korean languages, verbs come at the end of sentences, which means that the illocutionary act of a sentence cannot be determined until the whole sentence has been uttered. These languages often omit the subject of a sentence and are not specific in the numerals. Ellipses and incomplete sentences are abundant. The genuine ambiguity, however, comes from Asians' attitudes toward verbalization. Japanese can talk for hours without clearly expressing their opinion to another

(Morsbach, 1976). Even in ordinary conversation, a Japanese person may say *hai* (yes) without necessarily implying agreement. Frequently, *hai* is intended by the speaker, and is expected by the listener, to mean "I understand what you are saying."

Ambiguity of messages prompted cultures emphasizing high-context communication to develop strategies to decode the message accurately. Even in Western societies where meanings are relatively well elaborated, more can be meant than what is actually said (Grice, 1975). Particularly when the speaker attempts to trigger not a "standard" but a "generated implicature" by "exploiting the maxims of conversation" (Grice, 1975), interpretation depends a lot on the contextual knowledge. The implicature of even this nature in the West can be understood universally if proper context information is provided.

The ways in which Asians generate implicatures fall outside the scope of Grice's theory. As Yoshikawa (1978) observes, what is verbally expressed and what is actually intended are two different things. To understand the real intention, what one needs to employ are not the knowledge of conversational maxims and contextual information but pure intuition obtained through a lengthy history of contact with the speaker (i.e., *kan*).

Koreans have to develop *noon-chi* to figure out the intention, desire, mood, and attitude of the speaker from the ambiguous message (Lim & Choi, 1996). *Noon-chi*, which is literally translated as "eye-measure," is an integral part of communicative competence of Koreans. The ability to use *noon-chi* is different from person to person, and usually persons of more experiences use *noon-chi* better. Persons who do not have the proper abilities to use *noon-chi* often threaten the other's face by forcing the other to say explicitly something that may damage the other's respectability (Lim & Choi, 1996).

One of the major differences between the operation of *noon-chi* or *kan* and the process of generating implicature or reading between the lines is that, to those who have to use *noon-chi* to figure out the other's intended meaning, the mutual assumption that saying or doing *A* in the given context means *B* (Grice, 1975) is not available. Koreans who decide not to express their meanings explicitly do not necessarily want the other to figure out their meanings, or do not necessarily assume that the other will be able to figure out their intentions (Lim & Choi, 1996). In addition, the parties who have to use *noon-chi* to figure out the intention of the other do not necessarily have concrete clues about the intention. They have to go through the *noon-chi* operation, which makes use of all sorts of world knowledge, the knowledge of the other, the knowledge of the context, the history of their interactions, and verbal and nonverbal messages, if any. The process of operating *noon-chi*, in other words, is not routine but highly arbitrary. Thus, the interpretations generated by *noon-chi* mostly represent the perspective of the operator of *noon-chi*, that is, the hearer or observer (Lim & Choi, 1996). The interpretations sometimes are very different from what the other really intended.

Indirectness in the West is built on grammatical features such as longer grammatical structures and the subjunctive and conditional moods. That in the East, however, relies on the speaker's approach to communication such as avoiding verbalization and obscuring. Japanese do not say what they want and avoid precision and specification (Mizutani & Mizutani, 1987). Similarly, the Javanese culture manifests high degrees of "indirection" and "dissimulation" (Geertz, 1976). Javanese norms favor beating about the bush, not saying what is on one's mind, unwillingness to face issues in their naked truth, never saying what one really thinks, avoiding gratuitous truths, and never showing one's real feelings directly (Wierzbicka, 1991).

When Asians are placed in a situation where they have to verbalize their meanings, they do not have the luxury of grammatical indirectness devices. Their resort in this situation is the well-developed honorific system. Honorifics, by carrying certain degrees of respect for the other, compensate for the possible face-threat. When they are in a situation where the use of honorifics is inadequate (e.g., when they are speaking to a friend, when they are arguing, or when they speak in a Western language), they can be very direct.

Directness varies in Western societies. Wierzbicka (1991) reported that English cultural norms (as compared with Polish norms) favor "indirectness" in acts aimed at bringing about an action from the addressee. But as compared with some other languages such as Australian Aboriginal norms or African American norms, Anglo-Saxon cultural norms encourage "directness" in seeking information from the addressee (Abrahams, 1976; Eades, 1982; Sansom, 1980). Tannen (1981) and Blum-Kulka (1982) reported Greek social norms require a much higher level of indirectness in social interaction than American ones. On the contrary, the Israeli culture, as compared with the cultures of English-speaking societies, was reported to be generally more direct (Blum-Kulka, Danet, & Gherson, 1985). Israelis are less concerned with social distance, and therefore, their interaction style is oriented toward solidarity politeness. House and Kasper (1981) reported that German speakers were more direct than English speakers both in complaints and requests. Polish and many other European languages such as Russian, Serbo-Croatian, and Spanish are also very direct. Therefore, it may not be European languages but British English and North American English that emphasize the rights and the autonomy of individuals (Wierzbicka, 1991).

Validity of Cross-Cultural Theorizing

Despite differences in language use across cultures, constant efforts have been made to identify universal features. Most notable of these are a universal natural logic (Gordon & Lakoff, 1975), a universal logic of conversation (Grice, 1975), universal rules of indirectness (Searle, 1975), and a universal logic of politeness strategy selection (Brown & Levinson, 1987). Although the generalizations proposed in these works provide useful insights into mechanisms of language use, they should not be seen as absolute (Wierzbicka, 1991). For example, Searle (1975, p. 64) claimed that ordinary conversational requirements of politeness normally make it awkward to issue flat imperative sentences and explicit performatives and that politeness is the chief motivation for indirectness. Wierzbicka (1991), based on comparisons between a variety of languages including English, Italian, Russian, Polish, Yiddish, Hebrew, Japanese, Chinese, Korean, Walmatjari (an Australian Aboriginal language), criticized these claims, saying they are an illusion and simple manifestations of English conversational strategies and Anglo-Saxon cultural values. The principle of cooperation, the four maxims of conversation, and the implicature-generating mechanisms are also specific to the North American culture (Wierzbicka, 1991) or at the very most to low-context communication. Asians do not presuppose any principles or maxims to trigger implicatures, as evidenced by Japanese *kan* and Korean *noon-chi*.

Although Brown and Levinson (1987) claimed that their universal theory of politeness was based on a dozen languages from all quarters of the world, the theory reveals a strong anglocentric bias. Lim (1994) reported that the "wants" to be autonomous, respected, competent, and accepted (which roughly correspond to Brown and Levinson's negative and positive face-wants) represent only one of the five dimensions of Koreans' face-wants, namely, the self-sufficiency face. The other four dimensions are the decency face, including the image of being appropriate and well groomed; the integrity face, comprising the image of being trustworthy, discreet, and reasonable; the nobility face, including the image of being charitable, elegant, and prosperous; and the capability face, including the image of being socially successful. The two core principles of politeness, "avoidance of imposition" and "approval of the other," and numerous other specific tactics reflect clearly the authors' culture-specific perspective (Wierzbicka, 1991).

Anglocentrism, the dominant paradigm of today's cross-cultural pragmatics, allows English-speaking authors to make cross-cultural generalizations of their ethnographic knowledge with examinations of some hand-selected, isolated examples from other languages. To reach a valid generalization on a particular pragmatic feature, one has to compare the whole system of the pragmatic feature of one language with those of other languages. Researchers who attempted such a rigorous type of cross-cultural validation have always been greeted by culture-specific differences (Blum-Kulka, House, & Kasper, 1989; Emanatian, 1995; Fitch & Sanders, 1994; Suszczynska, 1999).

This does not mean that there are no universals in language use. Comparative studies always yield certain similarities among cultures. These similarities, however, seem to exist at atomic, semantic, or general levels, not at molecular, episodic, or specific levels as Gumperz and Levinson (1996) argued. Thus, the search for universals should focus more on the basic semantic elements or semantic primitives, and the study on specific uses of language or pragmatics should be more sensitive to cultural diversity.

REFERENCES

Abrahams, R. D. (1976). *Talking black*. Rowley, MA: Newbury House.

Abrahams, R. D. (1989). Black talking on the streets. In R. Bauman & J. Sherzer (Eds.), *Explorations in the ethnography of speaking* (pp. 240-262). Cambridge, UK: Cambridge University Press.

Barnlund, D. (1975). *Public and private self in Japan and the United States*. Tokyo: Simul.

Berlin, B., & Kay, P. (1969). *Basic color terms: Their universality and evolution*. Berkeley: University of California Press.

Bernstein, B. (1971). *Class, codes and control: Vol. 1. Theoretical studies toward a sociology of language*. London: Routledge & Kegan Paul.

Bernstein, B. (1972). Social class, language, and socialization. In P. P. Giglioli (Ed.), *Language and social context* (pp. 173-178). Middlesex, UK: Penguin.

Blum-Kulka, S. (1982). Learning to say what you mean in a second language: A study of the speech act performance of learners of Hebrew as a second language. *Applied Linguistics, 3,* 29-59.

Blum-Kulka, S., Danet, B., & Gherson, R. (1985). The language of requesting in Israeli society. In J. P. Forgas (Ed.), *Language and social situations* (pp. 113-139). New York: Springer.

Blum-Kulka, S., House, J., & Kasper, G. (1989). *Cross-cultural pragmatics: Requests and apologies*. Norwood, NJ: Ablex.

Boas, F. (1966). Introduction. In F. Boas (Ed.), *Handbook of American Indian languages* (Reprint ed., P. Holder, Ed., pp. 1-79). Lincoln: University of Nebraska Press. (Original work published 1911)

Brison, K. J. (1992). *Just talk: Gossip, meetings, and power in a Papua New Guinea village*. Berkeley: University of California Press.

Brown, P., & Levinson, S. (1987). *Politeness: Some universals in language usage*. Cambridge, UK: Cambridge University Press.

Brown, R., & Gilman, A. (1960). The pronouns of power and solidarity. In T. A. Sebeok (Ed.), *Style in language* (pp. 252-276). Cambridge, MA: MIT Press.

Clyne, M. G. (1994). *Inter-cultural communication at work: Cultural values in discourse.* Cambridge, UK, and New York: Cambridge University Press.

Dahl, O. (1995). When the future comes from behind: Malagasy and other time concepts and some consequences for communication. *International Journal of Intercultural Relations, 19,* 197-209.

Davis, K. A., & Henze, R. C. (1998). Applying ethnographic perspectives to issues in cross-cultural pragmatics. *Journal of Pragmatics, 30,* 399-419.

Eades, D. (1982). You gotta know how to talk: Information seeking in south-east Queensland Aboriginal society. *Australian Journal of Linguistics, 2,* 61-82.

Edwards, A. D. (1987). Language codes and classroom practice. *Oxford Educational Review, 12,* 237-247.

Emanatian, M. (1995). Metaphor and the expression of emotion: The value of cross-cultural perspectives. *Metaphor and Symbolic Activity, 10,* 163-182.

Ervin-Tripp, S. (1974). Sociolinguistic rules of address. In J. B. Pride & J. Holmes (Eds.), *Sociolinguistics* (pp. 225-240). Harmondsworth, UK: Penguin.

Ervin-Tripp, S. (1976). Is Sybil there? The structure of American English directives. *Language in Society, 5,* 25-66.

Ferroluzzi, G. E. (1992). If Whorf had known Tiruvalluvar: Universalism and cultural relativism in a famous work of ancient Tamil literature. *Anthropos, 87,* 391-406.

Fitch, K. L., & Sanders, R. E. (1994). Culture, communication, and preferences for directness in expression of directives. *Communication Theory, 4,* 219-245.

Fodor, J. A. (1983). *The modularity of mind.* Cambridge: MIT Press.

Geertz, C. (1976). *The religion of Java.* Chicago: Chicago University Press.

Goldstein, B. Z., & Tamura, K. (1975). *Japan and America: A comparative study in language and culture.* Rutland, VT: Charles E. Tuttle.

Gordon, D., & Lakoff, G. (1975). Conversational postulates. In P. Cole & J. L. Morgan (Eds.), *Syntax and semantics: Vol. 3. Speech acts* (pp. 83-106). New York: Academic Press.

Grice, H. P. (1975). Logic and conversation. In P. Cole & J. L. Morgan (Eds.), *Syntax and semantics: Vol. 3. Speech acts* (pp. 41-58). New York: Academic Press.

Gudykunst, W. B., & Kim, Y. Y. (1984). *Communicating with strangers: An approach to intercultural communication.* Reading, MA: Addison-Wesley.

Gumperz, J. J. (1982). *Discourse strategies.* Cambridge, UK: Cambridge University Press.

Gumperz, J. J., & Hymes, D. H. (Eds.). (1972). *Directions in sociolinguistics: The ethnography of communication.* New York: Holt, Rinehart & Winston.

Gumperz, J. J., & Levinson, S. C. (Eds.). (1996). *Rethinking linguistic relativity.* Cambridge, UK: Cambridge University Press.

Hall, E. T. (1976). *Beyond culture.* Garden City, NY: Doubleday/Anchor.

Hall, E. T., & Whyte, W. F. (1960). Intercultural communication. *Human Organization, 19,* 5-12.

Halliday, M. (1973). *Explorations in the functions of language.* New York: Elsevier.

Halliday, M. (1978). *Language as social semiotic: The social interpretation of language and meaning.* Baltimore: University Park.

Hasegawa, T., & Gudykunst, W. B. (1998). Silence in Japan and the United States. *Journal of Cross-Cultural Psychology, 29,* 668-684.

Hayward, R. J., & Lewis, I. M. (1996). *Voice and power: The culture of language in north-east Africa: Essays in honour of B. W. Andrzejewski.* London: School of Oriental and African Studies.

Heider, E. (1972). Universals in color naming and memory. *Journal of Experimental Psychology, 93,* 10-20.

Hijirida, K., & Sohn, H. M. (1986). Cross-cultural patterns of honorifics and sociolinguistic sensitivity to honorific variables: Evidence from English, Japanese, and Korean. *Papers in Linguistics, 19,* 365-401.

House, J., & Kasper, G. (1981). Politeness markers in English and German. In F. Coulmas (Ed.), *Conversational routine: Explorations in standardized communication situations and pre-*

patterned speech (pp. 157-185). The Hague, the Netherlands: Mouton.

Humboldt, K. W. von. (1903-1936). *Wilhelm von Humboldt's Werke* (A. Leitzmann, Ed.). 17 vols. Berlin: B. Behr.

Huttar, G., & Gregerson, K. K. (Eds.). (1985). *Pragmatics in non-Western perspective*. Dallas, TX: Summer Institute of Linguistics.

Hymes, D. H. (1971). Sociolinguistics and the ethnography of speaking. In E. Ardener (Ed.), *Social anthropology and language* (pp. 47-93). London: Tavistock.

Hymes, D. H. (1972). Models of the interaction of language and social life. In J. J. Gumperz & D. H. Hymes (Eds.), *Directions in sociolinguistics: The ethnography of communication* (pp. 35-71). New York: Holt, Rinehart & Winston.

Hymes, D. H. (1974). *Foundations in sociolinguistics: An ethnographic approach*. Philadelphia: University of Pennsylvania Press.

Kang, K. W., & Pearce, W. B. (1983). Reticence: A transcultural analysis. *Communication, 8,* 79-106.

Kashima, E. S., & Kashima, Y. (1998). Culture and language: The case of cultural dimensions and personal pronoun use. *Journal of Cross-Cultural Psychology, 29,* 461-486.

Kay, P., & McDaniel, C. K. (1978). The linguistic significance of the meanings of basic color terms. *Language, 54,* 610-646.

Keating, E. L. (1998). *Power sharing: Language, rank, gender, and social space in Pohnpei, Micronesia*. New York: Oxford University Press.

Keenan, E. (1974). Norm-makers, norm-breakers: Uses of speech by men and women in a Malagasy community. In R. Bauman & J. Sherzer (Eds.), *Explorations in the ethnography of speaking* (pp. 125-143). Cambridge, UK: Cambridge University Press.

Keesing, R. M. (1994). Theories of culture revisited. In R. Borofsky (Ed.), *Assessing cultural anthropology* (pp. 310-312). New York: McGraw-Hill.

Knapp, K., Enninger, W., & Knapp-Potthoff, A. (1987). *Analyzing intercultural communication*. Berlin: Mouton de Gruyter.

Kochman, T. (1981). *Black and white styles in conflict*. Chicago: University of Chicago Press.

Kuipers, J. C. (1998). *Language, identity, and marginality in Indonesia: The changing nature of ritual speech on the Island of Sumba*. Cambridge, UK: Cambridge University Press.

Labov, W. (1972a). *Language in the inner city: Studies in the black English vernacular*. Philadelphia: University of Pennsylvania Press.

Labov, W. (1972b). The logic of non-standard English. In P. P. Giglioni (Ed.), *Language and social context: Penguin modern sociology readings*. Harmondsworth, UK: Penguin.

Labov, W. (1975). Academic ignorance and black intelligence. In M. Maehr & W. Stallings (Eds.), *Culture, child, and school: Sociocultural influences on learning* (pp. 63-81). Monterey, CA: Brooks/Cole.

Lebra, T. S. (1976). *Japanese patterns of behavior*. Honolulu: University Press of Hawaii.

Lee, H. O., & Boster, F. J. (1992). Collectivism-individualism in perceptions of speech rate: A cross-cultural comparison. *Journal of Cross-Cultural Psychology, 23,* 377-388.

Lim, T. (1994). The structure of face and the determinants of face needs in Korea. *Korean Journal of Journalism and Communication Studies, 32,* 207-247.

Lim, T. (1997). *Speech communication*. Seoul: Yunam.

Lim, T., & Choi, S. (1996). Interpersonal relationships in Korea. In W. B. Gudykunst, S. Ting-Toomey, & T. Nishida (Eds.), *Communication in personal relationships across cultures* (pp. 122-136). Thousand Oaks, CA: Sage.

Lucy, J. A. (1992). *Language diversity and thought: A reformulation of the linguistic relativity hypothesis*. Cambridge, UK: Cambridge University Press.

Lucy, J. A. (1996). The scope of linguistic relativity: An analysis and review of empirical research. In J. J. Gumperz & S. C. Levinson (Eds.), *Rethinking linguistic relativity* (pp. 37-69). Cambridge, UK: Cambridge University Press.

Lucy, J. A., & Shweder, R. (1979). Whorf and his critics: Linguistic and nonlinguistic influences on color memory. *American Anthropologist, 81,* 581-615.

Malotki, E. (1983). *Hopi time: A linguistic analysis of the temporal categories in the Hopi language*. Berlin: Mouton.

Miller, G. R., & Steinberg, M. (1975). *Between people: A new analysis of interpersonal communication.* Chicago: Science Research Associates.

Mizutani, O., & Mizutani, N. (1987). *How to be polite in Japanese.* Tokyo: Japan Times.

Morsbach, H. (1976). Aspects of nonverbal communication in Japan. In L. Samovar & R. Porter (Eds.), *Intercultural communication: A reader* (2nd ed.). Belmont, CA: Wadsworth.

Newman, S. (1954). Semantic problems in grammatical systems and lexemes: A search for method. In H. Hoijer (Ed.), *Language in culture* (pp. 82-91). Chicago: University of Chicago Press.

Oliver, R. (1971). *Communication and culture in ancient India and China.* Syracuse, NY: Syracuse University Press.

Palmer, G. B. (1996). *Toward a theory of cultural linguistics.* Austin: University of Texas Press.

Philips, S. U. (1989). Warm Springs "Indian time": How the regulation of participation affects the progress of events. In R. Bauman & J. Sherzer (Eds.), *Explorations in the ethnography of speaking* (pp. 92-109). Cambridge, UK: Cambridge University Press.

Philipsen, G. (1992). *Speaking culturally: Explorations in social communication.* Albany: State University of New York Press.

Pinker, S. (1994). *The language instinct: How the mind creates language.* New York: William Morrow.

Rosch, E. (1977). Linguistic relativity. In P. N. Johnson-Laird & P. C. Wason (Eds.), *Thinking: Readings in cognitive science* (pp. 501-522). Cambridge, UK: Cambridge University Press.

Rosen, H. (1972). *Language and class: A critical look at the theories of Basil Bernstein.* Bristol, UK: Falling Wall.

Sanders, R. E. (1987). *Cognitive foundations of calculated speech: Controlling understandings in conversation and persuasion.* Albany: State University of New York Press.

Sansom, B. (1980). *The camp at Wallaby Cross: Aboriginal fringe dwellers in Darwin.* Canberra: Australian Institute of Aboriginal Studies.

Sapir, E. (1949). *The selected writings of Edward Sapir in language, culture, and personality* (D. G. Mandelbaum, Ed.). Berkeley: University of California Press. (Original work published 1924)

Schieffelin, B. B. (1990). *The give and take of everyday life: Language socialization of Kaluli children.* Cambridge, UK: Cambridge University Press.

Searle, J. (1975). Indirect speech acts. In P. Cole & J. L. Morgan (Eds.), *Syntax and semantics: Vol. 3. Speech acts* (pp. 59-82). New York: Academic Press.

Sherzer, J. (1987). A diversity of voices: Men's and women's speech in ethnographic perspective. In S. Philips, S. Steele, & C. Tanz (Eds.), *Language, culture, gender, and sex in comparative perspective* (pp. 95-120). New York: Cambridge University Press.

Sherzer, J., & Urban, G. (Eds.). (1986). *Native South American discourse.* New York: Mouton de Gruyter.

Smutkupt, S., & Barna, L. (1976). Impact of nonverbal communication in an intercultural setting: Thailand. In F. Casmir (Ed.), *International and intercultural communication annual* (Vol. 3). Falls Church, VA: Speech Communication Association.

Suleiman, Y. (1973). The Arabs and the West: Communication gap. In M. Prosser (Ed.), *Intercommunication among nations and peoples.* New York: Harper & Row.

Suszczynska, M. (1999). Apologizing in English, Polish and Hungarian: Different languages, different strategies. *Journal of Pragmatics, 31,* 1053-1065.

Suzuki, T. (1986). Language behavior in Japan: The conceptualization of personal relations. In T. S. Lebra & W. P. Lebra (Eds.), *Japanese culture and behavior* (Rev. ed., pp. 142-157). Honolulu: University Press of Hawaii.

Tamura, T., & Lau, A. (1992). Connectedness versus separateness: Applicability of family-therapy to Japanese families. *Family Process, 31,* 319-340.

Tannen, D. (1981). New York Jewish conversational style. *International Journal of the Sociology of Language, 30,* 133-149.

Waley, A. (Trans.). (1938). *The analects of Confucius.* New York: Vintage.

Wason, P., & Johnson-Laird, P. N. (Eds.). (1977). *Thinking.* Cambridge: Cambridge University Press.

Whorf, B. L. (1956). *Language, thought, and reality*. New York: John Wiley.

Wierzbicka, A. (1991). *Cross-cultural pragmatics: The semantics of human interaction*. Berlin: Mouton de Gruyter.

Wierzbicka, A. (1996). *Semantics: Primes and universals*. Oxford, UK: Oxford University Press.

Yoshikawa, M. (1978). Some Japanese and American cultural characteristics. In M. Prosser (Ed.), *The cultural dialogue* (pp. 220-251). Boston: Houghton Mifflin.

Yum, J. O. (1988). The impact of Confucianism on interpersonal relationships and communication patterns in East Asia. *Communication Monographs, 55*, 374-388.

Zaharna, R. S. (1995). Understanding cultural preferences of Arab communication patterns. *Public Relations Review, 21*, 241-255.

4

Nonverbal Communication Across Cultures

PETER A. ANDERSEN
San Diego State University

MICHAEL L. HECHT
Pennsylvania State University

GREGORY D. HOOBLER
Michigan State University

MAYA SMALLWOOD
Pennsylvania State University

Culture like nonverbal behavior tends to be elusive, normally out of our awareness, difficult to control, falsify, manipulate, erase, and has a potent influence in intercultural communication.

—*A. Wolfgang (1979, pp. 162-163)*

At the outset of the third millennium, it is a cliché to talk about globalization and the demise of distance. Global telecommunication, an interlinked world economy, increased travel for business and pleasure, and the continued worldwide movement of refugees and workers have brought people into contact like no time in world history. The technological revolution we are experiencing "will blur national boundaries and it will transform the nation state in a way humans have not witnessed for a millennium" (Andersen, 1999a, p. 540). But technology does not reduce the importance of face-to-face communication; relationships established on the telephone or Internet are frequently a prelude to face-to-face communication. For decades, people have been traveling in increasing numbers, and international trade is at an all-time high (Brown, Kane, & Roodman, 1994). The probability of encountering people from other cultures in our daily interactions is greater than ever before.

Intercultural interactions are always problematic. Linguistic barriers in many intercultural transactions are compounded by differences in nonverbal behavior. Andersen's (2000) review of research in intercultural nonverbal communication suggests that differences lie along eight nonverbal codes: chronemics, proxemics, kinesics, haptics, physical appearance, oculesics, vocalics, and olfactics. Thus, beyond language, multichannelled problems exist in interpreting nonverbal behavior of people from other cultures. Between any two cultures, thousands of potential differences exist, each fraught with opportunity for misunderstanding and confusion.

Nonverbal behavior is affected by many factors, some of which are innate and genetic, that produce cross-cultural similarities in nonverbal behavior (Brown, 1991; Ekman, 1972). Despite the considerable similarities, abundant differences also exist, most of which are the result of culture, "the manifold ways of perceiving and organizing the world that are held in common by a group of people and passed on interpersonally and intergenerationally" (Hecht, Andersen, & Ribeau, 1989, p. 163). Cultural differences are not random events; they occur because cultures developed with different geographies, climates, economies, religions, and histories, each exerting unique influence.

Most prior work on intercultural communication in general, and nonverbal communication in particular, has suffered from an atheoretical perspective that leaves the theorist or traveler with nothing more than thousands of useful but baffling anecdotes. This chapter employs a theory of nonverbal differ-

ences located in six intercultural dimensions. Led by the work of Hofstede, research on these cultural dimensions has gradually accumulated over the years into an impressive body of scholarship (see Andersen, 1988, 2000; Fernandez, Carlson, Stepina, & Nicholson, 1997; Gudykunst, 1988; Gudykunst et al., 1996; Gudykunst & Nishida, 1986; Hall, 1976, 1984; Hecht et al., 1989; Hofstede, 1984/2001; Merritt, 2000; Shackleton & Ali, 1990). From this considerable scholarly effort, six primary dimensions of culture have emerged that are described below including immediacy, individualism-collectivism, gender, power distance, uncertainty avoidance, and high and low context.

IMMEDIACY

Humans communicate interpersonal closeness through a series of actions, especially nonverbal actions, called immediacy behaviors. The immediacy dimension is anchored at one extreme by actions that simultaneously communicate warmth, closeness, approach, and accessibility and at the other extreme by behaviors expressing avoidance and distance (Andersen, 1985, 1998). Immediate behaviors include smiling, touching, eye contact, open body positions, closer distances, and more vocal animation. Some scholars have called these behaviors nonverbal involvement, intimacy, or expressiveness (Burgoon & LePoire, 1999; Floyd & Burgoon, 1999; Patterson, 1983). Others have focused on the accessibility aspect of immediacy and examined privacy regulation (Altman, 1975; Petronio, 1988). Research shows that in positive relationships, individuals tend to reciprocate immediate behaviors (Andersen & Andersen, 1984). Numerous summaries of intercultural immediacy studies have been published (Andersen, 1998, 1999b, 2000;

Patterson, Reidhead, Gooch, & Stopka, 1984).

Cultures that display considerable interpersonal closeness or immediacy are labeled "high-contact cultures" because people in these countries stand closer, touch more, and prefer more sensory stimulation than do people in lower-contact cultures (Hall, 1966). According to Patterson (1983), contact patterns permeate all aspects of everyday life and affect relationships. High-contact cultures (e.g., those of South Americans, southern and eastern Europeans, and Arabs) create immediacy by increasing sensory input, whereas low-contact cultures (e.g., those of Asians and northern Europeans) prefer less sensory involvement (Sussman & Rosenfeld, 1982). More recent research has shown that North America and Europe are probably high-contact cultures, whereas Asia is a low-contact culture (McDaniel & Andersen, 1998; Remland, Jones, & Brinkman, 1991). Whether a generational shift or internationalization has produced this change is unclear, but much of the Western world, including the United States, appears to be high-contact cultures.

Some cultures are higher contact than North America. A North American may feel anxious and violated by an Arab's spatial closeness, whereas the more "distant" style of the North American may alienate an Arab interactant (Almaney & Alwan, 1982; Cohen, 1987). The North American distance may leave the Arab suspicious of intentions due to the lack of olfactory contact (Almaney & Alwan, 1982). Similar differences are reported for people's tactile behavior in Latin America versus the United States (Shuter, 1976).

Most high-contact cultures are located in warmer countries, closer to the equator. Low-contact cultures are generally located in cooler climates at high latitudes (Andersen, 1999a). Most Arab countries, the Mediterra-nean, and Latin America are high-contact cultures (Mehrabian, 1971; Patterson, 1983; Scheflen, 1972; Van de Vliert, 1999). Australians and North Americans are moderate in their cultural contact level (Patterson, 1983). Low-contact cultures include most of northern Europe and Asia (Andersen, Lustig, & Andersen, 1987; McDaniel & Andersen, 1998; Mehrabian, 1971; Patterson, 1983; Scheflen, 1972). In the countries of the northern hemisphere, several studies have found that southerners within each country are much more immediate and expressive than northerners in the same country (Andersen et al., 1987, 1990; Pennebaker, Rimé, & Blankenship, 1996). Pennebaker et al. (1996) concluded that people living in cold climates spend more time dressing, storing food, and planning for winter, whereas people in warm climates have access to one another year-round. Similarly, Andersen et al. (1990) concluded,

In northern latitudes societies must be more structured, more ordered, more constrained and more organized if individuals are to survive harsh winter forces . . . in contrast southern latitudes may attract or produce a culture characterized by social extravagance that has no strong inclination to constrain or order their world. (p. 307)

Explanations for latitudinal variations have included energy level, climate, and metabolism (Andersen et al., 1987). Evidently, cultures in cooler climates tend to be more task-oriented and interpersonally "cool," whereas cultures in warmer climates tend to be more interpersonally oriented and interpersonally "warm." The harsh northern climates may explain this difference, because survival during a long winter requires a high degree of task orientation, cooperation, and tolerance of uncertainty. Cultures closer to the equator may not need to plan for winter, but they may need to conserve energy during the heat of summer (Hofstede, 1991). Even within the United States, warmer latitudes tend to contain higher-contact cultures (Andersen et al., 1987). Americans' migration to the Sunbelt may be one reason for the increased immediacy observed in recent studies.

Studies indicate that Asia is a low-immediacy, low-contact region (Barnlund, 1978; Klopf & Thompson, 1991; McDaniel & Andersen, 1998). The nonimmediacy of Asia does not fit the latitudinal pattern observed in most of the world. Asia may be a low-contact culture for other reasons including the influence of Confucianism with its emphasis on self-control, rectitude, decorum, and proper behavior (McDaniel & Andersen, 1998). The ancient origins of Asian culture may have proscribed public displays of emotion and interpersonal contact.

Geographical and ethnic considerations aside, immediacy plays a role in learning. Students from various cultural backgrounds within the United States and in noncontact and contact cultures respond positively to increased smiles, eye contact, and openness of teachers. Sanders and Wiseman (1990) reported that teacher immediacy was predictive of affective learning for white, Asian, and Hispanic students in the United States and of behavioral learning for black students. Although teachers from Puerto Rico and the United States were more nonverbally expressive than teachers from Australia and Finland, students in all four countries enjoyed the class more when teachers exhibited vocal variety, eye contact, and smiles (McCroskey, Fayer, Richmond, Sallinen, & Barraclough, 1996) and had higher perceived learning (McCroskey, Sallinen, Fayer, Richmond, & Barraclough, 1996).

Other studies show how nonverbal behavior communicates immediacy differently across cultures. Cline and Puhl (1984) reported that seating positions function differently in Taiwanese and U.S. cultures: Taiwanese generally prefer side-by-side seating to connect same-sex partners, and people from the United States generally prefer corner seating for intimate matters and use seating to connect opposite-sex partners and separate same-sex partners. Remland et al. (1991) found that French conversational partners sit farther apart yet are more direct in body orientation than Dutch and English partners. Ickes (1984), in a study of interracial (black-white) conversations in the United States, discovered that whites displayed more cues of interactional involvement and felt more stress than blacks. A study by Booth-Butterfield and Jordan (1987) found that gender might moderate this effect, with black women manifesting more positive cues when conversing with white women than vice versa. In a study of police-civilian interaction, Surinamese interactants exhibited more liveliness in body movements and smiled and laughed more often than their Dutch conversational counterparts, thus providing support for the "warmer" interactive nature of individuals who reside closer to the equator (Vrij & Winkel, 1991).

A group of cultural studies deals with verbal and nonverbal strategies for controlling accessibility and privacy. The strength of privacy needs is signaled by closed doors in the United States; soundproof, double doors in Germany (Hall, 1966); large doors in Norway; and trees at property lines in England and Canada (Altman & Gauvain, 1981). In contrast, paper walls in Japan denote a different view of privacy (Geertz, 1973), which may relate to the fact that Japanese mothers enter their children's rooms more often than do mothers in the United States (Omata, 1995). Certainly, many disparate studies of nonverbal cultural differences in particular behaviors are really differences in the immediacy of the culture that have numerous behavioral manifestations.

INDIVIDUALISM-COLLECTIVISM

A second basic cultural dimension is individualism-collectivism. Collectivistic cultures emphasize community, collaboration, shared interests, harmony, tradition, the public good, and maintaining face. Individualistic cultures emphasize personal rights and responsibilities, privacy, voicing one's own opinion, freedom, innovation, and self-expression.

In individualist societies, the ties between individuals are loose; everyone is expected to look after himself or herself and his or her immediate family. Conversely, in collectivist societies people are integrated into strong, cohesive ingroups, which throughout people's lifetime protect them in exchange for unquestioning loyalty (Hofstede, 1991, p. 51).

The degree of individualism or collectivism in a culture determines how people live together (alone, in families, or in tribes), their values, and their reasons for communicating (Andersen, 1985). Individualism is inextricably entwined with accessibility aspects of immediacy and the use of space. Extreme emphasis on owning space is based on individualism (Altman, 1975). Property ownership distances people, limits sensory stimulation, and regulates access to privacy.

Individualism is very characteristic of the United States (Bellah, Madsen, Sullivan, Swidler, & Tipton, 1985; Kim, 1994); the best and worst in U.S. culture can be attributed to individualism. Advocates of individualism have argued that it is the basis of freedom, creativity, and economic incentive. Nearly two centuries ago, Tocqueville (1835/1945) reported that the majority of Americans believe "that a man [or woman] by following his [or her] own interest, rightly understood, will be led to do what is just and good" (p. 409). Conversely, Bateson (1972) maintained that individual consciousness may pull humans out of their ecological niche and disrupt the systemic nature of life on Earth. Individualism has been blamed for alienation, loneliness, and materialism. The extreme individualism in the United States makes it difficult for its citizens to interact with those from less individualistic cultures (Condon & Yousef, 1983; Hofstede, 1991).

Western cultures are individualistic, so people rely on personal judgments and actions (Hofstede, 1991; Triandis, 1994). Eastern cultures emphasize harmony among people, and between people and nature, and value collective judgment (Gudykunst et al., 1996). Tomkins (1984) reported that an individual's psychological makeup is the result of this cultural dimension. He suggested that human beings, in Western civilization, have tended toward self-celebration, positive or negative. In Asian thought, another alternative is represented: harmony between humans and nature.

These cultural differences in individualism have been empirically supported by Hofstede (1984/2001) in 40 noncommunist countries. The 9 most individualistic, respectively, are the United States, Australia, Great Britain, Canada, the Netherlands, New Zealand, Italy, Belgium, and Denmark, all Western or European countries. The 9 least individualistic, respectively, are Venezuela, Colombia, Pakistan, Peru, Taiwan, Thailand, Singapore, Chile, and Hong Kong, all Asian or South American cultures.

Although the United States is the most individualistic country (Hofstede, 1984/2001), specific ethnic groups and geographic regions of the United States vary in their degree of individualism. Blacks place great emphasis on individualism (Collier, Ribeau, & Hecht, 1986; Hecht, Collier, & Ribeau, 1993; Hecht & Ribeau, 1984; Kochman, 1981), and

Mexican Americans place greater emphasis on relational solidarity (Hecht & Ribeau, 1984; Hecht, Ribeau, & Sedeno, 1990). But this is all relative, and by world standards even Chicanos in California constitute an individualistic culture.

A culture's individualism or collectivism affects nonverbal behavior in many ways. People in individualistic cultures are more distant proximally (Gudykunst et al., 1996). Collectivistic cultures are interdependent, and as a result they work, play, live, and sleep in close proximity to one another. Kinesic behavior tends to be more synchronized in collectivistic cultures. In urban individualistic cultures, family members often do their "own thing" on different schedules. People in individualistic cultures smile more than in normatively oriented cultures (Tomkins, 1984), probably because individualists are responsible for their relationships and their own happiness whereas in collectivistic cultures personal or interpersonal happiness is secondary. People in collectivist cultures suppress emotional displays that are contrary to the mood of the group, because maintaining group affect is a primary value (Andersen, 1988). People in individualistic cultures are encouraged to express emotions because individual freedom is of paramount value. These assumptions are supported by research on emotional expressiveness in individualistic and collectivistic cultures. Researchers (e.g., Bond, 1993; Matsumoto, 1990; Matsumoto, Tsutomo, Scherer, & Wallbott, 1988) found that expressions of Japanese and Chinese emotions are shorter and less intense than those of North Americans.

Individualistic cultures are more nonverbally affiliative (Andersen, 2000), and individuals must provide intimacy cues (Hofstede, 1984/2001). In the United States and other individualistic countries, affiliativeness, dating, flirting, small talk, and initial acquaintance are more important than in collectivist countries, where the social network is more fixed and less reliant on individual initiative than in the mobile U.S. society.

Individualistic and collectivistic cultures also use time differently. Hall (1984) distinguished between monochronistic patterns in individualistic cultures, in which one thing is done at a time, and polychronistic patterns in collectivistic cultures, in which multiple events are scheduled simultaneously. These time differences suggest that individualistic cultures are more task oriented in contrast to the relational and socioemotional orientation of collectivist cultures.

Personal individualism may transcend culture for certain variables. Schmidt (1983) compared the effects of crowding on people from an individualistic culture (the United States) and a collectivist culture (Singapore). The study examined the relationship among personal control, crowding annoyance, and stress, reporting similar findings for both cultures.

GENDER

Numerous studies have examined gender as an individual characteristic, but gender has been neglected as a cultural dimension. As conceptualized here, gender refers to the rigidity of gender roles. More rigid cultures influence members to behave within a narrow range of gender-related behaviors and stress traditional gender role identification. Within such a worldview, masculine traits are typically such attributes as strength, assertiveness, competitiveness, achievement, and ambitiousness, whereas feminine traits are such attributes as affection, compassion, nurturance, and emotionality (Andersen, 1988; Hofstede, 1984, 1998; Nasierowski & Mikula, 1998). In general, female communicators are more adaptive because they are more attentive to the silent, nonverbal cues, and cross-cultural research shows that young girls are expected to be more nurturant than boys, though there is variation from country to country (Hall, 1984). The masculinity of a culture is negatively correlated with the percentage of women in technical and professional jobs and positively correlated with segregation of the sexes in higher education (Hofstede, 1984).

The nine countries with the highest masculinity index scores, respectively, are Japan, Austria, Venezuela, Italy, Switzerland, Mexico, Ireland, Great Britain, and Germany (Hofstede, 1984). These countries lie in central Europe and the Caribbean, with the exception of Japan, Ireland, and Great Britain. The eight countries highest in feminine values, respectively, are Sweden, Norway, the Netherlands, Denmark, Finland, Chile, Portugal, and Thailand, mostly Scandinavian or South American cultures. Not surprisingly, Sweden has the highest rate of participation in the labor force by women (*Social and Labor Market Policy,* 2000). Why would South American cultures not manifest the typical Latin pattern of machismo? Hofstede (1984) suggests that machismo is present in the Caribbean region but not particularly evident in the remainder of South America.

Considerable research suggests that androgynous patterns of behavior (combinations of both feminine and masculine) result in more self-esteem, social competence, success, and intellectual development for both males and females. Buck (1984) has shown that males may harm their health by internalizing emotions rather than externalizing them as women often do. Jackson (1997) speaks of the cultural crossroads that black masculinity occupies, with black men alternately embracing and rejecting the more rigid gender roles of American mainstream culture and the more

androgynous and interdependent gender roles with their culture. It is probably not coincidental that more masculine countries display higher levels of stress (Hofstede, 1984). In egalitarian countries where women are economically important and where sexual standards for women are permissive, more relaxed vocal patterns are evident, and there is less tension between the sexes (Lomax, 1968).

POWER DISTANCE

Differences in intercultural communication may also be attributed to power distance (PD), the degree to which power, prestige, and wealth are unequally distributed in a culture. "Members of high power distance cultures see power as a basic fact in society, and stress coercive or referent power, while members of low power distance cultures believe power should be used only when it is legitimate and prefer expert or legitimate power" (Gudykunst & Matsumoto, 1996, p. 45). Cultures with high PD have control and influence concentrated in the hands of a few rather than equally distributed (Hofstede, 1984). Condon and Yousef (1983) distinguished among three cultural patterns: democratic, authority centered, and authoritarian. PD is highly correlated (.80) with authoritarianism (as measured by the F-scale) (Hofstede, 1984). PD may be better defined in terms of "varying orientations toward the obligations of social relationship" (Smith, Dugan, & Trompenaars, 1996, p. 231). This, based on Schwartz's (1994) terms of conservatism and egalitarian commitment, shifts the focus toward an individual's commitment to a group rather than on sociopolitical issues. Both conceptualizations hold implications for nonverbal communication and PD.

Countries highest in PD, respectively, are the Philippines, Mexico, Venezuela, India,

Singapore, Brazil, Hong Kong, France, and Colombia (Hofstede, 1984), all of which are South Asian and Caribbean countries (with the exception of France) that lie within the tropics, close to the equator. Gudykunst and Kim (1992) reported that both African and Asian cultures generally maintain hierarchical role relationships. Spencer-Oatley (1997) used British and Chinese tutors and graduate students to examine role relationships. Their findings revealed that British individuals had lower PD ratings, and Chinese individuals had higher PD ratings in tutor-student roles. The lowest PD countries, respectively, are Austria, Israel, Denmark, New Zealand, Ireland, Sweden, Norway, Finland, and Switzerland (Hofstede, 1984), all of which are of European origin and are middle-class democracies located at very high latitudes. The United States is lower than the median in PD.

A fundamental determinant of PD is the latitude of a country. Hofstede (1984) claimed that latitude and climate are two of the major forces shaping a culture because in colder climates technology is needed for survival. This produces a chain of events in which children are less dependent on authority and learn from people other than authority figures. In a study conducted at 40 universities throughout the United States, Andersen et al. (1990) reported a −.47 ecological correlation between latitude and intolerance for ambiguity and a −.45 ecological correlation between latitude and authoritarianism. Residents of the northern United States are less authoritarian and more tolerant of ambiguity, perhaps to ensure cooperation needed to survive the harsher climates. Andersen et al. (1990) used latitude, rainfall, storminess, and a multivariate climate index to account for 53% of the variance in PD predisposition.

The population of a country or a culture may be another predictor of PD. Generally, larger cultures score higher on PD (Lustig & Koester, 1999). As the size of any group

increases, it becomes unwieldy and difficult to manage informally. This is true of larger classrooms, larger governments, and larger organizations. In larger aggregations, informal relationships must yield to formal rules, bureaucracies, and hierarchical relationships. For cultures with large populations to function effectively, social and political hierarchies must be created, causing the PD factor to increase.

PD affects the nonverbal behavior of a culture. High PD cultures (e.g., India) may severely limit interaction. High PD countries often prohibit free interclass dating, marriage, and contact, which are taken for granted in low PD countries. Weitz (1974) suggested that oppressed people must become more skilled at decoding nonverbal behavior. In cultures with high PD, people are expected to show only positive emotions to others with high status and to display negative emotions to those with low status (Matsumoto, 1991; Porter & Samovar, 1998). In power-discrepant circumstances, subordinates show more bodily tension and smile more in an effort to appease superiors and appear polite (Andersen & Bowman, 1999). The continuous smiles of many Asians may be an effort to appease superiors or to produce smooth social relations, a product of being reared in a high PD culture. Finally, Bizman, Schwartzwald, and Zidon (1984) found that aggressive behavior toward minorities decreased when the minority was seen as having the power to retaliate, a factor that decreases power distance.

PD in a culture also affects paralinguistic or vocalic cues. Residents of low PD cultures are generally less aware that vocal loudness may be offensive to others (Andersen, 2000). North American vocal tones often are perceived as noisy, exaggerated, and childlike (Condon & Yousef, 1983).

Studies show that cultures differ in the signs of power. In the United States, downcast eyes and body position below that of another would probably be seen as subordinate. In Japanese culture, however, downcast eyes are a sign of attentiveness and agreement (Cambra & Klopf, 1979) and *teishiel* (or lower position) signals acceptance and respect and may be perceived as a sign that a person is trustworthy, loving, and accepting (Ishii, 1973). In the United States, power and status are typically achieved through monetary success and manifested by conspicuous material displays of materialism (Andersen & Bowman, 1999). Burgoon, Dillard, Doran, and Miller (1982) reported difference in the types of message strategies used in Asian and North American cultures. Key (1975) reported that American Indian children often feel that their white teachers are mean merely because their voices are louder than those in their own culture.

Cultural differences in nonverbal power behaviors contribute to misunderstandings. Eye gaze is a power cue in mainstream U.S. culture, and differences in patterns between black and white American communicators may lead to interactional difficulties. LaFrance and Mayo (1976, 1978) reported that black speakers look at their conversational partner less while listening than while speaking. The pattern for white communicators is the opposite (Kendon, 1967). In a black-white conversation, a black listener will look less than a white speaker expects, which suggests that the black listener is uninterested. Conversely, when the black interactant is talking, both parties will be looking more than each expects. Such long, mutual gazes are often interpreted as hostility. In this example, cultural patterning in power-related nonverbal cues may produce interpretations of disinterest and hostility. In addition, blacks decrease gaze in the presence of powerful people, whereas whites increase the amount of gaze in these situations, and the two ethnic groups differ in their interpretations of conversational regulators such as rising and falling inflections (Halberstadt, 1985).

Other power-related predictions, however, have not received support. Booth-Butterfield and Jordan (1987) predicted that black women, representing a minority group, would have less power and therefore adapt more than white females in interethnic conversations. This predication was not supported. Brown (1981), on the other hand, found that shoppers at a mall are more likely to walk through a black dyad that a white dyad, supporting the power differential assumption of Booth-Butterfield and Jordan. Researchers have to be careful not to equate societal positions with personal power, particularly in dyadic contexts and within cultures low on PD (e.g., the United States) or that encourage individual rather than cultural judgments of power. Gudykunst (1995) suggested that low-level egalitarianism of the individual would be associated with a high PD rating for the culture, and high-level egalitarianism of the individual would be associated with a low PD rating for the culture.

UNCERTAINTY AVOIDANCE

Uncertainty refers to the value placed on risk and ambiguity in a culture. Berger's (Berger & Calabrese, 1975) uncertainty reduction hypothesis has formed the theoretical basis for much cultural research in this area along with communication accommodation theory (Gallois, Giles, Jones, Cargile, & Ota, 1995) and expectancy violations theory (Burgoon, 1995). According to Gudykunst and Matsumoto (1996),

There is a strong desire for consensus in cultures high in uncertainty avoidance; deviant behavior is therefore not acceptable. Members of high uncertainty avoidance cultures also tend to display emotions more than do members of low uncertainty avoidance cultures. Members of low uncertainty avoidance cultures have lower stress levels and weaker superegos, and accept dissent and taking risks more than do members of high uncertainty avoidance cultures. (p. 42)

Countries show variation in their avoidance or tolerance of uncertainty. In some cultures, freedom produces uncertainty, which leads to stress and anxiety. These cultures may seek to avoid uncertainty by increasing rules of normative behavior. Other cultures are better able to tolerate freedom and diversity without excess stress or anxiety. Hofstede (1984) contends that a culture's rigidity and dogmatism are a function of the uncertainty avoidance dimension rather than the PD dimension. The countries most likely to avoid uncertainty and to be intolerant of ambiguity are Greece, Portugal, Belgium, Japan, Peru, France, Chile, Spain, and Argentina, respectively (Hofstede, 1984). mostly southern European and South American countries. Countries lowest in uncertainty avoidance and most tolerant of ambiguity are Singapore, Denmark, Sweden, Hong Kong, Ireland, England, India, the Philippines, and the United States, all based on northern European, Scandinavian, or South Asian cultures.

Hofstede (1984) reports that a country's neuroticism or anxiety scores are strongly correlated with uncertainty avoidance, and high uncertainty avoidance is negatively correlated with risk taking and positively correlated with fear of failure. Hofstede (1984) also reports that countries higher in uncertainty avoidance tend to be Catholic, and countries lower in uncertainty avoidance tend to be Protestant, Hindu, or Buddhist. Eastern religions and Protestantism tend to be less "absolute" than Catholicism. In addition, Andersen et al. (1990) reported that within the United States intolerance for ambiguity is much higher in southern states than in northern states, reflecting global patterns of latitude and tolerance.

Hofstede (1984) notes that people in high uncertainty avoidance cultures believe that "what is different is dangerous" (p. 119), whereas people in low uncertainty avoidance cultures tend to believe that "what is different, is curious" (p. 119). This concisely summarizes the incompatibility of persons from different cultural orientations to contextuality of meaning. During intercultural communication, these individuals engage in a process of adapting to each other's communication style, including use of nonverbal messages. A useful explanatory concept in describing this adaptation process is Gudykunst's (1995) anxiety/uncertainty management (AUM) theory.

Gudykunst and colleagues (Berger & Gudykunst, 1991; Gao & Gudykunst, 1990; Gudykunst, 1985, 1988; Gudykunst & Hammer, 1988; Gudykunst & Nishida, 1984) extended Berger's (Berger & Calabrese, 1975) uncertainty reduction theory to the intercultural context, culminating in Gudykunst's (1993, 1995) AUM theory. This theory seeks to explain the processes by which individuals communicate in intercultural and "stranger" situations (Gudykunst, 1995). The concept of the stranger refers to those who "are physically present and participate in a situation and, at the same time, are outside the situation because they are members of different groups" (Gudykunst, 1995, p. 10). Interacting with people outside of our group induces physiological arousal that is experienced as anxiety. Uncertainty and anxiety reduction is sought when future interaction is expected (Berger, 1979). The cognitive schemata involved in this determination are outlined in Andersen's (1998) cognitive valence theory.

Reduction of anxiety and uncertainty in these stranger encounters is achieved in part through adaptation to nonverbal communication behaviors. Compatibility in nonverbal communication is one key element to effective message interpretation, and misunderstandings frequently take place in intercultural communication because of nonverbal incongruity. Among the nonverbal behaviors that can be particularly difficult to adapt to are interpersonal distance, use of touch, amount of eye contact, and time boundaries. Countries high in uncertainty avoidance tend to show more emotions than countries low in uncertainty avoidance (Hofstede, 1984). Similarly, uncertainty avoidance is associated with accuracy of the recognition of emotions such as sadness and fear (Schimmack, 1996). Ducci, Arcuri, Georgis, and Sineshaw (1982) reported that familiarity with a culture aids in interpreting nonverbal expressions of emotion, although Koester and Otebe (1987) failed to validate this finding.

AUM theory has answered many of the questions we asked in a previous edition of the *Handbook of International and Intercultural Communication*. The process of intercultural adaptation predicts that nonverbal cues of dissimilarity will indeed increase uncertainty and that repeated interaction will result in reduced anxiety and uncertainty. Future research still needs to be conducted to empirically validate many of the axioms presented in AUM theory (Gudykunst, 1995).

HIGH AND LOW CONTEXT

A final important communication dimension is context (Hall, 1976, 1984). High-context (HC) communication relies mainly on the physical context or the relationship for information, with little explicitly encoded (Hall, 1976). "In a high-context culture such as that of Japan, meanings are internalized and there is a large emphasis on nonverbal codes" (Lustig & Koester, 1999, p. 108), whereas "in low-context cultures, people look for the meaning of others' behaviors in the messages that are plainly and explicitly coded" (p. 109). Lifelong friends often use HC or implicit messages that are nearly impossible for an outsider to understand. In these HC situa-

tions, the culture's information integrated from the environment, context, situation, and nonverbal cues gives the message meaning unavailable from explicit verbal utterances.

Low-context (LC) messages, in contrast to HC messages, provide most of the information in the explicit code itself (Hall, 1976). An LC message requires clear description, unambiguous communication, and a high degree of specificity. Unlike personal relationships that are HC message systems, institutions such as courts of law and formal systems such as mathematics or computer language require explicit LC systems because nothing can be taken for granted (Hall, 1984). Members of collectivistic cultures use higher-context messages; members of individualistic cultures use lower-context messages (Gudykunst & Matsumoto, 1996).

The lowest-context cultures are those of Germany, Switzerland, the United States, Sweden, Norway, Finland, Denmark, and Canada (Gudykunst & Kim, 1992; Hall, 1976, 1984). These cultures are preoccupied with specifies, details, and precise time schedules at the expense of context. They use behavior systems built around Aristotelian logic and linear thinking (Hall, 1984). Cultures that have some characteristics of both HC and LC systems include those of France, England, and Italy (Gudykunst & Kim, 1984), which are somewhat less explicit than other European and North American cultures.

The highest-context cultures are Chinese, Japanese, South Korean, Taiwanese, Native American, African American, Mexican American, and Latino (Elliott, Scott, Jensen, & McDonough, 1982; Gudykunst & Kim, 1992; Hall, 1976, 1984; Lustig & Koester, 1999). Even the Chinese language is an implicit HC system. To use a Chinese dictionary, one must understand thousands of characters that change meaning in combination with other characters. An excellent example of HC communication that is highly dependent on nonverbal messages is the Japanese tea cere-mony, in which even the subtlest behaviors are attributed with significant meaning (Jandt, 1995; Lustig & Koester, 1999).

Americans complain that the Japanese never "get the point" but fail to recognize that HC cultures must provide a context and set-ting, and let the point evolve (Hall, 1984). American Indian cultures with ancestral, mi-gratory roots in East Asia are remarkably like contemporary Oriental culture in several ways, especially in their need for HC (Hall, 1984). It is not surprising that most Latin American cultures, a fusion of Iberian (Portu-guese-Spanish) and Indian traditions, are also HC cultures. Southern and eastern Mediterra-nean people such as Greeks, Turks, and Arabs tend to have HC cultures as well.

Communication in HC cultures is generally perceived as direct, and communication in LC cultures is generally perceived as indirect as summarized in the following four principles. First, verbal communication and other ex-plicit codes are more prevalent in LC cul-tures such as the United States and northern Europe. People from LC cultures are often perceived as excessively talkative, belaboring the obvious and redundant, whereas people from HC cultures may be perceived as non-disclosing, sneaky, and mysterious (Andersen, 2000). Second, HC and LC cultures do not place the same emphasis on verbal communi-cation. Elliott et al. (1982) found that people in the United States perceived more verbal people as more attractive, but less verbal peo-ple were perceived as more attractive in Korea, a HC culture. Third, LC cultures, par-ticularly men in LC cultures, fail to perceive as much nonverbal communication as members of HC cultures. Nonverbal communication provides context for all communication (Watzlawick, Beavin, & Jackson, 1967), but people from HC cultures are particularly affected by contextual cues. Thus, facial ex-pressions, tension, movements, speed of

interaction, location of the interaction, and other subtle "vibes" are likely to be perceived by and have more meaning for people from HC cultures. Finally, people in HC cultures expect communicators to understand unarticulated moods, subtle gestures, and en-vironmental clues that people from LC cul-tures simply do not process (Hall, 1976). Worse, people from both cultural extremes fail to recognize these basic differences in be-havior, communication, and context and are quick to misattribute the causes for behavior.

In a study of farewell exchanges in airport departures, McDaniel and Andersen (1998) found interpersonal touch was a function of nationality rather than latitude, with Asians as the least tactile cultural group of all, reflecting the HC nature of Asian communication. Con-sistent with HC and LC communication pat-terns, individuals from the United States are much more likely to express immediacy overtly and explicitly through verbal commu-nication than are French or Japanese individu-als (Ting-Toomey, 1991). Examples of inter-personal situations where cultural context leads to misunderstandings also have been provided in the fields of health care (Singh, McKay, & Singh, 1998) and business commu-nication (Kim, Pan, & Park, 1998).

CONCLUSION

Over the past decade, scholars investigating nonverbal communication have increasingly used the theoretical framework outlined in this chapter. These six cultural dimensions are neither exhaustive nor discrete, but they do provide a conceptual framework by which the thousands of intercultural differences in non-verbal communication may be understood. This approach has moved the study of non-verbal communication beyond description of behavioral differences and into the realm of the meaning, functions, outcomes, and relationships.

Future research should employ this theoretical basis to pursue several research directions. First, the rich interplay among the dimensions of culture should be investigated. What are the differences between a high-immediacy, highly feminine culture; a low-immediacy, highly feminine culture; a high-immediacy, highly masculine culture; and a low-immediacy, highly masculine culture? In reality, cultures are influence by several of these dimensions simultaneously, so simple comparisons on a single dimension should yield to richer, multidimensional accounts.

Second, interactions among people who differ along cultural dimensions should be examined. What happens, for instance, when people in a high PD culture interact with people from a low PD culture? Thus far, most research on the culture dimension has emphasized cross-cultural differences in intra-cultural behavior rather than the interactions between people across different cultural dimensions.

Third, considerable evidence suggests that not all people in a culture share equally in the general traits of that culture. Some Americans are collectivistic and other oriented, and some Japanese are highly tactile. One should never attribute all of the characteristics of a culture to any individual with great certainty. "Conclusions about the nonverbal behavior of people from different cultures are generalized observations, not ironclad rules" (Andersen, 1999b, p. 103). Future studies should investigate why some members of a society do not seem to fully manifest the general tendencies of that culture.

Fourth, intercultural scholars should continue the search to situate culture in its most appropriate location. Certainly, culture is located in the behavior of individuals who share group similarities. Too often, however, nationality is confused with culture. Many

countries are balkanized or regionalized. Andersen et al. (1987, 1990), for instance, have shown that even the United States has distinct regional cultures, with the largest regional differences between north and south. Pennebaker et al. (1996) have demonstrated that north-south regional differences between northerners and southerners exist worldwide. Numerous studies have shown that ethnic groups within a given country represent different cultures.

We have attempted to explain differences in nonverbal communication through the lens of theoretical dimensions of culture. We believe that this approach is bound to bear the most conceptual fruit, not just for scholars and researchers but for business people and sojourners as well. To master a thousand nuances for each culture is impossible; to understand the underlying basis for thousands of nonverbal behaviors is a more manageable task.

REFERENCES

Almaney, A., & Alwan, A. (1982). *Communicating with the Arabs.* Prospect Heights, IL: Waveland.

Altman, I. (1975). *The environment and social behavior.* Monterey, CA: Brooks/Cole.

Altman, I., & Gauvain, M. (1981). A cross-cultural dialective analysis of homes. In L. Liben, A. Patterson, & N. Newcombe (Eds.), *Spatial representation and behavior across the life span.* New York: Academic Press.

Andersen, P. A. (1985). Nonverbal immediacy in interpersonal communication. In A. W. Siegman & S. Feldstein (Eds.), *Multichannel integrations of nonverbal behavior* (pp. 1-36). Hillsdale, NJ: Lawrence Erlbaum.

Andersen, P. A. (1988). Explaining intercultural differences in nonverbal communication. In L. A. Samovar & R. E. Porter (Eds.), *Intercultural communication: A reader.* Belmont, CA: Wadsworth.

Andersen, P. A. (1998). The cognitive valence theory of intimate communication. In M. T. Palmer

& G. A. Barnett (Eds.), *Progress in communication sciences: Vol. 14. Mutual influence in interpersonal communication: Theory and research in cognition, affect and behavior* (pp. 39-72). Stamford, CT: Ablex.

Andersen, P. A. (1999a). 1999 WSCA presidential address. *Western Journal of Communication, 63,* 339-543.

Andersen, P. A. (1999b). *Nonverbal communication: Forms and functions.* Mountain View, CA: Mayfield.

Andersen, P. A. (2000). Explaining intercultural differences in nonverbal communication. In L. A. Samovar & R. E. Porter (Eds.), *Intercultural communication: A reader* (9th ed., pp. 258-279). Belmont, CA: Wadsworth.

Andersen, P. A., & Andersen, J. F. (1984). The exchange of nonverbal communication. In L. A. Samovar & R. E. Porter (Eds.), *Intercultural communication: A reader.* Belmont, CA: Wadsworth.

Andersen, P. A., & Bowman, L. (1999). Positions of power: Nonverbal influence in organizational communication. In L. K. Guerrero, J. A. DeVito, & M. L. Hecht (Eds.), *The nonverbal communication reader: Classic and contemporary readings* (pp. 317-334). Prospect Heights, IL: Waveland.

Andersen, P. A., Lustig, M. W., & Andersen, J. F. (1987). Regional patterns of communication in the United States: A theoretical perspective. *Communication Monographs, 54,* 128-144.

Andersen, P. A., Lustig, M. W., & Andersen, J. F. (1990). Changes in latitude, changes in attitude: The relationship between climate and interpersonal communication predispositions. *Communication Quarterly, 38,* 291-311.

Barnlund, D. C. (1978). Communication styles in two cultures: Japan and the United States. In A. Kendon, R. M. Harris, & M. R. Key (Eds.), *Organizational behavior in face to face interaction* (pp. 427-456). The Hague, the Netherlands: Mouton.

Bateson, G. (1972). *Steps to an ecology of mind.* New York: Ballantine.

Bellah, R. N., Madsen, R., Sullivan, W. M., Swidler, A., & Tipton, S. (1985). *Habits of the heart: Individualism and commitment in American life.* New York: Harper & Row.

Berger, C. R. (1979). Beyond initial interactions. In H. Giles & R. St. Clair (Eds.), *Language and social psychology* (pp. 122-144). Oxford, UK: Basil Blackwell.

Berger, C. R., & Calabrese, R. (1975). Some explorations in initial interactions and beyond: Toward a developmental theory of interpersonal communication. *Human Communication Research, 1,* 99-112.

Berger, C. R., & Gudykunst, W. B. (1991). Uncertainty and communication. In B. Dervin & M. Voigt (Eds.), *Progress in communication sciences* (Vol. 10, pp. 21-66). Norwood, NJ: Ablex.

Bizman, A., Schwartzwald, J., & Zidon, A. (1984). Effects of the power to retaliate on physical aggression directed toward Middle-Eastern Jews, Western Jews, and Israeli-Arabs. *Journal of Cross-Cultural Psychology, 15,* 65-78.

Bond, M. H. (1993). Emotions and their expression in Chinese culture. *Journal of Nonverbal Behavior, 17,* 245-262.

Booth-Butterfield, M., & Jordan, F. (1987). *Verbal and nonverbal adaptation among racially homogeneous and heterogeneous groups.* Paper presented at the annual convention of the Speech Communication Association, Boston.

Brown, C. E. (1981). Shared space invasion. *Personality and Social Psychology Bulletin, 7,* 103-108.

Brown, D. E. (1991). *Human universals.* Philadelphia: Temple University Press.

Brown, L. R., Kane, H., & Roodman, D. M. (1994). *Vital signs 1994: The trends that are shaping our future.* New York: Norton.

Buck, R. (1984). *The communication of emotion.* New York: Guilford.

Burgoon, J. K. (1995). Cross-cultural and intercultural applications of expectancy violations theory. In R. L. Wiseman (Ed.), *Intercultural communication theory* (pp. 194-214). Thousand Oaks, CA: Sage.

Burgoon, J. K., & LePoire, B. A. (1999). Nonverbal cues and interpersonal judgements: Participant and observer perceptions of intimacy, dominance, composure, and formality. *Communication Monographs, 66,* 105-124.

Burgoon, M., Dillard, J. P., Doran, N. E., & Miller, M. D. (1982). Cultural and situational influences on the process of persuasive strategy selection. *International Journal of Intercultural Relations, 6,* 85-100.

Cambra, R. E., & Klopf, D. W. (1979). *A cross-cultural analysis of interpersonal needs.* Paper presented at the Speech Association Intercultural Communication Conference, Honolulu, HI.

Cline, R. J., & Puhl, C. A. (1984). Gender, culture, and geography: A comparison of seating arrangements in the United States and Taiwan. *International Journal of Intercultural relations, 8,* 199-219.

Cohen, R. (1987). Problems of intercultural communication in Egyptian-American diplomatic relations. *International Journal of Intercultural Relations, 11,* 29-47.

Collier, M. J., Ribeau, S. A., & Hecht, M. L. (1986). Intracultural rules and outcomes within three domestic cultures. *International Journal of Intercultural Relations, 10,* 439-457.

Condon, J. C., & Yousef, F. (1983). *An introduction to intercultural communication.* Indianapolis, IN: Bobbs-Merrill.

Ducci, L., Arcuri, L., Georgis, T., & Sineshaw, D. (1982). Emotion recognition in Ethiopia: The effect of familiarity with Western culture on accuracy of recognition. *Journal of Cross-Cultural Psychology, 13,* 340-351.

Elliott, S., Scott, M. D., Jensen, A. D., & McDonough, M. (1982). Perceptions of reticence: A cross-cultural investigation. In M. Burgoon (Ed.), *Communication yearbook 5.* New Brunswick, NJ: Transaction.

Ekman, P. (1972). Universal and cultural difference in the facial expression of emotion. In J. R. Cole (Ed.), *Nebraska symposium on motivation* (pp. 207-283). Lincoln: University of Nebraska Press.

Fernandez, D. R., Carlson, D. S., Stepina, L. P., & Nicholson, J. D. (1997). Hofstede's country classification 25 years later. *Journal of Social Psychology, 137,* 43-54.

Floyd, K., & Burgoon, J. K. (1999). Reacting to nonverbal expressions of liking: A test of interaction adaption theory. *Communication Monographs, 66,* 219-239.

Gallois, G., Giles, H., Jones, E., Cargile, A. C., & Ota, H. (1995). Accommodating intercultural encounters: Elaborations and extensions. In

R. L. Wiseman (Ed.), *Intercultural communication theory* (pp. 115-147). Thousand Oaks, CA: Sage.

Gao, G., & Gudykunst, W. B. (1990). Uncertainty, anxiety, and adaptation. *International Journal of Intercultural Relations, 14,* 301-317.

Geertz, C. (1973). *The interpretation of cultures.* New York: Basic Books.

Gudykunst, W. B. (1985). The influence of cultural similarity, type of relationship, and self-monitoring on uncertainty reduction processes. *Communication Monographs, 52,* 206-216.

Gudykunst, W. B. (1988). Uncertainty and anxiety: An extension of uncertainty reduction theory to intergroup communication. In Y. Y. Kim & W. B. Gudykunst (Eds.), *Theories in intercultural communication* (pp. 123-156). Newbury Park, CA: Sage.

Gudykunst, W. B. (1993). Toward a theory of effective interpersonal and intergroup communication: An anxiety/uncertainty management (AUM) perspective. In R. L. Wiseman & J. Koester (Eds.), *Intercultural communication competence* (pp. 33-71). Newbury Park, CA: Sage.

Gudykunst, W. B. (1995). Anxiety/uncertainty management (AUM) theory: Current status. In R. L. Wiseman (Ed.), *Intercultural communication theory* (pp. 8-58). Thousand Oaks, CA: Sage.

Gudykunst, W. B., & Hammer, M. R. (1988). Strangers and hosts. In Y. Y. Kim & W. B. Gudykunst (Eds.), *Cross-cultural adaptation* (pp. 106-139). Newbury Park, CA: Sage.

Gudykunst, W. B., & Kim, Y. Y. (1984). *Communicating with strangers: An approach to intercultural communication.* New York: Random House.

Gudykunst, W. B., & Kim, Y. Y. (1992). *Communicating with strangers: An approach to intercultural communication* (2nd ed.). New York: Random House.

Gudykunst, W. B., & Matsumoto, Y. (1996). Cross-cultural variability of communication in personal relationships. In W. B. Gudykunst, S. Ting-Toomey, & T. Nishida (Eds.), *Communication in personal relationships across cultures* (pp. 19-56). Thousand Oaks, CA: Sage.

Gudykunst, W. B., Matsumoto, Y., Ting-Toomey, S., Nishida, T., Kim, K., & Heyman, S. (1996). Influence of cultural individualism-collectivism, self-construals, and individual values on communication styles across cultures. *Human Communication Research, 22,* 510-543.

Gudykunst, W. B., & Nishida, T. (1984). Individual and cultural influence on uncertainty reduction. *Communication Monographs, 51,* 23-36.

Gudykunst, B. W., & Nishida, T. (1986). Attributional confidence in low- and high-context cultures. *Human Communication Research, 12,* 525-549.

Halberstadt, A. G. (1985). Race, socioeconomic status, and nonverbal behavior. In A. W. Siegman & S. Feldstein (Eds.), *Multichannel integrations of nonverbal behavior.* Hillsdale, NJ: Lawrence Erlbaum.

Hall, E. T. (1966). *The hidden dimension.* Garden City, NY: Doubleday.

Hall, E. T. (1976). *Beyond culture.* Garden City, NY: Doubleday/Anchor.

Hall, E. T. (1984). *The dance of life: The other dimension of time.* Garden City, NY: Doubleday/Anchor.

Hasegawa, T. H., & Gudykunst, W. B. (1998). Silence in Japan and the United States. *Journal of Cross-Cultural Psychology, 29,* 668-684.

Hecht, M. L., Andersen, P. A., & Ribeau, S. A. (1989). The cultural dimensions of nonverbal communication. In M. K. Asante & W. B. Gudykunst (Eds.), *Handbook of international and intercultural communication* (pp. 163-185). Newbury Park, CA: Sage.

Hecht, M. L., Collier, M. J., & Ribeau, S. A. (1993). *African-American communication: Ethnic identity and cultural interpretation.* Newbury Park, CA: Sage.

Hecht, M. L., & Ribeau, S. A. (1984). Ethnic communication: A comparative analysis of satisfying communication. *International Journal of Intercultural Relations, 8,* 135-151.

Hecht, M. L., Ribeau, S. A., & Sedeno, M. V. (1990). A Mexican American perspective on interethnic communication. *International Journal of Intercultural Relations, 14,* 31-55.

Hofstede, G. (1984). *Culture's consequences.* Beverly Hills, CA: Sage.

Hofstede, G. (1991). *Cultures and organizations: Software of the mind.* London: McGraw-Hill.

Hofstede, G. (1998). Masculinity/femininity as a dimension of culture. In G. Hofstede (Ed.), *Mas-culinity and femininity: The taboo dimension of national cultures* (pp. 3-28). Thousand Oaks, CA: Sage.

Hofstede, G. (2001). *Culture's consequences* (2nd ed.). Beverly Hills, CA: Sage.

Ickes, W. (1984). Compositions in black and white: Determinants of interaction in inter-racial dyads. *Journal od Personality and Social Psychology, 47,* 330-341.

Ishii, S. (1973). Characteristics of Japanese nonverbal communication behavior. *Communication, 2,* 163-180.

Jackson, R. L. (1997). Black "manhood" as xenophobe: An ontological exploration of the Hegelian dialectic. *Journal of Black Studies, 27,* 731-750.

Jandt, F. E. (1995). *Intercultural communication: An introduction.* Thousand Oaks, CA: Sage.

Kendon, A. (1967). Some functions of gaze direction in social interaction. *Acta Psychologia, 71,* 359-372.

Key, M. R. (1975). *Paralinguistics and kinesics.* Metuchen, NJ: Scarecrow.

Kim, D., Pan, Y., & Park, H. S. (1998). High- versus low-context culture: A comparison of Chinese, Korean, and American cultures. *Psychology & Marketing, 15,* 507-521.

Kim, U. (1994). Individualism and collectivism: Conceptual clarification and elaboration. In U. Kim, H. Triandis, Ç. Kâgitçibasi, S.-C. Choi, & G. Yoon (Eds.), *Individualism and collectivism: Theory, methods, and applications* (pp. 19-40). Thousand Oaks, CA: Sage.

Klopf, D. W., & Thompson, C. A. (1991). Nonverbal immediacy differences among Japanese, Finish and American university students. *Perceptual and Motor Skills, 73,* 209-210.

Kochman, T. (1981). *Black and white: Styles in conflict.* Chicago: University of Chicago Press.

Koester, J., & Otebe, M. (1987). *The relationship of cultural similarity, communication effectiveness and uncertainty reduction.* Paper presented at the annual convention of the Speech Communication Association, Boston.

LaFrance, M., & Mayo, C. (1976). Racial differences in gaze behavior during conversations: Two systematic observational studies. *Journal of Personality and Social Psychology, 33,* 547-552.

LaFrance, M., & Mayo, C. (1978). Gaze direction in interracial dyadic communication. *Ethnicity, 5,* 167-173.

Lomax, A. (1968). *Folk song style and culture.* New Brunswick, NJ: Transaction.

Lustig, M. W., & Koester, J. (1999). *Intercultural competence: Interpersonal communication across culture* (3rd ed.). New York: Longman.

Matsumoto, D. (1990). Cultural similarities and differences in display rules. *Motivation and Emotion, 14,* 195-214.

Matsumoto, D. (1991). Cultural influences on facial expressions of emotion. *Southern Communication Journal, 56,* 128-137.

Matsumoto, D., Tsutomo, K., Scherer, K., & Wallbott, H. (1988). Antecedents and reactions to emotions in the United States and Japan. *Journal of Cross-Cultural Psychology, 19,* 267-286.

McCroskey, J. C., Fayer, J. M., Richmond, V., Sallinen, A., & Barraclough, R. A. (1996). A multi-cultural examination of the relationship between nonverbal immediacy and affective learning. *Communication Quarterly, 44,* 297-307.

McCroskey, J. C., Sallinen, A., Fayer, J. M., Richmond, V., & Barraclough, R. A. (1996). Nonverbal immediacy and cognitive learning: A cross-cultural investigation. *Communication Education, 45,* 200-211.

McDaniel, E. R., & Andersen, P. A. (1998). Intercultural variations in tactile communication. *Journal of Nonverbal Communication, 22,* 59-75.

Mehrabian, A. (1971). *Silent messages.* Belmont, CA: Wadsworth.

Merritt, A. (2000). Culture in the cockpit: Do Hofstede's dimensions replicate? *Journal of Cross-Cultural Psychology, 31,* 283-301.

Nasierowski, W., & Mikula, B. (1998). Culture dimensions of Polish managers: Hofstede's indices. *Organization Studies, 19,* 495-509.

Omata, K. (1995). Territoriality in the house and its relationship to the use of rooms and the psychological well-being of Japanese married women. *Journal of Environmental Psychology, 15,* 147-154.

Patterson, M. L. (1983). *Nonverbal behavior: A functional perspective.* New York: Springer-Verlag.

Patterson, M. L., Reidhead, S. M., Gooch, M. V., & Stopka, S. J. (1984). A content-classified bibliography of research on the immediacy behaviors: 1965-1982. *Journal of Nonverbal Behavior, 8,* 360-393.

Pennebaker, J. W., Rimé, B., & Blankenship, V. (1996). Stereotypes of northerners and southerners: A cross-cultural test of Montesque's hypothesis. *Journal of Personality and Social Psychology, 70,* 372-380.

Petronio, S. (1988). *Communicative management of privacy: Process of negotiation between marital couples.* Paper presented at the annual convention of the Western Speech Communication Association, San Diego, CA

Porter, R. E., & Samovar, L. A. (1998). Cultural differences in emotional expression: Implications for intercultural communication. In P. A. Andersen & L. K. Guerrero (Eds.), *Handbook of communication and emotion: Research, theory, applications, and contexts* (pp. 452-472). San Diego, CA: Academic Press.

Remland, M. S., Jones, T. S., & Brinkman, H. (1991). Proxemic and haptic behavior in three European countries. *Journal of Nonverbal Behavior, 15,* 215-232.

Sanders, J. A., & Wiseman, R. L. (1990). The effects of verbal and nonverbal teacher immediacy on perceived cognitive, affective, and behavioral learning in the multicultural classroom. *Communication Education, 39,* 341-353.

Scheflen, A. E. (1972). *Body language and the social order.* Englewood Cliffs, NJ: Prentice Hall.

Schimmack, U. (1996). Cultural influences on the recognition of emotion by facial expressions: Individualistic or Caucasian cultures? *Journal of Cross-Cultural Psychology, 27,* 37-50.

Schmidt, D. E. (1983). Personal control and crowding stress: A test of similarity in two cultures. *Journal of Cross-Cultural Psychology, 14,* 221-239.

Schwartz, S. H. (1994). Cultural dimensions of values: Towards an understanding of national differences. In U. Kim, H. Triandis, Ç. Kâgitçibasi, S.-C. Choi, & G. Yoon (Eds.), *Individualism and* collectivism: Theory, methods, and applications (pp. 85-119). Thousand Oaks, CA: Sage.

Shackleton, V. J., & Ali, A. H. (1990). Work-related values of managers: A test of the Hofstede model. Journal of Cross-Cultural Psychology, 21, 109-118.

Shuter, R. (1976). Proxemics and tactility in Latin America. Journal of Communication, 26, 46-62.

Singh, N. N., McKay, J. D., & Singh, A. N. (1998). Culture and mental health: Nonverbal communication. Journal of Child and Family Studies, 7, 403-409.

Smith, P. B., Dugan, S., & Trompenaars, F. (1996). National culture and the values of organizational employees: A dimensional analysis across 43 nations. Journal of Cross-Cultural Psychology, 27, 231-264.

Social and labor market policy in Sweden. (2000). European parliament [Online]. Available: http://www.europarl.eu.int/sg/tree/en/default.htm

Spencer-Oatley, H. (1997). Unequal relationships in high and low power distant societies: A comparative study of tutor-student role relations in Britain and China. Journal of Cross-Cultural Psychology, 28, 284-302.

Sussman, N. M., & Rosenfeld, H. M. (1982). Influence of culture, language and sex on conversational distance. Journal of Personality and Social Psychology, 42, 66-74.

Ting-Toomey, S. T. (1991). Intimacy expressions in three cultures: France, Japan, and the United States. International Journal of Intercultural Relations, 15, 29-46.

Tocqueville, A. de. (1945). Democracy in America (Vol. 1, P. Bradley, Trans.). New York: Random House. (Original work published 1835)

Tomkins, S. S. (1984). Affect theory. In K. R. Scherer & P. Ekman (Eds.), Approaches to emotion. Hillsdale, NJ: Lawrence Erlbaum.

Triandis, H. C. (1994). Theoretical and methodological approaches to the study of collectivism and individualism. In U. Kim, H. Triandis, Ç. Kâgitçibasi, S.-C. Choi, & G. Yoon (Eds.), Individualism and collectivism: Theory, methods, and applications (pp. 41-51). Thousand Oaks, CA: Sage.

Van de Vliert, E. (1999). Gender role gaps, competitiveness, and temperature. In G. Hofstede (Ed.), Masculinity and femininity: The taboo dimension of national cultures (pp. 117-129). Thousand Oaks, CA: Sage.

Vrij, A., & Winkel, F. W. (1991). Cultural patterns in Dutch and Surinam nonverbal behavior: An analysis of simulated police/citizens encounters. Journal of Nonverbal Behavior, 15, 169-184.

Watzlawick, P., Beavin, J., & Jackson, D. (1967). Pragmatics of human communication. New York: Norton.

Weitz, S. (Ed.). (1974). Nonverbal communication: Readings and commentary. New York: Oxford University Press.

Wolfgang, A. (1979). The teacher and nonverbal behavior in the multicultural classroom. In A. Wolfgang (Ed.), Nonverbal behavior: Applications and cultural implications (pp. 159-174). New York: Academic Press.

5

Cultural Influences on the Expression and Perception of Emotion

DAVID MATSUMOTO
BRENDA FRANKLIN
JUNG-WOOK CHOI
DAVID ROGERS
HARUYO TATANI
San Francisco State University

Emotions are arguably some of the most important aspects of our lives, and psychologists, philosophers, and social scientists have, for many years, been concerned with them. They give meaning to life, serve as important motivators for our behaviors, and color our thoughts and cognitions. They are, indeed, the basic psychological fuel for growth, development, and action.

In this chapter, we review some of the major cross-cultural research that has been conducted on emotion, beginning with an overview of the study of emotion and culture in a historical perspective, and discussing the impact of this research on contemporary psychology. Then, we present a very brief review of a wide range of cross-cultural studies on emotion, spanning emotional expression, perception, experience, antecedents, appraisal,

physiology, and the concepts and definitions of emotion. We then focus on two areas of study—cross-cultural research on the expression and perception of emotion—highlighting what is known to date. Our goal is not only to provide the reader with a detailed review of this area of psychology but also to encourage scientists to get out of their boxes when thinking about this area and other areas of research.

EMOTION AND CULTURE IN HISTORICAL PERSPECTIVE AND THEIR IMPACT ON CONTEMPORARY PSYCHOLOGY

Emotion and culture have been objects of study and fascination not only by contemporary psychologists in recent history but also by philosophers and other thinkers for centuries. Indeed, emotions played a large role in the thinking and writing of Aristotle and Socrates (Russell, 1994) and were also well represented in the third-century Sanskrit text *Rasadhyaya* (Shweder & Haidt, 2000). Emotion was also central to many thinkers who were influential to modern psychology, such as Freud, Darwin, Erikson, Piaget, Bowlby, and many others.

Most modern-day studies of emotion and culture, however, find their roots in the work of Darwin, who inspired work on the expression of emotion and, as such, offered scientists a platform from which to measure emotions objectively, going beyond basic self-report, which psychologists tend to consider unreliable. Darwin's (1872/1998) thesis, summarized in *The Expression of the Emotions in Man and Animals,* suggested that emotions and their expressions had evolved across species and were evolutionarily adaptive, biologically innate, and universal across all human and even nonhuman primates.

This work, however, was not without criticism, including the lack of hard evidence that supported his claims. Between the time of Darwin's original writing and the 1960s, only seven studies attempted to address this gap in our knowledge. But these studies were methodologically flawed in a number of ways, so that unequivocal data speaking to the issue of the possible universality of emotional expression did not emerge (reviewed in Ekman, Friesen, & Ellsworth, 1972).

In the mid-1960s, Sylvan Tomkins, a pioneer in modern studies of human emotion, joined forces independently with Paul Ekman and Carroll Izard to conduct what have become known today as the universality studies (for reviews, see Ekman, 1973; Izard, 1971). These studies demonstrated the existence of six universal expressions—anger, disgust, fear, happiness, sadness, and surprise—as

judges all around the world agreed on what emotion was portrayed in the faces.

Yet the judgment studies in literate cultures conducted by Ekman and Izard were not the only evidence that came to bear on the question of emotion universality. Ekman and his colleague Wallace Friesen also demonstrated that judgments of preliterate cultures were consistent with universality, as were judgments of expressions posed by members of preliterate cultures (for a review, see Ekman, 1973). They also showed that the expressions that spontaneously occurred in reaction to emotion-eliciting films were universal (Ekman, 1972). Moreover, other scientists showed that the same expressions occur in nonhuman primates and congenitally blind individuals (Charlesworth & Kreutzer, 1973; Ekman, 1973) and correspond to similarities in emotion taxonomies in different languages around the world (Romney, Boyd, Moore, Batchelder, & Brazill, 1996; Romney, Moore, & Rusch, 1997). Thus, the universal basis for emotional expression is no longer debated in contemporary psychology, and it is considered a pancultural aspect of psychological functioning.

We also know, however, that people modify their expressions on the basis of *cultural display rules* (Ekman, 1972; Ekman & Friesen, 1969; Friesen, 1972), which are culturally prescribed rules, learned early in life, that dictate the management and modification of the universal expressions depending on social circumstance. The existence of these rules was demonstrated empirically in Ekman and Friesen's (Ekman, 1972) study of American and Japanese participants viewing stressful films alone and in the presence of an experimenter. Today, the existence of both universality and cultural display rules is well accepted in mainstream psychology (see also Fridlund's, 1997, view of display rules).

Universality implies that expressions provide an objective and reliable signal of emotion. Thus, both Ekman and Izard developed methods of measuring facial behaviors validly and reliably. In particular, Ekman and Friesen's (1978) facial action coding system (FACS) is widely recognized as the most comprehensive tool to analyze facial movements. The development of techniques such as FACS, along with the theoretical contributions of universal emotions, has led to a plethora of new research, theory, and application in the past 30 years. Studies using facial expressions of emotion as markers have addressed decades-old questions concerning the role and function of physiology in emotion, and studies involving faces and emotions have made substantial contributions to all areas of psychology, with applications in clinical, forensic, industrial, and organizational psychology. All of this has been made possible through the contributions of the original cross-cultural research on emotional expressions.

THE BREADTH OF CROSS-CULTURAL RESEARCH ON EMOTION

Not only have the original universality studies had a considerable impact on mainstream, contemporary psychology, they also have served as an important platform for continued work investigating the relation between culture and emotion. Many studies since Ekman and Izard's original research have tested the recognition of emotion in facial expressions across cultures. As one can see from the summary of studies investigating emotion recognition across cultures, there is considerable evidence that replicates the universality of the set of six emotional expressions originally reported by Ekman and Izard (see Table 5.1).

To be sure, all aspects of emotions have been studied cross-culturally. For instance, a number of studies have examined the antecedents

of emotions across cultures, reporting both cultural similarities and differences in antecedents and elicitors (Boucher & Brandt, 1981; Brandt & Boucher, 1985; Buunk & Hupka, 1987; Galati & Sciaky, 1995; Levy, 1973; Scherer, Matsumoto, Wallbott, & Kudoh, 1988; Scherer & Wallbott, 1994; Scherer, Wallbott, & Summerfield, 1983; see also a review by Mesquita & Frijda, 1992). Closely related to emotion antecedents is the topic of emotion appraisal, and a number of studies have reported cultural similarities and differences in this aspect of emotion as well (e.g., Mauro, Sato, & Tucker, 1992; Roseman, Dhawan, Rettek, Nadidu, & Thapa, 1995; Scherer, 1997a, 1997b).

Cultural influences on the subjective experience of emotion is also a topic that has received considerable attention (e.g., see reviews in Scherer & Wallbott, 1994; Wallbott & Scherer, 1986; see also work suggesting that emotion is a set of "socially shared scripts," Kitayama & Markus, 1994, 1995; Markus & Kitayama, 1991; Shweder, 1994; Wierzbicka, 1994), as has the topic of cultural similarities and differences in the concept of emotion (e.g., Levy, 1973, 1983; Lutz, 1983; Russell, 1991b). Another, relatively new area of cross-cultural research on emotion concerns the influence of culture on human physiology during emotional reactions (Ekman, Levenson, & Friesen, 1983; Levenson, Ekman, Heider, & Friesen, 1992; Tsai & Levenson, 1997), testing age-old questions concerning the role of physiology in emotional experience (see, e.g., James, 1890; Mandler, 1984).

Thus, cross-cultural studies on emotion have spanned a wide range of topics and have contributed important information to the literature on this aspect of human functioning. In the next two sections, we focus more specifically on a review of cross-cultural studies on the expression and perception of emotion, because they are arguably the most well-studied

Table 5.1 Summary of Contemporary Cross-Cultural Studies Examining the Recognition of Universal Facial Expressions of Emotion

Citation	Judge Cultures	Stimuli	Judgment Task	Major Findings
Biehl et al. (1997)	Hungarians, Poles, Japanese, Sumatrans, Americans, and Vietnamese	56 expressions from Matsumoto and Ekman (1988)	Forced-choice emotion categories	For all expressions, judges selected the intended emotion category at well above chance levels
Bormann-Kischkel, Hildebrand-Pascher, and Stegbauer (1990)	German 4-, 5-, 6-year-olds and adults	Seven Ekman and Friesen (1976) photos and two photos from Bullock and Russell (1984)	Matching with emotion category	4-year-olds correctly identified six emotions above chance levels; 5-year-olds correctly identified seven emotions above chance levels; 6-year-olds and university students correctly identified all emotions tested
Boucher and Carlson (1980)	Americans and Malays	25 American photos meeting Ekman criteria, and 42 photos of Malays with approximate criteria	Forced-choice emotion categories	Across all photos, judges selected the intended emotion category at well above chance levels
Chan (1985)	Hong Kong Chinese	Nine photos from Izard (1977)	Forced-choice emotion categories	Judges selected the intended emotion category at well above chance levels for all six universal emotions, as well as interest and shame
Ducci, Arcuri, Georges, and Sineshaw (1982)	Ethiopian high school students	28 photos from Ekman and Friesen (1976)	Forced-choice emotion categories (seven)	Judges selected the intended emotion category at well above chance levels for each of the six universal emotions
Ekman et al. (1987)	College students from Estonia, Germany, Greece, Hong Kong, Italy, Japan, Scotland, Sumatra, Turkey, and the U.S.	18 photos from Ekman and Friesen (1976)	Forced-choice emotion categories and multiple scalar ratings of emotion categories	All judges selected the intended emotion category at well above chance levels and gave the intended emotion category the highest intensity rating
Haidt and Keltner (1999)	Americans and East Indians	Universal emotions based on Ekman criteria, and other expressions	Free response and forced-choice emotion categories	For all universal expressions except contempt judged by Americans, judges selected the intended emotion category at above chance levels; similar findings obtained using free response
Kirouac and Dore (1982)	French-speaking Quebec individuals	110 photos from Ekman and Friesen (1976)	Forced-choice emotion categories	Judges selected the intended emotion category at well above chance levels for all universal emotions
Kirouac and Dore (1983)	French-speaking students in Quebec	96 photos from Ekman and Friesen (1976)	Forced-choice emotion categories	Judges selected the emotion category intended by the expressions at well above chance levels for all emotions
Kirouac and Dore (1985)	French-speaking individuals in Quebec	96 photos from Ekman and Friesen (1976)	Forced-choice emotion categories	Judges selected the emotion category intended by the expressions at well above chance levels for all emotions
Leung and Singh (1998)	Hong Kong Chinese children	24 photos from Ekman and Friesen (1975)	Matching with emotion-associated stories	Percentage of judges matching the expression with the emotion intended in the stories was well above chance for all six emotions tested

Study	Participants	Stimuli	Task	Results
McAndrew (1986)	Americans and Malays	30 photos from Ekman and Friesen (1975) presented tachistoscopically at 10 exposure times	Forced choice of six emotion categories	At 800 msec, all judges selected the intended emotion category at well above chance levels
Mandal, Saha, and Palchoudhury (1986)	Indians	Photos from Ekman and Friesen (1976)	Forced-choice emotion categories in Procedure 1, multiple scalar ratings of emotion categories in Procedure 2	For all six universal emotions, percentage of judges selecting the intended emotion category (Procedure 1) or giving the intended emotion the highest intensity rating (Procedure 2) was well above chance levels
Markham and Wang (1996)	Chinese and Australian children	18 photos from Ekman and Friesen (1976), and 18 Chinese facial expressions developed by Wang and Meng (1986)	Situation discrimination task and a situational inference task	Children from both cultures recognized the six universal emotions at above chance levels
Matsumoto (1990)	Americans and Japanese	14 expressions from Matsumoto and Ekman (1988)	Forced-choice emotion categories	Judges selected the intended emotion category at well above chance levels
Matsumoto (1992a)	Americans and Japanese	56 expressions from Matsumoto and Ekman (1988)	Forced-choice emotion categories	Judges selected the intended emotion category at well above chance levels
Matsumoto and Assar (1992)	Americans and Indians	56 expressions from Matsumoto and Ekman (1988)	Forced-choice emotion categories	Judges selected the intended emotion category at well above chance levels
Matsumoto and Ekman (1989)	Americans and Japanese	56 expressions from Matsumoto and Ekman (1988)	Multiple scalar ratings on emotion categories	Judges gave the highest intensity rating to the intended emotion category for all universal emotions except one
Matsumoto, Kasri, and Kooken (1999)	Americans and Japanese	56 expressions from Matsumoto and Ekman (1988)	Forced-choice emotion categories	Judges selected the intended emotion category at well above chance levels
Mazurski and Bond (1993, Experiment 2)	Australians	110 photos from Ekman and Friesen (1976)	Forced-choice emotion categories	Judges selected the intended emotion category for all universal emotions at well above chance levels
Mehta, Ward, and Strongman (1992)	Maori and Pakeha individuals	Maori and Pakeha poses of seven emotions and a neutral (coded by Ekman and Friesen's facial action coding system, or FACS)	Forced choice from 11 emotion categories	All emotions and neutral were recognized accurately at above chance levels
Russell, Suzuki, and Ishida (1993)	Canadians, Greeks, and Japanese	Seven slides from Matsumoto and Ekman (1988)	Open-ended emotion categories	For all emotions except contempt, the proportion of judges producing the intended emotion category was substantially greater than chance
Toner and Gates (1985)	Australians	110 slides from Ekman and Friesen (1976)	Six emotion categories and neutral	Overall, judges selected the intended emotion term at well above chance levels for all emotions

(continued)

95

Table 5.1 Continued

Citation	Judge Cultures	Stimuli	Judgment Task	Major Findings
Wallbott (1991)	Germans	28 slides from Ekman and Friesen (1976)	Scalar ratings of seven emotion categories	Proportion of judges rating the intended emotion category most intense was well above chance levels for each of the seven emotions tested
Wolfgang and Cohen (1988)	South and Central Americans, Canadians, Israelis, and Ethiopians	Wolfgang Interracial Facial Expressions Test (produced according to Ekman and Friesen criteria)	Forced-choice emotion categories	Overall, judges in all four groups selected the intended emotion term at well above chance levels for all emotions
Yik, Meng, and Russell (1998)	English-speaking Canadians, Cantonese-speaking Hong Kong Chinese, and Japanese-speaking Japanese	13 still photographs of facial expressions of babies	Freely produced emotion categories	Judges in all three groups produced the intended emotion category for happy photos, but not for any of the five other emotions
Yik and Russell (1999)	English-speaking Canadians, Cantonese-speaking Hong Kong Chinese, and Japanese-speaking Japanese	Six photos from Ekman and Friesen (1976), one photo from Matsumoto and Ekman (1988)	10 emotion categories statements	Judges in all three groups selected the intended emotion category at significantly above chance levels

NOTE: The inclusion criteria used in assembling these studies were as follows:

1. The study must have used full-face presentations of emotion with no distortion, using Ekman and Friesen or Izard related stimuli, or other stimuli provided there was a methodological check on the validity of the expressions to portray emotions.

2. The study must have included data from at least one non-U.S. sample; no within-country ethnic difference studies were included.

3. The study must have reported data for which recognition levels can be compared against chance.

4. The judges must have been non-mentally impaired.

areas of culture and emotion, producing many new and exciting findings over the past two decades.

EXPRESSION OF EMOTION ACROSS CULTURES

Contemporary cross-cultural research on emotional expression has examined different aspects of expression, including spontaneous expressions, self-reported expressions, self-reported display rules, and verbal expressions. Within each category, however, only a handful of studies have appeared in the literature. This is ironic, because cross-cultural and mainstream research in all areas of emotion owes a debt of gratitude to the original universality studies of expression. Nevertheless, the available research provides interesting and provocative information extending notions of universality in important ways.

Spontaneous Emotional Expressions in Infants

Cultural differences in spontaneous emotional expressions exist in infants under one year of age, despite some evidence for similarities in emotion socialization patterns. Camras et al. (1998), for example, examined spontaneously occurring expressions in 11-month-old Chinese, European American, and Japanese infants, indicating that the Chinese were less expressive than the European American and Japanese babies. Kanaya, Bradshaw, Nakamura, and Miyake (1987) and Kanaya, Nakamura, and Miyake (1989) examined the socialization of emotion focusing on how the regulation of American and Japanese infants' expressions is enculturated through the behavior of the mother. Mothers of both cultures were found to almost never display negative affect to their infants. When the infants

showed positive emotions, both American and Japanese mothers responded with the same kinds of slightly exaggerated expressions. These studies suggest similarities in socialization for these two cultures.

Spontaneous Emotional Expressions in Adults

Only two studies exist to date on spontaneous emotional expressions in adults, both of which demonstrate cultural similarities and differences. Waxer (1985) examined the facial expressions of American and Canadian game show contestants and found no differences in the kinds of emotions displayed. But American females were found to use their hands more than Canadian females, and American males smiled more than Canadian males. Matsumoto and Kupperbusch (2000) replicated and extended the original Ekman and Friesen display rules study by showing emotion eliciting stimuli to individualistic and collectivistic encoders, and videotaping their responses. When viewing negative film clips in the presence of an experimenter, collectivists showed less negative and more positive emotion, which is congruent with Ekman and Friesen's findings. But individualistic participants also appeared to mask their feelings in the presence of the experimenter, albeit to a much less extent.

Self-Reported Emotional Expression Across Cultures

Studies that have focused on self-reported emotional expression have yielded results that are contrary to traditional beliefs thought to govern individualistic and collectivistic cultures. Stephan, Stephan, and Cabezas De Vargas (1996) found that Americans felt more comfortable in expressing emotions to family members than to strangers, whereas Costa Ricans felt equivalent levels of comfort when expressing emotions to these groups. Stephan, Stephan, and Morrison Barnett (1998) also reported similar contradictions, in which the Japanese showed less concern for ingroup members than Americans, contrary to what is traditionally thought about collectivistic cultures. In addition, participants from the United States reported that they felt more comfortable expressing emotions to family members than to strangers, whereas those from Japan did not make this distinction.

Cultural Differences in Display Rules

Congruent with the original notions of display rules, there are considerable cultural differences in self-reported rules. Edelmann et al. (1987), for instance, reported cultural variations and explanations associated with the display of embarrassment in five countries (Greece, Italy, Spain, the United Kingdom, and West Germany). Using an American-Japanese comparison, Matsumoto (1990) suggested that cultural display rules differ systematically according to individualistic versus collectivistic differences in meaning of self-ingroup and self-outgroup relationships. Matsumoto, Takeuchi, Andayani, Kouznetsova, and Krupp (1998) extended these findings by reporting that individual differences in individualism and collectivism accounted for about 30% of the between-country differences among the United States, Japan, Korea, and Russia in display rules.

Several studies have measured self-reported expression and display rules concurrently in different contexts. Aune and Aune (1996) reported that Filipino Americans rated positive emotion expression and appropriateness higher than Japanese Americans did in romantic relationships; contrary to expectations, European Americans' ratings were as low or

lower than Japanese Americans' on all the expression and appropriateness measures. Matsumoto (1993) also found considerable differences in cultural display rules among four ethnic groups in the United States.

Cultural Differences in Verbal Expressions of Emotion

A number of studies have documented interesting cultural differences in the verbal expression of emotion. Wierzbicka (1998) compared Russian and Anglo cultures and revealed that Russians are much more emotionally expressive in their language compared with Anglos. Emanatian (1995) compared Tanzanian and English languages in the importance of the body in common metaphors of lust and sexual desire, indicating that both languages offer metaphors that include eating, hunger, and heat; some English metaphors, however, such as "there are other fish in the sea," have no equivalents in the Chagga language, because the geographical region where this language is spoken does not allow the catching of fish. Kuwano et al. (1991) examined differences between Japanese, Swedish, German, Chinese, and American languages regarding the appropriateness of the terms *loud, noisy,* and *annoying,* demonstrating cultural differences in the connotations of these words in these cultures.

PERCEPTION OF EMOTION ACROSS CULTURES

Within this area of research, there is a wide range of studies, many differing in the nature of the stimuli that are used as a basis to make emotion judgments. Some studies have examined the recognition of emotion in voice and vocal cues (e.g., Albas, McCluskey, & Albas, 1976; Beier & Zautra, 1972; Guidetti, 1991; Hatta & Nachshon, 1988; Matsumoto &

Kishimoto, 1983; McCluskey & Albas, 1981; McCluskey, Albas, Niemi, Cuevas, & Ferrer, 1975; Van Bezooijen, Otto, & Heenan, 1983), in general demonstrating that emotions can be recognized to a considerable degree, although it is often difficult to distinguish specific and discrete emotional states via voice. Other studies have examined cultural differences in judgments of body postures (e.g., Kudoh & Matsumoto, 1985; Matsumoto & Kudoh, 1987; Sogon & Masutani, 1989), indicating that emotional states can be inferred to some degree from body postures.

By far, the bulk of research in this area has been conducted using facial expressions of emotion as stimuli. In the remainder of this section, we review the major findings in the area of culture and emotion judgments involving facial expressions, describing, first, studies that show how countries and cultures are similar to, and then how they are also different from, each other when judging emotions. (Because of the wealth of material in these areas, we limit ourselves to a presentation of the major findings and articles; interested readers are referred to the original sources for more detail about them.) We then discuss the implications of these findings to future empirical and theoretical work on emotion and emotion judgments, giving researchers and students of emotion new ideas for unique and innovative research on emotion in the future.

Cultural Similarities in Emotion Judgments

Other universal expressions. The six universal expressions described earlier included only those that both Ekman and Izard had agreed were universal. In fact, Izard (1971, 1978) had suggested that other expressions were also universal, including interest-excitement and shame-humiliation. Some controversy, however, existed as to whether these were actually facial expressions or whether they were more reflective of head position or gaze direction. And in fact, the studies reviewed in Table 6.1 were not equivocal in their support for these expressions.

In the past decade, some studies have reported the existence of a universal contempt expression. Initial evidence from 10 countries including West Sumatra (Ekman & Friesen, 1986; Ekman & Heider, 1988) was later replicated by Matsumoto (1992b) in four countries, three of which were different from Ekman and Friesen's original ten. This finding received considerable attention and criticism (Izard & Haynes, 1988; Russell, 1991a), but these were later addressed by Ekman, O'Sullivan, and Matsumoto (1991a, 1991b), Rosenberg and Ekman (1995), and Biehl et al. (1997). Most recently, Haidt and Keltner (1999) reported the possible existence of a universal expression of embarrassment.

Relative intensity ratings. When comparing two expressions, people of different countries agree on which is more strongly expressed. Ekman et al. (1987) found that the 10 cultures in their study agreed 92% of the time. Matsumoto and Ekman (1989) replicated this finding by including comparisons across different poser types. These findings suggest that cultures judge emotions on a similar basis, despite differences in facial physiognomy, morphology, poser race, poser sex, or culturally prescribed rules governing the expression and perception of faces.

Association between perceived expression intensity and inferences about subjective experience. There is a strong, positive relationship between how strongly judges rate an expression and how much they believe the poser is feeling it (Matsumoto, Kasri, & Kooken, 1999). This link is a topic of considerable importance in contemporary theories of emotion. Some authors have claimed that the linkage between expression and experience is unfounded (e.g., Fernandez-Dols & Ruiz-Belda, 1997; Russell, 1997). Others, however, have argued that expressions and experience are intimately linked with each other, but need not always be coupled (Rosenberg & Ekman, 1994; see also the literature on the facial feedback hypothesis, reviewed by Matsumoto, 1987; Winton, 1986). The data from Matsumoto, Kasri, and Kooken (1999) clearly support notions of linkage.

Second mode of response in emotion recognition. People of different countries agree on the secondary emotions portrayed in an expression. For every country in Ekman et al.'s (1987) study, the secondary emotion for the disgust expressions was contempt, and for fear expressions surprise; for anger, the second mode varied depending on the photo, with disgust, surprise, and contempt as the second responses. Matsumoto and Ekman (1989) and Biehl et al. (1997) replicated these findings, suggesting pancultural agreement in the multiple meanings derived from universal faces. This agreement may exist because of overlap in the semantics of the emotion categories, antecedents and elicitors of emotion, or in the facial configurations themselves.

Perceived expressivity. People of different countries have similar stereotypes about the expressivity of other countries (Pittam, Gallois, Iwawaki, & Kroonenberg, 1995), agreeing about who is more or less expressive. The study by Waxer (1985) described above also speaks to this point.

Cultural Differences in Emotion Judgments

Emotion recognition. Although the original universality research showed that respondents recognized emotions at well over chance rates, no study ever reported perfect cross-national agreement. Matsumoto (1992a) formally tested Japanese and American judgments of emotion categories and found that recognition rates ranged from 64% to 99%, which were consistent with earlier universality studies. And in fact, many of the studies listed in Table 6.1 also report statistically significant differences in absolute levels of agreement across cultures.

Some writers have used cross-national differences in emotion recognition to argue against universality, criticizing the methodology used in judgment studies (Russell, 1991b, 1994, 1995), interpretations (Russell, 1994), and the use of language-specific terms for facial expressions of emotion (Wierzbicka, 1995). These concerns have been addressed by a number of writers (e.g., see Ekman, 1994; Izard, 1994; Romney et al., 1996; Romney et al., 1997; vanGeert, 1995; Winegar, 1995). It is also important to remember that the evidence for the universality of emotion also comes from research on nonhuman primates, infants, and congenitally blind individuals (e.g., Charlesworth & Kreutzer, 1973; Geen, 1992; Hauser, 1993). In addition, Rosenberg and Ekman (1995) presented data to suggest that even though judges cannot produce a discrete emotion category label that corresponds to the one intended by the researchers, they often understand the emotional connotations of the expression in the manner intended. Elsewhere (Yrizarry, Matsumoto, & Wilson Cohn, 1998), we have suggested at least five sources that would produce cultural differences in emotion perception even though the expression being judged may be universal. They include (1) semantic overlap in the linguistic categories and mental concepts related to emotion that are used in the judgment process, (2) overlapping facial components in the expressions, (3) cognitive overlap in events and experiences related to emotion, (4) personality biases in social cognition, and (5) culture.

More recent studies have attempted to uncover possible explanations for cross-national differences in judgments of emotion categories. For instance, Matsumoto (1992a) suggested that the differences in recognition rates are due to cultural differences in socially learned rules about how emotions could be recognized. Such a view allows for the examination of the influence of dimensions of culture on emotion judgments, a view that has received support from research described below.

Cross-national differences in emotion recognition rates and cultural dimensions. A number of studies support the notion that people of different cultures learn ways of perception management via *cultural decoding rules.* Matsumoto (1989), for instance, reported correlations between selected recognition data from 15 cultures reported in four studies and Hofstede's (1980, 1983) four cultural dimensions (power distance, uncertainty avoidance, individualism-collectivism, and masculinity-femininity. Differences in emotion perception as a function of cultural dimensions were also found in a meta-analysis by Schimmack (1996). Biehl et al. (1997) also reported cross-national differences in agreement (and in intensity ratings) that could not be explained adequately according to a Western/non-Western dichotomy, a division consistent with regional/country and racial/ethnic approaches to operationalizing culture. Rather, Biehl et al. discussed these differences in terms of possible underlying sociopsychological variables (i.e., those postulated by Hofstede, 1980, 1983) and the dimensional approach to culture advanced by Matsumoto (1989, 1990).

Attributions of personality based on smiles. The smile is a common signal for greeting, acknowledgment, showing acceptance, or mask-

ing emotions, and cultures may differ in their interpretations of it. Matsumoto and Kudoh (1993) obtained ratings from Japanese and Americans on smiling versus nonsmiling (i.e., neutral) faces with regard to intelligence, attractiveness, and sociability and indicated that the two cultures attribute different meanings to the smile.

Attributions of intensity. Ekman et al.'s (1987) study of 10 countries was the first to document cross-national differences in the intensity attributed to the facial expressions. Matsumoto and Ekman extended these findings by first developing a stimulus set composed of Asian and Caucasian posers (Matsumoto & Ekman, 1988) and presenting them to judges in the United States and Japan (Matsumoto & Ekman, 1989). For all but one emotion, Americans rated the expressions more intensely than the Japanese, regardless of the race of the poser. Because the differences were not specific to the poser, Matsumoto and Ekman (1989) interpreted the differences as a function of cultural decoding rules. Since then, other studies have replicated these findings (e.g., Biehl et al., 1997; Matsumoto, 1989, 1990).

Ethnic differences in intensity ratings. Differences exist in affect intensity, emotion judgments, display rule attitudes, and self-reported emotional expression among four ethnic groups in the United States (Matsumoto, 1993). Finding differences within an American sample (which is nearly always the comparison group in cross-cultural studies) clearly demonstrates the existence of within-country differences on emotion, and it urges us to consider meaningful psychological dimensions (e.g., individualism-collectivism, status differentiation) to explain cultural and individual differences in emotion expression and perception.

Inferences about emotional experiences underlying facial expressions of emotion. Cultural differences exist not only in judgments of external display but also of presumed subjective experience (Matsumoto, Kasri, & Kooken, 1999). These differences differ depending on the strength of the expression being judged (Matsumoto et al., 2000). In Matsumoto et al.'s (2000) study, for example, Americans rated external display significantly higher than internal experience when judging strong expressions, but there were no differences for the Japanese. On weak expressions, the Japanese rated internal experience higher than external display; there was no difference for the Americans. The researchers interpreted these findings as suggesting that for weaker expressions, Japanese may assume that a display rule is operating and may thus infer more emotion being felt than is actually displayed. When Americans see a weak expression, however, there need not be any such assumption; thus, they interpret the same amount of emotion felt as expressed. For strong expressions, Japanese may assume that the context was such that the expression was justified; thus, they infer a level of emotion felt that is commensurate with what is shown. When Americans see a strong expression, however, they know that there is a display rule to exaggerate one's feelings; thus, they compensate for this display rule by inferring less emotion felt.

Contribution of cultural dimensions to cross-national differences in emotion judgments. Recently, several writers have called for research that "unpackages" the effects of culture on psychological variables (e.g., Bond & Tedeschi, in press; Poortinga, van de Vijver, Joe, & van de Koppel, 1987; van de Vijver & Leung, 1997). Unpackaging refers to the identification of specific, psychological dimensions of culture that may account for between-country differences, their inclusion

and measurement, and the statistical estimation of the degree to which they actually account for between-country differences. Matsumoto et al.'s (2000) study described above did just that, obtaining data assessing individual-level differences in two major cultural constructs—individualism versus collectivism (IC; see Triandis, 1994, 1995, for review and relevance) and status differentiation (SD). They compared the effect sizes associated with the differences between external and internal ratings separately for Americans and Japanese between analyses with and without the IC and SD ratings as covariates and reported that approximately 90% of the variance in the rating differences was accounted for by these two cultural variables. Subsequent follow-ups further indicated that IC may contribute independent variance to this prediction. Thus, this study empirically demonstrated that the differences between Americans and Japanese on judgments of external and internal intensity may be almost entirely accounted for by cultural differences in IC and SD between the two cultures.

Summary

The evidence available to date suggests that perception can have both universal and culture-specific elements. Elsewhere (Matsumoto, 1996), we have suggested a mechanism similar to Ekman and Friesen's neurocultural theory of expression to describe how cultural similarities and differences in emotion perception or judgment can be obtained. This mechanism implies that judgments of emotion are affected by (1) a facial affect recognition program that is innate and universal (similar to Ekman and Friesen's facial affect program) and (2) culture-specific decoding rules that intensify, deintensify, mask, or qualify the perception (cf. Buck, 1984). When we perceive emotions in others, the expression is recognized through a process analogous to template matching with the universal facial prototypes of emotion. Before a judgment is rendered, however, that stimulus is also joined by learned rules about perceiving such expressions in others. The most recent research suggests that these rules may differ according to stable sociocultural dimensions such as IC and SD. This mechanism may be as basic to emotion communication across cultures as Ekman and Friesen's original neurocultural theory of expression.

CONCLUSION

Cross-cultural research over the past 30+ years has been pivotal in demonstrating the universality as well as culture-specificity of the expression and perception of emotion. These studies have had an enormous impact not only in the area of emotion but on psychology in general, as the pancultural expression and perception of emotion have come to be considered a fundamental and universal aspect of human psychological functioning. Cross-cultural findings in this area have served as the platform for new areas of research based on emotion in all other areas of psychology, and much of the information we have today on emotions in development, clinical work, psychopathology, social interaction, personality, and the like find their roots in the original universality studies. The study of emotion has been well accepted in mainstream psychology, and pre- and postdoctoral training programs exist to develop new scientists in this important area of study.

The next two decades promise to be even more exciting for research on culture and emotion. Interesting programs have sprung up all around the world, and in all disciplines of psychology. New technologies for mapping culture as a psychological construct on the individual level are being developed, as well

as ways to measure precisely moment-to-moment changes in our brains and bodies when we feel or judge emotion. Collectively, these endeavors will tell us more in the future about the relationship between culture and the physiology of emotion, the representation of display and decoding rules, emotion perception, and culture itself, in the brain. Research is also currently being done that elucidates the nature of the social meaning of emotions across cultures (e.g., Kitayama, Markus, & Matsumoto, 1995; cf. Kemper, 1978) and the differential and relative contribution of emotion and other factors in social interaction. In particular, the role of emotion and its perception in intercultural adjustment and adaptation are now being examined systematically, and preliminary evidence suggests that they are key to successful living, working, and playing across different cultural milieus (e.g., Bennett, 1993; Gudykunst, Matsumoto, Ting-Toomey, Nishida, Kim, & Heyman, 1996; Matsumoto, LeRoux, et al., 1999). Future research will also examine the contributions of folk psychology and other theories of mind that can aid in developing more comprehensive theories of display and decoding rules than are available today.

Emotion is one of the most exciting areas of study in psychology, and it is central to our understanding of people all around the world. Although we share emotions with nonhuman primates and other primitive relatives, it is our most endearing human quality, and future research will undoubtedly capture its place in our lives even better than we can today. Cross-cultural research in the future will certainly play a leading role toward this end.

REFERENCES

Albas, D. C., McCluskey, K. W., & Albas, C. A. (1976). Perception of the emotional content of speech: A comparison of two Canadian groups.

Journal of Cross-Cultural Psychology, 7, 481-490.

Aune, K. S., & Aune, R. K. (1996). Cultural differences in the self-reported experience and expression of emotions in relationships. *Journal of Cross-Cultural Psychology, 27* 67-81.

Beier, E. G., & Zautra, A. J. (1972). Identification of vocal communication of emotions across cultures. *Journal of Consulting and Clinical Psychology, 39,* 166.

Bennett, M. J. (1993). Towards ethnorelativism: A developmental model of intercultural sensitivity. In R. M. Paige (Ed.), *Education for the intercultural experience* (pp. 1-50). Yarmouth, ME: Intercultural Press.

Biehl, M., Matsumoto, D., Ekman, P., Hearn, V., Heider, K., Kudoh, T., & Ton, V. (1997). Matsumoto and Ekman's Japanese and Caucasian Facial Expressions of Emotion (JACFEE): Reliability data and cross-national differences. *Journal of Nonverbal Behavior, 21,* 3-22.

Bond, M. H., & Tedeschi, J. T. (in press). Polishing the jade: A modest proposal for improving the study of social psychology across cultures. In D. Matsumoto (Ed.), *Handbook of culture and psychology.* New York: Oxford University Press.

Bormann-Kischkel, C., Hildebrand-Pascher, S., & Stegbauer, G. (1990). The development of emotional concepts: A replication with a German sample. *International Journal of Behavioral Development, 13,* 355-372.

Boucher, J. D., & Brandt, M. E. (1981). Judgment of emotion: American and Malay antecedents. *Journal of Cross-Cultural Psychology, 12,* 272-283.

Boucher, J. D., & Carlson, G. E. (1980). Recognition of facial expression in three cultures. *Journal of Cross-Cultural Psychology, 11,* 263-280.

Brandt, M. E., & Boucher, J. D. (1985). Judgment of emotions from antecedent situations in three cultures. In I. Lagunes & Y. Poortinga (Eds.), *From a different perspective: Studies of behavior across cultures* (pp. 348-362). Lisse, the Netherlands: Swets & Zeitlinger.

Buck, R. (1984). *The communication of emotion.* New York: Guilford.

Bullock, M., & Russell, J. A. (1984). Preschool children's interpretation of facial expressions of emotion. *International Journal of Behavior Development, 7,* 193-214.

Buunk, B., & Hupka, R. B. (1987). Cross-cultural differences in the elicitation of sexual jealousy. *Journal of Sex Research, 23,* 12-22.

Camras, L. A., Oster, H., Campos, J., Campos, R., Ujie, T., Miyake, K., Wang, L., & Meng, Z. (1998). Production of emotional facial expressions in European American, Japanese, and Chinese infants. *Developmental Psychology, 34*(4), 616-628.

Chan, D. W. (1985). Perception and judgment of facial expressions among the Chinese. *International Journal of Psychology, 20,* 681-692.

Charlesworth, W. R., & Kreutzer, M. A. (1973). Facial expressions of infants and children. In P. Ekman (Ed.), *Darwin and facial expression* (pp. 91-168). New York: Academic Press.

Darwin, C. (1998). *The expression of the emotions in man and animals.* New York: Oxford University Press. (Original work published 1872)

Ducci, L., Arcuri, L., Georgis, T., & Sineshaw, T. (1982). Emotion recognition in Ethiopia: The effect of familiarity with Western culture on accuracy of recognition. *Journal of Cross-Cultural Psychology, 13,* 340-351.

Edelmann, R. J., Asendorpf, J., Contarello, A., Georgas, J., Villanueva, C., & Zammuner, V. (1987). Self-reported verbal and non-verbal strategies for coping with embarrassment in five European cultures. *Social Science Information, 26,* 869-883.

Ekman, P. (1972). Universals and cultural differences in facial expressions of emotion. In J. Cole (Ed.), *Nebraska Symposium on Motivation, 1971* (Vol. 19). Lincoln: University of Nebraska Press.

Ekman, P. (1973). *Darwin and facial expression.* New York: Academic Press.

Ekman, P. (1994). Strong evidence for universals in facial expressions: A reply to Russell's mistaken critique. *Psychological Bulletin, 115,* 268-287.

Ekman, P., & Friesen, W. V. (1969). Nonverbal leakage and clues to deception. *Psychiatry, 32,* 88-106.

Ekman, P., & Friesen, W. V. (1975). *Unmasking the face.* New York: Prentice Hall.

Ekman, P., & Friesen, W. V. (1976). *Pictures of facial affect*. Palo Alto, CA: Consulting Psychologists Press.

Ekman, P., & Friesen, W. V. (1978). *Facial action coding system*. Palo Alto, CA: Consulting Psychologists Press.

Ekman, P., & Friesen, W. V. (1986). A new pancultural facial expression of emotion. *Motivation and Emotion, 10,* 159-168.

Ekman, P., Friesen, W. V., & Ellsworth, P. (1972). *Emotion in the human face*. New York: Cambridge University Press.

Ekman, P., Friesen, W. V., O'Sullivan, M., Chan, A., Diacoyanni-Tarlatzis, I., Heider, K., Krause, R., LeCompte, W. A., Pitcairn, T., Ricci-Bitti, P. E., Scherer, K., Tomita, M., & Tzavaras, A. (1987). Universals and cultural differences in the judgment of facial expressions of emotion. *Journal of Personality and Social Psychology, 53,* 712-717.

Ekman, P., & Heider, K. G. (1988). The universality of a contempt expression: A replication. *Motivation and Emotion, 12,* 303-308.

Ekman, P., Levenson, R., & Friesen, W. V. (1983). Autonomic nervous system activity distinguishes between emotions. *Science, 221,* 1208-1210.

Ekman, P., O'Sullivan, M., & Matsumoto, D. (1991a). Confusions about context in the judgment of facial expression: A reply to "The contempt expression and the relativity thesis." *Motivation and Emotion, 15,* 169-184.

Ekman, P., O'Sullivan, M., & Matsumoto, D. (1991b). Contradictions in the study of contempt: What's it all about? Reply to Russell. *Motivation and Emotion, 15,* 293-296.

Emanatian, M. (1995). Metaphor and the expression of emotion: The value of cross-cultural perspectives. *Metaphor and Symbolic Activity, 10* (3), 163-182.

Fernandez-Dols, J. M., & Ruiz-Belda, M. A. (1997). Spontaneous facial behavior during intense emotional episodes: Artistic truth and optical truth. In J. A. Russell & J. M. Fernandez-Dols (Eds.), *The psychology of facial expression* (pp. 255-274). New York: Cambridge University Press.

Fridlund, A. J. (1997). The new ethology of human facial expressions. In J. A. Russell & J. M. Fernandez-Dols (Eds.), *The psychology of facial*

expression (pp. 103-129). New York: Cambridge University Press.

Friesen, W. V. (1972). *Cultural differences in facial expressions in a social situation: An experimental test of the concept of display rules.* Unpublished doctoral dissertation, University of California, San Francisco.

Galati, D., & Sciaky, R. (1995). The representation of antecedents of emotions in northern and southern Italy. *Journal of Cross-Cultural Psychology, 26,* 123-140.

Geen, T. (1992). Facial expressions in socially isolated nonhuman primates: Open and closed programs for expressive behavior. *Journal of Research in Personality, 26,* 273-280.

Gudykunst, W. B., Matsumoto, Y., Ting-Toomey, S., Nishida, T., Kim, K., & Heyman, S. (1996). The influence of culture, individualism-collectivism, self construals, and individual values on communication styles across cultures. *Human Communication Research, 22,* 510-543.

Guidetti, M. (1991). Vocal expression of emotions: A cross-cultural and developmental approach. *Annee Psycholgique, 91,* 383-396.

Haidt, J., & Keltner, D. (1999). Culture and facial expression: Open-ended methods find more expressions and a gradient of recognition. *Cognition and Emotion, 13,* 225-266.

Hatta, T., & Nachshon, I. (1988). Ear differences in evaluating emotional overtones of unfamiliar speech by Japanese and Israelis. *International Journal of Psychology, 23,* 293-302.

Hauser, M. (1993). Right hemisphere dominance for the production of facial expression in monkeys. *Science, 261,* 475-477.

Hofstede, G. (1980). *Culture's consequences: International differences in work-related values.* Beverly Hills, CA: Sage.

Hofstede, G. (1983). Dimensions of national cultures in fifty countries and three regions. In J. Deregowski, S. Dziurawiec, & R. Annis (Eds.), *Expiscations in cross-cultural psychology.* Lisse, the Netherlands: Swets & Zeitlinger.

Izard, C. (1971). *The face of emotion*. New York: Appleton-Century-Crofts.

Izard, C. E. (1977). *Human emotions*. New York: Plenum.

Izard, C. E. (1978). Emotions as motivations: Anevolutionary-developmental perspective. In

Nebraska Symposium on Motivation (Vol. 26, pp. 163-200). Lincoln: University of Nebraska Press.

Izard, C. E. (1994). Innate and universal facial expressions: Evidence from developmental and cross-cultural research. *Psychological Bulletin, 115,* 288-299.

Izard, C. E., & Haynes, O. M. (1988). On the form and universality of the contempt expression: A challenge to Ekman and Friesen's claim of discovery. *Motivation and Emotion, 12,* 1-16.

James, W. (1890). *Psychology.* New York: Holt.

Kanaya, Y., Bradshaw, D. L., Nakamura, C., & Miyake, K. (1987). Expressive behavior of Japanese mothers in response to their 5-month-old infants' negative and positive emotion expression. In *Research and Clinical Center for Child Development* (Annual Report No. 10, pp. 55-59).

Kanaya, Y., Nakamura, C., & Miyake, K. (1989). Cross-cultural study of expressive behavior of mothers in response to their 5-month-old infants' different emotion expression. *Research and Clinical Center for Child Development, Annual Rep. 11*(87-88), 25-31.

Kemper, T. D. (1978). *A social interactional theory of emotions.* New York: John Wiley.

Kirouac, G., & Dore, F. Y. (1982). Identification des expressions facials emotionalles par un echantillon Quebecois Francophone [Identification of emotional facial expressions by French speaking subjects in Quebec]. *International Journal of Psychology, 17,* 1-7.

Kirouac, G., & Dore, F. Y. (1983). Accuracy and latency of judgment of facial expressions of emotions. *Perceptual and Motor Skills, 57,* 683-686.

Kirouac, G., & Dore, F. Y. (1985). Accuracy of the judgment of facial expression of emotions as a function of sex and level of education. *Journal of Nonverbal Behavior, 9,* 3-7.

Kitayama, S., & Markus, H. R. (1994). *Emotion and culture: Empirical studies of mutual influence.* Washington, DC: American Psychological Association.

Kitayama, S., & Markus, H. R. (1995). Culture and self: Implications for internationalizing psychology. In N. R. Goldberger & J. B. Veroff (Eds.), *The culture and psychology reader* (pp. 366-383). New York: New York University Press.

Kitayama, S., Markus, H. R., & Matsumoto, D. (1995). Culture, self, and emotion: A cultural perspective on "self-conscious" emotions. In J. P. Tangney & K. W. Fischer (Eds.), *Self-conscious emotions: The psychology of shame, guilt, embarrassment, and pride* (pp. 439-464). New York: Guilford.

Kudoh, T., & Matsumoto, D. (1985). A cross-cultural examination of the semantic dimensions of body postures. *Journal of Personality and Social Psychology, 48,* 1440-1446.

Kuwano, S., Namba, S., Hashimoto, T., et al. (1991). Emotional expression of noise: A cross-cultural study. *Journal of Sound and Vibration, 151*(3), 421-428.

Leung, J. P., & Singh, N. N. (1998). Recognition of facial expressions of emotion by Chinese adults with mental retardation. *Behavior Modification, 22,* 205-216.

Levenson, R. W., Ekman, P., Heider, K., & Friesen, W. V. (1992). Emotion and autonomic nervous system activity in the Minangkabau of West Sumatra. *Journal of Personality and Social Psychology, 62,* 972-988.

Levy, R. I. (1973). *Tahitians.* Chicago: University of Chicago Press.

Levy, R. I. (1983). Introduction: Self and emotion. *Ethos, 11,* 128-134.

Lutz, C. (1983). Parental goals, ethnopsychology, and the development of emotional meaning. *Ethos, 11,* 246-262.

Mandal, M. K., Saha, G. B., & Palchoudhury, S. (1986). A cross-cultural study on facial affect. *Journal of Psychological Researches, 30,* 140-143.

Mandler, G. (1984). *Mind and body: Psychology of emotion and stress.* New York: Norton.

Markham, R., & Wang, L. (1996). Recognition of emotion by Chinese and Australian children. *Journal of Cross-Cultural Psychology, 27,* 616-643.

Markus, H. R., & Kitayama, S. (1991). Culture and the self: Implications for cognition, emotion, and motivation. *Psychological Review, 98,* 224-253.

Matsumoto, D. (1987). The role of facial response in the experience of emotion: More methodological problems and a meta-analysis. *Journal of Personality and Social Psychology, 52, 769-774.*

Matsumoto, D. (1989). Cultural influences on the perception of emotion. *Journal of Cross-Cultural Psychology, 20, 92-105.*

Matsumoto, D. (1990). Cultural similarities and differences in display rules. *Motivation and Emotion, 14, 195-214.*

Matsumoto, D. (1992a). American and Japanese cultural differences in the recognition of universal facial expressions. *Journal of Cross-Cultural Psychology, 23, 72-84.*

Matsumoto, D. (1992b). More evidence for the universality of a contempt expression. *Motivation and Emotion, 16, 363-368.*

Matsumoto, D. (1993). Ethnic differences in affect intensity, emotion judgments, display rule attitudes, and self-reported emotional expression in an American sample. *Motivation and Emotion, 17, 107-123.*

Matsumoto, D. (1996). *Unmasking Japan: Myths and realities about the emotions of the Japanese.* Stanford, CA: Stanford University Press.

Matsumoto, D., & Assar, M. (1992). The effects of language on judgments of facial expressions of emotion. *Journal of Nonverbal Behavior, 16, 85-99.*

Matsumoto, D., Consolacion, T., Yamada, H., Suzuki, R., Franklin, B., Paul, S., Ray, R., & Uchida, H. (2000). *American-Japanese cultural differences in judgments of emotional expressions of different intensities.* Manuscript submitted for publication.

Matsumoto, D., & Ekman, P. (1988). *Japanese and Caucasian Facial Expressions of Emotion (JACFEE) and Neutral Faces (JACNeuF)* [Slides]. (Available from the Human Interaction Laboratory, University of California, San Francisco, 401 Parnassus Avenue, San Francisco, CA 94143)

Matsumoto, D., & Ekman, P. (1989). American-Japanese differences in intensity ratings of facial expressions of emotion. *Motivation and Emotion, 13, 143-157.*

Matsumoto, D., Kasri, F., & Kooken, K. (1999). American-Japanese cultural differences in judgments of expression intensity and subjective experience. *Cognition and Emotion, 13, 201-218.*

Matsumoto, D., & Kishimoto, H. (1983). Developmental characteristics in judgments of emotion from nonverbal vocal cues. *International Journal of Intercultural Relations, 7, 415-424.*

Matsumoto, D., & Kudoh, T. (1987). Cultural similarities and differences in the semantic dimensions of body postures. *Journal of Nonverbal Behavior, 11, 166-179.*

Matsumoto, D., & Kudoh, T. (1993). American-Japanese cultural differences in attributions of personality based on smiles. *Journal of Nonverbal Behavior, 17, 231-243.*

Matsumoto, D., & Kupperbusch, C. (2000). *Idiocentric and allocentric differences in emotional expression and experience.* Manuscript submitted for publication.

Matsumoto, D., LeRoux, J., Ratzlaff, C., Tatani, H., Uchida, H., Kim, C., & Araki, S. (1999). *Development and validation of a measure of intercultural adjustment potential in Japanese sojourners: The Intercultural Adjustment Potential Scale (ICAPS).* Manuscript submitted for publication.

Matsumoto, D., Takeuchi, S., Andayani, S., Kouznetsova, N., & Krupp, D. (1998). The contribution of individualism-collectivism to cross-national differences in display rules. *Asian Journal of Social Psychology, 1, 147-165.*

Mauro, R., Sato, K., & Tucker, J. (1992). The role of appraisal in human emotions: A cross-cultural study. *Journal of Personality and Social Psychology, 62, 301-317.*

Mazurski, E. J., & Bond, N. W. (1993). A new series of slides depicting facial expressions of affect: A comparison with the Pictures of Facial Affect Series. *Australian Journal of Psychology, 45, 41-47.*

McAndrew, F. T. (1986). A cross-cultural study of recognition thresholds for facial expressions of emotion. *Journal of Cross-Cultural Psychology, 17, 211-224.*

McCluskey, K. W., & Albas, D. C. (1981). Perception of the emotional content of speech by Canadian and Mexican children, adolescents, and adults. *International Journal of Psychology, 16, 119-132.*

McCluskey, K. W., Albas, D. C., Niemi, R., Cuevas, C., & Ferrer, C. (1975). Cross-cultural differences in the perception of the emotional content of speech: A study of the development of sensitivity in Canadian and Mexican children. *Developmental Psychology, 11, 551-555.*

Mehta, S. D., Ward, C., & Strongman, K. (1992). Cross-cultural recognition of posed facial expressions of emotion. *New Zealand Journal of Psychology, 21,* 74-77.

Mesquita, B., & Frijda, N. H. (1992). Cultural variations in emotions: A review. *Psychological Bulletin, 112,* 197-204.

Pittam, J., Gallois, C., Iwawaki, S., & Kroonenberg, P. (1995). Australian and Japanese concepts of expressive behavior. *Journal of Cross-Cultural Psychology, 26,* 451-473.

Poortinga, Y. H., van de Vijver, F. J. R., Joe, R. C., & van de Koppel, J. M. H. (1987). Peeling the onion called culture: A synopsis. In Ç. Kâgitçibasi (Ed.), *Growth and progress in cross-cultural psychology* (pp. 22-34). Berwyn, PA: Swets North America.

Romney, A. K., Boyd, J. P., Moore, C. C., Batchelder, W. H., & Brazill, T. J. (1996). Culture as shared cognitive representations. *Proceedings from the National Academy of Sciences, 93,* 4699-4705.

Romney, A. K., Moore, C. C., & Rusch, C. D. (1997). Cultural universals: Measuring the semantic structure of emotion terms in English and Japanese. *Proceedings of the National Academy of Sciences, 94,* 5489-5494.

Roseman, I. J., Dhawan, N., Rettek, S. I., Nadidu, R. K., & Thapa, K. (1995). Cultural differences and cross-cultural similarities in appraisals and emotional responses. *Journal of Cross-Cultural Psychology, 26,* 23-48.

Rosenberg, E. L., & Ekman, P. (1994). Coherence between expressive and experiential systems in emotion. *Cognition and Emotion, 8,* 201-229.

Rosenberg, E. L., & Ekman, P. (1995). Conceptual and methodological issues in the judgment of facial expressions of emotion. *Motivation and Emotion, 19,* 111-138.

Russell, J. A. (1991a). The contempt expression and the relativity thesis. *Motivation and Emotion, 15,* 149-184.

Russell, J. A. (1991b). Culture and the categorization of emotions. *Psychological Bulletin, 110,* 426-450.

Russell, J. A. (1994). Is there universal recognition of emotion from facial expression? A review of cross-cultural studies. *Psychological Bulletin, 115,* 102-141.

Russell, J. A. (1995). Facial expressions of emotion: What lies beyond minimal universality? *Psychological Bulletin, 118,* 379-391.

Russell, J. A. (1997). Reading emotions from and into faces: Resurrecting a dimensional-contextual perspective. In J. A. Russell & J. M. Fernandez-Dols (Eds.), *The psychology of facial expression* (pp. 295-320). New York: Cambridge University Press.

Russell, J. A., Suzuki, N., & Ishida, N. (1993). Canadian, Greek, and Japanese freely produced emotion labels for facial expressions. *Motivation and Emotion, 17,* 337-351.

Scherer, K. (1997a). Profiles of emotion antecedent-appraisal: Testing theoretical predictions across cultures. *Cognition and Emotion, 11,* 113-150.

Scherer, K. (1997b). The role of culture in emotion-antecedent appraisal. *Journal of Personality and Social Psychology, 73,* 902-922.

Scherer, K., Matsumoto, D., Wallbott, H., & Kudoh, T. (1988). Emotional experience in cultural context: A comparison between Europe, Japan, and the USA. In K. Scherer (Ed.), *Facets of emotion: Recent research* (pp. 5-30). Hillsdale, NJ: Lawrence Erlbaum.

Scherer, K. R., & Wallbott, H. G. (1994). Evidence for universality and cultural variation of differential emotion response patterning. *Journal of Personality and Social Psychology, 66,* 310-328.

Scherer, K. R., Wallbott, H. G., & Summerfield, A. B. (Eds.). (1983). *Experiencing emotion: A cross-cultural study.* Cambridge, UK: Cambridge University Press.

Schimmack, U. (1996). Cultural influences on the recognition of emotion by facial expressions: Individualist or Caucasian cultures? *Journal of Cross-Cultural Psychology, 27,* 37-50.

Shweder, R. A. (1994). Are there basic emotions? In P. Ekman & R. J. Davidson (Eds.), *The nature* of emotion: *Fundamental questions. Series in affective science* (pp. 5-47). New York: Oxford University Press.

Shweder, R. A., & Haidt, J. (2000). The cultural psychology of the emotions: Ancient and new. In M. Lewis & J. Haviland (Eds.), *The handbook of emotions* (pp. 325-414). New York: Guilford.

Sogon, S., & Masutani, M. (1989). Identification of emotion from body movements: A cross-cultural study of Americans and Japanese. *Psychological Reports, 65,* 35-46.

Stephan, C. W., Stephan, W. G., & Morrison Barnett, S. (1998). Emotional expression in Japan and the United States: The nonmonolithic nature of individualism and collectivism. *Journal of Cross-Cultural Psychology, 29,* 728-748.

Stephan, W. G., Stephan, C. W., & Cabezas De Vargas, M. (1996). Emotional expression in Costa Rica and the United States. *Journal of Cross-Cultural Psychology, 27,* 147-160.

Toner, H. L., & Gates, G. R. (1985). Emotional traits and recognition of facial expressions of emotion. *Journal of Nonverbal Behavior, 9,* 48-66.

Triandis, H. C. (1994). *Culture and social behavior.* New York: McGraw-Hill.

Triandis, H. C. (1995). *Individualism and collectivism.* Boulder, CO: Westview.

Tsai, J. L., & Levenson, R. W. (1997). Cultural influences of emotional responding: Chinese American and European American dating couples during interpersonal conflict. *Journal of Cross-Cultural Psychology, 28,* 600-625.

Van Bezooijen, R., Otto, S., & Heenan, T. (1983). Recognition of vocal expressions of emotion. *Journal of Cross-Cultural Psychology, 14,* 387-406.

van de Vijver, F. J. R., & Leung, K. (1997). *Methods and data analysis for cross-cultural research.* Thousand Oaks, CA: Sage.

vanGeert, P. (1995). Green, red, and happiness: Towards a framework for understanding emotion universals. *Culture and Psychology, 1,* 259-268.

Wallbott, H. G. (1991). Recognition of emotion from facial expression via imitation? Some indirect evidence for an old theory. *British Journal of Social Psychology, 30,* 207-219.

Wallbott, H. G., & Scherer, K. (1986). How universal and specific is emotional experience? Evidence from 27 countries on five continents. *Social Science Information, 25,* 763-795.

Wang, L., & Meng, Z. (1986). A preliminary study of discrimination on facial expressions of adults. *Acta-Psychologica-Sincia, 18,* 349-355.

Waxer, P. H. (1985). Video ethology: Television as a data base for cross-cultural studies in nonverbal displays. *Journal of Nonverbal Behavior, 9,* 111-120.

Wierzbicka, A. (1994). Semantic universals and primitive thought: The question of the psychic unity of humankind. *Journal of Linguistic Anthropology, 4,* 23-49.

Wierzbicka, A. (1995). Emotion and facial expression: A semantic perspective. *Culture and Psychology, 1,* 227-258.

Wierzbicka, A. (1998). Russian emotional expression. *Ethos, 26*(4), 456-483.

Winegar, L. (1995). Moving toward culture-inclusive theories of emotion. *Culture and Psychology, 1,* 269-277.

Winton, W. M. (1986). The role of facial response in self-reports of emotion: A critique of Laird. *Journal of Personality and Social Psychology, 50,* 808-812.

Wolfgang, A., & Cohen, M. (1988). Sensitivity of Canadians, Latin Americans, Ethiopians, and Israelis to interracial facial expressions of emotions. *International Journal of Intercultural Relations, 12,* 139-151.

Yik, M. S. M., Meng, Z., & Russell, J. A. (1998). Adults' freely produced emotion labels for babies' spontaneous facial expressions. *Cognition and Emotion, 12,* 723-730.

Yik, M. S. M., & Russell, J. A. (1999). Interpretation of faces: A cross-cultural study of a prediction from Fridlund's theory. *Cognition and Emotion, 13,* 93-104.

Yrizarry, N., Matsumoto, D., & Wilson Cohn, C. (1998). American and Japanese multi-scalar intensity ratings of universal facial expressions of emotion. *Motivation and Emotion, 22,* 315-327.

6

Cognition and Affect in Cross-Cultural Relations

COOKIE WHITE STEPHAN
WALTER G. STEPHAN
New Mexico State University

Cross-cultural relations are characterized by misunderstandings, misinterpretations, and miscommunications. People commonly misconstrue or misconceive the behaviors of individuals from other cultures because they view these behaviors within the framework of the values, beliefs, and norms of their own culture. The reason these problems arise is that cultures differ in the ways in which they construct and respond to social reality (Brislin, Cushner, Cherrie, & Yong, 1986). In this chapter, we present a conceptual model regarding the role of cognition and affect in cross-cultural interactions. Then, we explore the social science literature to help explain the ways in which the components of the model can have negative effects on cross-cultural interactions. Finally, we use the model as a framework to consider a number

of remedies for the problems created by cultural differences.

Our working model is presented in Figure 6.1. We argue that individuals' cognitions and affective responses are determined in large part by their cultural background and the contexts in which they find themselves. The primary way in which culture influences individual cognition is by creating the cognitive structures that are used to process information. The symbolic aspects of culture—language, socialization practices, norms, roles, laws, and so on—are of primary importance in creating these structures. These symbolic aspects of culture influence the worldview of individuals within the culture, creating a vision that is typically taken for granted and that usually goes unexamined

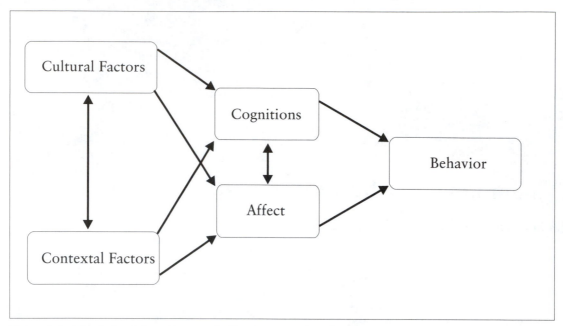

Figure 6.1   The Role of Cognitions and Affect in Intercultural Relations

and unchallenged. Differing worldviews are the root cause of most cross-cultural miscommunications and misunderstandings.

Culture also shapes affect and its expression. It does so by influencing what stimuli take on affective significance, defining the socially acceptable emotions, and specifying the circumstances under which they may be expressed. In addition, culture has an indirect effect on affect by establishing routines that, when disrupted, cause emotional reactions.

Situational contexts also influence cognition and affect. Members of particular cultures bring their shared views to the situations they enter, but the specific cognitions that are activated depend on the situational context. Context influences affect by directly causing emotional reactions such as pleasure and pain, through the associations it creates to prior emotional reactions, and by evoking emotion through empathy and other responses to people.

Cognition and affect have a reciprocal influence on one another. Associationist models

of the relationships between cognition and affect argue that nodes of cognitive and affective information are interconnected by a series of links varying in strength and direction (Stephan & Stephan, 1996). Activating any node activates the other nodes to which it is connected. Thus, encountering an outgroup member may activate many different cognitions and various types of affect. The activation of interconnected cognitions and affect occurs automatically and is typically outside of awareness. However, even when no preexisting network of connections between cognition and affect exists, cognitions can evoke affect (e.g., an appraisal of an outgroup member as threatening evokes fear) and affect can evoke cognitions (e.g., a person angered by an outgroup member may consider ways of seeking redress).

Cognition and affect have a direct impact on behavior in cross-cultural interactions. Behavior may be influenced by cognitions, affect, or a combination of both. For example, behavior might be determined predominantly by expectations generated on the basis of the stereotype of the group, a cognitive factor. Alternatively, behavior might be determined primarily by affective responses to the group, such as contempt or mistrust.

Clearly, individual differences among members of any given culture exist, both in cognitions and affective responses. However, because our concern is with culturally shaped patterns of behavior, in this chapter we disregard these individual differences, even though we acknowledge their importance. In the next section, we present concepts and theories to help explain the ways in which cognition and affect influence cross-cultural interaction.

THE INFLUENCE OF COGNITION AND AFFECT ON CROSS-CULTURAL INTERACTIONS

We discuss each of the components of the model in turn, including contextual factors, cognition, and affect.

Contextual Factors Relevant to Cross-Cultural Relations

Both cultural interpretations of contexts and the conditions of contact have important effects on cross-cultural relations. All cross-cultural encounters take place in specific contexts that are likely to be construed differently by people from different cultures (Smith & Bond, 1999). For example, people from both individualistic and collectivistic societies routinely violate the norms of each other's societies in cross-cultural interactions. Collectivists often perceive individualists to be too intimate, whereas individualists frequently feel that collectivists behave too distantly. In general, contextual factors are viewed as more important in collectivist than in individualist cultures and, for this reason, behavior differs

more from situation to situation in the former type of culture (Triandis, 1995).

A wide range of contextual factors influence both cognition and affect. For example, the long tradition of studying the contact hypothesis has yielded an impressive array of situational factors that promote positive intergroup relations (Amir, 1976; Stephan, 1987). Many studies of the contact hypothesis also provide information about situations that are likely to lead to negative interpretations and affective responses. Thus, competition, unequal status, conflicting goals, and a lack of support by relevant authorities lead to negative intergroup relations. Contact that involves unbalanced group representation can likewise have negative effects. Unfortunately, many cross-cultural interactions are characterized by such negative contextual factors.

Other contextual factors that clearly have a negative influence on cognition and affect include conflict and situations that are perceived to be unjust, such as those involving inequities or relative deprivation (Leung & Stephan, 2001; Markus & Lin, 1999). In addition, situations that involve uncertainty, feelings of threat, or frustration most likely have negative consequences on cognition and affect.

It is very important to note, however, that even in the absence of negative contextual factors, cross-cultural interaction may still be characterized by misunderstandings and misinterpretations due to cultural differences in worldviews. That is, cultural differences can create negative cross-cultural relations, even under optimal contact conditions.

Cognitions Relevant to Cross-Cultural Relations

In our model, cultural and contextual factors combine to influence cognition. Theorists and researchers have identified a number of cognitive elements of cross-cultural relations that can have a potentially detrimental impact.

They include ethnocentrism, stereotypes, cognitive biases, and social identity concerns.

Ethnocentrism

All groups are ethnocentric; that is, they subscribe to "the view of things in which one's own group is the center of everything, and all others are scaled or rated with reference to it" (Sumner, 1906, p. 13). One consequence of ethnocentrism is that people base their expectations regarding cross-cultural interaction on their own culture's norms and rules regarding social interaction (Brislin et al., 1986). This process often leads to an almost complete misunderstanding of the values, intentions, statements, and actions of others, thereby turning attempts at cross-cultural communication into serious miscommunications. Wiseman, Hammer, and Nishida (1989) have found that ethnocentrism is negatively related to three components important to cross-cultural communication competence: cultural-specific understanding of the other, cultural-general understanding, and positive regard for the other.

Another consequence of ethnocentrism is that one's own group's norms, values, and behaviors are seen as moral, good, and proper, whereas those of groups that differ from one's own often are seen as immoral, wrong, and improper. Ethnocentrism also leads people to exaggerate group differences. Ethnocentric cultural groups see themselves as superior to other groups, which are treated as inferior (LeVine & Campbell, 1972). In addition, ethnocentrism is often characterized by negative affective reactions to outgroups, such as distrust, hostility, and contempt.

Research indicates that cultural differences in ethnocentrism exist (Bond, 1988). In general, ethnocentrism is lower in countries with a social integrationist value structure (strong belief in tolerance of others, harmony with others) than in countries with a cultural inwardness value structure (sense of cultural superiority, respect for tradition). Thus, the extent to which ethnocentrism complicates cross-cultural interaction depends on the level of ethnocentrism of the countries represented in the interaction.

Stereotypes

Stereotypes are all too often overgeneralized, inaccurate, and negative (Hamilton & Sherman, 1996; Oakes, Haslam, & Turner, 1994). Unfortunately, they are frequently used to dominate, disparage, or dehumanize members of outgroups. Cultural stereotypes are created through socialization, media portrayals, norms, and laws (e.g., statutes regarding outgroup marriage), as well as through direct experience. The particular traits in a cultural stereotype that are activated depend on the situational context (Oakes et al., 1994). The stereotype activated on a battleground is different from that prompted at a concert. Although the stereotype of a given culture often differs between ingroup and outgroup members, sometimes the stereotype is held consensually. For instance, Americans and Russians agree on the stereotype of Americans, but they disagree on the stereotype of Russians (Stephan, Ageyev, Coates-Shrider, Stephan, & Abalakina, 1994). However, even when there is descriptive consensus, there may not be evaluative consensus (Peabody, 1999). That is, the two cultures may differ in the evaluation of the traits in the stereotype. Usually, it is the outgroup stereotype that is viewed negatively, but there is evidence of negative autostereotyping in some countries such as Hungary and Russia (Mlicki & Ellemers, 1996; Stephan et al., 1994).

One function of stereotypes is the creation of order out of the chaos of social reality. Stereotypes provide guidelines for cross-cultural interaction and expectations for the behavior of others. People often base their behavior toward outgroup members on stereotype-related expectancies. The members of the outgroup may respond to being treated in this manner by acting in ways that confirm the initial expectancies (Snyder, 1992). For instance, an American who perceives that the British are reserved may be so tentative and cool that the Britisher responds in kind. That is, the expectation becomes the reality—a self-fulfilling prophecy.

Cognitive Biases

A number of cognitive biases exist in the way in which individuals evaluate themselves and others, and these biases have implications for cross-cultural interactions. When group stereotypes are activated, either consciously or unconsciously, they typically lead to biased processing of information, and this bias is stronger for well-developed stereotypes, such as those about nationality and race (Stangor & McMillan, 1992). Stereotypes are maintained in part by the tendency for people to better remember expectancy-confirming information about social groups than expectancy-disconfirming information (Fyock & Stangor, 1994; Stangor & McMillan, 1992). These biases affect the information that is noticed, remembered, stored in long-term memory, and recalled. Another memory bias, illusory correlation, leads people to remember that members of minority groups have engaged in negative behaviors more frequently than they actually have (Hamilton & Rose, 1980). They also tend to remember negative information about outgroup members if it is consistent with their negative feelings toward them (Higgins & King, 1981). An additional cognitive bias that maintains stereotypes is the tendency to discount evidence that contradicts

the stereotype by attributing disconfirming behaviors to situational factors.

Biases associated with attributional tendencies also vary across cultures. In individualistic cultures people often fall prey to the *fundamental attribution error*, the tendency to attribute the behavior of others to internal traits. However, in collectivistic cultures people emphasize situational causes of behavior to a greater extent than in individualistic cultures because they see behavior as more dynamic and driven by contextual factors (Morris & Peng, 1994). These attributional preferences have an intriguing consequence. They lead people from collectivistic cultures to expect positive behaviors from others to a greater degree than do people from individualistic cultures (Ybarra & Stephan, 1999). This bias occurs because people in collectivistic cultures believe that situational factors are important determinants of behavior and the situational pressures that exist in most contexts favor positive behaviors.

A bias also occurs for the attributions made to explain positive and negative behaviors. People tend to blame outgroup members more than ingroup members for negative behaviors and give more credit for positive behaviors to ingroup than outgroup members. This bias has been labeled the ultimate attribution error (Hewstone & Jaspars, 1982; Pettigrew, 1979). It is relevant to cross-cultural interactions because individuals often disconfirm each other's expectancies that are based on their own culture. Because these disconfirmations often involve behaviors that are regarded as negative, unfavorable trait attributions about the other person are likely to be made (e.g., an American will think a Greek neighbor is nosy because the neighbor asks how much she paid for her dress). These negative trait attributions may then feed into negative self-fulfilling prophecies. Smith and Bond (1999) argue that the ultimate attribution error should be less likely to occur in vertical collectivistic societies than in other types of societies. In these cultures, disadvantaged groups should be relatively more likely to accept the legitimacy of their lower status.

Finally, there appear to be cultural differences in the attributions people make to explain their own behavior. The attributions that people in individualistic cultures make for their own behavior are often self-serving (Snyder, Stephan, & Rosenfield, 1978). In contrast, the attributions that people in collectivistic cultures make for their own behavior depend to a greater extent on the audience. Both modesty and self-serving biases have been found in collectivistic cultures (Smith & Bond, 1999).

Social Identity

Social identity theorists have argued that the desire to maintain a positive self-image motivates people to favorably evaluate the groups to which they belong and, in the process of doing so, disparage outgroups (Abrams & Hogg, 1990; Tajfel & Turner, 1986). In addition, the more important the group identity, the stronger the tendency to treat outgroup members as having uniform characteristics. At the same time, individuals with strong group identification perceive their group as more dissimilar from the outgroup.

Perceiving the outgroup as dissimilar contributes to disliking the other group (Byrne, 1971). Thus, cultural and contextual factors that heighten the salience of cultural identity are likely to have negative effects on cross-cultural relations, leading to avoidance or rejection of outgroup members.

Affect and Cross-Cultural Relations

Negative affective responses to intergroup interaction pose major problems for cross-cultural relations. Among the most common negative affective responses are anxiety, uncertainty, feelings of injustice, and the negative affect associated with prejudice (e.g., feelings of hatred). We also explore the effect of moods on cognitive processes and behavior.

Intergroup Anxiety and Anxiety/Uncertainty Management

Intergroup anxiety often arises during interactions with outgroup members (Gudykunst, 1995; Stephan & Stephan, 1985, 1996; Stephan, Stephan, & Gudykunst, 1999). In such situations, people may be anxious about possible negative consequences of the interaction. People fear negative psychological consequences (e.g., confusion, frustration, feeling incompetent), negative behavioral consequences (e.g., being exploited, harmed), negative evaluations by outgroup members (e.g., being rejected or ridiculed), and negative evaluations by ingroup members (e.g., rejection, being identified with outgroup members). Intergroup anxiety has been shown to predict prejudice toward members of other cultures, immigrant groups, and racial and ethnic groups in a multicultural society (Stephan & Stephan, 2000).

Gudykunst's anxiety/uncertainty management (AUM) model applies to all levels of communication, from the interpersonal to the cross-cultural. In this theory, it is argued that the primary tasks necessary for effective cross-cultural communication are managing the anxiety and uncertainty people have about predicting others' attitudes, feelings, and behaviors (Gudykunst, 1995). Individuals can communicate effectively to the extent that they are able to manage their anxiety and accurately predict and explain others' attitudes, feelings, and behaviors. Gudykunst believes that people have minimum and maximum thresholds for uncertainty and anxiety and that either too much or too little uncertainty and anxiety hampers cross-cultural communication. Anxiety and uncertainty have been found to be associated with one another in a number of studies, and several studies have shown that anxiety and uncertainty are associated with communication effectiveness (Gudykunst & Nishida, 2001; Hubbert, Gudykunst, & Guerrero, 1999).

The type of information that people seek to reduce uncertainty about others varies by culture. In collectivistic cultures, where assumptions are based largely on group membership, group-based information is most useful (Gudykunst & Nishida, 1986a). Conversely, in individualistic cultures, where assumptions rest more on individual characteristics, person-based information is sought. Both self-disclosure and frequency of communication are associated with uncertainty reduction in individualistic, but not collectivistic, cultures (Gudykunst & Nishida, 1986b; Sanders, Wiseman, & Matz, 1991).

Affective Responses to Injustice

Feelings of injustice often arise as a consequence of negative cross-cultural interactions. One cross-cultural study of psychological reactions to injustice found that the same set of emotional reactions characterized 25 different cultures (Mikula, Scherer, & Athenstaedt, 1998). In this study, injustice was reported to be a very common cause of anger, disgust, sadness, fear, shame, and guilt. It seems likely that the type of injustice that elicits these emotions differs across cultures. In individualistic cultures, injustice directed at the individual is probably more likely to provoke anger than injustice directed at the ingroup, but the reverse is likely to be true in collectivistic cultures. For instance, Sprecher (1986) found that American students commonly responded to interpersonal injustice with anger.

Another study conducted in the United States found that feelings of envy due to injustice were linked to hostility (Smith, Parrott, Ozer, & Moniz, 1994). These investigators contrast envy, which they regard as an essentially private and not socially acceptable emotional reaction to injustice, with resentment, which they regard as a more public and socially acceptable emotional reaction to injustice. It is possible that members of collectivistic cultures, with their greater emphasis on the control and display of emotions, would be more prone to envy as a reaction to injustice, whereas those from individualistic cultures might be more prone to resentment.

Prejudice

Negative affect is at the heart of prejudice, and intergroup prejudice is strongly associated with cross-cultural ineffectiveness, communication incompetence, and maladjustment. Several theories of the causes of prejudice are useful in understanding the bases of negative cross-cultural interactions. These include realistic group conflict and symbolic bases of prejudice.

Realistic group conflict. Realistic group conflict theory argues that group antagonisms arise from competition for scarce resources, such as territory, wealth, or natural resources (LeVine & Campbell, 1972; Sherif, 1966). Considerable empirical work has demonstrated a relationship between threats to the political or economic power of the ingroup and prejudice directed toward the outgroup (Ashmore & Del Boca, 1976; Bobo, 1988). Perceived conflicts can be as important in producing prejudice as actual realistic conflicts.

Symbolic bases of prejudice. A number of recent theories have suggested that prejudice is no longer based on presumed biological inferiority but rather on contradictions among groups' fundamental values and attitudes. These contradictions can stem from presumed value and attitude differences between the ingroup and the outgroup (Sears, 1988), the conflict between unacknowledged negative affect toward outgroups and egalitarian values (Gaertner & Dovidio, 1986), or positive and negative feelings held simultaneously (Katz, Wachenhut, & Hass, 1986). These theories have been applied to a wide variety of groups who suffer from prejudice and discrimination, where these value, attitude, and affect contradictions have been shown to be powerful predictors of behavior.

Effects of Mood

Moods can have an impact on cognitive processes and behavior. For instance, the arousal created by anxiety can lead to a reliance on simplified (heuristic) information processing (Baron, Burgess, Kao, & Logan, 1990; Wilder & Shapiro, 1989). One reason for these effects is that high levels of arousal undermine processing capacity, as do very low levels of arousal. Thus, both high and low levels of arousal can lead to an increased reliance on stereotypes (Bodenhausen, 1993).

Moods have also been found to affect the perception of outgroups. In one study, students in a positive mood were more likely to stereotype members of a racial outgroup than students in a neutral or negative mood, apparently because good moods undercut people's motivation to process information carefully (Park & Banaji, 2000). In a related study, both happy and angry students were more likely to stereotype an ethnic outgroup than students in a neutral mood (Bodenhausen, 1990). Other studies have found that moods affect recall, although the effects of mood on recall vary a great deal (Blaney, 1986; Mineka & Nugent, 1995). One common pattern is mood-congruent recall. For example, people in a negative mood may recall negative information about others better than positive information. Because negative mood and high arousal are common in cross-cultural interac-

tions, people may both tend to rely on stereotypes and recall negative information about others.

In the final section, we consider remedies that have been developed for cross-cultural communication and cross-cultural relations problems.

REMEDIES FOR CROSS-CULTURAL RELATIONS PROBLEMS

The problems created by maladaptive cognitive and affective responses to cross-cultural interaction can be addressed in cross-cultural relations training programs. We use information regarding the concepts and theories we have just reviewed to formulate suggestions concerning ways to mitigate cross-cultural relations problems. Although most techniques of improving cross-cultural relations attempt to create change by altering both cognition and affect, we first discuss concepts and theories that are related primarily to cognitions and then consider those that are related primarily to affect. The discussion of remedies begins with the concepts and theories presented in the first half of the chapter, although additional concepts and theories relevant to improving cross-cultural relations are also introduced.

Cognitive Concepts and Theories

In this section, we discuss ways of reducing the impact of ethnocentrism, stereotypes, cognitive biases, social identity concerns, and cultural differences on cross-cultural relations. We also discuss the ways in which concepts from the theory of reasoned action are relevant to improving cross-cultural relations.

Ethnocentrism

Ethnocentrism creates cross-cultural relations problems in part because people expect others to think and behave as they do. Ignorance of the other culture is a major cause of cross-cultural relations problems (Stephan & Stephan, 1984). These problems can be addressed through didactic programs that present information in a nonevaluative manner. Presenting the practical reasons for the beliefs and values of the other culture should minimize negative reactions to cultural differences. Valid cultural information can replace unrealistic expectations with more realistic ones.

Cultural information can also be acquired through experiential techniques (Goldstein & Smith, 1999; Gudykunst, Guzley, & Hammer, 1996). Using these techniques, individuals can learn to confront a world that is different from their own. They may be asked to act appropriately in this unfamiliar cultural context and perform assigned tasks. These techniques facilitate the acquisition of new norms, values, and behaviors (Weeks, Pedersen, & Brislin, 1982).

Cultural sensitizers can be used to provide information about other cultures. Cultural sensitizers use specific instances of cross-cultural misunderstanding or conflict to teach people about the subjective culture of another group. That is, they learn about the norms, values, and beliefs that typically remain hidden from outsiders (Cushner & Landis, 1996; Triandis, 1972).

Stereotypes

Members of stereotyped groups can prevent self-fulfilling prophecies by counteracting them, if they are aware of others' negative expectations and have been trained to do so (Cohen & Roper, 1972). People are especially likely to counteract self-fulling prophecies if they believe that they do not possess the stereotyped trait (Swann & Ely, 1984).

People sometimes avoid changing their stereotypes by subtyping—breaking a larger group down into smaller subcategories (Rothbart & John, 1985). Providing contact with a diverse array of outgroup members makes the process of subtyping more difficult and creates more differentiated perceptions of outgroup members (Langer, 1989).

Cognitive Biases

Expectancy-based cognitive biases can be weakened if people engage in systematic processing of expectancy-disconfirming information and then attribute the cause of the disconfirming behaviors to internal factors (Crocker, Hannah, & Weber, 1983). Internal attributions are most likely to be made if many different outgroup members engage in the disconfirming behavior and it occurs frequently in a variety of settings (Mackie, Allison, Worth, & Asuncion, 1992; Rothbart & John, 1985). In addition, training people in the logic of making statistically valid inferences reduces their tendency to stereotype groups (Schaller, Asp, Rosell, & Heim, 1996).

Social Identity

One way to reduce problems stemming from ingroup bias is by creating a strong identification with an overarching social category. Identifying with superordinate groups such as regional alliances or humankind itself converts cultures that had considered themselves to be ingroups and outgroups into a single group with a shared identity (Dovidio, Kawakami, & Gaertner, 2000; Sherif, Harvey, White, Hood, & Sherif, 1961).

Another technique of mitigating the negative effects of ingroup bias is to remind people of the multiple social categories to which they belong (Hewstone, Islam, & Judd, 1993; Vanbeselaere, 1991). Every individual simultaneously belongs to numerous social categories (e.g., sex and age, as well as nationality), and these social categories overlap with those of others in a criss-crossing pattern. The belief that the outgroup differs significantly from the ingroup can also be changed by increasing the perception of the similarity of the outgroup to the ingroup (Byrne, 1971).

Dimensions of Cultural Difference

Theories about major dimensions of cultural differences, such as individualism and collectivism, can provide information on the underlying causes of the behavior of people from other cultures. This use of "culture theory" allows interventions to be based on the most relevant cultural characteristics, and it makes these differences seem more intelligible and thus more acceptable (Bhawuk & Triandis, 1996).

Theory of Reasoned Action

In the theory of reasoned action, it is argued that people's intentions to behave are a function of their attitudes toward the act and their subjective norms, which are the perceptions people have of the attitudes of important others (Fishbein & Ajzen, 1975). According to this theory, it should be possible to increase positive cross-cultural behaviors by modifying people's attitudes about the outcomes of such behaviors and by altering their perceptions of relevant subjective norms. Creating a positive climate for cultural interaction can also change perceptions of the outcomes of cross-cultural interaction and alter people's beliefs about the attitudes of important others (e.g., other members of their ingroup).

Affective Concepts and Theories

The next set of concepts and theories we discuss is more closely related to affect, al-

though cognitions invariably play a role as well. We discuss perceived threats, anxiety, uncertainty, dissonance theory, social learning theory, empathy, compunction theory, and contact theory.

Perceived Threats

Because symbolic threats are created by the belief that others possess dissimilar values and beliefs (Sears, 1988; Stephan & Stephan, 2000), information about overriding human values common to all cultures should decrease prejudice based on symbolic threats. Realistic threats arise because other cultural groups are perceived to be competing for scarce resources with one's own group (Bobo, 1988; Stephan et al., 1999; Stephan & Stephan, 2000). Information regarding the exaggerated nature of people's beliefs concerning the scarcity of resources, as well as the creation of superordinate identities, should reduce prejudice based on perceived realistic conflict.

Anxiety and Uncertainty

Training programs based on Gudykunst's AUM model teach people to manage anxiety and uncertainty in cross-cultural interactions (Gudykunst et al., 1996). This type of training might involve exercises to evoke anxiety, followed by acquiring techniques to manage anxiety. It might also include techniques to manage uncertainty. Anxiety and uncertainty might also be reduced by didactic learning.

Dissonance Theory

Dissonance theory is based on the idea that when people behave in ways that contradict their customary views of themselves, they experience a negative affective state (dissonance), which they try to reduce (Aronson, 1997). If people who are ethnocentric, prejudiced, or biased toward members of another culture behave in positive ways toward members of this group, they will be motivated to change their previously prejudicial attitudes to be consistent with their current behavior (Leippe & Eisenstadt, 1994; Monteith, 1993). Also, if people are presented with discrepancies between their positive values and their negative behaviors directed toward outgroup members, they may change their behaviors to be consistent with their values (Grube, Mayton, & Ball-Rokeach, 1994). However, techniques based on dissonance may not be as effective in collectivistic cultures as they are in individualistic cultures because people in collectivistic cultures expect their behavior to vary by context (Heine & Lehman, 1997).

Social Learning Theory

Social learning theory is concerned with learned associations between objects and affect, including associations between cultural groups and affective responses to them (Bandura, 1986). Cross-cultural relations programs can modify the associations between outgroups and negative affect by providing people with vicarious or direct positive experiences with outgroup members. Some cross-cultural relations programs have leaders from a variety of cultures model behavior toward one another that they wish their trainees to learn.

Empathy

Empathy for outgroup members can be an effective tool to improve cross-cultural relations (Batson et al., 1997; Stephan & Finlay, 1999). Learning about people from another culture can elicit both cognitive and emotional empathy (Davis, 1996; Stephan & Finlay, 1999). Cognitive empathy involves learning to understand the perspective of the other group. Cognitive empathy can be created by presenting information using a didactic approach.

In cross-cultural relations programs, emotional empathy consists primarily of compassion-related emotions that arise from a feeling of concern for the suffering of others. Hearing first-person accounts can activate emotional empathy, as can role-playing exercises (Weiner & Wright, 1973).

Compunction Theory

People can learn to regulate their use of stereotypes. In social compunction theory, it is argued that people in all societies are exposed to the prevailing racial, ethnic, religious, and cultural stereotypes during socialization (Devine, 1989; Devine, Monteith, Zuwerink, & Elliot, 1991). Although these stereotypes tend to be automatically activated in cross-cultural interactions, their influence can be consciously overcome. If people are motivated to overcome their tendency to stereotype others, they can learn to use the guilt feelings they experience when their stereotypes are activated as a cue to suppress the negative effects of stereotyping (Monteith, 1993; Monteith, Zuwerink, & Devine, 1994).

Contact

Contact theory concerns the conditions under which face-to-face interaction leads to changes in both cognition and affect. Cross-cultural relations programs can maximize their effectiveness by fostering the following conditions. The interactions should be cooperative in nature, and the cooperation should result in favorable outcomes (Blanchard, Adelman, & Cook, 1975). Cross-cultural contact should be nonsuperficial and voluntary (Stephan & Stephan, 1984). It should offer people the opportunity to get to know one another as individuals (Amir, 1976), and attempts should be made to create conditions in which friendships can be established (Pettigrew, 1998). The contact should also be supported by the relevant authority figures

(Allport, 1954). If the trainees are from low power distance cultures, trainers should try to ensure that equal status conditions prevail within the contact setting (Riordan, 1978). In addition, the group identities of the participants must be made salient if the positive interpersonal effects resulting from intergroup contact are to generalize to outgroup members who are not a part of the training (Hewstone, 1996; Pettigrew, 1998).

SUMMARY

We have argued that cognition and affect play a crucial role in cross-cultural interactions because cultures differ in the cognitive schemata they employ to create meaning from social reality and they have differing patterns of affective responses to this reality. These cognitive and affective responses to social reality are influenced by cultural differences, and they are responsive to contextual factors such as those outlined in the contact hypothesis. Research indicates that ethnocentrism, social identity concerns, stereotypes, and cognitive biases create problems in cross-cultural interactions, but these problems can be remedied in cross-cultural training programs. Similarly, anxiety, uncertainty, feelings of injustice, prejudice, and other negative affective reactions to cross-cultural contact can create problems during cross-cultural encounters, but these too can be counteracted through effective training.

REFERENCES

Abrams, D., & Hogg, M. A. (1990). *Social identity theory*. New York: Springer-Verlag.

Allport, G. W. (1954). *The nature of prejudice*. Reading, MA: Addison-Wesley.

Amir, Y. (1976). The role of intergroup contact in change of prejudice and race relations. In P. Katz

& D. A. Taylor (Ed.), *Towards the elimination of racism* (pp. 245-308). New York: Pergamon.

Aronson, E. (1997). The theory of cognitive dissonance: The evolution and vicissitudes of an idea. In E. Harmon-Jones & J. S. Mills (Eds.), *Cognitive dissonance theory: Revival with revisions and controversies* (pp. 20-35). Oxford, UK: Basil Blackwell.

Ashmore, R. D., & Del Boca, F. K. (1976). Psychological approaches to understanding intergroup conflict. In P. A. Katz (Ed.), *Towards the elimination of racism* (pp. 73-124). New York: Pergamon.

Bandura, A. (1986). *The social foundations of thought and action*. Englewood Cliffs, NJ: Prentice Hall.

Baron, R. S., Burgess, M. L., Kao, C. F., & Logan, H. (1990, May). *Fear and superficial social processing: Evidence of stereotyping and simplistic persuasion*. Paper presented at the annual convention of the Midwestern Psychological Association, Chicago.

Batson, C. D., Polycarpou, M. P., Harmon-Jones, E., Imhoff, H. J., Mitchener, E. C., Bednar, L. L., Klein, T. R., & Highberger, L. (1997). Empathy and attitudes: Can feeling for a member of a stigmatized group improve feelings toward the group? *Journal of Personality and Social Psychology, 72*, 105-118.

Bhawuk, D. P. S., & Triandis, H. C. (1996). The role of culture theory in the study of culture and intercultural training. In D. Landis & R. S. Bhagat (Eds.), *Handbook of intercultural training* (2nd ed., pp. 17-34). Thousand Oaks, CA: Sage.

Blanchard, F. A., Adelman, L., & Cook, S. W. (1975). Effect of group success and failure upon interpersonal attraction in cooperating interracial groups. *Journal of Personality and Social Psychology, 31*, 1020-1030.

Blaney, P. H. (1986). Affect and memory: A review. *Psychological Bulletin, 99*, 229-246.

Bobo, L. (1988). Group conflict, prejudice, and the paradox of contemporary racial attitudes. In P. A. Katz & D. A. Taylor (Eds.), *Eliminating racism* (pp. 85-116). New York: Plenum.

Bodenhausen, G. V. (1990). Stereotypes as judgmental heuristics: Evidence in circadian variations in discrimination. *Psychological Science, 1,* 319-322.

Bodenhausen, G. V. (1993). Emotions, arousal, and stereotypic judgments: A heuristic model of affect and stereotyping. In D. M. Mackie & D. L. Hamilton (Eds.), *Affect, cognition, and stereotyping* (pp. 13-37). New York: Academic Press.

Bond, M. H. (1988). Finding universal dimensions of individual variation in multicultural studies of values: The Rokeach and Chinese value surveys. *Journal of Personality and Social Psychology, 55,* 1009-1015.

Brislin, R. W., Cushner, K., Cherrie, C., & Yong, M. (1986). *Intercultural interactions.* Beverly Hills, CA: Sage.

Byrne, D. (1971). *The attraction paradigm.* New York: Academic Press.

Cohen, E., & Roper, S. (1972). Modification of interracial interaction disability: An application of status characteristics theory. *American Sociological Review, 37,* 643-657.

Crocker, J., Hannah, D. B., & Weber, R. (1983). Person memory and causal attributions. *Journal of Personality and Social Psychology, 44,* 55-66.

Cushner, K., & Landis, D. (1996). The intercultural sensitizer. In D. Landis & R. S. Bhagat (Eds.), *Handbook of intercultural training* (2nd ed., pp. 185-202). Thousand Oaks, CA: Sage.

Davis, M. H. (1996). *Empathy.* Boulder, CO: Westview.

Devine, P. G. (1989). Stereotypes and prejudice: Their automatic and controlled components. *Journal of Personality and Social Psychology, 56,* 5-19.

Devine, P. G., Monteith, M. J., Zuwerink, J. R., & Elliot, A. J. (1991). Prejudice with and without compunction. *Journal of Personality and Social Psychology, 60,* 817-830.

Dovidio, J. F., Kawakami, K., & Gaertner, S. L. (2000). Reducing contemporary prejudice: Combating explicit and implicit bias at the individual and intergroup level. In S. Oskamp (Ed.), *Reducing prejudice and discrimination* (pp. 137-163). Mahwah, NJ: Lawrence Erlbaum.

Fishbein, M., & Ajzen, I. (1975). *Belief, attitude, intention, and behavior.* Reading, MA: Addison-Wesley.

Fyock, J., & Stangor, C. (1994). The role of memory biases in stereotype maintenance. *British Journal of Social Psychology, 33,* 331-343.

Gaertner, S. L., & Dovidio, J. F. (1986). The aversive form of racism. In J. F. Dovidio & S. L. Gaertner (Eds.), *Prejudice, discrimination, and racism* (pp. 61-90). Orlando, FL: Academic Press.

Goldstein, D. L., & Smith, D. H. (1999). The analysis of the effects of experiential training on sojourners' cross-cultural adaptability. *International Journal of Intercultural Relations, 23,* 157-173.

Grube, J. W., Mayton, D. M., & Ball-Rokeach, S. J. (1994). Inducing change in values, attitudes, and behaviors: Belief system theory and the method of value self-confrontation. *Journal of Social Issues, 50,* 1253-1273.

Gudykunst, W. B. (1995). Anxiety/uncertainty management (AUM) theory: Development and current status. In R. L. Wiseman (Ed.), *Intercultural communication theory* (pp. 8-58). Thousand Oaks, CA: Sage.

Gudykunst, W. B., Guzley, R. M., & Hammer, M. R. (1996). Designing intercultural training. In D. Landis & R. S. Bhagat (Eds.), *Handbook of intercultural training* (2nd ed., pp. 61-80). Thousand Oaks, CA: Sage.

Gudykunst, W. B., & Nishida, T. (1986a). Attributional confidence in low- and high-context cultures. *Human Communication Research, 12,* 525-549.

Gudykunst, W. B., & Nishida, T. (1986b). The influence of cultural variability on perceptions of communication behavior associated with relationship terms. *Human Communication Research, 13,* 147-166.

Gudykunst, W. B., & Nishida, T. (2001). Anxiety, uncertainty, and perceived effectiveness of communication across relationships and cultures. *International Journal of Intercultural Relations, 25,* 55-72.

Hamilton, D. L., & Rose, T. (1980). Illusory correlation and the maintenance of stereotype beliefs. *Journal of Personality and Social Psychology, 39,* 832-845.

Hamilton, D. L., & Sherman, S. J. (1996). Perceiving persons and groups. *Psychological Review, 103,* 336-355.

Heine, S. J., & Lehman, D. R. (1997). Culture, dissonance, and self-affirmation. *Personality and Social Psychology Bulletin, 23,* 389-400.

Hewstone, M. (1996). Contact and categorization. In C. N. Macrae, C. Stangor, & M. Hewstone (Eds.), *Foundations of stereotypes and stereotyping* (pp. 323-368). New York: Guilford.

Hewstone, M., Islam, M. R., & Judd, C. M. (1993). Models of crossed categorization and intergroup relations. *Journal of Personality and Social Psychology, 64,* 779-793.

Hewstone, M., & Jaspars, H. (1982). Intergroup relations and attribution processes. In H. Tajfel (Ed.), *Social identity and intergroup relations* (pp. 99-133). Cambridge, UK: Cambridge University Press.

Higgins, E. T., & King, G. (1981). Accessibility of social constructs: Information processing consequences of individual and contextual variables. In N. Cantor & J. F. Kihlstrom (Eds.), *Personality, cognition, and social interaction* (pp. 69-122). Hillsdale, NJ: Lawrence Erlbaum.

Hubbert, K., Gudykunst, W. B., & Guerrero, S. (1999). Intergroup communication over time. *International Journal of Intercultural Relations, 23,* 13-46.

Katz, I., Wachenhut, J., & Hass, R. G. (1986). Racial ambivalence, value duality, and behavior. In J. F. Dovidio & S. L. Gaertner (Eds.), *Prejudice, discrimination, and racism* (pp. 35-60). New York: Academic Press.

Langer, E. (1989). *Mindfulness.* Reading, MA: AddisonWesley.

Leippe, M. R., & Eisenstadt, D. (1994). Generalization of dissonance reduction: Decreasing prejudice through induced compliance. *Journal of Personality and Social Psychology, 67,* 395-413.

Leung, K., & Stephan, W. G. (2001). Social justice from a cultural perspective. In D. Matsumoto (Ed.), *Handbook of culture and psychology.* New York: Oxford University Press.

LeVine, R. A., & Campbell, D. T. (1972). *Ethnocentrism.* New York: John Wiley.

Mackie, D. M., Allison, S. T., Worth, L. T., & Asuncion, A. G. (1992). Social decision making processes: The generalization of outcome-biased counter-stereotypic inferences. *Journal of Experimental Social Psychology, 28,* 23-42.

Markus, H. R., & Lin. L. R. (1999). Conflictways: Cultural diversity in the meanings and practices of conflict. In D. A. Prentice & D. T. Miller (Eds.), *Cultural divides: Understanding and overcoming group conflict* (pp. 303-333). New York: Russell Sage Foundation.

Mikula, G., Scherer, K. R., & Athenstaedt, U. (1998). The role of injustice in the elicitation of differential emotional reactions. *Personality and Social Psychology Bulletin, 24,* 769-783.

Mineka, S., & Nugent, K. (1995). Mood-congruent memory biases in anxiety and depression. In D. L. Schacter (Ed.), *Memory distortion: How minds, brains, and societies reconstruct the past* (pp. 173-193). Cambridge, MA: Harvard University Press.

Mlicki, P., & Ellemers, N. (1996). Being different or being better? National stereotypes and identifications of Polish and Dutch students. *European Journal of Social Psychology, 26,* 97-114.

Monteith, M. J. (1993). Self-regulation of prejudiced responses: Implications for progress in prejudice-reduction efforts. *Journal of Personality and Social Psychology, 65,* 469-485.

Monteith, M. J., Zuwerink, J. R., & Devine, P. G. (1994). Prejudice and prejudice reduction: Classic challenges, contemporary approaches. In P. G. Devine, D. L. Hamilton, & T. M. Ostrom (Eds.), *Social cognition* (pp. 324-346). San Diego: Academic Press.

Morris, M. W., & Peng, K. P. (1994). Culture and cause: American and Chinese attributions for social and physical events. *Journal of Personality and Social Psychology, 67,* 949-971.

Oakes, P. J., Haslam, S. A., & Turner, J. C. (1994). *Stereotyping and social reality.* Cambridge, MA: Blackwell.

Park, J., & Banaji, M. R. (2000). Mood and heuristics: The influence of happy and sad states on sensitivity and bias in stereotyping. *Journal of Personality and Social Psychology, 78,* 1005-1023.

Peabody, D. (1999). Nationality characteristics: Dimensions for comparison. In Y. Lee, C. R. McCauley, & J. G. Draguns (Eds.), *Personality and perception across cultures.* Mahwah, NJ: Lawrence Erlbaum.

Pettigrew, T. F. (1979). The ultimate attribution error: Extending Allport's cognitive analysis of prejudice. *Personality and Social Psychology Bulletin, 5,* 461-476.

Pettigrew, T. F. (1998). Intergroup contact theory. *Annual Review of Psychology, 49,* 65-85.

Riordan, C. (1978). Equal-status interracial contact: A review and revision of the concept. *International Journal of Intercultural Relations, 2,* 161-185.

Rothbart, M., & John, O. P. (1985). Social categorization and behavioral episodes: A cognitive analysis and the effects of intergroup contact. *Journal of Social Issues, 41,* 81-104.

Sanders, J., Wiseman, R., & Matz, I. (1991). Uncertainty reduction in acquaintance relationships in Ghana and the United States. In S. Ting-Toomey & F. Korzenny (Eds.), *Cross-cultural interpersonal communication.* Newbury Park, CA: Sage.

Schaller, M., Asp, C. H., Rosell, M. C., & Heim, S. J. (1996). Training in statistical reasoning inhibits the formation of erroneous group stereotypes. *Personality and Social Psychology Bulletin, 22,* 829-844.

Sears, D. O. (1988). Symbolic racism. In P. A. Katz & D. A. Taylor (Eds.), *Eliminating racism* (pp. 53-84). New York: Plenum.

Sherif, M. (1966). *In common predicament.* Boston: Houghton Mifflin.

Sherif, M., Harvey, O. J., White, B. J., Hood, W. R., & Sherif, C. W. (1961). *Intergroup conflict and cooperation.* Norman: University of Oklahoma Press.

Smith, P. B., & Bond, M. H. (1999). *Social psychology across cultures* (2nd ed.). Boston: Allyn & Bacon.

Smith, R. H., Parrott, W. G., Ozer, D., & Moniz, A. (1994). Subjective injustice and inferiority as predictors of hostile and depressive feelings of anger. *Personality and Social Psychology Bulletin, 20,* 705-711.

Snyder, M. (1992). Motivational foundations of behavioral confirmation. In M. Zanna (Ed.), *Advances in experimental social psychology* (Vol. 25, pp. 67-114). Orlando, FL: Academic Press.

Snyder, M., Stephan, W., & Rosenfield, D. (1978). Attributional egotism. In J. Harvey, W. Ickes, & R. Kidd (Eds.), *New directions in attribution research* (Vol. 2, pp. 91-120). New York: John Wiley.

Sprecher, S. (1986). The relationship between equity and emotions in close relationships. *Social Psychology Quarterly, 49,* 309-321.

Stangor, C., & McMillan, D. (1992). Memory for expectancy-congruent and expectancy-incongruent information: A review of the social and social developmental literatures. *Psychological Bulletin, 111,* 42-61.

Stephan, W. G. (1987). The contact hypothesis in intergroup relations. In C. Hendrick (Ed.), *Group processes and intergroup relations* (pp. 13-40). Newbury Park, CA: Sage.

Stephan, W. G., Ageyev, V. S., Coates-Shrider, L., Stephan, C. W., & Abalakina, M. (1994). On the relationship between stereotypes and prejudice: An international study. *Personality and Social Psychology Bulletin, 20,* 277-284

Stephan, W. G., & Finlay, K. A. (1999). The role of empathy in improving intergroup relations. *Journal of Social Issues, 55,* 729-744.

Stephan, W. G., & Stephan, C. W. (1984). The role of ignorance in intergroup relations. In N. Miller & M. B. Brewer (Eds.), *Groups in contact* (pp. 229-257). New York: Academic Press.

Stephan, W. G., & Stephan, C. W. (1985). Intergroup anxiety. *Journal of Social Issues, 41,* 157-175.

Stephan, W. G., & Stephan, C. W. (1996). *Intergroup relations.* Boulder, CO: Westview.

Stephan, W. G., & Stephan, C. W. (2000). An integrated threat theory of prejudice. In S. Oskamp (Ed.), *Reducing prejudice and discrimination* (pp. 23-46). Hillsdale, NJ: Lawrence Erlbaum.

Stephan, W. G., Stephan, C. W., & Gudykunst, W. B. (1999). Anxiety in intergroup relations: A comparison of anxiety/uncertainty management theory and integrated threat theory. *International Journal of Intercultural Relations, 23,* 613-628.

Sumner, W. G. (1906). *Folkways.* Boston: Ginn.

Swann, W. B., Jr., & Ely, R. J. (1984). A battle of wills: Self-verification versus behavioral confirmation. *Journal of Personality and Social Psychology, 46,* 1287-1302.

Tajfel, H., & Turner, J. C. (1986). *The social identity theory of intergroup behavior.* In S. Worchel & W. G. Austin (Eds.), *Psychology of intergroup relations* (2nd ed., pp. 33-47). Chicago: Nelson-Hall.

Triandis, H. C. (1972). *The analysis of subjective culture*. New York: John Wiley.

Triandis, H. C. (1995). *Individualism and collectivism*. Boulder, CO: Westview.

Vanbeselaere, N. (1991). The different effects of simple and crossed categorizations: A result of the category differentiation process or of differential category salience? *European Review of Social Psychology, 2*, 247-278.

Weeks, W. W., Pedersen, P. B., & Brislin, R. W. (1982). *A manual of structured experiences for cross-cultural learning*. Yarmouth, ME: Intercultural Press.

Weiner, M. J., & Wright, F. E. (1973). Effects of undergoing arbitrary discrimination upon subsequent attitudes toward a minority group. *Journal of Applied Social Psychology, 3*, 94-102.

Wilder, D. A., & Shapiro, P. N. (1989). Role of competition-induced anxiety in limiting the beneficial aspect of positive behavior by an outgroup member. *Journal of Personality and Social Psychology, 56*, 60-69.

Wiseman, R., Hammer, M. R., & Nishida, H. (1989). Predictors of intercultural communication competence. *International Journal of Intercultural Relations, 13*, 349-370.

Ybarra, O., & Stephan, W. G. (1999). Attributional orientations and the prediction of behavior: The attribution-prediction bias. *Journal of Personality and Social Psychology, 76*, 718-727.

7

Cross-Cultural Face
Concerns and Conflict Styles
Current Status and Future Directions

STELLA TING-TOOMEY
California State University, Fullerton

JOHN G. OETZEL
University of New Mexico

Conflict is an emotionally frustrated experience in conjunction with perceived incompatibility of values, expectations, face concerns, conflict styles, goals, scarce resources, and/or outcomes between a minimum of two interdependent parties. Intercultural conflict involves emotional frustrations or mismatched expectations that stem, in part, from cultural group membership differences. To understand the intercultural conflict negotiation process, we have to first understand cross-cultural diverse approaches that people bring with them in expressing their different values, norms, face-saving orientations, goal emphasis, and conflict styles in handling a conflict episode (Ting-Toomey & Oetzel, 2001). Conflict is an inevitable aspect of human relatedness, especially in intercultural situations. Cultures, with the mediating factor of situation, socialize individuals to develop preferences for particular facework and conflict behaviors in particular situations. As a result, cultural differences in conflict communication can exacerbate a conflict encounter. Thus, understanding cross-cultural differences in face concerns and conflict behavior is the first step in developing an inclusive multicultural community.

Research on cross-cultural face concerns and conflict styles has flourished over the past

AUTHORS' NOTE: We thank William Gudykunst for his thoughtful comments on an earlier version of this chapter.

127

15 years. The purpose of this chapter is to review the extant literature on cross-cultural face concerns, face behaviors, and conflict styles. We identify major findings and trends, and we suggest directions for future cross-cultural facework and conflict style research. Conflict is an emotionally laden, face-threatening experience. Individuals in recurring conflicts often have to deal with substantive, relational, and identity issues. Conflict negotiation involves both subtle and explicit conflict moves and countermoves. The developmental process involves different face-saving, face-attacking, and face-recouping conflict strategies. The interaction process also involves the use of different conflict styles in approaching (i.e., fight) or side-stepping (i.e., flight) the conflict issue to avoiding the other conflict party altogether.

The chapter is developed in four sections. First, we review the literature on cross-cultural face concerns and face behaviors. Second, we identify research patterns in cross-cultural conflict styles. Third, we use conflict face-negotiation theory (Ting-Toomey, 1985, 1988) to link face concerns, facework behaviors, and conflict styles. Fourth, we offer directions for future research in the areas of face concerns and conflict styles.

EXPLANATORY VARIABLES

Before reviewing the relevant research on cross-cultural face concerns and conflict styles, we briefly describe the variables often used to explain cross-cultural differences in face concerns, facework, and conflict behaviors: individualism-collectivism (IC), power distance, and self construals (for a detailed discussion, see Gudykunst and Lee, Chapter 2 in this volume).

Individualism-Collectivism and Power Distance

Two cultural-level variables have been examined in cross-cultural facework and conflict styles: IC and power distance. We briefly define these concepts here. The contrast of individualism and collectivism is the major concept used to identify cultural differences (Hofstede, 1991; Hui & Triandis, 1986; Triandis, 1995). *Individualism* is a cultural pattern that consists of loosely linked individuals who view themselves as independent of collectives and who give priority to their personal goals over the goals of others (Triandis, 1995). *Collectivism* is a cultural pattern consisting of closely linked individuals who see themselves as part of one or more collectives (family, coworkers, tribe, nation) and are willing to give priority to the goals of these collectives over their own personal goals (Triandis, 1995). *Power distance* is "the extent to which the less powerful members of institutions and organizations within a country expect and accept that power is distributed unequally" (Hofstede, 1991, p. 28). Individuals in small power distance cultures believe that individuals are relatively equal, make efforts to diminish status, and distribute power evenly. In contrast, individuals in large power distance cultures emphasize status differences between members and accept uneven power distributions.

Conflict behavior is learned within the primary socialization process of one's cultural or ethnic group. Individuals learn the norms and scripts for appropriate and effective conflict conduct in their immediate cultural environment. However, individuals also enact behaviors that vary from the predominant cultural framework of a society. Essentially, cultural values have both a direct and an indirect effect on facework behaviors that is mediated through individual-level factors (Gudykunst et al., 1996; Kim et al., 1996).

Self Construal

Self construal is a key individual factor that focuses on individual variation within and between cultures (Markus & Kitayama, 1991). *Self construal* is one's self-image and is composed of an independent self and an interdependent self (Markus & Kitayama, 1991). The independent construal of self involves the view that an individual is a unique entity with an individuated repertoire of feelings, cognitions, and motivations. In contrast, the interdependent construal of self involves an emphasis on the importance of relational connectedness (Markus & Kitayama, 1991).

Self construal is the individual-level equivalent of the cultural variability dimension of IC (Gudykunst et al., 1996). For example, Gudykunst et al. (1996) argue that independent self construal is predominantly associated with people of individualistic cultures, whereas interdependent self construal is predominantly associated with people of collectivistic cultures. However, both dimensions of self exist within each individual, regardless of cultural identity. In individualistic cultures, there may be more communication situations that evoke the need for independent-based decisions and behaviors. In group-based cultures, there may be more situations that demand the sensitivity for interdependent-based decisions and actions. The manner in which individuals conceive of their self-images—independent versus interdependent selves—in a particular conflict situation should have a profound influence on what types of facework behaviors and conflict styles they would use in a conflict episode. In addition, the interpretations or appraisals they engage in—in attributing their conflict opponents' identity motivations in particular conflict scenes—should cast a strong influence on the face-related conflict negotiation process.

CROSS-CULTURAL FACE CONCERNS AND FACEWORK

Face is the claimed sense of favorable social self-worth and the estimated other-worth in an interpersonal situation (Ting-Toomey & Kurogi, 1998). It is a symbolic resource in social interaction because this resource can be threatened, enhanced, maintained, and bargained over. Face is a cluster of identity and relational-based issues that simmer and surface before, during, and after the conflict process. Face is associated with identity respect, disrespect, dignity, honor, shame, guilt, status, and competence issues. Face has simultaneous affective (e.g., feelings of guilt and shame), cognitive (e.g., appraising how much to give and receive face), and behavioral (e.g., different facework tactics such as "shaming" or "apology" tactics) levels.

Rogan and Hammer (1994) suggest that face consists of three dimensions: (a) locus of face, concern for self or other; (b) face valence, whether face is being defended, maintained, or honored; and (c) temporality, whether face is being restored or proactively protected. We focus on locus of face in our discussion because it is the primary dimension of face and it determines an individual's interest and the direction of the subsequent facework messages (Ting-Toomey & Cole, 1990). *Self-face* is the concern for one's own image, and *other-face* is the concern for another's image. Although most prior research has focused only on these two loci of face, a third concern, mutual-face, is also relevant. *Mutual-face* is the concern for both parties' images and/or the "image" of the relationship (Ting-Toomey & Kurogi, 1998). Mutual-face reflects a separate concern away from the individual parties and thus reflects a separate locus of face.

Although face is a universal phenomenon, how we frame the situated and affective meaning of face (and how we enact facework) differ from one culture to the next. Culture-specific theoretical efforts (e.g., Bond, 1991; Earley, 1997; Gao, 1998, on Chinese facework; Garcia, 1996, on Mexican facework; Katriel, 1986, on Israeli Sabra facework; Lim & Choi, 1996, on Korean facework; Morisaki & Gudykunst, 1994, on Japanese facework) have been developed in a wide range of cultures. Culture-specific lenses complement a culture-general framework in analyzing conflict-related facework behaviors across cultures. In this section, we review studies that have compared the face concerns in perceived conflict situations in a variety of cultures.

National Cultures Analysis

IC and self construals are the predominant variables to explain cross-cultural differences in face concerns. Leung (1987) examined the preferences for resolving conflict by Hong Kong Chinese and U.S. Americans. Specifically, 96 students and 72 nonstudents from each culture were asked to describe how they would resolve a conflict with a good friend and colleague. Leung found that the Chinese preferred bargaining and negotiation more than U.S. Americans because these procedures were perceived as reducing the animosity between the parties. Essentially, the Chinese were concerned with the mutual-face concerns of the parties more than the U.S. Americans.

In a more inclusive study, Ting-Toomey et al. (1991) studied the face concerns of 965 students in a hypothetical conflict episode involving a student group project across five national cultures: China ($n = 117$), Japan ($n = 197$), South Korea ($n = 207$), Taiwan ($n = 224$), and the United States ($n = 220$ European Americans). The United States represented individualism, and the other four cultures represented collectivism. The findings included the following: (a) Chinese, Korean, and Taiwanese reported higher degree of other-face than the U.S. students; (b) U.S.

Americans had a higher degree of other-face than the Japanese; (c) U.S. Americans, Chinese, and Taiwanese reported a higher degree of self-face than the Koreans; and (d) Japanese reported a higher degree of self-face than the other four cultures.

National Cultures and Self Construal Analysis

Two recent studies demonstrate the importance of both national culture and self construal for face concerns. Oetzel et al. (2000) studied the face concerns of 765 students in a recalled acquaintance conflict in four national cultures: China, Germany, Japan, and the United States. Germany and the United States were identified as the individualistic cultures, and China and Japan were identified as the collectivistic cultures. The major findings were as follows: (a) Chinese have higher self-, other-, and mutual-face concerns than the other three national cultures; (b) Japanese have higher other-face concern than Germany; (c) Japanese have lower self-face concerns than the other cultures; and (d) self construals provided a better explanation of face concerns with independent self construal positively correlated with self-face and interdependent self construal positively correlated with other- and mutual-face. In a second study, the researchers (Oetzel, Ting-Toomey, & Chew, 1999) examined the face concerns in 411 participants in a recalled conflict with a parent or sibling in Germany, Japan, Mexico, and the United States. The authors found that Japanese had a lower self-face concern than the other three national cultures, and self construals provided a better explanation of face concerns with independent self construal positively correlated with self-face and interdependent self construal positively correlated with other- and mutual-face.

In summary, the extant literature reveals clear patterns of relationships for cross-cultural face concerns. Specifically, self-face concern is related positively to individualism and independent self construals, whereas other-face and mutual-face concerns are related positively to collectivism and interdependent self construals. There have been exceptions (e.g., Japanese self-face in Ting-Toomey et al., 1991; Chinese self-face in Oetzel et al., 2000), but the larger face concern patterns hold true across a wide range of Western and Asian cultures. In addition, self construals provide a better explanation of face concerns than does cultural-level IC.

Cross-Cultural Facework Research

A closely related concept to conflict style is facework. *Facework* is "the actions taken to deal with the face-wants of one and/or the other" (Lim, 1994, p. 211). During conflict, facework has a variety of functions. Facework is employed to resolve a conflict, exacerbate a conflict, avoid a conflict, threaten or challenge another person's position, protect a person's image, and so on. These functions are part of the process of maintaining and upholding face. However, facework is not equivalent to conflict styles. Conflict styles primarily focus on resolving substantive goals (at least in the existing U.S. conflict literature), whereas facework includes the management of identity, relational, and substantive conflict goals. For example, facework can occur during or after the conflict to manage identity image issues (e.g., "We should really learn to compromise for the sake of the senior manager" or "I'll let you win this time, but you owe me in the next round."). Conflict management styles can include a variety of facework behaviors. For example, the integrating conflict style reflects a need for solution closure in conflict and involves both parties working together to substantively resolve the issue (Rahim, 1983). Facework behaviors that are consistent with

the integrating style may include (but are not limited to) listening to the other person, respecting the feelings of the other, and sharing personal viewpoints in a face-sensitive manner. In sum, facework can be distinguished from conflict style in that the former involves specific behaviors that focus on a person's (or others') claimed image as it relates to identity, relational, and substantive goals above and beyond the conflict situation. The latter involves a general pattern of behavior during a conflict encounter with attempts to address and resolve substantive issues as a key priority.

In comparison to cross-cultural face concerns research, there are fewer studies that have investigated cross-cultural face behaviors in conflict. We were able to identify six studies. Three of these use IC as the primary explanatory variable; two use IC, self construals, and power distance; and one employs face concerns. For example, Lindsley and Braithwaite (1996) investigated the facework norms for intercultural conflicts between Mexicans and U.S. Americans in maquiladoras (offshore assembly plants). The authors conducted 20 ethnographic interviews and used observations in touring seven plants. They found that Mexicans have a norm of supporting the other's approval face and for using indirect communication styles. In contrast, U.S. Americans did not follow these norms and reflected a direct, self-face orientation. They found evidence of these norms in manager-manager communication, manager-employee communication, and international manager-manager communication.

Tsai and Levenson (1997) examined emotional expression in discussion about relationship conflict. Thus, they indirectly tested for affective and relational face issues. The authors asked 22 Chinese American and 20 European American college-age dating couples to self-report their affect concerning conversations about conflict in their relationships. The findings of the study included the following: (a) Chinese Americans revealed less positive affect than European Americans, and (b) Chinese and European Americans did not differ in negative affect display.

Tata (2000) investigated the influence of culture and hierarchical level on face concerns and account giving in conflict-inducing situations. Participants (89 Mexican Americans and 104 European Americans) completed a self-report instrument about face concerns, likelihood of using certain accounts, and perceived effectiveness of these accounts in regards to delivering bad news to a supervisor and a subordinate. The author found that account giving and face concerns varied by hierarchical level more for Mexican Americans than European Americans. Specifically, when communicating with a subordinate, Mexican Americans reported less emphasis on other-face concerns and greater likelihood of using aggravating accounts (consistent with a dominating or forcing style) compared with European Americans. When communicating with a superior, Mexican Americans reported greater emphasis on other-face concerns and greater use of mitigating accounts (consistent with an obliging or integrating style) than European Americans. The results illustrate that Mexican Americans appear to hold a larger power distance value compared with European Americans.

Multiple Explanatory Factors on Facework

Oetzel et al.'s (1999) study of conflicts with family members in Germany, Japan, Mexico, and the United States investigated facework behaviors in conjunction with IC, self construals, and power distance. They investigated a variety of facework tactics including (a) aggression, (b) problem solving, (c) third-party help, (d) apologizing, (e) defending one's position, (f) respecting the other, (g) pretending the conflict does not exist, (h) remaining calm, (i)

giving in to the other party, (j) expressing emotions, and (k) private discussion.

The authors found that

1. Germans tend to use direct, confrontal facework strategies and do not avoid conflict; Japanese pretend conflict does not exist and do not defend their positions overtly; Mexicans use a variety of strategies to confront and resolve the conflict, as well as pretending the conflict does not exist; and U.S. Americans also use a variety of strategies to confront and resolve the conflict.

2. The more interdependent the individuals' self construal, the more likely they will use problem solving, respect, apologizing, third-party help, remaining calm, private discussion, and giving in, and the less likely they will use aggression.

3. The larger the individuals' power distance, the more likely they will use aggression, third-party help, and pretending.

4. Self construal was a better predictor of facework behaviors than was IC or power distance.

Oetzel et al. (2000) also considered 11 types of facework behaviors, IC, self construals, and power distance in their study of Chinese, Germans, Japanese, and U.S. Americans. The researchers uncovered that

1. Chinese tend to use a variety of avoiding and obliging behaviors and aggression; Germans use a direct, confrontal approach; Japanese avoid direct confrontation, and U.S. Americans use respect and expression of feelings to resolve conflicts.

2. The more independent the individuals' self construal, the more likely they will

use defensive facework tactics and attempting to remain calm; and the more interdependent the individuals' self construal, the more likely they will use problem solving, respect, apologizing, pretending, remaining calm, private discussion, and giving in, and the less likely they will use aggression, defending, and expressing.

3. The larger the individuals' power distance, the more likely they will use aggression, defending, apologizing, pretending, third-party help, and giving in.

4. Self construal was a better predictor of facework behaviors than IC or power distance.

Oetzel, Ting-Toomey, Yokochi, Matsumoto, and Takai (in press) further extended this research by examining the relationship between face concerns and face behaviors in their study of acquaintance conflicts for students in China, Germany, Japan, and the United States. Oetzel and his colleagues measured three face concerns and 11 facework strategies. In the pancultural analysis, self-face concerns predicted aggression, defending, and third-party strategies in a positive manner. Furthermore, other-face concerns predicted problem solving, apologizing, remaining calm, private discussion, and giving in via a positive manner. Finally, mutual-face concerns predicted respecting and problem solving in a positive manner and aggression in a negative manner.

CROSS-CULTURAL CONFLICT STYLES

The majority of research on cross-cultural facework and conflict focuses on conflict style. We organize this section using the major concepts employed to explain cross-cultural conflict style differences: defining conflict styles, IC, power distance, self construals, and face concerns. At the end of this section, we summarize and integrate the findings regarding these four variables.

Defining Conflict Styles

Conflict style is one of the key communication behaviors that we use to manage face concerns and face threats. *Conflict style* refers to general tendencies or modes of patterned responses to conflict in a variety of antagonistic interactive situations (Putnam & Poole, 1987; Sternberg & Soriano, 1984; Ting-Toomey, 1997). Conflict styles provide an overall picture of a person's general communication orientation toward conflict. Individuals often have one or two predominant conflict styles or tendencies in managing everyday conflict. However, they also modify and tailor their conflict approaches based on situational factors. Thus, conflict style is an integrative combination of traits (e.g., cultural background and personality) and states (e.g., situational factors such as ingroup-outgroup conflict and conflict salience) (TingToomey & Oetzel, 2001). There are numerous approaches for explaining conflict styles, but the primary approach is the five-style model based on two dimensions (Blake & Mouton, 1964; Rahim, 1983, 1992; Thomas & Kilmann, 1974). Rahim's (1983) conceptualization of conflict styles has been used systematically because of its compatibility with face-negotiation theory (Ting-Toomey, 1988).

Rahim bases his classification of conflict styles on the two conceptual dimensions of concern for self and concern for others. The first dimension illustrates the degree (high or low) to which a person seeks to satisfy his or her own interest or own face need. The second dimension represents the degree (high or low) to which a person desires to incorporate the other's conflict interest. The two dimensions combine for five styles of handling conflict: integrating, compromising, dominating, obliging, and avoiding. Briefly, the *integrating* style reflects a need for solution closure in conflict and involves high concern for self and high concern for other in conflict substantive negotiation. The *compromising* style involves a give-and-take concession approach to reach a midpoint agreement concerning the conflict issue. The *dominating* style emphasizes conflict tactics that push for one's own position or goal above and beyond the other person's conflict interest. The *obliging* style is characterized by a high concern for the other person's conflict interest above and beyond one's own conflict interest. Finally, the *avoiding* style involves eluding the conflict topic, the conflict party, or the conflict situation altogether.

Individualism-Collectivism and Conflict Styles

The influence of cultural IC on cross-cultural conflict styles is well-documented in a variety of settings and cultures. The majority of studies compare other (or another) collectivistic cultures with the individualistic United States. We organize this review by focusing on Asia, the Middle East, Latin America, and within the United States. We review exemplars from each region.

Asia. Several studies look at one culture compared with the United States. Ohbuchi and his colleagues (Ohbuchi, Fukushima, & Tedeschi, 1999; Ohbuchi & Takahashi, 1994) compare Japanese (collectivists) and U.S. Americans (individualists) conflict tactics in interpersonal conflicts. For example, Ohbuchi et al. (1999) had 264 U.S. Americans and 207 Japanese self-report their social goals, resource goals, and conflict tactics in regards to a recalled interpersonal conflict. Social goals included relationship, justice, and identity as-

pects, whereas resource goals focused on economic and personal gain. Conflict tactics included conciliation (i.e., integration), assertion (i.e., dominating), avoidance, and third-party intervention. The authors found that Japanese used avoidance more and assertion less than U.S. Americans. Furthermore, U.S. Americans were oriented strongly to achieving justice, whereas Japanese were oriented strongly to maintain relationships.

China and Vietnam have also been compared with the United States. Chiu and Kosinski (1994) studied the conflict style preferences of 266 business students from Hong Kong ($n = 142$) and the United States ($n = 124$). The authors found that Hong Kong Chinese were less direct, assertive, and confrontal in conflict situations than U.S. Americans (i.e., European Americans). Dsilva and Whyte (1998) researched the conflict styles of Vietnamese refugees in south Louisville, Kentucky. The authors conducted focus groups with the refugees, held interviews with four opinion leaders, and completed a content analysis of letters to the editors of local newspapers. The authors found that the refugees have a collectivistic, high-context communication style and that they tend to avoid conflict to maintain peace and tranquility.

Several studies compare multiple Asian cultures with the United States. For example, Morris et al. (1998) investigated conflict styles in four national cultures: China, India, the Philippines, and the United States. They asked 454 MBA students (100 in China, 160 in India, 62 in the Philippines, and 132 in the United States) to self-report their general conflict styles in management situations. The authors found that Chinese use avoiding more than the other three cultures, and U.S. Americans use competing more than the other three cultures.

Ting-Toomey et al. (1991) investigated conflict styles in the five national cultures. They found that

1. U.S. Americans, Chinese, and Taiwanese reported using dominating styles more than Japanese and Koreans.

2. Japanese reported using integrating less than the other four cultures.

3. Chinese and Taiwanese reported using obliging styles more than U.S. Americans, Japanese, and Koreans.

4. Chinese reported using avoiding styles more than Taiwanese, who reported using avoiding more than the other three cultures.

5. Japanese reported using compromising less than the other four cultures, and Chinese reported using compromising more than U.S. Americans, Koreans, and Taiwanese.

Middle East. Three studies illustrate the comparison between several Middle Eastern nations and the United States. Kozan (1989) compared the conflict styles of managers in Turkey, Jordan, and the United States. He asked 215 Turkish managers and 134 Jordanian managers to describe their predominant style for managing conflict with subordinates. He then compared these ratings to a prior study on U.S. managers (Rahim, 1986). Kozan found that

1. Turkish managers reported using collaborating (i.e., integrating) more than forcing (i.e., dominating), and compromising and forcing more than avoiding, and avoiding more than accommodating (i.e., obliging).

2. Jordanian managers reported using collaborating more than compromising, compromising more than accommodating, and avoiding more than forcing.

3. Managers from Turkey, Jordan, and the United States all preferred collaborating compared with other styles.

4. U.S. managers were more likely to report using accommodating than Jordanian and Turkish managers, whereas Turkish managers were more likely to report using forcing than U.S. and Jordanian managers.

Elsayed-Ekhouly and Buda (1996) conducted a study comparing Arab Middle Eastern managers with U.S. managers. The authors included the self-reports of the general conflict styles of 913 Arab managers (from Egypt, Saudi Arabia, and the United Arab Emirates) and 144 U.S. managers. The authors found that U.S. managers reported using dominating and obliging more and integrating and avoiding less than Arab managers. The difference in obliging cannot be explained by IC. However, the power distance between these groups does help explain the results for obliging. Specifically, Arab nations are large power distance cultures, whereas the United States is a relatively small power distance culture. Managers in large power distance cultures are not likely to use obliging because it would cause them to appear weak and not in power.

Finally, Kozan and Ergin (1998) investigated the preference of individuals from Turkey and the United States for third-party help during conflict. They had 60 students in Turkey and 60 students in the United States participate in a prisoner's dilemma type game. The participants were able to communicate directly with their adversary or through an intermediary. Turkish participants preferred the intermediary, whereas U.S. participants preferred direct communication. The authors argue that the results are consistent with IC. Specifically, the collectivist Turkish participants likely preferred the third party in order to avoid conflict and preserve group harmony, whereas the individualistic U.S. participants likely preferred direct communication in order to maximize rewards.

Latin America. We review two studies to illustrate cross-cultural differences in Latin America. One recent study compares Mexico and U.S. conflict styles. Gabrielidis, Stephan, Ybarra, Dos Santos Pearson, and Villareal (1997) examined four conflict styles: accommodation (i.e., obliging), avoidance, collaboration (i.e., integrating), and competition (i.e., dominating). The authors asked the participants (103 Mexican students and 91 U.S. American students) to think about how they managed conflict with friends, family members, and coworkers. U.S. Americans were more concerned with their own outcomes (competition and collaboration) and less concerned with others' outcomes (avoidance and accommodation) than were Mexicans.

Graham (1985) investigated the negotiating style in Brazil, Japan, and the United States. He videotaped six experienced businessmen from each of these three cultures in a negotiation simulation. Specifically, there were nine negotiations, three from each culture. Graham found that Brazilians touch more, gaze more, interrupt more, make more extreme first offers, make greater concessions, and take more time to negotiate than either the U.S. Americans or Japanese. Essentially, the Brazilian style is more expressive than the other cultures. This style is consistent with the Brazilian focus on interpersonal relationships. The contrast between Japanese and Brazilian collectivism is that Brazilians view emotional expression as a means to establish and maintain relationships, whereas Japanese view overt emotional expression as negative because it will hinder relational harmony.

United States. A number of studies compare conflict styles of ethnic groups within the United States and use IC as the explanatory factor. We review two exemplars here. Cox, Lobel, and McLeod (1991) studied the effects of IC on people's cooperative and competitive choices made during a prisoner's dilemma game. They assigned research participants to either an all-European American group or to a culturally diverse group (four members, one each from African American, Asian American, European American, and Latino American ethnic groups). The authors found that groups composed of members with a collectivistic cultural tradition (i.e., Asian American, Hispanic American, and African American) displayed more cooperative choices than groups composed of members with an individualistic cultural tradition.

A second study investigated the conflict styles of four U.S. ethnic groups in an acquaintance conflict. Ting-Toomey et al. (2000) included 662 participants from African American ($n = 135$), Asian American ($n = 181$), European American ($n = 194$), and Latino American ($n = 152$) groups. They used a self-report questionnaire to measure ethnic and cultural identity and conflict styles. In regards to individualism and collectivism, the authors found that individuals with a strong cultural identity (i.e., identifying with the larger, individualistic U.S. culture) use integrating, compromising, and emotional expression more than individuals with a weak cultural identity.

Power Distance and Conflict Styles

Two studies directly examine power and conflict styles. Smith, Dugan, Peterson, and Leung (1998) examined managers' espoused values for handling disagreements in 23 national cultures. The authors used Hofstede's (1991) score to indicate the countries' level of power distance and asked managers what resources they use to handle disagreement. The authors found that (a) the larger the power distance, the more frequent outgroup disagreements; (b) the smaller the power distance, the more likely a manager uses peers to handle disagreements; and (c) the smaller the power distance, the more likely a manager uses subordinates to handle disagreements. These findings illustrate that in small power distance cultures, managers minimize status difference (i.e., using horizontal facework; Ting-Toomey & Kurogi, 1998) during conflict and rely on peers and subordinates to assist in mediating disagreements. However, the authors did not find that in large power distance cultures individuals rely more on their superiors for advice (i.e., using vertical facework; Ting-Toomey & Kurogi, 1998) in handling these disagreements.

More specifically, Rahim and Buntzman (1989) examined the power bases (reward, legitimate, expert, and referent) (French & Raven, 1959) of 301 participants who were business students and members of the U.S. workforce. The authors found that (a) reward power is correlated positively with integrating and avoiding; (b) legitimate power is correlated positively with dominating; (c) expert is correlated positively with integrating and dominating, and negatively correlated with avoiding; and (d) referent power is correlated positively with integrating, obliging, and compromising, and negatively correlated with dominating. Furthermore, it appears that these power bases relate directly to face concern issues. Specifically, expert and legitimate power are related to self-face concerns because these power bases emphasize that the appropriate and correct conflict responses are held by the manager. In contrast, reward and referent powers are related to other-face concerns because these power bases focus on building a smooth facework relationship between the manager and employee.

Self Construals and Conflict Styles

Independent and interdependent self construals are parsimonious ways to explain conflict styles because of the direct measurement of individual tendencies afforded by considering self construals. Oetzel (1998a, 1998c) compared the communication patterns of 14 homogeneous European American groups, 10 homogeneous Japanese groups, and 13 heterogeneous groups composed of two Japanese and two European Americans working on a decision-making task. Oetzel used self construals to explain the conflict strategies used by groups and group members. He asked participants to complete a self construal measure (Gudykunst et al., 1996) and then videotaped the interaction of the group members. Oetzel found that (a) groups composed of members with high independent self construals were more likely to use competitive tactics and less likely to use cooperative tactics than groups composed of members with low independent self construals, and (b) because of their self construals, European Americans initiated more conflicts and used more competitive conflict tactics than did Japanese in these groups.

In another study of group communication, Oetzel (2001) explored the relationship between member self construals and cooperation in groups of varying levels of diversity (in terms of age, gender, and ethnicity). The 36 total groups were composed of three to six undergraduate students in the United States engaged in three group tasks relevant to a course in which the students were enrolled. Oetzel found that the average interdependent self construal of the group members is associated positively with cooperation during group interaction.

Furthering this line of research, Oetzel (1998b) expanded the focus of cooperation and competition to include a variety of conflict styles. He asked 234 European American and 115 Latino American students to report their self construals and conflict styles in a hypothetical group situation. He found that (a) self construal is a better predictor of conflict styles than is ethnic background; (b) dominating conflict styles are associated positively with independent self construals, whereas avoiding, obliging, and compromising conflict styles are associated positively with interdependent self construals; and (c) integrating conflict styles are associated positively with both self construals, but more strongly with interdependence than independence.

Finally, one study has examined the combination of the two self construal dimensions that results in four self construal types: biconstrual (high on both dimensions), independent orientation (high independent, low interdependent), interdependent orientation (low independent, high interdependent), and weak construal (low on both dimensions). Ting-Toomey, Oetzel, and Yee-Jung (2001) investigated the self construals and conflict styles of 662 participants from four ethnic groups in the United States who recalled an acquaintance conflict. The authors found that (a) biconstruals, independents, and interdependents use integrating and compromising conflict styles more than weak construals; (b) biconstruals use an emotionally expressive style more than weak construals; (c) biconstruals use the dominating conflict style more than interdependents and weak construals; (d) interdependents and weak construals use third-party help more than biconstruals and independents; and (e) weak construals use a neglecting (i.e., passive-aggressive) style more than biconstruals, independents, and interdependents. Results were interpreted from a conflict face-negotiation perspective.

FACE-NEGOTIATION THEORY AS AN EXPLANATORY FRAMEWORK

Why are face concerns such salient issues in a conflict negotiation process? Face is closely tied with identity, relational, and emotional issues before, during, and after a conflict episode. Conflict is a face-threatening process because it involves the unfolding contact of two selves. The conception of self is a fragile resource that can be trampled on by the other conflict party via abusive words or passive-aggressive actions. The emotions that are tied to the construction of self and face (e.g., pride and shame) are also at a most vulnerable stage during a conflict episode. When conflict needs, goals, face-saving orientations, and conflict styles create recurring clashes, face issues are at stake.

Ting-Toomey (1988) developed face-negotiation theory to provide the conceptual linkage among cultural variability dimensions (e.g., IC), face concerns, facework behaviors, and conflict styles. Face concerns are about identity respect and identity threat issues in any anxiety-inducing conflict situations. Facework behaviors are communication behaviors enacted to protect either self-image or other-image, or both.

Basic Assumptions

The basic assumptions of face-negotiation theory (Ting-Toomey, 1985, 1988; Ting-Toomey & Kurogi, 1998) are summarized as follows: (a) People in all cultures try to maintain and negotiate face in all communication situations; (b) the concept of face becomes especially problematic in anxiety-laden or goal-frustrated situations (such as embarrassment situations and conflict situations) when the situated identities of the communicators are called into question; and (c) the cultural variability dimensions of IC and power distance, in conjunction with other individual, relational, and situational factors, influence the use of various facework and conflict styles in intergroup and interpersonal conflicts.

Ting-Toomey and Kurogi (1998) explain that face behaviors and conflict styles are learned within the primary socialization of an individual's cultural groups, such as nationality, ethnicity, and sex. The spectrums of IC and small-large power distance are two major value dimensions used to identify these types of cultural differences (Hofstede, 1991; Hui & Triandis, 1986; Triandis, 1995). Overall, research by Ting-Toomey and associates (Cocroft & Ting-Toomey, 1994; Ting-Toomey et al., 1991; Trubisky, Ting-Toomey, & Lin, 1991) indicates that individualists tend to use more self-oriented face-saving strategies, such as dominating to protect-self interests, and collectivists tend to use more other-oriented face-saving strategies, such as avoiding and obliging to maintain relational harmony.

Overall, previous studies (e.g., Lindsley & Braithwaite, 1996; Oetzel et al., 2000; Oetzel et al., in press) paint a clear picture of the relationship between cross-cultural face concerns and facework behaviors. Self-face is associated positively with dominating-type facework behaviors; other-face is associated positively with integrating-, avoiding-, and obliging-type facework behaviors; and mutual-face is associated positively with integrating-type facework behaviors and negatively with dominating-type behaviors. In addition, members of individualistic cultures tend to use facework behaviors that are low-context and direct, emphasize self-face, and reflect individual conflict goals. Members of collectivistic cultures tend to employ facework behaviors that are high-context and indirect, support the other's face, and preserve relational and network harmony. Finally, power distance plays a role in facework in that members of large power distance cultures differentiate their behavior depending on whether the other party is a superior or a subordinate. Members of small power distance cultures do not appear to make such strong distinctions in comparison to members of large power distance cultures. They tend to use a more impartial approach (i.e., principle of fairness) to conflict rather than a benevolent approach (i.e., principle of status) to managing differences

between superiors and subordinates (Ting-Toomey & Oetzel, 2001).

Relationship Between Face Concerns and Conflict Styles

Face concerns are also closely related to different cross-cultural conflict styles because in the updated face-negotiation theory (Ting-Toomey & Kurogi, 1998), Propositions 23 to 26 clearly linked the different face concerns with specific conflict communication styles. For example, Proposition 23 states: "Self-face maintenance is associated positively with dominating or competing conflict management style" (p. 200). Proposition 24 states: "Other-face maintenance is associated positively with avoiding or obliging conflict management style" (p. 200). The factor of "face concerns" on conflict styles has not been as well researched as IC and self construals because it is often assumed and not directly measured. For example, Oetzel (1998b) assumed that independent self construal and dominating conflict styles are related because of a high concern for self-face. However, one study that we reviewed earlier provides direct evidence of the relationship between face concerns and conflict styles.

Ting-Toomey et al.'s (1991) study of students from China, Japan, South Korea, Taiwan, and the United States examined both face concerns and conflict styles. In the pancultural analysis, the authors found a positive relationship between self-face and dominating conflict styles and positive relationships between other-face and avoiding, obliging, integrating, and compromising conflict styles. In the individual cultures, China, South Korea, and Taiwan followed the pancultural pattern. In the United States, integrating was associated with self-face; in Japan, integrating was associated with both self- and other-face. The authors argue that these findings suggest that the face concern leading to integrating may be based on substantive and relational aspects. That is, in individualistic cultures, a high self-face concern is linked closely with substantive issues and results in dominating or integrating (i.e., for the sake of substantive closure) conflict styles. In collectivistic cultures, a high other-face concern is tied closely with relational issues and results in avoiding, obliging, or integrating (i.e., for the sake of preserving relational harmony) conflict styles. Japan is recognized as a moderate collectivistic culture (Hofstede, 1991) with strong individualistic tendencies displayed especially by university students.

In summary, the review of literature finds some clear patterns about cross-cultural differences in facework and conflict styles. Specifically, individualism and independent self construals lead to self-face concerns, which result in dominating and competing conflict styles. On the other hand, collectivism and interdependent self construals lead to other- and mutual-face concerns, which result in avoiding, obliging, and integrating conflict styles. Small power distance is associated negatively with obliging conflict style and using subordinates to resolve conflicts, but positively with using peers to resolve conflicts. Although these general patterns are illustrative, it is important to note that there are differences between regions of the world and within regions. For example, Asian collectivism results in an obliging conflict style, whereas Middle Eastern collectivism does not. In addition, within Asia, Chinese use avoiding conflict style more than Indians and Filipinos. Chinese in China and Taiwan also tend to use dominating style more than Japanese, and Japanese use integrating style less than Chinese and Koreans. Within the Middle East, Turkish managers use dominating style more than Jordanian managers. These findings demonstrate that there are both etic and emic differences in the use of conflict styles within and between

cultural regions. Cultural value dimensions, together with individual-level and situational-level analysis, may yield the most fruitful directions for future research in face concerns and conflict styles within and across cultures.

FUTURE DIRECTIONS

The review of the existing literature reveals several areas needing future research. In some cases, the future directions are the result of areas that have not been addressed. We organize this section with five suggested directions: situation, power distance, face concerns, emotions, and conflict styles.

Situation

First, the study of face-negotiation in conflict would benefit by investigating the influence of situations. Argyle, Furnham, and Graham (1981) describe a situation as "the sum of features of the behavior system for the duration of a social encounter" (p. 3). Miller, Cody, and McLaughlin (1994) expand by explaining that situations are inextricably woven with interaction goals. The goals that a person has in a particular conflict situation affect his or her conflict behavior. For example, we may emphasize relationship maintenance as an important conflict goal with others in close relationships, and emphasize the achievement of instrumental goals as a top priority when interacting with strangers.

Wilson, Aleman, and Leatham (1996) provide insight into how situational goals influence face concerns during compliance gaining. They examined the face-threatening acts of 303 students in one of three compliance-gaining situations: giving advice, asking favors, and enforcing an unfulfilled obligation. They found that participants were more concerned with the autonomy face of the other in advice giving and asking favor situations than when enforcing obligations. Furthermore, the participants were more likely to persist in enforcing situations than the other situations because there was a greater concern for the goal of gaining compliance than the goal of threatening face.

There are a variety of situational features that can affect face concerns, facework, and conflict styles. Ting-Toomey and Oetzel (2001) propose a culture-based situational model of conflict. They focus on ingroup/outgroup boundaries, relational parameters, conflict goal assessments, and conflict intensity as situational features that frame face behaviors and conflict styles. Some preliminary evidence exists to illustrate the importance of situation on face concerns. Oetzel et al. (1999) found that students in conflict with siblings were more likely to use aggression, third-party help, and private discussion and less likely to use interpersonal respect than were students in conflict with parents. Oetzel et al. (2000) found that U.S. Americans in a conflict with a close other were more likely to have a higher other-face concern than U.S. Americans in a conflict with a distant other. Comparatively, Germans in a conflict with a distant other were more likely to have a higher self-face concern (e.g., less apologizing behaviors) than Germans in a conflict with a close other. However, it should be noted that in both of these studies, national culture and self construal better explain face concerns and facework behaviors than did level of intimacy or familial relation. Thus, further work is needed to understand the situational effect on face and facework in cross-cultural and intercultural conflicts.

Power Distance

The majority of research on cross-cultural conflict has relied on IC or self construals. Although IC is the most important dimension of cultural variability (Triandis, 1995), power distance is also a useful dimension for explaining cross-cultural differences. As we illustrated in the review of literature, there are very few studies comparing cultures of varying power distances in their use of conflict styles and facework behaviors.

It is imperative for researchers not to assume that national culture results in individuals' feelings about power distance (i.e., ecological fallacy). Rather, researchers need to measure attitudes toward power distance directly (e.g., Earley & Erez, 1997). Smith et al. (1998) explain that one possible reason they did not find a relationship between power distance and relying on supervisors for handling disagreements is that individual scores of power distance were not captured. This practice is particularly troubling when there is a small sample size as is the case in a few of Smith et al.'s 23 countries (e.g., *n* as small as 34). A small sample size is subject to individual variation much more than a large sample size. Regardless, direct measurements of power distance are likely to result in more robust findings than relying on Hofstede's (1991) scores for countries.

Face Concerns

A third omission of research regarding cross-cultural conflict is the focus primarily on self- and other-face. However, the valence and temporality are also important dimensions for understanding how individuals complete the process of face-negotiation during and after the actual conflict negotiation process across cultures. Ting-Toomey and Kurogi (1998) have numerous propositions regarding face valence and temporality that have not been investigated to date.

The lack of investigations on face valence and temporality may be a by-product of the methods used in the majority of research on cross-cultural conflict. The majority of the studies we have reviewed (exceptions include

Lindsley & Braithwaite, 1996; Oetzel, 1998a, 1998c) rely on self-report measures of face behavior in hypothetical or recalled conflicts. The use of these methods does not allow researchers to examine the developmental process of face-negotiation—making it particularly difficult to study temporality. The study of conflict face-negotiation would benefit by examining actual interaction via procedures such as interaction analysis or discourse analysis to understand the ways in which individuals defend and maintain face, as well as whether they are proactive or reactive in managing face. In addition, post-conflict interviews can elicit the logic or narrative accounts that individuals use to justify their facework behaviors during a conflict.

Emotions

If we dig deeper, face concerns are directly linked to emotionally based identity issues in conflict. Face concerns are basically about unmet identity needs and mismatched identity expectations of how one wants to be treated. When face needs are not met, conflict parties experience devaluations or identity disconfirmations. Conflict is an emotionally loaded experience when either one or both parties believe that their identity images are blocked or thwarted. Recurring conflict issues are often about identity and relationship issues more so than substantive conflict issues. Emotions frame identity facework negotiation process. Individuals in a wide variety of conflict situations can choose to express their emotions directly or indirectly, or suppress their conflict emotions altogether.

Two emotions that may indicate the salience of face concerns are shame and pride. According to Scheff (1990), all human beings desire secure social bonds via approval and inclusion. Because face involves the need for approval and inclusion on a relational level,

respect for face is one way to maintain secure social bonds, and disrespect for face is a reflection of a broken social bond. Thus, pride and shame communicate the state of our social bond to the self and the other. Pride and shame then would be associated with self- and other-face.

It seems logical to reason that shame is experienced when face is threatened and pride is restored when face is enhanced in any conflict situations. The emotions of shame versus pride, guilt versus forgiveness, and contempt versus respect form some of the complex emotions that underlie facework negotiation during and after a conflict. These are affective responses experienced and generated in reaction to others and related to the cognitive appraisals of the worthiness of self-face and other-face in conflict. More collaborative research efforts are needed to identify the emotional responses and cognitive appraisal process in face-threatening, face-recouping, face-honoring, and face-compensating conflict moves in different cultures.

Conflict Styles

Several scholars have critiqued the conceptualization of conflict style typologies (Kim & Leung, 2000; Ting-Toomey, 1988; Ting-Toomey & Kurogi, 1998). For example, Ting-Toomey (1988) critiqued some of the conflict style research as follows: "Unfortunately, amidst the enthusiastic debate between three-style and five-style approaches to conflict, interpersonal and organizational conflict researchers typically have failed to provide cross-cultural evidence for both their theoretical and methodological claims over the various styles of conflict negotiation" (p. 221). In addition, Ting-Toomey (1985, 1988, 1997) and Kim and Leung (2000) have illustrated the Western bias in the conflict management literature. Specifically, obliging and avoiding

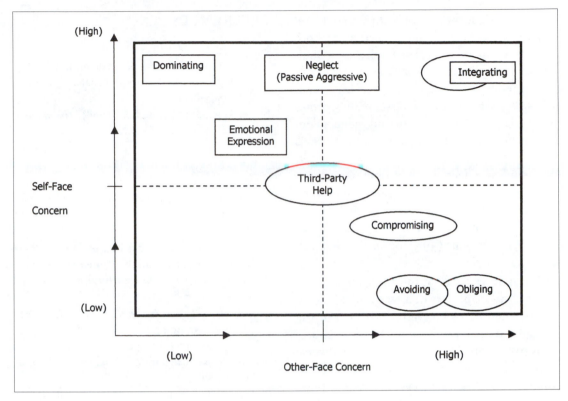

Figure 7.1   An Eight-Style Conflict Grid: An Intercultural Approach

styles often take on a Western slant of being negatively disengaged (i.e., "placating" or "flight" from the conflict scene). However, members of collectivistic cultures do not necessarily perceive obliging and avoiding conflict styles as negative. These two styles are typically employed by collectivists to maintain mutual-face interests and relational network interests (Ting-Toomey, 1988).

Furthermore, scholars have critiqued the five-style models of conflict management for not covering the subtle nuances and variants in conflict management (Ting-Toomey et al., 2000). As a result, Ting-Toomey et al. (2000) chose to add three other conflict styles to account for the potentially rich areas of cultural and ethnic differences in conflict: emotional expression, third-party help, and neglect. Emotional expression refers to using one's

emotions to guide communication behaviors during conflict. Third-party help involves using an outsider to mediate the conflict. Neglect is characterized by using passive-aggressive responses to sidestep the conflict but at the same time get an indirect reaction from the other conflict party.

The research reviewed in this chapter helps to illustrate the manner in which individuals across diverse cultures (e.g., China, Germany, Japan, Mexico, and the United States, including African Americans, Asian Americans, European Americans, and Latino Americans) approach conflict. Based on these studies, we propose a new model of conflict styles (Ting-Toomey & Oetzel, 2001) (see Figure 7.1).

As illustrated in the figure, avoiding, obliging, and compromising are reflective of high other-face concerns and an interdependent self. Integrating is based on both high self- and other-face concerns and reflective of both independent and interdependent selves. Similarly, the use of a third party to mediate a conflict is reflective of these same concerns, but as a middle-of-the-road style. Dominating comes from high self-face concern and independent self, whereas emotional expression is also a high self-face concern and independent self but to a lesser degree than is dominating conflict style. Finally, passive-aggressive (i.e., neglect) is a high self-face/independent self and a moderate amount of other-face and interdependent self (Ting-Toomey & Oetzel, 2001).

Overall, we feel that this model provides a more accurate picture of how conflict is being approached across cultures. We believe the model provides a starting point for a culture-sensitive approach to conceptualize diverse face concerns and conflict styles across cultures. However, we also recognize that there are emic meanings and interpretations of different conflict styles that are not captured by our model. Future researchers will be wise to investigate both the emic and etic facets of different conflict styles and facework tactics.

In conclusion, there is a moderate amount of research on cross-cultural face concerns, facework, and conflict styles, especially in regards to IC and self construals. However, more research is needed to determine the importance of situational and affective aspects of face concerns and conflict styles across ethnic groups and across a diverse range of cultures. In addition, face valence, temporality, and competence are important dimensions for cross-cultural conflict research. The future directions we specify will help to expand conflict face-negotiation theory. More studies are also needed to expand the research boundaries of cross-cultural conflict styles and to examine adaptive *intercultural* conflict styles in a diverse range of intimate and nonintimate conflict settings.

REFERENCES

Argyle, M., Furnham, A., & Graham, J. A. (1981). *Social situations.* Cambridge, UK: Cambridge University Press.

Blake, R. R., & Mouton, J. S. (1964). *The managerial grid.* Houston, TX: Gulf.

Bond, M. (1991). *Beyond the Chinese face.* Hong Kong: Oxford University Press.

Chiu, R. K., & Kosinski, F. A. (1994). Is Chinese conflict-handling behavior influenced by Chinese values? *Social Behavior and Personality, 22,* 81-90.

Cocroft, B.-A., & Ting-Toomey, S. (1994). Facework in Japan and the United States. *International Journal of Intercultural Relations, 18,* 469-506.

Cox, T. H., Lobel, S. A., & McLeod, P. L. (1991). Effects of ethnic group cultural differences on cooperative and competitive behavior on a group task. *Academy of Management Journal, 34,* 827-847.

Dsilva, M. U., & Whyte, L. O. (1998). Cultural differences in conflict styles: Vietnamese refugees and established residents. *Howard Journal of Communications, 9,* 57-68.

Earley, P. C. (1997). *Face, harmony, and social structure: An analysis of organizational behavior across cultures.* New York: Oxford University Press.

Earley, P. C., & Erez, M. (1997). *The transplanted executive.* New York: Oxford University Press.

Elsayed-Ekhouly, S. M., & Buda, R. (1996). Organizational conflict: A comparative analysis of conflict style across cultures. *International Journal of Conflict Management, 7,* 71-81.

French, J. R. P., & Raven, B. (1959). The bases of social power. In D. Cartwright (Ed.), *Social studies in power* (pp. 150-167). Ann Arbor, MI: Institute for Social Research.

Gabrielidis, C., Stephan, W. G., Ybarra, O., Dos Santos Pearson, V. M., & Villareal, L. (1997). Preferred styles of conflict resolution: Mexico and the United States. *Journal of Cross-Cultural Psychology, 28,* 661-677.

Gao, G. (1998). An initial analysis of the effects of face and concern for "other" in Chinese interpersonal communication. *International Journal of Intercultural Relations, 22,* 467-482.

Garcia, W. (1996). Respeto: A Mexican base for interpersonal relationships. In W. B. Gudykunst, S. Ting-Toomey, & T. Nishida (Eds.), *Communication in personal relationships across cultures* (pp. 137-155). Thousand Oaks, CA: Sage.

Graham, J. (1985). The influence of culture on the process of business negotiations: An exploratory study. *Journal of International Business Studies, 85,* 81-96.

Gudykunst, W. B., Matsumoto, Y., Ting-Toomey, S., Nishida, T., Kim, K. S., & Heyman, S. (1996). The influence of cultural individualism-collectivism, self construals, and individual values on communication styles across cultures. *Human Communication Research, 22,* 510-543.

Hofstede, G. (1991). *Cultures and organizations: Software of the mind.* London: McGraw-Hill.

Hui, C. H., & Triandis, H. C. (1986). Individualism-collectivism: A study of cross-cultural researchers. *Journal of Cross-Cultural Psychology, 17,* 225-248.

Katriel, T. (1986). *Talking straight: Dugri speech in Israeli Sabra culture.* Cambridge, UK: Cambridge University Press.

Kim, M. S., Hunter, J. E., Miyahara, A., Horvath, A., Bresnahan, M., & Yoon, H. (1996). Individual- vs. cultural-level dimensions of individualism and collectivism: Effects on preferred conversational styles. *Communication Monographs, 63,* 28-49.

Kim, M. S., & Leung, T. (2000). A multicultural view of conflict management styles: Review and critical synthesis. In M. Roloff (Ed.), *Communication yearbook 23* (pp. 227-269). Thousand Oaks, CA: Sage.

Kozan, M. K. (1989). Cultural influences on styles of handling interpersonal conflicts: Comparisons among Jordanian, Turkish, and U.S. managers. *Human Relations, 42,* 787-799.

Kozan, M. K., & Ergin, C. (1998). Preference for third-party help in conflict management in the United States and Turkey: An experimental study. *Journal of Cross-Cultural Psychology, 29,* 525-539.

Leung, K. (1987). Some determinants of reactions to procedural models for conflict resolution: A

cross-national study. *Journal of Personality and Social Psychology, 53,* 898-908.

Lim, T.-S. (1994). Facework and interpersonal relationships. In S. Ting-Toomey (Ed.), *The challenge of facework: Cross-cultural and interpersonal issues* (pp. 209-229). Albany: State University of New York Press.

Lim, T.-S., & Choi S. (1996). Interpersonal relationships in Korea. In W. B. Gudykunst, S. Ting-Toomey, & T. Nishida (Eds.), *Communication in personal relationships across cultures* (pp. 122-136). Thousand Oaks, CA: Sage.

Lindsley, S. L., & Braithwaite, C. A. (1996). "You should 'wear a mask' ": Facework norms in cultural and intercultural conflict in maquiladoras. *International Journal of Intercultural Relations, 20,* 199-225.

Markus, H., & Kitayama, S. (1991). Culture and the self: Implications for cognition, emotion, and motivation. *Psychological Review, 98,* 224-253.

Miller, L. C., Cody, M. J., & McLaughlin, M. L. (1994). Situations and goals as fundamental constructs in interpersonal communication research. In M. L. Knapp & G. R. Miller (Eds.), *Handbook of interpersonal communication* (2nd ed., pp. 162-198). Thousand Oaks, CA: Sage.

Morisaki, S., & Gudykunst, W. B. (1994). Face in Japan and the United States. In S. Ting-Toomey (Ed.), *The challenge of facework* (pp. 47-93). Albany: State University of New York Press.

Morris, M. W., Williams, K. Y., Leung, K., Larrick, R., Mendoza, M. T., Bhatnagar, D., Li, J., Kondo, M., Luo, J.-L., & Hu, J.-C. (1998). Conflict management style: Accounting for cross-national differences. *Journal of International Business Studies, 29,* 729-748.

Oetzel, J. G. (1998a). Culturally homogeneous and heterogeneous groups: Explaining communication processes through individualism-collectivism and self-construal. *International Journal of Intercultural Relations, 22,* 135-161.

Oetzel, J. G. (1998b). The effects of self-construals and ethnicity on self-reported conflict styles. *Communication Reports, 11,* 133-144.

Oetzel, J. G. (1998c). Explaining individual communication processes in homogeneous and heterogeneous groups through individualism-collectivism and self-construal. *Human Communication Research, 25,* 202-224.

Oetzel, J. G. (2001). Self-construals, communication processes, and group outcomes in homogeneous and heterogeneous groups. *Small Group Research, 32,* 19-54.

Oetzel, J. G., Ting-Toomey, S., & Chew, M. (1999, November). *Face and facework in conflicts with parents and siblings: A cross-cultural comparison of Germans, Japanese, Mexicans, and U.S. Americans.* Paper presented at the annual meeting of the National Communication Association, Chicago.

Oetzel, J. G., Ting-Toomey, S., Masumoto, T., Yokochi, Y., Pan, X., Takai, J., & Wilcox, R. (2000, May). *Face and facework in conflict: A cross-cultural comparison of China, Germany, Japan, and the United States.* Paper presented at the annual meeting of the International Communication Association, Acapulco, Mexico.

Oetzel, J. G., Ting-Toomey, S., Yokochi, Y., Matsumoto, T., & Takai, J. (in press). A typology of facework behaviors in conflicts with best friends and relative strangers. *Communication Quarterly.*

Ohbuchi, K., Fukushima, O., & Tedeschi, J. T. (1999). Cultural values in conflict management: Goal orientation, goal attainment, and tactical decision. *Journal of Cross-Cultural Psychology, 30,* 51-71.

Ohbuchi, K., & Takahashi, Y. (1994). Cultural styles of conflict management in Japanese and Americans: Passivity, covertness, and effectiveness of strategies. *Journal of Applied Social Psychology, 24,* 1345-1366.

Putnam, L. L., & Poole, M. S. (1987). Conflict and negotiation. In F. M. Jablin, L. L. Putnam, K. H. Roberts, & L. W. Porter (Eds.), *Handbook of organizational communication* (pp. 549-599). Newbury Park, CA: Sage.

Rahim, M. A. (1983). A measure of styles of handling interpersonal conflict. *Academy of Management Journal, 26,* 368-376.

Rahim, M. A. (1986). Referent role and styles of handling interpersonal conflict. *Journal of Social Psychology, 125,* 79-86.

Rahim, M. A. (1992). *Managing conflict in organizations* (2nd ed.). Westport, CT: Praeger.

Rahim, M. A., & Buntzman, G. F. (1989). Supervisory power bases, styles of handling conflict with subordinates, and subordinate compliance and satisfaction. *Journal of Psychology, 123,* 195-210.

Rogan, R. G., & Hammer, M. R. (1994). Crisis negotiations: A preliminary investigation of facework in naturalistic conflict discourse. *Journal of Applied Communication Research, 22,* 216-231.

Scheff, T. (1990). *Microsociology: Discourse, emotion, and social structure.* Chicago: University of Chicago Press.

Smith, P. B., Dugan, S., Peterson, M. F., & Leung, K. (1998). Individualism-collectivism and the handling of disagreement: A 23-country study. *International Journal of Intercultural Relations, 22,* 351-367.

Sternberg, R. J., & Soriano, L. J. (1984). Styles of conflict resolution. *Journal of Personality and Social Psychology, 47,* 115-126.

Tata, J. (2000). Implicit theories of account-giving: Influence of culture and gender. *International Journal of Intercultural Relations, 24,* 437-454.

Thomas, K. W., & Kilmann, R. H. (1974). *Thomas-Kilmann conflict MODE instrument.* New York: XICOM, Tuxedo.

Ting-Toomey, S. (1985). Toward a theory of conflict and culture. In W. Gudykunst, L. Stewart, & S. Ting-Toomey (Eds.), *Communication, culture, and organizational processes* (pp. 71-86). Beverly Hills, CA: Sage.

Ting-Toomey, S. (1988). Intercultural conflict styles: A face-negotiation theory. In Y. Y. Kim & W. B. Gudykunst (Eds.), *Theories in intercultural communication* (pp. 213-235). Newbury Park, CA: Sage.

Ting-Toomey, S. (1997). Intercultural conflict competence. In W. Cupach & D. Canary (Eds.), *Competence in interpersonal conflict* (pp. 120-147). New York: McGraw-Hill.

Ting-Toomey, S., & Cole, M. (1990). Intergroup diplomatic communication: A face-negotiation perspective. In F. Korzenny & S. Ting-Toomey (Eds.), *Communicating for peace: Diplomacy and negotiation* (pp. 77-95). Newbury Park, CA: Sage.

Ting-Toomey, S., Gao, G., Trubisky, P., Yang, Z., Kim, H. S., Lin, S.-L., & Nishida, T. (1991). Culture, face maintenance, and styles of handling interpersonal conflict: A study in five cultures. *International Journal of Conflict Management, 2,* 275-296.

Ting-Toomey, S., & Kurogi, A. (1998). Facework competence in intercultural conflict: An updated face-negotiation theory. *International Journal of Intercultural Relations, 22,* 187-225.

Ting-Toomey, S., & Oetzel, J. G. (2001). *Managing intercultural conflict effectively.* Thousand Oaks, CA: Sage.

Ting-Toomey, S., Oetzel, J. G., & Yee-Jung, K. (2001). Self construal types and conflict management styles. *Communication Reports.*

Ting-Toomey, S., Yee-Jung, K., Shapiro, R., Garcia, W., Wright, T., & Oetzel, J. G. (2000). Cultural/ ethnic identity salience and conflict styles. *International Journal of Intercultural Relations, 23,* 47-81.

Tsai, J. L., & Levenson, R. W. (1997). Cultural influences on emotional responding: Chinese American and European American dating couples during interpersonal conflict. *Journal of Cross-Cultural Psychology, 28,* 600-625.

Triandis, H. (1995). *Individualism and collectivism.* Boulder, CO: Westview.

Trubisky, P., Ting-Toomey, S., & Lin, S.-L. (1991). The influence of individualism-collectivism and self-monitoring on conflict styles. *International Journal of Intercultural Relations, 15,* 65-84.

Wilson, S. R., Aleman, C. G., & Leatham, G. B. (1996). Identity implications of influence goals: A revised analysis of face-threatening acts and application to seeking compliance with same-sex friends. *Human Communication Research, 25,* 64-96.

8

Issues in Cross-Cultural Communication Research

WILLIAM B. GUDYKUNST
California State University, Fullerton

Gudykunst and Lee (Chapter 2, this volume) argue that cross-cultural studies of communication should be theory based. Research designed to test cross-cultural theories and hypotheses must be methodologically sound.[1] Over the years, an extensive body of knowledge about conducting cross-cultural research has been generated (e.g., Berry, Poortinga, & Pandey, 1997; Brislin, Lonner, & Thorndike, 1973; Enber & Enber, 2000; Lonner & Berry, 1986; Triandis & Berry, 1980; van de Vijver, in press; van de Vijver & Leung, 1997a, 2000). Most of the work written on cross-cultural research focuses on specific methods of data collection and analysis (e.g., field research, surveys). The vast majority of the work on cross-cultural methods does not place cross-cultural research in the context of theories designed to explain variability in communication across cultures. My purpose in this chapter is to outline some of the issues that are important in conducting theory-based research on crosscultural communication. I, therefore, focus on broad methodological issues, not specific research methods.

METHODOLOGICAL ISSUES IN CONDUCTING THEORY-BASED RESEARCH

In this section, I focus on central methodological issues (not specific methods) critical to conducting sound theory-based crosscultural communication research: conduct-

AUTHOR'S NOTE: This chapter is adapted from Gudykunst (2000). I want to thank Michael Bond and George Barnett for their comments on an earlier version of the chapter.

ing emic versus etic research, making theoretical predictions, designing cross-cultural research, isolating the effects to be studied, establishing equivalence, developing derived etic measures, and establishing reliability and validity of measures.

Conducting Emic Versus Etic Research

The distinction between the emic and etic approaches to studying culture and behavior can be traced to Pike's (1966) discussion of phonetics (vocal utterances that are universal) and phonemics (culturally specific vocal utterances). Berry (1980, pp. 11-12) presents a succinct summary of the distinction between the emic and etic approaches to research:

Emic Approach	Etic Approach
Studies behavior from within the system	Studies behavior from a position outside the system
Examines only one culture	Examines many cultures, comparing them
Structure discovered by the analyst	Structure created by the analyst
Criteria are relative to internal characteristics	Criteria are considered absolute or universal

Researchers tend to use one of the two approaches exclusively, and the two approaches often are linked to the qualitative versus quantitative debate in the social sciences.

Emic analyses often are equated with the use of qualitative methods of research, and etic analyses often are equated with the use of quantitative methods of research. More generally, an emic approach often is associated with subjectivist meta-theoretical assumptions (e.g., nominalism, antipositivism, volunteerism; Burrell & Morgan, 1979), and etic research often is associated with objectivist meta-theoretical assumptions (e.g., realism, positivism, determinism; Burrell & Morgan,

1979). Neither the extreme subjectivist nor the extreme objectivist assumptions, however, are defensible. The only reasonable meta-theoretical assumptions are between the two extremes. Both emic and etic approaches are needed for methodologically sound cross-cultural research. The approach used *must* depend on the research question being posed. I believe that the questions researchers pose should drive their methods; the methods researchers use should *not* drive the questions they pose. Because the focus of this chapter is on conducting theory-based cross-cultural research, the emphasis throughout the remainder of the chapter is on etic research (incorporating emic issues where appropriate).

Making Theoretical Predictions

The dimensions of cultural variability (e.g., individualism-collectivism) and the individual-level factors (e.g., self construals) that mediate the influence of dimensions of cultural variability should be used to make theoretical predictions in cross-cultural research (see Gudykunst & Lee, this volume). It is critical that cultural- and individual-level effects be differentiated. Cultural-level effects must be derived from the norms and rules of the cultures being studied. This means that specific norms and rules should be isolated, and these norms and rules must be linked to the dimensions of cultural variability in order to make cultural-level predictions. The predictions must involve communication behavior that results from the cultural norms or rules. To illustrate, there are cultural-level rules guiding reward allocation (Leung & Bond, 1984). Members of collectivistic cultures (e.g., Chinese), for example, prefer to use "equality" rules (i.e., divide rewards equally) with ingroup members but not with outgroup members. Members of individualistic cultures (e.g., U.S. Americans), in contrast, use "equity" rules (i.e., make rewards based on performance) with both ingroup and outgroup members.

Specific aspects of communication may not be a function of only one dimension of cultural variability. To illustrate, interaction with strangers may be a function of individualism-collectivism *and* uncertainty avoidance. Individuals from collective cultures would be expected to differ in how they interact with strangers depending on whether their culture is low or high in uncertainty avoidance. Those from high uncertainty avoidance cultures would probably avoid strangers as much as possible because they see strangers' behaviors as unpredictable or cultural rules prescribe how to interact with strangers. Those from low uncertainty avoidance cultures, in contrast, might be inclined to interact with strangers because they view ambiguity as "interesting."

Individual-level effects are linked to factors that mediate the effect of cultural dimensions (e.g., self construals mediate the effect of cultural individualism-collectivism). To illustrate, specific communication styles that individuals use are not linked to cultural norms or rules; rather, they are a function of individuals' self construals (see Gudykunst et al., 1996).

Designing Theory-Testing Research

Cross-cultural studies are not *true experiments* (see Campbell & Stanley, 1966). True experiments require that respondents are assigned randomly to conditions of the independent variable(s). Obviously, cultures cannot be assigned randomly to dimensions of cultural variability and respondents cannot be assigned randomly to cultures. Cross-cultural studies generally fit the design that Campbell and Stanley refer to as a nonequivalent control group design or a static group comparison (see

Malpass & Poortinga, 1986, for a discussion of specific designs used in cross-cultural research). These designs have numerous threats to internal validity (i.e., rival explanations for the results; see Campbell & Stanley, 1966). Analyzing data from cross-cultural studies as true experiments can yield misleading results (see Poortinga & Malpass, 1986, for a discussion of the problems in making inferences). Differences that emerge in cross-cultural studies may be due to the dimensions of cultural variability being studied, or there may be rival hypotheses based on education, literacy, issues of equivalence, and so on.

In designing cross-cultural studies, it is important to isolate potential rival hypotheses in advance and design studies in ways that they can be ruled out. "A feasible strategy is to identify the most likely variables that may account for expected cultural differences and measure these variables in the study" (van de Vijver & Leung, 1997b, pp. 260-261).

The method used to sample the cultures in which data are collected is an important design issue. Van de Vijver and Leung (1997b) isolate three possible sampling methods: convenience, systematic, and random. Most cross-cultural studies use convenience sampling. Cultures are selected because researchers have contacts in the cultures being studied, or they will be visiting the cultures. The cultures selected, however, may not be ideal representatives of the dimensions of cultural variability being studied. Systematic sampling involves selecting cultures in a theory-driven way. Ideally, cultures as far apart on the cultural dimensions being studied are selected. If individualism-collectivism is being studied, for example, cultures that are highly individualistic and highly collectivistic are selected. Random sampling involves selecting cultures in a random way. Using this approach makes it difficult to test dimensions of cultural variability, but it is useful for testing universals or pancultural theories.

Even though individuals cannot be assigned randomly to cultures, they can be assigned randomly to other conditions within cultures. This may be important in testing theoretical predictions based on dimensions of cultural variability. To illustrate, if researchers are interested in the influence of cultural individualism-collectivism on behavior, they need to collect data in individualistic and collectivistic cultures. In addition, researchers may want to "manipulate" interaction with members of ingroups and outgroups within cultures in a laboratory experiment or on a survey because predictions based on individualism-collectivism would suggest that there is more variability in ingroup-outgroup communication in collectivistic cultures than in individualistic cultures.[2]

Isolating the Theoretical Effects Being Studied

Researchers often mistakenly assume that culture has only one type of effect on behavior. This is not the case. If responses to a set of items are considered, culture can have two different types of effects on data (Leung & Bond, 1989). First, culture can affect the relationships among the items. Two items, for example, may be uncorrelated in one culture, positively correlated in another culture, and negatively correlated in a third. This is referred to as the *patterning* effect of culture. If the correlations are similar across cultures, the relationship has cross-cultural generalizability. If the correlations are different, explanations for the differences must be generated. Second, culture can affect how "average" members of different cultures respond to items. This is referred to as the *location* or *positioning* effect of culture. The same correlations may exist between two items in two cultures, but average members of the cultures may respond differently to the items.

To establish dimensions of variation at the cultural level, mean scores for cultures on a series of items from individuals from a large number of cultures are either factor analyzed or clustered using nonmetric multidimensional scaling. These procedures isolate a location or positioning effect for culture, and only a location or positioning effect (Leung & Bond, 1989). Alternatively, a pancultural analysis can be conducted. This type of analysis can yield both a location or positioning effect and a patterning effect for culture. Neither procedure allows for dimensions at the individual level to be isolated.

To isolate dimensions at the individual level, an *isoregion* analysis must be conducted (Leung & Bond, 1989). To conduct an isoregion analysis, the data are first standardized within individuals. The within-individual standardized scores are then standardized within cultures to eliminate the location or positioning effect for culture. If the resulting data are factor analyzed, the factors are "pure" because there is no location or positioning effect for culture. There is, however, still a patterning effect for culture in the data. This procedure allows researchers to examine cultural differences at the individual level or to ignore culture and look for universals at the individual level.

The effects that researchers need to isolate depend on the research questions or hypotheses they pose. If the questions/hypotheses focus on universal patterns of behavior, the pattern effect must be the focus. If, on the other hand, researchers are interested in how behavior differs in individualistic and collectivistic cultures, the location or positioning effect must be the focus.

Whatever effect researchers are studying, they must not just report statistical tests of significance. It is critical that researchers report the effect size (e.g., the amount of variance explained) when they analyze the results of their studies. Cross-cultural research is sufficiently well developed that studies should yield more than small effect sizes (e.g., more than 5% to 10% of the variance should be explained).

Establishing Equivalence

"If comparisons are to be legitimately made across cultural boundaries, it is first necessary to establish equivalent bases upon which to make comparisons" (Lonner, 1979, p. 27). Equivalence refers to equality in quantity, value, meaning, and so forth. At least five types of equivalence must be addressed: functional, conceptual, linguistic, metric, and sample equivalence. Lack of equivalence in any of these areas can provide rival hypotheses to explain results in cross-cultural studies.

Functional equivalence. Functional equivalence involves the relationship between specific observations and the inferences that are made from the observations. Goldschmidt (1966) argues that activities must have similar functions if they are to be used for purposes of comparison. Without equivalent functions, communication across cultures is incomparable.

One area of research in which functional equivalence is of concern is research on communication apprehension (e.g., fear of communication; Klopf & Cambra, 1979). Although communication apprehension is viewed as undesirable in the United States where the concept was developed, this view is not shared in Japan or Korea where reticence is valued. Any comparisons of this phenomenon must take these functional differences into account. Lack of functional equivalence is a rival hypothesis to the dimension(s) of cultural variability being studied in explaining the results of a cross-cultural study.

Conceptual equivalence. Functional equivalence involves equivalence at the macro or cultural level. Conceptual equivalence, in contrast, "focuses upon the presence (or absence) of meanings that individuals attach to specific stimuli" (Lonner, 1979, p. 27). Sears (1961) argues that researchers must discover the meaning of concepts within the cognitive systems of the members of the culture(s) being examined.

When studying concepts that first appear unique to one culture (e.g., *amae, sasshi, ishin denshin* in Japan; assertiveness, communication apprehension in the United States), for example, it is necessary to begin by looking at emic conceptualizations of the concepts. Once the concepts have been analyzed using an emic analysis, cross-cultural studies can begin. It is critical, however, to take one additional step and to generate etic conceptualizations of concepts that are compatible with culturally specific emic conceptualizations (i.e., derived etic conceptualizations).

An alternative approach is to use emic operationalizations of concepts to test etic models. Triandis, Malpass, and Davidson (1973), for example, suggest that a three-stage process be used in cross-cultural studies. First, researchers develop etic constructs that appear to be universal. Second, researchers develop emic measures of the constructs and validate them. Third, use the emic operationalizations to study the etic constructs across cultures. This procedure works well for constructs that are "universal," but it does not work as well in studying constructs that at first glance appear to be culturally specific. For these constructs, the procedure outlined earlier (i.e., developing derived etic conceptualizations) is needed. Lack of conceptual equivalence becomes a rival hypothesis to the dimension(s) of cultural variability being studied in explaining the results in a cross-cultural study.

Linguistic equivalence. Linguistic (or translation) equivalence focuses on the language used in questionnaires, interviews, and field observations and instructions used in research (see Brislin, 1976, for a discussion of translation issues). Administration of research instruments in a language of one culture to people in another culture for whom this language is not a native language yields data that are not equivalent. Even if the respondents are bilingual in the original language of the research instrument, the data are not equivalent. Research instruments must be administered in the respondents' native language, and the forms used in different cultures must be linguistically equivalent. Lack of linguistic equivalence is a rival hypothesis to the dimension(s) of cultural variability being studied in explaining the results of cross-cultural research.

The most widely used method to establish linguistic equivalence is back-translation. This procedure generally involves one bilingual translating the instrument from the first language into the second and another bilingual back-translating the instrument into the first language. Variations in original wording and the back-translation must then be reconciled.

Brislin (1976) argues that research instruments need to be decentered where "material in one language is changed so that there will be a smooth, natural sounding version in the second language. The result of de-centering contrasts with the awkward, stilted versions common when material in one language is taken as the final content that must be translated with minimal change into another language" (p. 222). This can be very difficult when multiple cultures are involved.

Metric equivalence. Closely related to linguistic equivalence is the issue of metric equivalence, establishing that the score levels obtained in one culture are equivalent to score levels obtained in another culture. To illustrate, research suggests that Asians do not use extreme scores (e.g., *strongly agree* or *strongly*

disagree) as much as U.S. Americans. Asians, therefore, may score lower on scales constructed from questionnaires because of their response tendencies, not real cultural differences (e.g., Chen, Lee, & Stevenson, 1995; Peng, Nisbett, & Wong, 1997).

Poortinga (1975) argues that there are at least three alternative interpretations of differences in scores between two cultures: (1) The differences exist and are real, (2) the test measures qualitatively different aspects of the concept (this is related to conceptual and linguistic equivalence), and (3) the test measures quantitatively different aspects of the concept. Without establishing metric equivalence, the second and third interpretations become rival hypotheses to explain differences observed across cultures. Minimally, both raw and standardized scores should be examined in cross-cultural studies to ensure metric equivalence. Lack of metric equivalence is a rival hypothesis to the dimension(s) of cultural variability being studied in explaining the results of cross-cultural studies.

Sample equivalence. The final equivalence is sample equivalence. It is important that comparable samples are used when cross-cultural comparisons are made. Brislin and Baumgardner (1971) point out that most cross-cultural studies use samples of convenience, rather than random samples. Because random samples generally are not feasible in cross-cultural research, steps need to be taken to ensure that samples are as equivalent as possible.

One way to demonstrate that the samples are as equivalent as possible is to gather as much data on the respondents that is relevant to the study and compare the data across samples. To illustrate, basic demographic information on the samples (e.g., sex, age, education, ethnicity, social class) can help establish equivalence. Also, other variables that might be related to the dependent variables could be collected. If, for example, communication in ingroups and outgroups is being studied, the intimacy of the ingroup and outgroup relationships and frequency of contact with ingroup and outgroup members should be assessed. Lack of sample equivalence is a rival hypothesis to the dimension(s) of cultural variability being studied in explaining the results of cross-cultural studies.

Related to sample equivalence is the issue of whether the samples used actually represent the dimensions of cultural variability being studied (this issue is discussed in more detail below). Samples from Japan and the United States, for example, should be checked to ensure that the respondents from Japan are more collectivistic than those from the United States, and samples from the United States need to be checked to ensure they are more individualistic than those from Japan. Gudykunst and Nishida (1999) argue that this often is problematic because Japanese college students demonstrate high levels of individualism and when selected "manipulation checks" (e.g., self construals) are used, Japanese samples may be more individualistic than U.S. samples. Researchers using etic approaches must be careful to ensure that their samples are indeed representative of the dimensions they are studying.

Developing Derived Etic Measures

Often when researchers study communication across cultures, they assume that a concept from one culture exists in another culture and that it is similar. These researchers then may use a measure developed in one culture (e.g., a measure of communication apprehension developed in the United States) in the other culture without any changes. This procedure often is referred to as *imposed* etic

(Berry, 1969) or *pseudo* etic (Triandis et al., 1973). Imposed or pseudo etic measurement can create problems (see issues of equivalence discussed earlier). To develop equivalent measures, *derived* etic (Berry, 1969) measurement is necessary.

Developing derived etic measures is a time-consuming process. Emic aspects of the concept under study must be generated in each culture in which data are being collected (e.g., by intensive interviews or open-ended surveys). The culture-specific and universal aspects of the concept must be integrated into one measure, translated, and pretested in each culture. Based on the pretest, items that are inappropriate in one or more cultures are discarded and a final measure developed (for an example, see Hasegawa & Gudykunst's, 1998, study of silence). The final instrument is presented to a new sample in all the cultures.

To isolate possible dimensions of the concept being studied, the resulting data must be standardized within cultures before they are factor analyzed (to remove the location or positioning effect).[3] To illustrate, if researchers are studying self construals across cultures, they might expect two factors to emerge in the analysis: independent and interdependent self construals. When the within-culture standardized data are factor analyzed, the factors that emerge are the derived etic measure. These factors will be common to all the cultures. Culture-specific items will not load on the factors isolated. Within-culture factor analysis can be performed to isolate culture-specific factors.

Establishing Reliability and Validity

As indicated earlier, culture has a patterning effect on data. That is, culture can influence the relationships (e.g., correlations) among items and variables. This has clear implications for establishing the reliability and validity of measures being used in cross-cultural studies.

Calculating reliability and validity involves correlating responses to individual items and variables. These correlations may be influenced by the patterning effect of culture. Items A and B, for example, may be correlated positively in one culture, correlated negatively in another, and uncorrelated in a third. The patterning effect can lead to very different levels of reliability and validity (e.g., when concurrent validity is established) in different cultures. This suggests that reliability and validity must be established within each culture studied separately. Pancultural assessment of reliability and validity is meaningless.

PROBLEMS IN CURRENT CROSS-CULTURAL RESEARCH

There are numerous problems in the current cross-cultural research being conducted in communication. In this section, I focus on problems in conducting theory-based cross-cultural research.[4]

Cultures Studied

The vast majority of cross-cultural communication research involves comparisons of Asian and Western cultures. One reason for this is that there are more Asian scholars trained in communication to serve as collaborators than there are researchers in other cultures (e.g., Arab, Latin, and African cultures). Clearly, there is a need for more research examining communication in non-Asian cultures. To make generalizations about the dimensions of cultural variability, cultures from many different world regions must be studied (see Bond, 1998).

Generalizations made regarding Asian collectivists may or may not apply to non-Asian collectivistic cultures (e.g., Arab, Latin, and African cultures). Collectivism in Africa (e.g., communalism), for example, may have a different influence on communication than collectivism in Asia. Similarly, generalizations from the United States, England, and Australia may not generalize to other individualistic cultures (e.g., Germany, Norway). There is a clear need for studies of communication in a variety of individualistic and collectivistic cultures. Without such studies, it is impossible to make firm generalizations about the effects of cultural individualism-collectivism (or other dimensions of cultural variability).

Use of Only One Dimension of Cultural Variability

Most cross-cultural studies use only one dimension of cultural variability to explain communication across cultures. Individualism-collectivism is the dimension used most widely in cross-cultural research. Individualism-collectivism often is used when there is *not* a clear linkage between individualism-collectivism and the specific communication behavior under study. Only communication linked to the ingroup-outgroup distinction is probably related to cultural individualism-collectivism. Communication linked to the ingroup-outgroup distinction, however, also may be related to other dimensions of cultural variability. If individuals are of unequal status, for example, cultural power distance also should affect communication. Also, if the individuals' genders differ, cultural masculinity-femininity should influence communication.

Many aspects of communication are affected by more than one dimension of cultural variability (Gudykunst & Ting-Toomey, 1988). To understand communication with strangers, for example, it probably is necessary to use both individualism-collectivism and uncertainty avoidance. Members of collectivistic cultures, for example, respond differently to strangers depending on whether they come from low uncertainty avoidance or high uncertainty avoidance cultures (see Gudykunst & Bond, 1997). Furthermore, when Asian cultures are studied, it is particularly important to use multiple dimensions of cultural variability. Asian cultures tend to be collectivistic, but some of the differences among them are a function of differences in uncertainty avoidance (see Gudykunst & Bond, 1997).

Number of Cultures Studied

The vast majority of cross-cultural studies involve comparing communication in only two cultures. One reason for this trend is the difficulty of forming research teams involving more than two cultures. Another difficulty involves problems in developing derived etic measures in multiple cultures. Also, the more cultures in which data are collected, the longer it takes to complete the research.

Studying communication in more than two cultures is necessary to test the effect of dimensions of cultural variability on communication. To ensure that communication is due to cultural individualism-collectivism, for example, at least four cultures are needed (two predominantly individualistic and two predominantly collectivistic). There must be consistency of responses within at least two individualistic and two collectivistic cultures, and differences between the individualistic and collectivistic cultures. Without at least four cultures, the results may be due to unique aspects of the cultures studied rather than the dimensions of cultural variability studied. This is complicated when communication is a function of more than one dimension of cultural variability.

If communication is a function of more than one dimension of cultural variability, at least eight cultures are needed to adequately test theoretical hypotheses. To illustrate, assume communication is theoretically predicted to be a function of individualism-collectivism and masculinity-femininity. To test such predictions, samples from eight cultures are needed: two predominantly individualistic, masculine cultures; two predominantly individualistic, feminine cultures; two predominantly collectivistic, masculine cultures; and two predominantly collectivistic, feminine cultures. Also, the aspect of communication under study needs to be linked clearly to specific cultural norms/rules, because individualism-collectivism and masculinity-femininity tendencies exist in all cultures.

Ignoring Individual-Level Mediators of Cultural-Level Phenomena

The vast majority of cross-cultural studies do not include individual-level factors that mediate the influence of the cultural dimension(s) under study. Future research must take the individual-level factors into consideration.

As indicated earlier, some behavior is a function of cultural norms and rules, and some is due to individual variability within cultures. The only way that these differential effects can be isolated is if individual-level mediators of the cultural dimension under study are included in the research (this requires derived etic measures of these mediators). Including individual-level mediators is also important because they allow researchers to determine if their samples are representative of the cultural dimension under study.[5]

Representativeness of Respondents

Most cross-cultural researchers do not present clear evidence that their respondents are representative of the cultural-level processes studied (this is not an issue in all studies; e.g., political advertisements). When samples are collected in individualistic and collectivistic cultures, for example, the respondents in collectivistic cultures often are highly individualistic (see Gudykunst & Nishida, 1999; Triandis, Bontempo, Villareal, Asai, & Lucca, 1988). This is especially problematic with student samples.

When the samples are not representative of the cultures from which they were drawn, conclusions regarding dimensions of cultural variability are questionable. Members of collectivistic cultures who emphasize an independent self construal and do not emphasize an interdependent self construal will not necessarily follow the ingroup norms, and their behaviors, therefore, may not be representative of collective cultures. When the results of a study are inconsistent with theoretical hypotheses, lack of representativeness of the respondents becomes a rival hypothesis for the results that cannot be ruled out unless individual-level mediators are measured. It is imperative that individual-level mediators of cultural processes be included in the analyses when samples are not representative of the dimensions of cultural variability under study (e.g., a sample from Japan is more individualistic than a sample from the United States).

Methods of Data Analysis

Many different analytic procedures have been used in cross-cultural studies of communication in recent years. Many of the analyses treat culture and individual-level mediators of cultural variability as if they were at the same level of analysis. They are not; culture is not an individual trait. The analytic procedures used need to recognize they are at different levels.

As indicated earlier, individual-level mediators of the dimensions of cultural variability (e.g., self construals when individualism-collectivism is used) need to be assessed when dimensions of cultural variability are used to make theoretical predictions to ensure that the samples represent the dimensions under study. Also, dimensions of cultural variability and individual-level mediators may be used to make predictions in the same study. Most studies also tend to examine more than one related dependent variable. Given these conditions, multivariate analysis of covariance (MANCOVA) is the most appropriate method of data analysis.

In conducting a MANCOVA, culture (e.g., Japan/United States) and any manipulated variables (e.g., ingroup/outgroup communication) should be treated as the independent variables. Individual-level mediators of the dimensions of cultural variability used to make predictions should be treated as covariates. If the manipulation check indicates that the samples do not represent the dimensions of cultural variability being studied (e.g., a sample from Japan scores higher on independent self construal than a U.S. sample), then the covariates should be entered into the analysis before the main effect. By doing this, the effect of the lack of representativeness of the samples will be statistically "controlled" so that the effect of culture can be examined.

If researchers hypothesize that the individual-level mediators are better predictors of the dependent variables than culture, MANCOVA also can be used. Two analyses could be used. First, compute the effect of culture on the dependent variables without the individual level mediators included as covariates, and examine the multivariate variance explained (e.g., 1 – Wilks's lambda). Second, compute a MANCOVA with the individual-level mediators included as covariates, and examine the multivariate variance explained by culture. If the individual-level mediators are the best predictors, the variance explained by culture should decrease from Analysis 1 to Analysis 2, and the variance explained by the covariates should be larger than the variance explained by culture in Analysis 2.

No matter how the initial analyses are conducted when individual-level mediators are included, follow-up analyses must be conducted within cultures. The results for the covariates in MANCOVA, for example, only tell researchers the effect of the individual-level mediators across the cultures studied. Culture, however, has a patterning effect on data. The individual-level mediators, therefore, may have different effects on the dependent variables within cultures. This can be determined only by examining the effects within cultures (e.g., regression analyses can be conducted within cultures).

Use of Only One Method

Most cross-cultural studies use only one type of data (e.g., survey) to test hypotheses. If multiple methods are not used, it is possible that the results are due to the methods used. To illustrate, Asian respondents may not use the response end-points (e.g., *strongly agree* or *strongly disagree*) in surveys (e.g., Chen et al., 1995). As indicated earlier, in this situation differences in the mean scores obtained may be due to the way Asians respond to surveys rather than to cultural differences in behavior (response differences can be taken into consideration in data analysis by using standardized scores). Other problems emerge when respondents in one culture are unfamiliar with stimulus material that members of another culture see regularly (e.g., many cognitive tests).

Closely related to the use of one method is the use of only etic or emic approaches. To fully understand behavior across cultures, however, both emic and etic measures are needed. Etic measures allow us to understand commonalities across cultures, and emic measures allow us to understand unique aspects of behavior within cultures.

Ideally, multiple methods should be used to study behavior across cultures. Multiple methods allow researchers to rule out methods effects as a rival hypothesis for findings. Multiple methods also allow for *triangulation* of research findings (e.g., finding results that support a hypothesis using different methods).

CONCLUSION

It is impossible to discuss research methods in isolation from theory. The methods that researchers use are based on the meta-theoretical assumptions they make and the theories they use to guide their thinking. Conducting methodologically sound cross-cultural research requires the cooperation of culturally diverse research teams. The research teams need to be committed to working together on common lines of research over a period of time, not just one study. Only when a team of researchers works together over a period of time can the researchers develop methodologically sound procedures for conducting cross-cultural research that will contribute to our theoretical understanding of culture and communication.

NOTES

1. *Cross-cultural* and *intercultural* are used as interchangeable. They are, nevertheless, different. Cross-cultural research involves comparing behavior in two or more cultures (e.g., comparing self-

disclosure in Japan, the United States, and Iran when individuals interact with members of their own culture). Intercultural research involves examining behavior when members of two or more cultures interact (e.g., examining self-disclosure when Japanese and Iranians communicate with each other). Intercultural behavior often is compared with intracultural behavior (e.g., behavior within a culture). To illustrate, Iranian self-disclosure when communicating with Japanese might be compared with Iranian communication with other Iranians. Understanding cross-cultural differences in behavior is a prerequisite for understanding intercultural behavior. I, therefore, focus on issues of conducting cross-cultural research in this chapter. See Barnett's chapter in this volume for a discussion of methods for studying intercultural communication.

2. Obviously, there should be a "manipulation check" for the manipulated variable.

3. In his review of this chapter, Michael Bond indicated that he factor analyzes the average correlation matrices to achieve the same result.

4. All research involves trade-offs. One problem may be accepted to control for another. There are few, if any, studies that are problem free, including my own.

5. This is an important issue. If researchers find, for example, that self construals do not fit the expected pattern, this does not mean that self construals are not solid individual-level indicators of cultural individualism-collectivism. Rather, it probably means that the samples are not representative of cultural individualism-collectivism.

REFERENCES

Berry, J. (1969). On cross-cultural comparability. *International Journal of Psychology, 4,* 119-128.

Berry, J. (1980). Introduction to methodology. In H. C. Triandis & J. Berry (Eds.), *Handbook of cross-cultural psychology* (Vol. 2, pp. 1-28). Boston: Allyn & Bacon.

Berry, J. W., Poortinga, Y. H., & Pandey, J. (Eds.). (1997). *Handbook of cross-cultural psychology: Vol. 1. Theory and method* (2nd ed.). Boston: Allyn & Bacon.

Bond, M. H. (1998). Social psychology across cultures. In J. Adair, D. Belanges, & K. Dion (Eds.), *Advances in psychological science* (Vol. 1, pp. 137-150). Sussex, UK: Psychology Press.

Brislin, R. (1976). *Translation: Application and research.* New York: Gardner.

Brislin, R., & Baumgardner, S. (1971). Non-random sampling of individuals in cross-cultural research. *Journal of Cross-Cultural Psychology, 2,* 397-400.

Brislin, R., Lonner, W., & Thorndike, R. (1973). *Cross-cultural research methods.* New York: John Wiley.

Burrell, G., & Morgan, G. (1979). *Sociological paradigms and organizational analysis.* London: Heinemann.

Campbell, D., & Stanley, J. (1966). *Experimental and quasi-experimental designs for research.* Chicago: Rand McNally.

Chen, C. S., Lee, S. Y., & Stevenson, H. (1995). Response style and cross-cultural comparisons of rating scales among East Asians and North American students. *Psychological Science, 6,* 170-175.

Enber, C., & Enber, M. (2000). *Cross-cultural research methods.* Walnut Creek, CA: AltaMira.

Goldschmidt, W. (1966). *Comparative functionalism.* Berkeley: University of California Press.

Gudykunst, W. B. (2000). Methodological issues in conducting theory-based cross-cultural research. In H. Spencer-Oatey (Ed.), *Culturally speaking* (pp. 293-315). London: Cassell Academic.

Gudykunst, W. B., & Bond, M. H. (1997). Intergroup relations. In J. W. Berry, M. H. Segall, & Ç. Kâgitçibasi (Eds.), *Handbook of cross-cultural psychology: Vol. 3. Social behavior and applications* (2nd ed., pp. 119-161). Boston: Allyn & Bacon.

Gudykunst, W. B., Matsumoto, Y., Ting-Toomey, S., Nishida, T., Kim, K. S., & Heyman, S. (1996). The influence of cultural individualism-collectivism, self construals, and individual values on communication styles across cultures. *Human Communication Research, 22,* 510-543.

Gudykunst, W. B., & Nishida, T. (1999). The influence of culture and strength of cultural identity on individual values in Japan and the United

States. *Intercultural Communication Studies, 9,* 1-18.

Gudykunst, W. B., & Ting-Toomey, S. (with Chua, E.) (1988). *Culture and interpersonal communication.* Newbury Park, CA: Sage.

Hasegawa, T., & Gudykunst, W. B. (1998). Silence in Japan and the United States. *Journal of Cross-Cultural Psychology, 29,* 668-684.

Klopf, D., & Cambra, R. (1979). Communication apprehension among college students in America, Australia, Japan, and Korea. *Journal of Psychology, 102,* 27-31.

Leung, K., & Bond, M. (1989). On the empirical identification of dimensions for cross-cultural comparisons. *Journal of Cross-Cultural Psychology, 20,* 133-151.

Leung, K., & Bond, M. H. (1984). The impact of cultural collectivism on reward allocation. *Journal of Personality and Social Psychology, 49,* 793-804.

Lonner, W. (1979). Issues in cross-cultural psychology. In A. Marsella, A. Tharp, & T. Cibrowski (Eds.), *Perspectives in cross-cultural psychology* (pp. 17-45). New York: Academic Press.

Lonner, W., & Berry, J. (Eds.). (1986). *Field methods in cross-cultural research.* Beverly Hills, CA: Sage.

Malpass, R., & Poortinga, Y. (1986). Strategies for design and analysis. In W. Lonner & J. Berry (Eds.), *Field methods in cross-cultural research* (pp. 47-84). Beverly Hills, CA: Sage.

Peng, K., Nisbett, R., & Wong, N. (1997). Validity problems comparing values across cultures and possible solutions. *Psychological Methods, 2,* 329-344.

Pike, K. (1966). *Language in relation to a unified theory of the structure of human behavior.* The Hague: Mouton.

Poortinga, Y. (1975). Limitations of intercultural comparisons of psychological data. *Netherlands Tijschrift voor de Psychologie, 30,* 23-39.

Poortinga, Y., & Malpass, R. (1986). Making inferences from cross-cultural data. In W. Lonner & J. Berry (Eds.), *Field methods in cross-cultural psychology* (pp. 17-46). Beverly Hills, CA: Sage.

Sears, R. (1961). Transcultural variables and conceptual equivalence. In B. Kaplan (Ed.), *Studying personality cross-culturally* (pp. 445-455). Evanston, IL: Row & Petersen.

Triandis, H. C., & Berry, J. (Eds.). (1980). *Handbook of cross-cultural psychology: Methodology* (Vol. 2). Boston: Allyn & Bacon.

Triandis, H. C., Bontempo, R., Villareal, M., Asai, M., & Lucca, N. (1988). Individualism-collectivism: Cross-cultural studies on self-ingroup relationships. *Journal of Personality and Social Psychology, 54,* 323-338.

Triandis, H. C., Malpass, R., & Davidson, A. (1973). Cross-cultural psychology. *Biennial Review of Anthropology, 24,* 1-84.

van de Vijver, F. (in press). The evolution of cross-cultural research methods. In D. Matsumoto (Ed.), *Handbook of culture and psychology.* New York: Oxford University Press.

van de Vijver, F., & Leung, K. (1997a). *Methods and data analysis for cross-cultural research.* Thousand Oaks, CA: Sage.

van de Vijver, F., & Leung, K. (1997b). Methods and data analysis of comparative research. In J. W. Berry, Y. H. Poortinga, & J. Pandey (Eds.), *Handbook of cross-cultural psychology: Vol. 1. Theory and method* (2nd ed., pp. 257-300). Boston: Allyn & Bacon.

van de Vijver, F., & Leung, K. (2000). Methodological issues in psychological research on culture. *Journal of Cross-Cultural Psychology, 31,* 33-51.

PART II

Intercultural Communication

Introduction

William B. Gudykunst

The focus of this section is intercultural communication. Intercultural communication generally is conceptualized as communication between people from different national cultures, and many scholars limit it to face-to-face communication. I view intercultural communication as one "type" of intergroup communication (i.e., communication between members of different social groups). Intergroup communication includes many types of communication that may not be included under the rubric of intercultural communication; for example, communication between able-bodied and disabled, intergenerational communication, communication between members of different social classes, and interracial/interethnic communication.

In deciding on the content of this part, it was necessary to limit what was covered because of space limitations. Since one thing that intercultural, international, and development communication share in common is a focus on culture, I decided to limit the content to intercultural communication. There is extensive research in many areas of intergroup communication that is related to the content of this part. Braithwaite and Thompson (2000), for example, edited a handbook on communication with the disabled. Similarly, Williams and Nussbaum (2001) summarize research on intergenerational communication across the life span.

There are several recent analyses of interracial/interethnic communication. I, therefore, decided not to include chapters on it here. Ellis (1999), for example, examines how ethnicity and social class influence discourse processes. Hecht's (1998) volume contains analyses of how prejudice is communicated in interracial communication. Leets and Giles (1997) examine the effects of harmful speech in intergroup encounters. Milhouse, Asante, and Nwosu's (2001) edited volume contains contributions that focus on various aspects of interracial communication.

Given the space limitations, I had to limit the intercultural communication topics examined in this part. The previous edition of the *Handbook* contained a chapter on intercultural training. Since there have been several recent reviews on this topic (e.g., Brislin & Horvath, 1997; Cargile & Giles, 1996; Landis & Bhagat, 1996), I decided to omit it here.

Two other areas that ideally would have been included if space allowed are intercultural communication in small-group and organizational contexts. There are, however, recent reviews of these areas of research. Granrose and Oskamp's (1997) volume, for example, contains several studies of communication in intercultural small groups, and Oetzel, Burtis, Chew Sanchez, and Pérez's (2001) review research on communication in intercultural small groups. There also have been several recent analyses of intercultural issues in organizations (e.g., Chemers, Oskamp, & Costanzo, 1995; Earley, 1997; Punnett & Shenkar, 1995; Wiseman & Shuter, 1994).

One area of research I would like to have included, but did not, is power in intercultural communication. Power is an important aspect of many intercultural encounters, but not all encounters. Unfortunately, there is insufficient research on power in intercultural interactions on which to base a chapter. I hope this is not true when the next edition of the *Handbook* is published.

Given what is not included in this part, I turn attention to what is included. The first chapter is my review of intercultural communication theories (I wrote this chapter because

the original author could not complete the chapter on time, and it was too late to find another author). I summarize 15 theories, divided into five categories: theories focusing on effective outcomes, theories focusing on accommodation or adaptation, theories focusing on identity negotiation, theories focusing on communication networks, and theories focusing on acculturation or adjustment. The majority of these theories are published in volumes of the *International and Intercultural Communication Annual* that focus on theories (Gudykunst, 1983; Kim & Gudykunst, 1988; Wiseman, 1995).

The second chapter is Wiseman's analysis of intercultural communication competence. Wiseman examines the conceptualization of intercultural communication competence and reviews several exemplar theories of competence. Many of these theories are contained in the volume of the *International and Intercultural Communication Annual* that he edited on this topic (Wiseman & Koester, 1993). He also overviews areas of research related to intercultural communication competence (e.g., second-language competence) and proposes areas where future research is needed.

The third chapter is Abrams, O'Connor, and Giles's review of identity and intergroup communication. Given the nature of identities, the authors of this chapter use an intergroup perspective. Abrams et al. examine the major research on the influence of identity on communication. They isolate propositions that summarize the research reviewed. They conclude by proposing a framework for future research that includes both objective and subjective components of identity. Camilleri and Malewska-Peyre's (1997) analysis of socialization and identity strategies across cultures complements the material covered in this chapter.

The fourth chapter is Chen's review of research on communication in intercultural relationships. Since there is not a chapter on cross-cultural comparisons of communication in relationships, she begins with a brief review of this research. Next, Chen analyzes research on communication in intercultural relationships, including dating and marital relationships. Chen concludes by proposing a dialectical perspective that she uses to integrate previous research and suggest areas for future research. Gudykunst and Bond's (1997) review of research on intergroup relationships across cultures and Gareis's (1999) review of research on intercultural friendships complement Chen's review.

The fifth chapter is Kim's review of research on intercultural adaptation. She examines both short-term and long-term adaptation. Kim reviews the major lines of research, focusing on research looking at adaptation as a "problem" and adaptation as a "growth" process. She isolates the major indicators and predictors of adaptation. Kim's (2001) book updates her theory and contain a summary of the vast majority of research conducted on communication acculturation. Berry and Sam (1997) and Ward (2001) provide complementary reviews of acculturation from psychological perspectives. Ward argues for an integrated theory of acculturation. Sussman (2000) examines how cultural identities change as a function of cultural transitions. The processes Sussman isolates are related directly to Kim's discussion of adaptation as a "growth" process.

The final chapter is Barnett and Lee's analysis of issues in intercultural communication research. The authors present a structural model of intercultural communication based on networks. They also briefly summarize research on intercultural networks (also see the network theories in Gudykunst's "Intercultural Communication Theories" chapter). Barnett and Lee conceptualize the major problems in conducting intercultural communication research, and discuss issues of globalization and intercultural communication

research. They argue that interpersonal and mediated channels of communication often need to be studied together.

Taken together, the chapters in this section of the *Handbook* provide reviews of the major theories and lines of research in intercultural communication. The chapter authors provide well-thought-out suggestions for future research. I hope readers will use these chapters as resources in developing theories and conducting research on intercultural communication.

REFERENCES

Berry, J., & Sam, D. (1997). Acculturation and adaptation. In J. W. Berry, M. H. Segall, & Ç. Kâgitçibasi (Eds.), *Handbook of cross-cultural psychology: Vol. 3. Social behavior and applications* (2nd ed., pp. 291-326). Boston: Allyn & Bacon.

Braithwaite, D., & Thompson, T. (Eds.). (2000). *Handbook of communication and people with disabilities*. Hillsdale, NJ: Lawrence Erlbaum.

Brislin, R., & Horwath, A.-M. (1997). Cross-cultural training and multicultural education. In J. W. Berry, M. H. Segall, & Ç. Kâgitçibasi (Eds.), *Handbook of cross-cultural psychology: Vol. 3. Social behavior and applications* (2nd ed., pp. 327-370). Boston: Allyn & Bacon.

Camilleri, C., & Malewska-Peyre, H. (1997). Socialization and identity strategies. In J. W. Berry, P. R. Dasen, & T. S. Saraswathi (Eds.), *Handbook of cross-cultural psychology: Vol. 2. Basic processes and human development* (2nd ed., pp. 41-68). Boston: Allyn & Bacon.

Cargile, A., & Giles, H. (1996). Intercultural communication training. In B. Burleson (Ed.), *Communication yearbook 19* (pp. 385-424). Thousand Oaks, CA: Sage.

Chemers, M., Oskamp, S., & Costanzo, M. (Eds.). (1995). *Diversity in organizations*. Thousand Oaks, CA: Sage.

Earley, P. C. (1997). *Face, harmony, and social structure: An analysis of organizational behavior across cultures*. New York: Oxford University Press.

Ellis, D. (1999). *Crafting society.* Hillsdale, NJ: Lawrence Erlbaum.

Gareis, E. (1999). Adult friendship: Examples of intercultural patterns. In M. Roloff (Ed.), *Communication yearbook 22* (pp. 431-468). Thousand Oaks, CA: Sage.

Granrose, C., & Oskamp, S. (Eds.). (1997). *Cross-cultural work groups.* Thousand Oaks, CA: Sage.

Gudykunst, W. B. (Ed.). (1983). *Intercultural communication theory.* Beverly Hills, CA: Sage.

Gudykunst, W. B., & Bond, M. H. (1997). Intergroup relations across cultures. In J. W. Berry, M. H. Segall, & Ç. Kâgitçibasi (Eds.), *Handbook of cross-cultural psychology: Vol. 3. Social behavior and applications* (2nd ed., pp. 119-162). Boston: Allyn & Bacon.

Hecht, M. (Ed.). (1998). *Communicating prejudice.* Thousand Oaks, CA: Sage.

Kim, Y. Y. (2001). *Becoming intercultural.* Thousand Oaks, CA: Sage.

Kim, Y. Y., & Gudykunst, W. B. (Eds.). (1988). *Theories in intercultural communication.* Newbury Park, CA: Sage.

Landis, D., & Bhagat, R. (Eds.). (1996). *Handbook of intercultural training* (2nd ed.). Thousand Oaks, CA: Sage.

Leets, L., & Giles, H. (1997). Harmful speech in intergroup encounters. In M. Roloff (Ed.), *Communication yearbook 22* (pp. 91-138). Thousand Oaks, CA: Sage.

Milhouse, V., Asante, M. K., & Nwosu, P. (Eds.). (2001). *Transcultural realities.* Thousand Oaks, CA: Sage.

Oetzel, J., Burtis, T., Chew Sanchez, M., & Pérez, F. (2001). Investigating the role of communication in culturally diverse work groups. In W. B. Gudykunst (Ed.), *Communication yearbook 25* (pp. 237-270). Mahwah, NJ: Lawrence Erlbaum.

Punnett, B., & Shenkar, D. (Eds.). (1995). *Handbook for international management research.* Cambridge, UK: Basil Blackwell.

Sussman, N. (2000). The dynamic nature of cultural identity throughout cultural transitions. *Personality and Social Psychology Review, 4,* 355-373.

Ward, C. (2001). The A, B, Cs of acculturation. In D. Matsumoto (Ed.), *Handbook of culture and psychology* (pp. 411-445). New York: Oxford University Press.

Williams, A., & Nussbaum, J. (2001). *Intergenerational communication across the lifespan.* Hillsdale, NJ: Lawrence Erlbaum.

Wiseman, R. L. (Ed.). (1995). *Intercultural communication theory.* Thousand Oaks, CA: Sage.

Wiseman, R. L., & Koester, J. (Eds.). (1993). *Intercultural communication competence.* Newbury Park, CA: Sage.

Wiseman, R. L., & Shuter, R. (Eds.). (1994). *Communication in multinational organizations.* Thousand Oaks, CA: Sage.

9

Intercultural Communication Theories

WILLIAM B. GUDYKUNST
California State University, Fullerton

Theorizing about intercultural communication has made tremendous progress in the past 20 years. When I completed my doctorate, there were no theories of intercultural communication.[1] Initial attempts to theorize about interpersonal communication between people from different cultures were included in the first thematic volume of the *International and Intercultural Communication Annual* published by Sage (Gudykunst, 1983).[2] Most of the chapters in the volume were initial attempts at theorizing about intercultural communication. By the time the second volume of the *Annual* on theory was published (Kim & Gudykunst, 1988), theorizing had increased in sophistication and there were theories supported by lines of research. There was another leap in the quality of theorizing when the most recent volume of the *Annual* on theory was published (Wiseman, 1995).[3] Today, there are at least 15 theories covering different aspects of intercultural communication.

Gudykunst and Nishida (1989) used Burrell and Morgan's (1979) distinction between objectivist and subjectivist approaches to theory to compare theories in intercultural communication. Objectivists, for example, see a "real world" external to individuals, look for regularities in behavior, and see communication as "determined" by situations and environments. Subjectivists, in contrast, contend that there is no "real world" external to individuals, try to understand individual communicators' perspectives, and view communication as a function of "free will." Gudykunst and Nishida suggest that extreme objectivist or subjectivist perspectives are not defensible. They argue that both approaches are

---

EDITORS' NOTE: This chapter was scheduled to be written by another author, who could not complete it by the deadline. By the time this person dropped out, it was too late to find another author. The chapter, however, is too important to drop. The section editor, therefore, wrote the chapter.

necessary to understand intercultural communication and that the ideal is to eventually integrate the two perspectives.

My purpose in this chapter is to summarize the major theories of intercultural communication.[4] When possible, I summarize all of the propositions in the theories. Many theories, however, are too complicated to present all propositions. For these theories, I provide broad overviews. I divide the theories into five categories that are not necessarily mutually exclusive: (1) theories focusing on effective outcomes, (2) theories focusing on accommodation or adaptation, (3) theories focusing on identity management or negotiation, (4) theories focusing on communication networks, and (5) theories focusing on acculturation or adjustment. Both objectivistic and subjectivistic theories are included. The majority of the theories, however, are objectivistic. Very few of the theorists attempt to integrate objectivistic and subjectivistic assumptions.[5] I begin with theories that focus on effective outcomes.

THEORIES FOCUSING ON EFFECTIVE OUTCOMES

One goal of theorizing is to explain specific outcomes. One outcome that intercultural theorists have used in developing theories is effective communication and effective group decisions. Three theories fit in this category: (1) cultural convergence theory (e.g., Barnett & Kincaid, 1983), (2) anxiety/uncertainty management theory (e.g., Gudykunst, 1995), and (3) effective group decision making theory (e.g., Oetzel, 1995).

Cultural Convergence

Cultural convergence theory (Barnett & Kincaid, 1983; Kincaid, 1988) is based on Kincaid's (1979; also see Rogers & Kincaid, 1981) convergence model of communication.[6] Kincaid (1979) defines communication as "a process in which two or more individuals or groups share information in order to reach a mutual understanding of each other and the world in which they live" (p. 31). He argues that mutual understanding can be approached but never perfectly achieved. "By means of several iterations of information-exchange, two or more individuals may converge towards a more mutual understanding of each other's meaning" (p. 32).

Barnett and Kincaid (1983) use the convergence model of communication to develop a mathematical theory of the effects of communication on cultural differences. They argue that "the laws of thermodynamics predict that all participants in a closed system will converge over time on the mean collective pattern of thought if communication is allowed to continue indefinitely" (p. 175). Information that is introduced from outside the system can delay convergence or reverse it (i.e., lead to divergence). They present a mathematical model that predicts the convergence of the collective cognitive states of members of two cultures whose members are interacting. Kincaid's (1979) convergence model applies to individual-level communication, and Barnett and Kincaid's mathematical theory applies to group-level phenomena (e.g., culture).

Kincaid (1987, 1988) presents the theory in verbal form. Kincaid (1988) summarizes the theory in two theorems and three hypotheses. Theorem 1, for example, states that "in a relatively closed social system in which communication among members is unrestricted, the system as a whole will tend to *converge* over time toward a state of greater cultural *uniformity*" (p. 289). The system will tend to diverge toward diversity when communication is restricted (Theorem 2). The hypotheses apply the theorems to the case of immigrant groups and native/host cultures.

Kincaid, Yum, Woelfel, and Barnett (1983) tested the predictions of cultural convergence theory for Korean immigrants in Hawaii. The data fit the equations presented by Barnett and Kincaid (1983). Convergence theory has been applied to communication and development (Buck, Kincaid, Nichter, & Nichter, 1983) and the study of communication networks (Rogers & Kincaid, 1981).

Anxiety/Uncertainty Management

Gudykunst (1985) extends Berger and Calabrese's (1975) uncertainty reduction theory (URT) to intergroup encounters as the first step in developing anxiety/uncertainty management (AUM) theory. Gudykunst and Hammer (1988) used uncertainty (e.g., the inability to predict or explain others' attitudes, behavior, or feelings) and anxiety (e.g., feelings of being uneasy, tense, worried, or apprehensive) to explain intercultural adjustment (see adjustment section below).

Gudykunst (1988) proffered a general theory using uncertainty and anxiety to explain effective interpersonal and intergroup communication (i.e., minimize misunderstandings). Intercultural communication is one type of intergroup communication in AUM theory. Gudykunst (1988) uses Simmel's (1908/1950) notion of "the stranger" (e.g., individuals who are present in a situation but are not members of the ingroup) as a central organizing concept. This initial version of the theory included 13 abstract axioms (11 dealing with effective communication and 2 focusing on cross-cultural variability). Gudykunst (1990) applied the axioms of the 1988 version of the theory to diplomacy, a special case of intergroup communication.

Gudykunst (1993) expanded AUM theory using a competency framework (Note: The

label "AUM" was first used in this version). Gudykunst specified the meta-theoretical assumptions of the theory in this version. The assumptions underlying the theory avoid the extreme objectivist or subjectivist positions (e.g., he assumes that individuals' communication is influenced by their cultures and group memberships, but they also can choose how they communicate when they are mindful). Furthermore, Gudykunst expanded the number of axioms (49) in the theory to make the theory easier to understand (see Reynolds, 1971) and easier to apply.[7] This version of the theory also incorporates minimum and maximum thresholds for uncertainty and anxiety. Finally, Gudykunst integrated Langer's (1989) notion of mindfulness as a moderating process between AUM and effective communication in this version.

The most recent version of AUM theory designed to explain effective interpersonal and intergroup communication is Gudykunst (1995). This version is a modification of Gudykunst (1993) using a different organizing framework (see Figure 9.1), and incorporating cultural variability in AUM processes (see Gudykunst & Lee, Chapter 2 in this volume, for a discussion of the cultural variability part of the theory).

Following Lieberson (1985), Gudykunst (1995) argues that there are *basic* and *superficial* causes of effective communication. He contends that anxiety and uncertainty management are the basic causes of effective communication, and the effect of other variables (e.g., ability to empathize, attraction to strangers) on effective communication is mediated through anxiety and uncertainty management. The extent to which individuals are mindful of their behavior moderates the influence of their anxiety and uncertainty management on their communication effectiveness. Gudykunst (1995) suggests that dialectical processes are involved in AUM (e.g., the uncertainty dialectic involves novelty and

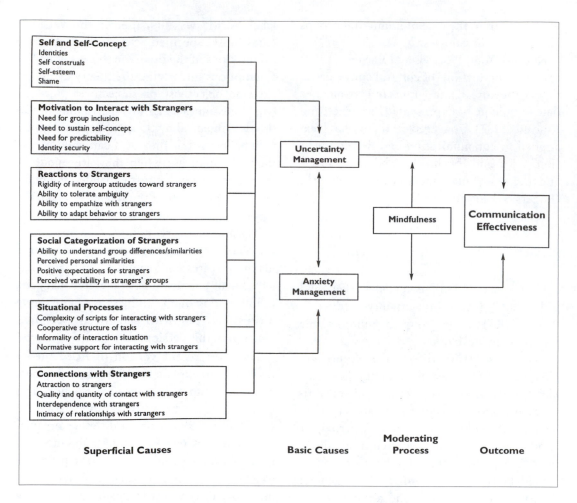

Figure 9.1.   A Schematic Representation of Anxiety/Uncertainty Management Theory
SOURCE: Gudykunst and Nishida (2001).

predictability), but these processes have not been elaborated.

There is extensive research supporting AUM theory. Gudykunst and Shapiro (1996), for example, examine differences in AUM processes in intragroup and intergroup relationships. Hubbert, Gudykunst, and Guerrero (1999) report that anxiety and uncertainty influence perceived effectiveness of communication over time, and unreported data from this study suggest that perceived effectiveness of communication at one point in time affects anxiety and uncertainty the next time individuals interact. Gudykunst and Nishida (2001)

demonstrate that anxiety and uncertainty influence perceived effectiveness of communication in ingroup and outgroup relationships in Japan and the United States.

Effective Group Decision Making

Oetzel (1995) proposes a theory of effective decision making in intercultural groups. Oetzel integrates Hirokawa and Rost's (1992) vigilant interaction theory (VIT) and Ting-Toomey's (1988) cross-cultural theory of face-negotiation and conflict management.

Hirokawa and Rost (1992) assume that the way members of groups talk about things (e.g., problems) associated with group decisions influences how they think about things associated with the decisions they must make. How group members think about things associated with the decisions they make influences the quality of their decisions. A group's final decision is a result of "a series of interrelated subdecisions" (p. 270). Oetzel (1995) suggests that VIT may be limited to monocultural groups in the United States because different outcomes are emphasized in individualistic and collectivistic cultures.[8] He, therefore, defines decision effectiveness in terms of quality and appropriateness.

Oetzel's (1995) theory contains 14 propositions. The initial set of propositions focuses on homogeneous (e.g., monocultural) and heterogeneous (e.g., intercultural) groups. He contends that when members of homogeneous groups activate independent self construals, they emphasize task outcomes; when they activate interdependent self construals, they emphasize relational outcomes (P1). Members of homogeneous groups who activate independent self construals are less likely to reach consensus and will have more conflict and manage it less cooperatively than members of homogeneous groups who activate interdependent self construals (P3, P5, P6). Member contributions tend to be more equal in homogeneous groups and members are more committed to the group than are members in heterogeneous groups (P2, P4).

Oetzel (1995) contends that when most members activate independent self construals, they tend to use dominating conflict strategies. When most members activate interdependent self construals, in contrast, they tend to use avoiding, compromising, or obliging conflict strategies (P7). Groups that use cooperative styles to manage conflict make more effective decisions than groups that use competing or avoiding styles (P8). Groups in

which members activate personal identities make better decisions than groups in which members activate social identities (P9).

Oetzel's (1995) theory suggests that the more equal member contributions and the more group members are committed to the group and its decision, the more effective the decisions (P10, P11, P12). Consensus decisions are more effective than majority or compromise decisions (P13). Finally, Oetzel believes that the "fundamental requisites" of VIT apply to intercultural groups: Groups that understand the problem, establish "good" criteria, develop many alternatives, and examine the positive/negative consequences of the alternatives make more effective decisions than those that do not (P14).

Not all propositions in Oetzel's (1995) theory have been tested. There is, however, research to support several of the propositions (e.g., Oetzel, 1998). Oetzel, Burtis, Chew Sanchez, and Pérez (2001) summarize research related to the theory.

THEORIES FOCUSING ON ACCOMMODATION OR ADAPTATION

Another goal on which theorists focus is how communicators accommodate or adapt to each other. There are three theories that fit this category: (1) communication accommodation theory (e.g., Gallois, Giles, Jones, Cargile, & Ota, 1995), (2) intercultural adaptation theory (e.g., Ellingsworth, 1988), and (3) co-cultural theory (e.g., Orbe, 1998b).

Communication Accommodation

Communication accommodation theory (CAT) originated in Giles's (1973) work on accent mobility. CAT began as speech accommodation theory (SAT; e.g., Giles & Smith,

1979). SAT proposed that speakers use linguistic strategies to gain approval or to show distinctiveness in their interactions with others. The main strategies communicators use based on these motivations are speech convergence or divergence. These are "linguistic moves" to decrease or increase communicative distances, respectively.

Giles, Mulac, Bradac, and Johnson (1987) expanded SAT in terms of the range of phenomena covered and relabeled it CAT. Coupland, Coupland, Giles, and Henwood (1988) adapted CAT to intergenerational communication and incorporated additional modifications to the theory (e.g., conceptualizing speaker strategies as based on an "addressee focus" and incorporating addressees' attributions about speakers' behavior). Gallois, Franklyn-Stokes, Giles, and Coupland (1988) adapted Coupland et al.'s (1988) model to intercultural communication. This modification integrated predictions from ethnolinguistic identity theory (ELIT; e.g., Giles & Johnson, 1987) and emphasized the influence of situations on intercultural communication.

Gallois et al. (1995) updated the 1988 version of the theory, incorporating research that had been conducted and cross-cultural variability in accommodative processes. This version of the theory contains 17 propositions, with several propositions subdivided into two based on the processes that are occurring (e.g., when interlocutors are evaluated positively or negatively). It is impossible to summarize all of the propositions in the space available. I, therefore, outline the theory (Gallois et al., 1988) and present representative propositions. The theory is diagrammed in Figure 9.2.[9]

CAT begins with the *sociohistorical context* of the interaction. This includes the relations between the groups having contact and the social norms regarding contact (intercultural contact is one type of intergroup contact in

CAT). This component also includes cultural variability.

The second component of CAT is the communicators' *accommodative orientation*; their tendencies to perceive encounters with outgroup members in interpersonal terms, intergroup terms, or a combination of the two. There are three aspects to accommodative orientations: (1) "intrapersonal factors" (e.g., social identities, personal identities), (2) "intergroup factors" (e.g., factors that reflect communicators' orientations to outgroups such as perceived ingroup vitality), and (3) "initial orientations" (e.g., perceived potential for conflict, long-term accommodative motivation toward outgroups).

The perceived relations between groups influence communicators' tendencies to perceive encounters as interpersonal or intergroup (P1). Similarly, members of dominant groups who have insecure social identities and perceive threats with outgroups tend to perceive convergence by members of subordinate groups negatively (P3). Also, individuals who are dependent on their groups and feel solidarity with them tend to see encounters in intergroup terms and tend to emphasize linguistic markers of their groups (P8a).

The third component in CAT is the *immediate situation*. There are five aspects to the immediate situation: (1) "sociopsychological states" (e.g., communicators' interpersonal or intergroup orientation in the situation), (2) "goals and addressee focus" (e.g., motivations in the encounter, conversational needs, relational needs), (3) "sociolinguistic strategies" (e.g., approximation, discourse management), (4) "behavior and tactics" (e.g., language, accent, topic), and (5) "labeling and attributions." The five aspects of the immediate situation are interrelated.

Proposition 13b illustrates the propositions regarding the immediate situation: "When intergroup concerns are salient, speakers are likely to attempt to attune (or counterattune)

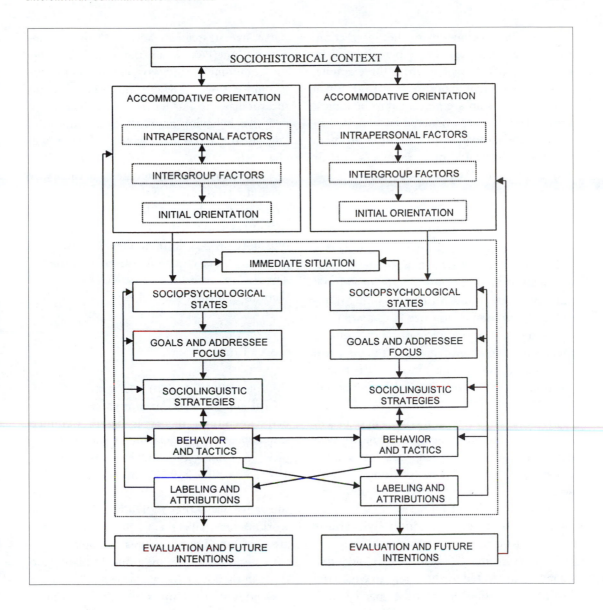

Figure 9.2. A Diagram of Communication Accommodation Theory
SOURCE: Gallois, Giles, Jones, Cargile, and Ota (1995). Used with permission of the authors and Sage Publications.

to their interlocutors through approximation, interpretability, discourse management, and interpersonal control strategies using group-marked behavior and behavior relevant to group differences and intergroup role relations" (Gallois et al., 1995, p. 145). Convergence and divergence are viewed as approxi-

mation strategies in this version of the theory. Proposition 13a focuses on when interpersonal factors are important in intergroup encounters.

The final component of CAT is *evaluation and future intentions.* The propositions here focus on communicators' perceptions of their interlocutors' behavior in the interaction. Convergent behavior that is perceived to be based on "benevolent intent," for example, tends to be evaluated positively (P15a). When interlocutors who are perceived to be typical group members are evaluated positively, individuals are motivated to communicate with the interlocutors and other members of their groups in the future (P16a).

Intercultural Adaptation

Ellingsworth (1983) assumes that all communication involves some degree of cultural variability. He suggests that explaining intercultural communication needs to start from interpersonal communication and cultural factors need to be incorporated. Ellingsworth presents "a rational generation of theory in a form that is subject to empirical examination" (p. 195).[10]

Ellingsworth's (1983) theory is designed to explain how communicators adapt to each other in "purpose-related encounters." He isolates eight "laws" (i.e., "ongoing relationships by which units affect one another," p. 201). Examples of Ellingsworth's laws are "Adaptation of communication style affects invocation of culture-based belief differences" (L2, p. 202) and "The burden of adaptive behavior is affected by the extent to which the setting favors one or the other participant" (L4, p. 202).

Based on the eight laws and the units in the theory, Ellingsworth (1983) generates 10 propositions (he notes that more could be generated). The propositions suggest that functionally adapting communication (P1) and equity in adaptation (P2) facilitate task completion. Nonfunctional adaptive communication leads to invocation of cultural differences (P3) and slowing task completion (P4). When communicators have to cooperate, there is equity in adapting communication (P5). Using

persuasive strategies leads to adapting communication (P6). When the situation favors one communicator (P7) or one communicator has more power (P8, P9), the other communicator has the burden to adapt. The more adaptive behavior in which communicators engage, the more their cultural beliefs will change (P10).

Ellingsworth (1988) updated the theory by expanding discussion of the laws and propositions in the theory. The theory, however, remains essentially the same (e.g., one less law, one more proposition). To date, I know of no research directly attributable to this theory. The theory, nevertheless, provides clear predictions that can be tested.

Co-Cultural

Orbe (1998a, 1998b) uses a phenomenological approach to develop co-cultural theory. Co-cultural theory is based in muted group theory (e.g., social hierarchies in society privilege some groups over others; Ardener, 1975; Kramarae, 1981) and standpoint theory (e.g., specific positions in society provide subjective ways that individuals look at the world; Smith, 1987). Co-cultures include but are not limited to nonwhites, women, people with disabilities, gay men and lesbians, and those in the lower social classes.

Orbe (1998b) points out that "in its most general form, co-cultural communication refers to interactions among underrepresented and dominant group members" (p. 3). The focus of co-cultural theory is providing a framework "by which co-cultural group members negotiate attempts by others to render their voices muted within dominant societal structures" (p. 4). Two premises guide co-cultural theory: (1) Co-cultural group members are marginalized in the dominant societal structures, and (2) co-cultural group members use certain communication styles to achieve success when confronting the "oppressive dominant structures."

Orbe (1998b) argues that co-cultural group members generally have one of three goals for their interactions with dominant group members: (1) assimilation (e.g., become part of the mainstream culture), (2) accommodation (e.g., try to get the dominant group members to accept co-cultural group members), or (3) separation (e.g., rejecting the possibility of common bonds with dominant group members). Other factors that influence co-cultural group members' communication are "field of experience" (e.g., past experiences), "abilities" (e.g., individuals' abilities to enact different practices), the "situational context" (e.g., where are they communicating with dominant group members), "perceived costs and rewards" (e.g., the pros and cons of certain practices), and the "communication approach" (i.e., being aggressive, assertive, or nonassertive).

Orbe (1998a, 1998b) isolates 26 practices (e.g., ways members of "marginalized groups" negotiate their muted group status," 1998b, p. 8) co-cultural group members use in their interaction with dominant group members. The practices used are a function of the co-cultural group members' goals and communication approaches. The combination of these yields nine communication orientations in which different practices tend to be used: (1) Nonassertive separation involves practices of "avoiding" and "maintaining interpersonal barriers"; (2) nonassertive accommodation involves practices of "increasing visibility" and "dispelling stereotypes"; (3) nonassertive assimilation involves practices of "emphasizing commonalities," "developing positive face," "censoring self," and "averting controversy"; (4) assertive separation involves practices of "communicating self," "intragroup networking," "exemplifying strengths," and "embracing stereotypes"; (5) assertive accommodation involves practices of "communicating self," "intragroup networking," "utilizing

liaisons," and "educating others"; (6) assertive assimilation involves practices of "extensive preparation," "overcompensating," "manipulating stereotypes," and "bargaining"; (7) aggressive separation involves practices of "attacking" and "sabotaging others"; (8) aggressive accommodation involves practices of "confronting" and "gaining advantage"; and (9) aggressive assimilation involves practices of "dissociating," "mirroring," "strategic distancing," and "ridiculing self."

THEORIES FOCUSING ON IDENTITY NEGOTIATION OR MANAGEMENT

Another goal that theorists use as a focus of their work is negotiating identities in intercultural interactions. These theories address adaptation of identities and not specific communication behaviors (as in the preceding section). Three theories focus on identity: (1) identity management theory (Cupach & Imahori, 1993), (2) identity negotiation theory (Ting-Toomey, 1993), and (3) cultural identity theory (Collier & Thomas, 1988).

Identity Management

Cupach and Imahori's (1993) identity management theory (IMT) is based in interpersonal communication competence, and the authors believe it generalizes to intercultural competence.[11] IMT is based in the work of Goffman (1967) on self-presentation and facework.

Cupach and Imahori (1993) view identity as providing "an interpretive frame for experience" (p. 113). Identities provide expectations for behavior and motivate individuals' behavior. Individuals have multiple identities, but Cupach and Imahori view cultural (based on Collier & Thomas, 1988; see below) and relational identities (e.g., identities within specific relationships) as central to identity management. Following Collier and Thomas, Cupach and Imahori view identities as varying as a function of scope (e.g., number of individuals who share identity), salience (e.g., importance of identity), and intensity (e.g., strength identity is communicated to others). They differentiate intercultural communication (e.g., interlocutors have different cultural identities) and intracultural communication (e.g., interlocutors share cultural identities).

Cupach and Imahori (1993) argue that aspects of individuals' identities are revealed through the presentation of face (e.g., situated identities individuals claim). They contend "the maintenance of face is a natural and inevitable *condition* of human interaction" (p. 116). In IMT, "interpersonal communication competence should include the ability of an individual to successfully negotiate mutually acceptable identities in interaction" (p. 118, italics omitted). The ability to maintain face in interactions is one indicator of individuals' interpersonal communication competence. Cupach and Imahori believe this extends to intercultural communication competence as well.

Cupach and Imahori (1993) argue that because individuals often do not know much about others' cultures, they manage face in intercultural encounters using stereotypes. Stereotyping, however, is face threatening because it is based on externally imposed identities. The result is a dialectic tension regarding three aspects of face: (1) fellowship face versus autonomy face, (2) competence face versus autonomy face, and (3) autonomy face versus fellowship or competence face. Intercultural communication competence involves successfully managing face, which involves managing these three dialectical tensions.

Cupach and Imahori (1993) contend that competence in developing intercultural relationships goes through three phases. The first phase involves "trial and error" processes of finding identities on which communicators share some similarities. The second phase involves enmeshment of the identities of the participants into "a mutually acceptable and convergent relational identity, in spite of the fact that their cultural identities are still divergent" (p. 125). The third phase involves renegotiating identities. "Competent intercultural interlocutors use their narrowly defined but emerging relational identity from the second phase as the basis for renegotiating their separate cultural identities" (p. 127). Cupach and Imahori argue that the three phases are "cyclical," and individuals in intercultural relationships may go through the three phases for each aspect of their identities that are relevant to their relationships.

Identity Negotiation

Ting-Toomey (1993) argues that intercultural communication competence is "the effective identity negotiation process between two interactants in a novel communication episode" (p. 73). She makes eight assumptions: (1) Everyone has multiple images concerning a sense of self; (2) cultural variability influences the sense of self; (3) self-identification involves security and vulnerability; (4) identity boundary regulation motivates behavior; (5) identity boundary regulation involves a tension between inclusion and differentiation; (6) individuals try to balance self, other, and group memberships; (7) managing the inclusion-differentiation dialectic influences the coherent sense of self; and (8) a coherent sense of self influences individuals' communication resourcefulness (i.e., "the knowledge and ability to apply cognitive, affective, and behavioral resources appropriately, effectively, and creatively in diverse interaction situations," p. 74). The theory is diagrammed in Figure 9.3.[12]

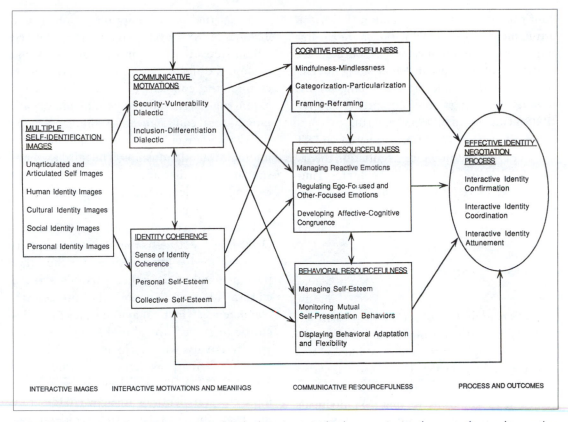

NOTE: This figure represents two interactants, to reflect the dynamic nature of such communication; there may, of course, be more than two people.

Figure 9.3.   A Diagram of Identity Negotiation Theory

SOURCE: Ting-Toomey (1993). Used with permission of the author and Sage Publications.

Ting-Toomey (1993) includes 20 propositions in identity negotiation theory (INT). She argues that the more secure individuals' self-identifications are, the more they are open to interacting with members of other cultures (P1). The more vulnerable individuals feel, the more anxiety they experience in these interactions (P2). Individuals' vulnerability is affected by their needs for security (P3). The more individuals need inclusion, the more they value ingroup and relational boundaries (P4). The more individuals need differentiation, the more distance they place between the self and others (P5).

Individuals' resourcefulness in negotiating identities is affected by effectively managing the security-vulnerability (P6) and inclusion-

differentiation (P7) dialectics. The more secure individuals' self-identifications, the greater their identity coherence (P8) and global self-esteem (P9). The greater individuals' self-esteem (P10) and the greater their membership collective esteem (P11), the more resourceful they are when interacting with strangers.

Individuals' motivation to communicate with strangers influences the degree to which they seek out communication resources (P12). The greater individuals' cognitive (P13), affective (P14), and behavioral (P15) resourcefulness, the more effective they are in identity negotiation. The more diverse individuals' communication resources are, the more effective they are in interactive identity confirmation (P16), coordination (P17), and attunement (P18). Finally, the more diverse individuals' communication resources, the more flexible they are in "co-creating interactive goals" (P19) and "in developing mutual identity meanings and comprehensibility" (P20) (Ting-Toomey, 1993, p. 110).

Ting-Toomey's (1999) text is based on INT and her cross-cultural face-negotiation theory (see Gudykunst & Lee, this volume; Ting-Toomey & Oetzel, this volume). The text contains research that supports the theory.

Cultural Identity

Collier and Thomas (1988) present an "interpretive" theory of how cultural identities are managed in intercultural interactions (see also Collier, 1998). Their theory is stated in six assumptions, five axioms, and one theorem. The assumptions are that (1) individuals "negotiate multiple identities in discourse" (p. 107); (2) intercultural communication occurs "by the discursive assumption and avowal of differing cultural identities" (p. 107); (3) intercultural communication competence involves managing meanings coherently and engaging in rule following (i.e., appropriate) and outcomes that are positive (i.e., effective); (4) intercultural communication competence involves negotiating "mutual meanings, rules, and positive outcomes" (p. 112); (5) intercultural communication competence involves validating cultural identities (i.e., identification with and perceived acceptance into a group that has shared systems of symbols and meanings as well as norms/rules for conduct," p. 113); and (6) cultural identities vary as a function of scope (e.g., how general identities are), salience (e.g., how important identities are), and intensity (e.g., how strongly identities are communicated to others).

Given the six assumptions, Collier and Thomas (1988) develop five axioms. The first axiom states that "the more that norms and meanings differ in discourse, the more intercultural the contact" (p. 112). The second axiom suggests that the more individuals have intercultural communication competence, the better they are able to develop and maintain intercultural relationships. The third axiom is similar to the first and states that "the more that cultural identities differ in the discourse, the more intercultural the contact" (p. 115).

The fourth axiom in Collier and Thomas's (1988) theory suggests that the more one person's ascribed cultural identity for the other person matches the other person's avowed cultural identity, the more the intercultural competence. The final axiom states that "linguistic references to cultural identity systematically covary with sociocontextual factors such as participants, type of episode, and topic" (p. 116). The theorem claims that the more cultural identities are avowed, the more important they are relative to other identities.

THEORIES FOCUSING ON COMMUNICATION NETWORKS

Network theories are based on the assumption that individuals' behavior is influenced by relationships between individuals rather than the characteristics of the individuals. "In network theory, the main focus is on positions and social relationships, rather than beliefs or internalized norms. Also, the focus is on series of interconnecting relationships, rather than static, bounded groups" (Yum, 1988, p. 240). These theories focus on explaining linkages between people from different cultures.[13] Three theories focus on networks: (1) outgroup communication competence theory (Kim, 1986), (2) intracultural versus intercultural networks theory (Yum, 1988), and

(3) networks and acculturation theory (Smith, 1999).

Networks and Outgroup Communication Competence

Kim (1986) uses a personal network approach to explain outgroup communication competence. Personal networks emphasize the links between individuals. She argues that "one of the most important aspects of a personal network is ego's conscious and unconscious reliance on the network members for perceiving and interpreting various attributes and actions of others (and of self)" (p. 90).

Kim (1986) assumes that having outgroup members in individuals' personal networks and the nature of these outgroup ties influence their outgroup communication competence. Theorem 1 states that "a higher level of heterogeneity of a personal network is associated with a higher level of ego's overall outgroup communication competence" (p. 93). This theorem suggests that having outgroup members in individuals' personal networks facilitates outgroup communication competence.

Theorem 2 in Kim's (1986) theory proposes that "a higher level of centrality of outgroup members in a personal network is associated with higher level of the ego's outgroup communication competence" (p. 93). This theorem suggests that having outgroup members in central positions in individuals' personal networks facilitates outgroup communication competence. Theorem 3 contends that "a higher level of an ego's tie strength with outgroup members is associated with a higher level of his/her ego's outgroup communication competence" (p. 94). This theorem suggests that the more frequent the contact and the closer the ties individuals have with outgroup members, the more their outgroup communication competence.

Intracultural Versus Intercultural Networks

Yum's (1988) theory is designed to explain the differences in individuals' intracultural and intercultural networks. She begins with the assumption that there is more variance in behavior between cultures than within cultures. There are six theorems in Yum's theory.

Yum's (1988) first theorem posits that intercultural networks tend to be radial (e.g., individuals are linked to others who are not linked to each other) and intracultural networks tend to be interlocking (e.g., individuals are linked to others who are linked to each other). Theorem 2 predicts that intracultural networks are more dense (e.g., the ratio of actual direct links to number of possible links) than intercultural networks.

Yum's (1988) third theorem proposes that intracultural networks are more multiplex (e.g., multiple messages flow through linkages) than intercultural networks. Theorem 4 states that "intercultural network ties are more likely to be weak ties than strong ties" (p. 250). Strong ties involve frequent and close contact (e.g., friendships). Links between acquaintances and people with whom individuals have intermittent role relationships (e.g., hairdressers) tend to be weak ties.

Theorem 5 in Yum's (1988) theory states that "the roles of liaison and bridge will be more prevalent and more important for network connectedness in intercultural networks than in intracultural networks" (p. 251). Liaisons are individuals who link cliques (e.g., a group of connected individuals) but are not members of any of the cliques. Bridges are individuals who link cliques and are members of one of the cliques. Both are "intermediaries" and can form indirect linkages between members of different groups.

Yum's (1988) final theorem suggests that "transitivity will play a much smaller role in creating intercultural networks than intra-cultural networks" (p. 252). Transivity occurs when "my friend's friends are my friends" (p. 252). Because intercultural networks tend to be uniplex and involve weak ties, they do facilitate forming networks with friends of outgroup members in the network.

Networks and Acculturation

Smith's (1999) theory links social networks to immigrant acculturation.[14] The theory consists of seven assumptions about the nature of networks and seven propositions. The first proposition states that "intercultural identity strategies are discernible within social network structures" (p. 646, italics omitted in all propositions). This proposition suggests that immigrants tend to be linked to those individuals who define their identities (e.g., other immigrants from their cultures or host nationals). The second proposition suggests that "culturally influenced perceptions shape the function and experienced nature of social networks" (p. 647). This proposition claims that the way immigrants experience their social networks is influenced by their native cultures.

Smith's (1999) third proposition states that "as socio-structural heterogeneity increases, the probability of acculturation increases" (p. 647).[15] This proposition suggests that the more host nationals are in immigrants' social networks, the more likely immigrants are to acculturate. The fourth proposition claims that the "rate of change in an intercultural social network is a dynamic function dependent on the stage of integration with the host community" (p. 648). This proposition suggests that as immigrants become integrated into host communities, their social networks change. Proposition 5 contends that "structural constraints will impact the size of inter-cultural networks, in turn affecting the adjustment process" (p. 648). This proposition

suggests that factors such as where immigrants live and their social class influence their abilities to form intercultural networks and acculturate.

Smith's (1999) sixth proposition states that "as density increases, the provision of diverse resources within the net decreases, thereby affecting socialization/acculturation" (p. 650). This proposition suggests that dense networks (e.g., links connected to each other) decreases immigrants abilities to obtain the resources needed for acculturation. The final proposition contends that "intercultural networks will be less dense, with more radial ties in cultures reflecting a contextual-based relationship norm than those found in cultures reflecting a person-based relationship norm" (p. 650).[16]

THEORIES FOCUSING ON ACCULTURATION AND ADJUSTMENT

The acculturation of immigrants and the adjustment of sojourners have been of interest to intercultural communication scholars for nearly 50 years. Only in recent years, however, have formal theories focusing on communication been proposed. Three theories are examined in this section: (1) communication acculturation theory (e.g., Kim, 1988, 2001), (2) anxiety/uncertainty management theory of adjustment (e.g., Gudykunst, 1998a), and (3) communication in assimilation, deviance, and alienation states theory (McGuire & McDermott, 1988).[17]

Communication Acculturation

Kim has been developing her theory of communication and acculturation for more than 20 years. The first version of the theory appeared in a causal model of Korean immigrants' acculturation to Chicago (Kim, 1977). She has refined the theory several times using an open-system perspective (e.g., Kim, 1979, 1988, 1995, 2001; Kim & Ruben, 1988). Two of the major changes incorporated into the theory are adding the "stress, adaptation, and growth dynamics" that immigrants go through and focusing on immigrants becoming "intercultural." In addition, the current version of the theory attempts to portray "cross-cultural adaptation as a collaborative effort, in which a stranger and the receiving environment are engaged in a joint effort" (Kim, 1995, p. 192).

The current version of Kim's (2001) theory contains three assumptions based on open-systems theory, 10 axioms, and 21 theorems. The axioms are "lawlike" statements about relationships between units in the theory. Theorems are derived from the axioms. A structural model of the theory is presented in Figure 14.4 in Chapter 14, this volume.

The first five axioms are broad principles of cross-cultural adaptation: (A1) Acculturation and deculturation are part of the cross-cultural adaptation process, (A2) the stress-adaptation-growth dynamic underlies the adaptation process, (A3) intercultural transformations are a function of the stress-adaptation-growth dynamic, (A4) the severity of the stress-adaptation-growth dynamic decreases as strangers go through intercultural transformations, and (A5) functional fitness and psychological health result from intercultural transformations. The final five axioms deal with the reciprocal relationship between intercultural transformations and host communication competence (A6), host communication activities (A7),[18] ethnic communication activities (A8), environmental conditions (A9), and strangers' predispositions (A10).

The first three theorems posit relationships between host communication competence and host communication activities (positive, T1), ethnic communication activities (negative, T2), and intercultural transformations (positive, T3).[19] Host interpersonal and mass communication activities are related to ethnic communication activities (negative, T4) and intercultural transformations (positive, T5). Ethnic interpersonal and mass communication activities are related negatively to intercultural transformations (T6).

The next three theorems relate host receptivity and conformity pressure to host communication competence (positive, T7), host communication activities (positive, T8), and ethnic communication activities (negative, T9). Ethnic group strength is related to host communication competence (negative, T10), host communication activities (negative, T11), and ethnic communication activities (positive, T12). Ethnic proximity is related to host communication competence (positive, T16), host communication activities (positive, T17), and ethnic communication activities (negative, T18).

Strangers' preparedness for change is related to host communication competence (positive, T13), host communication activities (positive, T14), and ethnic communication activities (negative, T15). Strangers' adaptive personalities are related to host communication competence (positive, T19), host communication activities (positive, T20), and ethnic communication activities (negative, T21).

Kim's (2001) theory is based on extensive research with immigrants to the United States. She has conducted research with Korean immigrants, Indochinese refugees, Japanese Americans, and Mexican Americans, among others. This research, as well as other research compatible with the theory, is summarized in Kim (2001).

Anxiety/Uncertainty Management

Defining strangers is a figure-ground phenomena. The effective communication versions of AUM theory (e.g., Gudykunst, 1995) are written from the perspective of individuals communicating with strangers (e.g., others approaching individuals' ingroups). The adjustment version of the theory is written from the perspective of strangers (e.g., sojourners) entering new cultures and interacting with host nationals.

As indicated earlier, the original version of AUM theory (the label "AUM," however, was not used) was a theory of adjustment (Gudykunst & Hammer, 1988).[20] This theory led to the first effective communication version of the theory (Gudykunst, 1988). The most recent effective communication version (Gudykunst, 1995) was adapted to adjustment (Gudykunst, 1998a). The current adjustment version includes comparable axioms to the 1995 version of the effective communication version, plus two additional axioms focusing specifically on adjustment (i.e., pluralistic tendencies in the host culture decreases and permanence of stay increases strangers' anxiety). The focus here is on the most recent version of the adjustment theory (Gudykunst, 1998a).

When strangers enter a new culture, they have uncertainty about host nationals' attitudes, feelings, beliefs, values, and behaviors (Gudykunst, 1998a). Strangers need to be able to predict which of several alternative behavior patterns hosts will employ. Strangers also need to be able to explain hosts' attitudes, feelings, and behaviors. Whenever strangers try to figure out why hosts behaved the way they did, strangers are engaging in explanatory uncertainty reduction.

When strangers communicate with hosts, strangers experience uncertainty and anxiety (Gudykunst, 1998a). Anxiety is the tension, feelings of being uneasy, or apprehension strangers have about what will happen when they communicate with hosts (Stephan & Stephan, 1985). The anxiety strangers experience when they communicate with hosts is based on negative expectations.

To adjust to other cultures, strangers do not want to try to totally reduce their anxiety and uncertainty (Gudykunst, 1995). At the same time, strangers cannot communicate effectively with hosts if their uncertainty and anxiety are too high.[21] If uncertainty is too high, strangers cannot accurately interpret hosts' messages or make accurate predictions about hosts' behaviors.[22] When anxiety is too high, strangers communicate on automatic pilot and interpret hosts' behaviors using their own cultural frames of reference. Also, when anxiety is too high, the way strangers process information is very simple, thereby limiting their ability to predict hosts' behaviors. When uncertainty is too low, strangers become overconfident that they understand hosts' behaviors and do not question whether their predictions are accurate. When anxiety is too low, strangers are not motivated to communicate with hosts.

If strangers' anxiety is high, they must mindfully manage their anxiety to communicate effectively and adjust to the host cultures. Managing anxiety requires that strangers become mindful (e.g., create new categories, be open to new information, be aware of alternative perspectives). When strangers have managed their anxiety, they need to try to develop accurate predictions and explanations for hosts' behaviors. When strangers communicate on automatic pilot, they predict and interpret hosts' behaviors using their own frames of reference. When strangers are mindful, in contrast, they are open to new information and aware of alternative perspectives (e.g., hosts' perspectives; Langer, 1989), and they, therefore, can make accurate predictions.

Lieberson (1985) argues that it is necessary to isolate basic and superficial causes of the phenomenon being explained (e.g., effective communication, intercultural adjustment). In AUM theory, managing uncertainty and anxiety are the basic causes of strang-

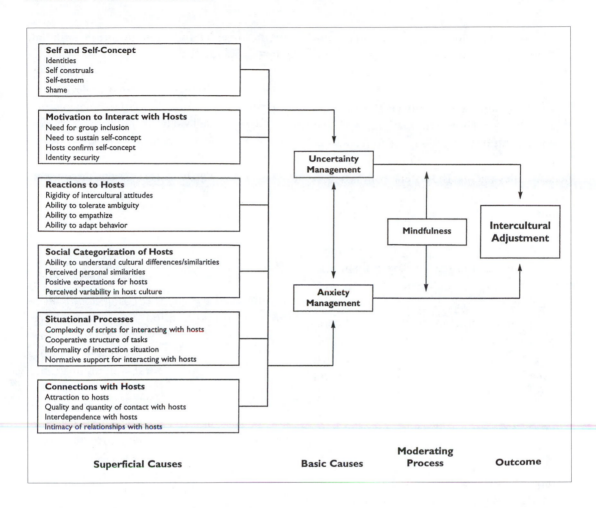

Figure 9.4. A Schematic of the Anxiety/Uncertainty Management Theory of Intercultural Adjustment

ers' intercultural adjustment. The amount of uncertainty and anxiety strangers experience in their interactions with hosts is a function of many superficial causes (e.g., self-concepts, motivation, reactions to hosts, social categorization, situational processes, connections with hosts). Research suggests that the superficial causes of adjustment (e.g., ability to adapt behavior) are linked to adjustment through uncertainty and anxiety (e.g., Gao & Gudykunst, 1990; Hammer, Wiseman, Rasmussen, & Bruschke, 1998). The AUM theory of adjustment is diagrammed in Figure 9.4.

Assimilation, Deviance, and Alienation States

McGuire and McDermott (1988) argue that assimilation and adaptation are not permanent outcomes of the adaptation process; rather, they are temporary outcomes of the communication process.[23] The reason is that everyone, no matter how well they are integrated into their cultures, deviates from social norms and rules at some point. They contend that "individuals (or groups) have achieved the assimilation state when their perceptions are receiving positive reinforcement from others' communications . . . the group accomplishes an assimilation state when an individual conforms to expected norms" (p. 93, italics omitted).

McGuire and McDermott (1988) contend that the hosts' response to immigrants' deviation from cultural norms is neglectful communication. Neglectful communication involves negative messages or the absence of messages. When immigrants are not deviant or engage in assimilative communication (e.g., interact with hosts, increase fluency in host languages), host nationals respond with assimilative communication (e.g., praise immigrants' behavior, being available to interact with immigrants).

When immigrants are in a deviance state, they experience tension with their new cultures (McGuire & McDermott, 1988). Host nationals tend to respond with neglectful communication (e.g., low level of communication, negative feedback). One possible response to host nationals' neglectful communication is for immigrants to become alienated from the host cultures. Alienation involves feelings of "normlessness and social isolation" (p. 101). Immigrants, therefore, may feel that they cannot accomplish their goals and are being excluded from the host cultures. This does not, however, necessarily "involve hostility, aggression or conflict" (p. 101).

The way host nationals respond to immigrants when immigrants feel alienated influences whether immigrants stay in an alienated state. If host nationals respond in a way to strengthen alienation (e.g., refusing to interact with immigrants, being obscene, ridiculing immigrants), immigrants are likely to withdraw from host cultures, be hostile toward the host cultures, or refuse to use the host languages.

McGuire and McDermott (1988) argue that the way host nationals and immigrants respond to neglectful communication is similar. They conclude that

> changes in the amount or kind of deviance or amount or kind of neglectful communication will push an individual toward or into either the alienation or the assimilation state. . . . Alienation or assimilation, therefore, of a group or an individual, is an outcome of the relationship between deviant behavior and neglectful communication. (p. 103)

CONCLUSION

As indicated earlier, theorizing about intercultural communication has improved tremendously in recent years. Several issues, however, still need to be addressed in future theorizing on intercultural communication.

First, the vast majority of the theories proposed to date are objectivistic in nature. Only two of the theorists included here claim to have developed subjectivistic theories. Some objectivistic theories include subjectivistic components (e.g., mindfulness in AUM), but the general trend is for the two types of theorizing not to be integrated. Clearly, there is a need for more subjectivistic theorizing and for integrating subjectivistic and objectivistic theories.

Second, the vast majority of the theorists were born in the United States. Researchers born in other cultures, however, have contributed to several of the lines of research on which the theories are based (e.g., Todd Imahori, Young Yun Kim, Stella Ting-Toomey, June Ock Yum). There may be theories of intercultural communication published in languages other than English of which I am not aware. The omission of theorists from outside the United States may be a function of the role of theory in scholarship in different cultures (e.g., developing theories often is not emphasized in many cultures). There is, nevertheless, a need for theories developed by scholars outside the United States.

Third, the issue of power is not incorporated in very many of the theories constructed to date. Clearly, power plays a role in many, but not all, intercultural encounters. Reid and Ng (1999), for example, describe the relationships among language, power, and intergroup relations. Power needs to be incorporated in theories of intercultural communication. Berger (1994) examines power in interpersonal communication, and his analysis provides one starting point for looking at power in intercultural communication.

Fourth, many of the theories proposed to date are compatible with each other. Many of the theories proposed have different scopes and boundary conditions. This allows for the possibility of integration. Gallois et al. (1995), for example, indicate that CAT can incorporate other theoretical positions but do not present specifics (e.g., one possibility is cocultural theory, which is not inconsistent with CAT). Similarly, Cupach and Imahori's (1993) theory appears to be theoretically compatible with Collier and Thomas's (1988) theory. Gudykunst (1995) suggests that dialectical theory can be integrated with AUM. I believe that integrating theories, especially objectivistic and subjectivistic theories, will increase our ability to understand intercultural communication.

Finally, there is little or no published research supporting some of the theories presented (e.g., Cupach & Imahori, 1993; Ellingsworth, 1983, 1988; Kim, 1986; McGuire & McDermott, 1988; Smith, 1999; Yum, 1988). Given the state of theorizing in intercultural communication, conducting atheoretical research is unwarranted. Research designed to test the theories presented is needed to advance the state of our understanding of intercultural communication, not more atheoretical research.

NOTES

1. Hall (1976) had been published, and this could be considered a cross-cultural theory of communication but not an intercultural theory.

2. This volume was based on an "Action Caucus" I organized at the Speech Communication Association convention two years earlier. The volume included both cross-cultural and intercultural theorizing. Prior to the publication of the volume, there was a theory of communication and intercultural adaptation (Kim, 1977).

3. Another volume of the annual that Wiseman edited on intercultural competence also included theories (Wiseman & Koester, 1993).

4. Wiseman (Chapter 11 in this volume) discusses some of the same theories in his analysis of intercultural communication competence.

5. I have not included theoretical discussions that are not developed into full theories (e.g., Martin & Nakayama's, 1999, discussion of dialectical processes). I also have not included rhetorical approaches to intercultural communication (e.g., Gonzalez & Tanno, 2000). Cross-cultural theories are discussed in Gudykunst and Lee's chapter in this volume.

6. This theory could have been discussed in the acculturation section. It is discussed here because the convergence model of communication focuses on mutual understanding, an effective outcome.

7. The large number of axioms often is viewed as violating the principle of parsimony. This, however, is not the case. The principle of parsimony essentially suggests that if two theories explain the same phenomena, select the simpler explanation.

8. For discussions of individualistic and collectivistic cultures and self construals, see Gudykunst and Lee's chapter in this volume.

9. I want to thank Cindy Gallois and her colleagues for permission to use this figure.

10. He uses procedures outlined by Dubin (1969) to generate his theory.

11. Cupach and Imahori do not present formal propositions.

12. I want to thank Stella Ting-Toomey for permission to use the figure.

13. Two theories could have been presented in other sections. Kim's theory could have been included in the section on effective outcomes, and Smith's theory could have been included in the acculturation section. Yum's theory, however, does not fit any of the other categories.

14. Given the focus, this theory could have been included in the next section. As indicated earlier, my categories are not mutually exclusive.

15. One problem with Smith's theory is that the propositions are not stated in a consistent form. The third proposition, for example, links variables and the first two do not.

16. This proposition is different in kind from the other propositions in that it adds a cross-cultural comparison to the proposition, which is not present in the others.

17. I have not included work that is not a complete theory and work that does not focus on communication (e.g., Ady, 1995; Nishida, 1999).

18. Host and ethnic communication activities include interpersonal and mass communication components.

19. The direction of the posited relationship in the theorems are given in parentheses.

20. Witte (1993) recasts the theory using her fear appeal theory.

21. In the 1995 version of the theory, I discuss the idea of minimum and maximum thresholds for uncertainty and anxiety (see also Gudykunst, 1998b; Gudykunst & Kim, 1997). This idea has practical implications in training. To illustrate, trainees can be taught to isolate their maximum thresholds for anxiety (i.e., that point at which if anxiety increases they are more concerned with their anxiety than with what is happening in the situation in which they find themselves). Once trainees know the physical symptoms associated with their maximum thresholds (e.g., the amount of "butterflies" in their stomach), they can isolate a point that is slightly lower and use the physical symptoms associated with this point as an indicator that they should become mindful.

22. I only use behavior here (and below), but the claim also applies to hosts' feelings, attitudes, values, and so on.

23. McGuire and McDermott do not present formal theoretical propositions.

REFERENCES

Ady, J. C. (1995). Toward a differential demand model of sojourner adjustment. In R. L. Wiseman (Ed.), *Intercultural communication theory* (pp. 92-114). Thousand Oaks, CA: Sage.

Ardener, S. (1975). *Perceiving women.* London: Malaby.

Barnett, G. A., & Kincaid, D. L. (1983). Cultural convergence. In W. B. Gudykunst (Ed.), *Intercultural communication theory* (pp. 171-194). Beverly Hills, CA: Sage.

Berger, C. R. (1994). Power, dominance, and social interaction. In M. Knapp & G. Miller (Eds.), *Handbook of interpersonal communication* (2nd ed., pp. 450-507). Thousand Oaks, CA: Sage.

Berger, C. R., & Calabrese, R. (1975). Some explorations in initial interactions and beyond. *Human Communication Research, 1,* 99-112.

Buck, E., Kincaid, D. L., Nichter, M., & Nichter, M. (1983). Development communication in the cultural context: Convergence theory and community participation. In W. Dissanayake & A. Said (Eds.), *Communications research and cultural values* (pp. 106-126). Singapore: Asian Mass Communication and Information Centre.

Burrell, G., & Morgan, G. (1979). *Sociological paradigms and organizational analysis.* London: Heinemann.

Collier, M. J. (1998). Researching cultural identity. In D. Tanno & A. Gonzalez (Eds.), *Communication and identity across cultures* (pp. 122-147). Thousand Oaks, CA: Sage.

Collier, M. J., & Thomas, M. (1988). Cultural identity. In Y. Y. Kim & W. B. Gudykunst (Eds.), *Theories in intercultural communication* (pp. 99-120). Newbury Park, CA: Sage.

Coupland, N., Coupland, J., Giles, H., & Henwood, K. (1988). Accommodating the elderly. *Language in Society, 17,* 1-41.

Cupach, W. R., & Imahori, T. (1993). Identity management theory. In R. L. Wiseman & J. Koester (Eds.), *Intercultural communication competence* (pp. 112-131). Newbury Park, CA: Sage.

Dubin, R. (1969). *Theory-building.* New York: Free Press.

Ellingsworth, H. W. (1983). Adaptive intercultural communication. In W. B. Gudykunst (Ed.), *Intercultural communication theory* (pp. 195-204). Beverly Hills, CA: Sage.

Ellingsworth, H. W. (1988). A theory of adaptation in intercultural dyads. In Y. Y. Kim & W. B. Gudykunst (Eds.), *Theories in intercultural communication* (pp. 259-279). Newbury Park, CA: Sage.

Gallois, C., Franklyn-Stokes, A., Giles, H., & Coupland, N. (1988). Communication accommodation in intercultural encounters. In Y. Y. Kim & W. B. Gudykunst (Eds.), *Theories in intercultural communication* (pp. 157-185). Newbury Park, CA: Sage.

Gallois, C., Giles, H., Jones, E., Cargile, A., & Ota, H. (1995). Accommodating intercultural encounters. In R. L. Wiseman (Ed.), *Intercultural communication theory* (pp. 115-147). Thousand Oaks, CA: Sage.

Gao, G., & Gudykunst, W. B. (1990). Uncertainty, anxiety, and adaptation. *International Journal of Intercultural Relations, 14,* 301-317.

Giles, H. (1973). Accent mobility: A model and some data. *Anthropological Linguistics, 15,* 87-105.

Giles, H., & Johnson, P. (1987). Ethnolinguistic identity theory. *International Journal of the Sociology of Language, 68,* 66-99.

Giles, H., Mulac, A., Bradac, J., & Johnson, P. (1987). Speech accommodation theory. In M. McLaughlin (Ed.), *Communication yearbook 10* (pp. 13-48). Newbury Park, CA: Sage.

Giles, H., & Smith, P. (1979). Accommodation theory. In H. Giles & R. St. Clair (Eds.), *Language and social psychology* (pp. 45-65). Oxford, UK: Basil Blackwell.

Goffman, E. (1967). *Interaction ritual: Essays on face-to-face behavior.* Garden City, NY: Anchor.

Gonzalez, A., & Tanno, D. (Eds.). (2000). *Rhetoric in intercultural contexts.* Thousand Oaks, CA: Sage.

Gudykunst, W. B. (Ed.). (1983). *Intercultural communication theory.* Beverly Hills, CA: Sage.

Gudykunst, W. B. (1985). A model of uncertainty reduction in intergroup encounters. *Journal of Language and Social Psychology, 4,* 79-98.

Gudykunst, W. B. (1988). Uncertainty and anxiety. In Y. Y. Kim & W. B. Gudykunst (Eds.), *Theories in intercultural communication* (pp. 123-156). Newbury Park, CA: Sage.

Gudykunst, W. B. (1990). Diplomacy: A special case of intergroup communication. In F. Korzenny & S. Ting-Toomey (Eds.), *Communicating for peace* (pp. 19-39). Newbury Park, CA: Sage.

Gudykunst, W. B. (1993). Toward a theory of effective interpersonal and intergroup communication. In R. L. Wiseman & J. Koester (Eds.), *Intercultural communication competence* (pp. 33-71). Newbury Park, CA: Sage.

Gudykunst, W. B. (1995). Anxiety/uncertainty management (AUM) theory. In R. L. Wiseman (Ed.), *Intercultural communication theory* (pp. 8-58). Thousand Oaks, CA: Sage.

Gudykunst, W. B. (1998a). Applying anxiety/uncertainty management (AUM) theory to intercultural adjustment training. *International Journal of Intercultural Relations, 22,* 227-250.

Gudykunst, W. B. (1998b). *Bridging differences* (3rd ed.). Thousand Oaks, CA: Sage.

Gudykunst, W. B., & Kim, Y. Y. (1997). *Communicating with strangers* (3rd ed.). New York: McGraw-Hill.

Gudykunst, W. B., & Hammer, M. R. (1988). Strangers and hosts: An uncertainty reduction based theory of intercultural adaptation. In Y. Y. Kim & W. B. Gudykunst (Eds.), *Cross-cultural adaptation* (pp. 106-139). Newbury Park, CA: Sage.

Gudykunst, W. B., & Nishida, T. (1989). Theoretical perspectives for studying intercultural communication. In M. K. Asante & W. B. Gudykunst (Eds.), *Handbook of international and intercultural communication* (pp. 17-46). Newbury Park, CA: Sage.

Gudykunst, W. B., & Nishida, T. (2001). Anxiety, uncertainty, and perceived effectiveness of communication across relationships and cultures. *International Journal of Intercultural Relations, 25,* 55-72.

Gudykunst, W. B., & Shapiro, R. (1996). Communication in everyday interpersonal and intergroup encounters. *International Journal of Intercultural Relations, 20,* 19-45.

Hall, E. T. (1976). *Beyond culture.* Garden City, NY: Doubleday/Anchor.

Hammer, M. R., Wiseman, R. L., Rasmussen, J., & Bruschke, J. (1998). A test of uncertainty/anxiety reduction theory: The intercultural adaptation context. *Communication Quarterly, 46,* 309-326.

Hirokawa, R., & Rost, K. (1992). Effective groups decision-making in organizations. *Management Communication Quarterly, 5,* 267-288.

Hubbert, K., Gudykunst, W. B., & Guerrero, S. (1999). Intergroup communication over time. *International Journal of Intercultural Relations, 23,* 13-46.

Kim, Y. Y. (1977). Communication patterns of foreign immigrants in the process of acculturation. *Human Communication Research, 4,* 66-77.

Kim, Y. Y. (1979). Toward an interactive theory of communication acculturation. In B. Ruben (Ed.), *Communication yearbook 3* (pp. 435-453). New Brunswick, NJ: Transaction.

Kim, Y. Y. (1986). Understanding the social structure of intergroup communication. In W. B. Gudykunst (Ed.), *Intergroup communication* (pp. 86-95). London: Edward Arnold.

Kim, Y. Y. (1988). *Communication and cross-cultural adaptation.* Clevendon, UK: Multilingual Matters.

Kim, Y. Y. (1995). Cross-cultural adaptation: An integrative theory. In R. L. Wiseman (Ed.), *Intercultural communication theory* (pp. 170-194). Thousand Oaks, CA: Sage.

Kim, Y. Y. (2001). *Becoming intercultural: An integrative theory of communication and cross-cultural adaptation.* Thousand Oaks, CA: Sage.

Kim, Y. Y., & Gudykunst, W. B. (Eds.). (1988). *Theories in intercultural communication.* Newbury Park, CA: Sage.

Kim, Y. Y., & Ruben, B. (1988). Intercultural transformations. In Y. Y. Kim & W. B. Gudykunst (Eds.), *Theories in intercultural communication* (pp. 299-322). Newbury Park, CA: Sage.

Kincaid, D. L. (1979). *The convergence model of communication.* Honolulu, HI: East-West Communication Institute.

Kincaid, D. L. (1987). The convergence theory of communication, self-organization, and cultural evolution. In D. L. Kincaid (Ed.), *Communication theory from Eastern and Western perspectives* (pp. 209-221). New York: Academic Press.

Kincaid, D. L. (1988). The convergence theory of intercultural communication. In Y. Y. Kim & W. B. Gudykunst (Eds.), *Theories in intercultural communication* (pp. 280-298). Newbury Park, CA: Sage.

Kincaid, D. L., Yum, J. O., Woelfel, J., & Barnett, G. (1983). The cultural convergence of Korean immigrants in Hawaii. *Quality and Quantity, 18,* 59-78.

Kramarae, C. (1981). *Women and men speaking.* Rowley, MA: Newbury House.

Langer, E. (1989). *Mindfulness.* Reading, MA: Addison-Wesley.

Lieberson, S. (1985). *Making it count: The improvement of social research and theory.* Berkeley: University of California Press.

Martin, J. N., & Nakayama, T. K. (1999). Thinking dialectically about culture and communication. *Communication Theory, 9,* 1-25.

McGuire, M., & McDermott, S. (1988). Communication in assimilation, deviance, and alienation states. In Y. Y. Kim & W. B. Gudykunst (Eds.), *Cross-cultural adaptation* (pp. 90-105). Newbury Park, CA: Sage.

Nishida, H. (1999). A cognitive approach to intercultural communication based on schema theory. *International Journal of Intercultural Relations, 23,* 753-777.

Oetzel, J. (1998). Culturally homogeneous and heterogeneous groups. *International Journal of Intercultural Relations, 22,* 135-161.

Oetzel, J., Burtis, T., Chew Sanchez, M., & Pérez, F. (in press). Investigating the role of communication in culturally diverse work groups. In W. B. Gudykunst (Ed.), *Communication yearbook 25* (pp. 237-270). Hillsdale, NJ: Lawrence Erlbaum.

Oetzel, J. G. (1995). Intercultural small groups: An effective decision-making theory. In R. L. Wiseman (Ed.), *Intercultural communication theory* (pp. 247-270). Thousand Oaks, CA: Sage.

Orbe, M. P. (1998a). *Constructing co-cultural theory.* Thousand Oaks, CA: Sage.

Orbe, M. P. (1998b). From the standpoint(s) of traditionally muted groups: Explicating a co-cultural communication theoretical model. *Communication Theory, 8,* 1-26.

Reid, S., & Ng, S. H. (1999). Language, power, and intergroup relations. *Journal of Social Issues, 55*(1), 119-139.

Reynolds, P. (1971). *A primer in theory construction.* Indianapolis, IN: Bobbs-Merrill.

Rogers, E., & Kincaid, D. L. (1981). *Communication networks.* New York: Free Press.

Simmel, G. (1950). The stranger. In K. Wolff (Ed. & Trans.), *The sociology of Georg Simmel* (pp. 402-408). New York: Free Press. (Original work published 1908)

Smith, D. E. (1987). *The everyday world as problematic: A feminist sociology of knowledge.* Boston: Northeastern University Press.

Smith, L. R. (1999). Intercultural network theory. *International Journal of Intercultural Relations, 23,* 629-658.

Stephan, W., & Stephan, C. (1985). Intergroup anxiety. *Journal of Social Issues, 41*(3), 157-166.

Ting-Toomey, S. (1988). Intercultural conflict styles. In Y. Y. Kim & W. B. Gudykunst (Eds.), *Theories in intercultural communication* (pp. 213-238). Newbury Park, CA: Sage.

Ting-Toomey, S. (1993). Communicative resourcefulness: An identity negotiation theory. In R. L. Wiseman & J. Koester (Eds.), *Intercultural communication competence* (pp. 72-111). Newbury Park, CA: Sage.

Ting-Toomey, S. (1999). *Communicating across cultures.* New York: Guilford.

Wiseman, R. L. (Ed.). (1995). *Intercultural communication theory.* Thousand Oaks, CA: Sage.

Wiseman, R. L., & Koester, J. (Eds.). (1993). *Intercultural communication competence.* Newbury Park, CA: Sage.

Witte, K. (1993). A theory of cognition and negtive affect: Extending Gudykunst and Hammer's theory of uncertainty and anxiety reduction. *International Journal of Intercultural Relations, 17,* 197-216.

Yum, J. O. (1988). Network theory in intercultural communication. In Y. Y. Kim & W. B. Gudykunst (Eds.), *Theories in intercultural communication* (pp. 239-258). Newbury Park, CA: Sage.

10

Intercultural Communication Competence

RICHARD L. WISEMAN
California State University, Fullerton

Intercultural communication (ICC) competence (or related constructs such as effectiveness, success, and adaptation) has been the focus of a number of studies since the term was probably introduced by researchers interested in overseas technical assistants and Peace Corps volunteers (Gardner, 1962; Hoselitz, 1954). Since then, ICC competence has been investigated in studies with such diverse conceptual foci as sojourner adjustment, immigrant acculturation, intergroup contact, culture shock, cross-cultural training, social change, international management, and foreign student advising (cf. Benson, 1978; Brislin, 1981; Gudykunst, Wiseman, & Hammer, 1977; Landis & Brislin, 1983; Rogers, 1983; Stening, 1979). The research in this area has been such that attempts to synthesize and report many of the findings have taken the forms of textbooks (Gudykunst, 1998; Lustig & Koester, 1999; Wiseman & Koester, 1993), a journal issue (Martin, 1989), chapters reporting the "state of the art" (Cargile & Giles, 1996; Chen & Starosta, 1996), and even a meta-analysis of a number of studies in the area (Bradford, Allen, & Beisser, 2000).

The purpose of the present chapter is not to duplicate extant reviews of the literature, nor is it to provide a new exhaustive review of the many studies on ICC competence. Rather, the purpose is to delineate some of the choices (either explicit or tacit) that a scholar must make in an investigation of ICC competence. These choices have been arrayed to correspond to the steps in designing a research study. First, the chapter examines issues regarding the conceptualization of ICC competence—how is it to be conceived, defined, and identified? Second, issues regarding metatheory are discussed—what is the nature of the concept (ontology), what is its importance (axiology), and what are the ways of knowing about it (epistemology)? At this point, a number of illustrative theories are introduced to depict the influences of one's meta-theory on the investigation of a phenomenon. Third, the essay examines the choices one can make in actually studying ICC competence—methodological concerns such as unit of analysis, data collection method, and measurement tools. Finally, posited interrelationships between ICC competence and other constructs are discussed to provide the heuristic bases for future research.

CONCEPTUALIZATION OF INTERCULTURAL COMMUNICATION COMPETENCE

ICC competence has been conceptualized in a variety of ways. Early in the history of scholarship on the construct, the conceptualizations varied according to the researcher's theoretical orientation or specific sample being studied. Some of these conceptualizations were labeled as cross-cultural adjustment, cross-cultural adaptation, intercultural understanding, overseas success, personal growth/adjustment, cross-cultural effectiveness, and satisfaction with overseas experience (see, e.g., Guthrie & Zektick, 1967; Harris, 1975; Ruben & Kealey, 1979). In the past two decades, there has been a growing consensus on a conceptualization of ICC competence. As a reflection of this consensus and for the purposes of this chapter, ICC competence involves the knowledge, motivation, and skills to interact effectively and appropriately with members of different cultures. There are a number of implications entailed in this conceptualization.

Different Cultures

The conceptualization of culture has undergone considerable change in the field of ICC

scholarship. Some researchers take a more traditional approach at defining culture and typically use characteristics such as race, nationality, ethnicity, or geographic region to operationalized culture (e.g., Bradford, Kane, & Meyers, 1999; Dean & Popp, 1990; Oetzel et al., 2000). Other scholars focus on culture as a "learned set of shared interpretations about beliefs, values, and norms, which affect the behaviors of a relatively large group of people" (Lustig & Koester, 1999, p. 30). With this shift of focus, the operationalization of culture is not where members were born or the color of their skin, but on the commonalities in and interpretations of their behaviors. Taking this tack, operationalizations of culture could include elderly people (Fox & Giles, 1993; Herek & Giles, 2000), individuals with physical disabilities (Braithwaite, 1991; Wiseman, Emry, & Morgan, 1987), individuals who are deaf (Shearer, 1984), sexual orientations (Herek, 1991), or genders (Tannen, 1990). Certainly, the latter approach opens more subpopulations to investigation; however, the problem becomes one of determining sufficient distinctive features to delineate *different* cultures.

A number of theoretical solutions have been proffered to help resolve this problem. One possible solution comes from Gudykunst and Lim (1986), who suggest qualitative distinctions based on the salience of individual versus group characteristics in influencing the nature of individuals' attributions and their communication. If there is a greater preponderance of individual characteristics, the communication is considered more interpersonal, whereas if group characteristics predominate, the communication is considered intergroup. Another possible solution is the reliance on cultural dimensions, for example, individualism-collectivism (Triandis, 1995), independent/interdependent self construals (Markus & Kitayama, 1991), or high/low power distance

(Hofstede, 1980). With the use of these cultural dimensions, the operationalization of culture moves from a more typological and discrete format to one that is based on *degrees* of differences on cultural dimensions. Finally, a third solution involves the symbolic interactionist principle of self-referencing; namely, the operationalization of culture is based on one's own self-identity (Collier & Thomas, 1988). With this approach, it becomes important to measure how communicators define their own identities, be those identities ethnic, social, or cultural. Although the measures of self-identities still need some refinement, several research studies have had success taking this tack at conceptualizing and operationalizing culture (e.g., Gao, Schmidt, & Gudykunst, 1994; Rubin & Hewstone, 1998).

Effectively and Appropriately

What criteria should be used to judge ICC competence? A growing number of communication scholars have embraced Spitzberg's (1988) answer to this question: "Competent communication is interaction that is perceived as effective in fulfilling certain rewarding objectives in a way that is also appropriate to the context in which the interaction occurs" (p. 68). In other words, *competent* communication consists of behaviors that are regarded as effective and appropriate. Effective communication suggests that people are able to achieve desired personal outcomes. To do so, competent communicators should be able to control and manipulate their social environment to obtain those goals. This presumes that competent communicators are able to identify their goals, assess the resources necessary to obtain those goals, accurately predict the other communicator's responses, choose workable communication strategies, enact those communication strategies, and finally,

accurately assess the results of the interaction (Parks, 1976).

Appropriate communication entails the use of messages that are expected in a given context and actions that meet the expectations and demands of the situation. This criterion for communication competence requires the interactant to demonstrate an understanding of the expectations for acceptable behavior in a given situation. Appropriate communicators must recognize the constraints imposed on their behavior by different sets of rules (Lee, 1979), avoid violating those rules with inappropriate (e.g., impolite, abrasive, or bizarre) responses (Getter & Nowinski, 1981), and enact communication behaviors in an appropriate (e.g., clear, truthful, considerate, responsive) manner (Allen & Wood, 1978).

The two criteria of effectiveness and appropriateness combine to influence the quality of the interaction. In his recent formulation on ICC competence, Spitzberg (2000) suggested four possible communication styles that may result from the combinations of the extremes of the two criteria:

1. *Minimizing* communication is both inappropriate and ineffective and would obviously be of a low communicative quality.

2. *Sufficing* communication is appropriate but ineffective; that is, it is highly accommodating and does nothing objectionable but also accomplishes no personal objectives. Here Spitzberg suggested that the sufficing style is sufficient to meet the basic demands of the context, but it accomplishes nothing more.

3. *Maximizing* communication occurs when an individual is effective in achieving personal goals but at the cost of being highly inappropriate contextually. This style may include verbal aggression,

Machiavellian behavior, deception, the infringement of others' rights, or the degradation of others.

4. *Optimizing* communication occurs when interactants simultaneously achieve their personal goals and fulfill the normative expectations of the context.

Although this two-by-two analysis of discrete, binary combinations of the two criteria may be a bit simplistic, it helps to provide insight into the dialectics of the competence criteria in social episodes.

To Interact

We now come to the active aspect of our conceptualization of ICC competence. When communicators interact, they are co-orienting and coordinating their behaviors (verbal and nonverbal) to accomplish social functions, obtain personal goals, and conform to the normative expectations of the situation. To the extent that the communicators do these activities effectively and appropriately, they are considered *competent* communicators.

There has been considerable variation in the foci on communicative behaviors across investigations on ICC competence. In an early study, Ruben (1976) identified seven dimensions of communication related to one's effectiveness in overseas assignments: display of respect, interaction posture, orientation to knowledge, empathy, role behavior, interaction management, and tolerance for ambiguity. These general behaviors were subsequently operationalized in both self-report and observer measures and applied to the evaluation of overseas technical assistance personnel (Kealey, 1989; Ruben & Kealey, 1979), Japanese student sojourners (Nishida, 1985), and ICC workshop participants (Hammer, 1984).

In another early study, Hammer, Gudykunst, and Wiseman (1978) examined the intercultural effectiveness among American sojourners in terms of their educational experiences in other nations. Based on a measure consisting of 24 general behaviors posited to be instrumental in one's intercultural effectiveness, a factor analysis of the sojourners' responses determined three basic factors: ability to deal with psychological stress, ability to communicate effectively, and ability to establish interpersonal relationships. Subsequent research found some support for the culture-general character of these factors, as well as some evidence for some culture-specific aspects (Abe & Wiseman, 1983; Gudykunst & Hammer, 1984; Hammer, 1987; Wiseman & Abe, 1984).

A number of other research programs—with different results and sets of recommended communicative behaviors—could be reviewed (e.g., Harris, 1977; Hwang, Chase, & Arden-Ogle, 1985; Smith, 1966); however, issues of comparability, consistency, and generalizability emerge. Spitzberg and Kube (1988) recognized these problems and advocated an approach to reconciling these varying research foci. One of the steps in this reconciliation involves recognizing that some behaviors are very specific and concrete (molecular), whereas others are more general and traitlike (molar). Besides striving for consistency on the level of focus, Spitzberg (1989) also recommended consistency in the evaluation of the behavior being examined. Based on some of Lonner's (1980) research on cross-cultural universals, Spitzberg suggested four dimensions: "*Valence* (i.e., evaluation/affiliation), *Potency* (i.e., power relations), *Surgency* (i.e., activity/intensity), and *Socialization* (i.e., the extent to which a person is cognizant of, and rational about, the larger cultural context and rules of conduct involved)" (p. 251). Researchers should strive for consistency in terms of level of resolution of behavior (molar-molecular) and cultural members' affect toward the behavior.

Martin (1993) extended Spitzberg's recommendation for consistency on the level of resolution of behavior by developing a three-level typology. The most global type of behavior consists of high-order cognitive and behavioral processes, including global encoding/decoding skills, understanding cultural rules, and linguistic competence. Research by Brislin (1981), Bond (1988), Pruegger and Rogers (1993), and Triandis (1977) are illustrative of investigations on high-order cognitive and behavioral processes. The second type of behavior consists of midrange constructs (similar to Spitzberg's notion of molar concepts), including interaction management, social relaxation, empathy, assertiveness, sociability, politeness, and rule conformity. Research on these molar concepts can be illustrated with studies by Chen and Starosta (1997, 1998), Collier (1988), Koester and Olebe (1988), Spitzberg and Cupach (1989), and Wiemann (1977). The third and most specific level of resolution for behavior consists of molecular overt behaviors, for example, head nods, facial expressions, and proxemic orientations. Molecular behavior has been examined by Coker and Burgoon (1987), Kowner and Wiseman (2000), Li (1999), Martin and Hammer (1989), and Milhouse (1993). To enhance the comparability and thus the generalizability of findings regarding behavior related to ICC competence, researchers should be mindful of the levels of resolution for the behavior they are investigating and cultural members' evaluations of those behaviors.

Knowledge, Motivation, and Skills

ICC competence is not something innate within us, nor does it occur accidentally. Rather, there are necessary conditions that must exist before we are consciously and consistently competent in our intercultural interactions. Spitzberg and Cupach (1984) isolated three conditions: knowledge, motivation, and skills. If an interactant is lacking one of these conditions, the likelihood of competent intercultural communication is significantly diminished.

Knowledge refers to our awareness or understanding of requisite information and actions to be interculturally competent. A knowledgeable communicator needs information about the people, the communication rules, the context, and the normative expectations governing the interaction with the member of the other culture. Without this information, the communicator will invariably make misattributions, choose incorrect communication strategies, violate rules of etiquette, or cause the loss of face for self or other. Furthermore, the unknowing communicator may not be able to correctly ascribe the reasons for the errors or be able to remedy them. To obtain the needed knowledge to communicate competently, individuals need to be sensitive to the feedback from others (Berger, 1979) as well as be cognitively flexible to accommodate that feedback (Gudykunst, 1992). Thus, this knowledge component entails the body of information one needs as well as the cognitive schemata needed to assimilate that knowledge to be competent intercultural communicators.

Motivation refers to the set of feelings, intentions, needs, and drives associated with the anticipation of or actual engagement in intercultural communication. Factors such as anxiety, perceived social distance, attraction, ethnocentrism, and prejudice can influence an individual's decision to communicate with another. If our fears, dislikes, and anxieties predominate our affect toward the other, we will have negative motivation, and we will be likely to avoid the interaction, even if we feel we have the requisite knowledge and skills to perform. However, if our confidence, interest, likes, and good intentions predominate our affect toward the other, we will have positive motivation and will seek out and engage in interaction with the other (Morreale, Spitzberg, & Barge, 2001). Thus, competent communicators must learn to reduce the negative influences and increase the positive influences on their motivation to communicate with members of different cultures.

Skills refer to the actual performance of the behaviors felt to be effective and appropriate in the communication context. For Spitzberg (2000), skills must be repeatable and goal oriented. If a person accidentally produces a behavior that is perceived as competent, this would not be adequate, because the person may not be able to replicate the same behavior with the same effect. The person needs to be able to perform the script fluently and with cause (i.e., an appropriate rationale for its performance). This brings us to the notion that skills must be goal oriented. There must be some teleological basis for the performance, or else it is just behavior, not *skilled* behavior. The goals may be personal, dyadic, social, or contextual.

We will return to these three components—knowledge, motivation, and skills—later in this chapter. At this junction, though, it is important to note that competent intercultural communication requires all three components. Furthermore, these three components can be influenced through education, experience, and guided practice such that we can all learn to be competent intercultural communicators.

META-THEORIES
AND THEORIES

Given the above conceptualization of ICC competence, we are now ready to discuss different meta-theories and illustrative substantive theories that aspire to explain or predict ICC competence. A meta-theory is a set of assumptions that a researcher makes regarding the nature of the concept (ontology), what is important about the concept and its relationship with other human phenomena (axiology), and how the concept should be investigated (epistemology). Although new meta-theories may emerge in the future or other distinctions among the extant meta-theories can be made, there seems to be some agreement that three major meta-theories characterize communication research: the covering laws, systems, and human action perspectives (Hawes, 1977; Infante, Rancer, & Womack, 1997).

Of the three meta-theories, the covering laws perspective is the oldest and most frequent in communication theory and research. There are a number of common assumptions made by covering laws scholars (Infante et al., 1997):

1. Phenomena can be known through empirical means; that is, they are observable, measurable, and quantifiable.

2. There are regularities in our physical and social environments that can be observed or discovered. These regularities often transcend time, culture, and situation and are known as *laws* (Berger, 1977).

3. Underlying these regularities is the notion of causality, namely, cause-and-effect relationships. To explain or predict phenomena, we need to understand the causes of, or at least the antecedents to, those phenomena.

4. The goal of covering laws research is to discover regularities (laws) that have maximum generalizability.

The systems meta-theory was introduced to the communication discipline via the physical and biological sciences. The central contribution of systems theory is the notion that communication process is an integrated system consisting of interdependent units working together to adapt to a changing environment (Monge, 1977). A number of sensitizing concepts are important:

1. Communication systems are open systems; that is, they interact with their social and physical environments.

2. Communication is hierarchical; that is, it consists of subsystems and supra-systems.

3. Systems strive for balance or homeostasis. Changes in the environment or within the system create a drive in the system to restore balance.

4. Systems are teleological; that is, they are programmed to obtain specific goals.

One strength of systems meta-theory is that it attempts to focus on a broad range of interactions and relationships within a communication event to better understand the event.

The human action meta-theory represents a reaction against the strict logical positivism of the covering laws theory. For human action theorists, reality is not discovered in an objective world, but rather, reality is a subjective experience. To understand a person's communication, the researcher needs to understand the communicator's perception of the event (Cushman & Whiting, 1972). Thus, human action theorists focus on the actor's *interpretation* of the communication event and the way the communication event is related to the actor's goals. The relationship between communication and the actor's goals is usually depicted in terms of rules that associate goals with certain normatively expected instrumental behavior. The human action researcher attempts to explore actors' meanings, interpretations, and the rules governing their behavior.

These meta-theories provide a diversity of perspectives to assist scholars in better understanding communication. As Pearce (1977) argued,

> The effects of disciplinary diversity are favorable, provided that the various strands of the discipline are not insulated from each other. . . . The ability to articulate meta-theoretical assumptions is necessary to exploit the value of disciplinary diversity and is best attained by generating a corpus of materials which formally examine the meta-theoretical alternatives available to theorists and researchers. (p. 3)

To illustrate the contributions of these various strands of meta-theories, we will now explore representative substantive theories for each of the three meta-theories.

Covering Laws Theories

A number of substantive theories have emerged from the covering laws perspective. Two of those theories concerned with ICC competence are Gudykunst's (1993, 1995) anxiety/uncertainty management (AUM) theory and Ting-Toomey's (1988; Ting-Toomey & Kurogi, 1998) face-negotiation theory. An exploration of these two theories will enlighten our understanding of the covering laws perspective as well as the construct of ICC competence.

In Gudykunst's (1993, 1995) AUM theory, effective communication is related to one's ability to minimize misunderstandings with members of other cultures (i.e., "strangers"; cf. Simmel, 1908/1950). To the extent that misunderstandings arise, we feel uncertainty about the other and the situation. This uncertainty subsequently evokes anxiety within us, which, in turn, creates a drive to reduce our uncertainty and increase our mindfulness (Langer, 1989). Consistent with the covering laws meta-theory, these basic processes are invariant across situation, culture, or time.

The management of uncertainty and anxiety is the core of Gudykunst's AUM theory. This core mediates the influence of other variables and effective communication. Although uncertainty and anxiety are considered the basic causal influences on effective communication, other variables (e.g., self-concept, social categorization processes, motivations to communicate) are considered "superficial causes" (Lieberson, 1985). Consistent with the covering laws meta-theory, Gudykunst carefully developed axioms hypothesizing causal linkages between these superficial causes and uncertainty/anxiety and between uncertainty/anxiety and effective communication. Research on these axioms has found support for the model (Gao & Gudykunst, 1990; Gudykunst & Shapiro, 1996; Hammer, Wiseman, Rasmussen, & Bruschke, 1998).

Although a complete review of the elaborated model is beyond the scope of this chapter (see Gudykunst, Chapter 10 in this volume, for an elaboration of the model), it is worth noting that cognitive, motivational, and behavioral factors impinge on one's levels of anxiety and/or uncertainty. Once individuals feel sufficient levels of anxiety, they are, in turn, motivated to reduce their uncertainty via uncertainty reduction strategies (e.g., asking questions, disclosing). By reducing their uncertainty in making predictions about strangers, they will presumably reduce misunderstandings and increase their ICC effectiveness. Given the articulateness of the AUM theory, it should prove to be a heuristic source for future research.

Ting-Toomey's (1988) face-negotiation theory is concerned with the relational and appropriateness dimensions of our communication. Ontologically, competent intercultural communication involves issues regarding losing face and saving face. Face refers to one's sense of a favorable social self-worth, and facework consists of the communication that "people use to regulate their social dignity and

to support or challenge the other's social dignity" (Ting-Toomey & Kurogi, 1998, p. 188). It is felt that face and facework are universal phenomena; however, the actual strategies engaged in fulfilling face and facework vary culturally.

To warrant the causal connections among the variables of face, facework, cultural dimensions, and contextual factors, Ting-Toomey (1994) has conceptualized competence in facework as the integration of three core dimensions, namely, knowledge, mindfulness, and communication skills in managing self-face and other-face concerns. By knowledge, Ting-Toomey is referring to a deep-structure awareness of the nature and rules of the cultures involved in a particular situation. This awareness would include the cultural members' predispositions for face, relational goals, and communication strategies. Mindfulness involves "attending to one's internal assumptions, cognitions, and emotions and simultaneously attuning attentively to the other's assumptions, cognitions, and emotions while focusing the five senses" (Ting-Toomey & Kurogi, 1998, p. 203). We need to be more mindful of ourselves and others to effectively monitor our ethnocentrism and biases. Ting-Toomey's conceptualization of interaction skills is consistent with our conceptualization of ICC competence as noted above, in that interaction skills refer to "our abilities to communicate appropriately, effectively, and adaptively in a given situation" (Ting-Toomey & Kurogi, 1998, p. 204). Interaction skills are operationalized as mindful listening, mindful observation, facework management, trust building, and collaborative dialogue. As can be seen in this brief review of Ting-Toomey's face-negotiation theory (see Gudykunst and Lee, Chapter 2 in this volume, for more detail), competent intercultural communication emphasizes the relationships and appropriateness (axiology).

Systems Theories

As noted above, the systems meta-theory conceives of communication as an open system consisting of interrelated subsystems, all working to achieve some goal or purpose. Two substantive theories are representative of the systems orientation: Spitzberg's (2000) model of ICC competence and Kim's (1995) cross-cultural adaptation theory. Although the systems in the two theories vary in teleological intent, the systems are similar in their meta-theoretical orientation.

Based on a significant program of research and theorizing, Spitzberg (2000) presented his systems model of ICC competence. ICC competence is "an impression that behavior is appropriate and effective in a given context" (p. 375). Thus, the two standards of appropriateness and effectiveness are goals for competent intercultural communication. Three subsystems are operative: (1) The *individual* system is composed of the characteristics, traits, skills, and predispositions of the communicators; (2) the *episodic* system includes "those features of a particular Actor that facilitate competence interaction on the part of a specific Co-actor in a specific episode of interaction" (p. 376); and (3) the *relational* system includes those aspects of competence that affect the span of a relationship rather than just that particular episode. These systems are hierarchical in that each level is subsumed by another (i.e., the individual system is subsumed by the episodic system, which, in turn, is subsumed by the relational system).

For each of the three subsystems in Spitzberg's model, the components of knowledge, motivation, and skills are perceived as influencing communicative competence. At the individual level, communicator confidence, reward-relevant efficacy beliefs, and approach dispositions are positively associated with communicator motivation. At the episodic level, the actor's competence, attrib-uted status, and fulfillment of the coactor's expectancies are posited to increase the co-actor's impression of the actor's competence. Finally, at the relational level, mutual fulfillment of autonomy and intimacy needs, mutual attraction, mutual trust, and relational network integration are hypothesized to be positively associated with relational competence.

Spitzberg (2000) emphasized that one subsystem is insufficient in obtaining ICC competence. Even if a person is highly knowledgeable, motivated, and skilled, another from a different culture may reject his or her perceived competence and thus there would be a low probability of competent interaction (Bourhis, Moïse, Perreault, & Senécal, 1997). ICC competence is contingent on the optimal interrelationship of the individual, episodic, and relational systems.

Young Kim's program of research resulting in her cross-cultural adaptation theory spans nearly 25 years (Kim, 1995, 2001). The theory attempts to (1) describe the *process* of cross-cultural adaptation and (2) explain the *structure* of the process and the key variables that influence the degree to which individuals adapt to new and unfamiliar cultures. Because adaptation is a dynamic process involving both internal (intrapersonal) and external (social/environmental) variables, Kim advocates a systems approach at understanding the adaptation process because systems are best suited for representing the complex interrelationships involved in adaptation.

Kim (1995) characterized adaptation as a three-step process: stress-adaptation-growth. Consistent with the systems meta-theory, a challenge to the homeostasis (balance) of the system is introduced in the form of stress on the newcomer. The newcomer may feel culture shock, avoidance, hostility, or selective attention. Stress motivates the person to adapt to the host environment to restore homeostasis. This adaptation is accomplished through acculturation (learning) and deculturation (unlearning). From these learning processes, adaptation occurs in the form of an internal transformation of growth. The process of growth is not a simple linear one but rather a helical one characterized by ups and downs in the stress-adaptation process. The major variables in this process are host communication competence, host social communication, ethnic social communication, environment, and predisposition (see Gudykunst, Chapter 10 in this volume, for an elaboration of these systemic variables). These five variables constitute the structure of cross-cultural adaptation and interact to facilitate or inhibit intercultural transformation.

Human Action Theories

The human action meta-theory focuses on actors' meanings, interpretations, and the rules governing their behavior. In the present case, we are interested in human action theories that explore actors' meanings, interpretations, and rules for ICC competence. Because this meta-theory is one of the most recent of the emergent paradigms, there are fewer substantive theories representative of the human action perspective. However, two substantive theories should provide insight into this meta-theory as well as its approach to ICC competence: Collier's (1988, 1996) cultural identity theory and Cupach and Imahori's (1993) identity management theory.

In Collier's (1996) cultural identity theory, the constructs of culture and cultural identity are defined as concepts that emerge through interaction with others, and they take the forms of patterns of meanings, interpretations, and rules for behaviors. Consistent with human action meta-theory, the emphasis is on the subjective experience and one's interpretations for behavior (Geertz, 1973). Furthermore, one's cultural identity is negotiated

along two dimensions of rules: a constitutive dimension (consisting of symbols, interpretations, and meanings) and a normative dimension (consisting of guidelines for behavior and competencies for conduct). Individuals co-create and coordinate their meanings and rules to learn and enact their cultural identities. Thus, competent intercultural communication requires that individuals understand the meanings, rules, and codes for interacting appropriately.

Epistemologically, communication competence is identified by asking members of a culture to identify appropriate, rule-following behavior and to describe outcomes that arise from conforming to and violating those rules (Collier, 1989). This approach presumes a principle in human action theory, namely, the "open souls doctrine," which suggests that individuals are mindful of their behavior and can explain the reasons for it (Harré & Secord, 1972). The rules for behavior can vary in scope (breadth) and salience (relative importance). Information on the sanctions for rule violations is helpful in providing evidence for the force or strength of the rule (Pearce & Cronen, 1980), as well as providing insight as to how behavior is deemed appropriate or inappropriate. Procedurally, human action researchers ask cultural informants open-ended questions about their behavior, perceived (in)appropriateness, and rationales for their actions. From this corpus of data, the action researcher then attempts to find patterns or themes that emerge from the text. The strengths of human action research appear to be its heuristic value and its representational validity (i.e., the consistency of the results with the actors' judgments).

Another example of the human action meta-theory is Cupach and Imahori's (1993; see also Gudykunst's chapter in this volume) identity management theory. Identity management theory is significantly influenced by the work of Goffman (1967) and is akin to Collier's

(1989) cultural identity theory. According to Cupach and Imahori (1993), identity "gives one a sense of one's own ontological status and serves as an interpretive frame for experience" (p. 113). In contrast to interpersonal communication, intercultural communication poses additional complexity in the management of the actors' identities because each actor possesses salient but separate cultural identities. These salient and separate cultural identities need to be negotiated, maintained, and/or supported by both actors. Based on Brown and Levinson's (1978) work on politeness, the management of cultural identities is a form of facework.

Ontologically, communication competence is a matter of successfully negotiating mutually acceptable identities during the process of interaction. Competent intercultural communicators must be able to reconcile three dialectical tensions: (1) supporting one's own face or other's face, (2) supporting competence face (e.g., ingratiation, empowerment) or autonomy face (e.g., respecting other's privacy, independence), and (3) confirming other's separate cultural identity (heightening cultural differences) or negotiating a mutually defined cultural identity (minimizing separate cultural differences). The last dialectical tension is similar to communication accommodation theory's notions of divergence versus convergence (Giles, Mulac, Bradac, & Johnson, 1987). To the extent that communicators effectively and appropriately negotiate the three dialects, they are perceived as interculturally competent. Furthermore, it should be noted that face, facework, and dialectical orientations are never static—they are constantly in flux and must continually be renegotiated if the relationship is to stay healthy.

Given this discussion of meta-theories and representative substantive theories, we are now ready to examine some of the decisions the researcher of ICC competence must make in terms of methodology.

METHODOLOGICAL ISSUES

Methodology involves one's decisions about what to investigate, how to design the line of inquiry, what data collection techniques to use, on whom to collect data, and what sense to make of the data. Obviously, one's conceptualization of the topic of research, one's meta-theoretical orientation (ontology, axiology, and especially, epistemology), and one's particular substantive theoretical approach all influence the choices one makes. This section of the chapter explores some of the options available in making decisions about methodology.

Lustig and Spitzberg (1993) proposed a creative approach at understanding methodological decisions using a set of journalist's *topoi* (i.e., *what, who, when, where,* and *why* decisions in researching ICC competence). In terms of what is being investigated, at least three issues need to be addressed: (1) level of abstraction: microscopic interaction behaviors, mezzoscopic behaviors (e.g., politeness rituals, speech acts), or macroscopic behaviors (e.g., conflict styles, empathy levels); (2) level of analysis: behaviors, social artifacts, individuals, groups, or cultures; and (3) type of comparison made among the particular attributes or behaviors: typicality, variability, associations with other variables, or patterns of differences in behavior among individuals, groups, or cultures.

In terms of who is the locus of competence evaluation, Lustig and Spitzberg (1993) suggested the issue is one of whether to collect data from the actor, coactor, or an uninvolved observer. The problem is that the perceptions of these three parties are often inconsistent (Jacobson & Moore, 1981). The solution advocated is to let the researcher decide the perceptual locus, that is, who is in the best position to make the perceptions. If it involves internal attributions and psychological orientations, the actor may be in the best position, whereas if it involves public behavior, the coactor or uninvolved observer may be in the best position to make judgments. In terms of the when issue, the decision is whether to conceptualize competence as an episodic or dispositional phenomenon. Episodic phenomena are more situation specific or context specific, whereas dispositional phenomena tend to be viewed as cross-situational traits. Another aspect of when to collect data involves whether to collect cross-sectional or longitudinal data. Certainly, if a researcher is interested in the process nature of competence (e.g., phases), longitudinal data would be preferable.

Lustig and Spitzberg (1993) viewed the where issue as a contextual one. Is ICC competence dependent on the particular context (e.g., business, academia, tourism), or does it transcend contexts (i.e., a universal trait)? Hammer, Nishida, and Wiseman (1996) provided a cogent argument for accounting for the contextual effects on ICC competence. Finally, in terms of the why issue, Lustig and Spitzberg (1993) admonished past researchers for not considering the cultural and social implications of their research on ICC competence. If the researcher is attempting to design a training program, improve cultural relationships, or enhance an individual's image, there will be implications for how to research the construct. ICC competence researchers need to take these implications into consideration.

CONSTRUCTS RELATED TO INTERCULTURAL COMMUNICATION COMPETENCE

Although it is beyond the scope of this chapter to review all of the research demonstrating ICC competence's relationships with relevant social and psychological constructs, it may be helpful for future researchers to provide a cursory review of some of the findings on these relationships. As a means for organizing this brief review, the chapter will consider constructs related to the knowledge, motivation, and skill components of ICC competence.

The knowledge component of competence is conceptualized as the information necessary to interact appropriately and effectively, and the requisite cognitive orientation to facilitate the acquisition of such information. In terms of the necessary information, research has found positive associations between ICC competence and awareness of the other culture (Wiseman, Hammer, & Nishida, 1989), self-awareness (Gudykunst, Yang, & Nishida, 1987), and host language fluency (Giles, 1977). These forms of knowledge increase the intercultural communicator's understanding of other and self in order to facilitate making accurate predictions and attributions. Favorable cognitive orientations have been found in terms of open-mindedness (Adler, 1975), nonjudgmentalness (Ruben, 1976), self-monitoring ability (Snyder, 1987), problem-solving ability (Brislin, 1981), and cognitive complexity (Wiseman & Abe, 1985). These orientations facilitate perspective taking and adaptation to new information.

In terms of the motivation component of competence, a number of variables have been found to influence one's affect toward others and intercultural communication. Positive associations have been found between ICC competence and intercultural sensitivity (Chen & Starosta, 1998, 2000), positive affect toward the other culture (Randolph, Landis, & Tzeng, 1977), social relaxation (Gudykunst & Hammer, 1988; Sanders & Wiseman, 1993), and empathy toward others (Chen & Tan, 1995; Ruben, 1976). A negative association has been found for ethnocentrism (Neuliep & McCroskey, 1997; Nishida, Hammer, & Wiseman, 1998). These evaluative elements (both positive and negative valence) seem to operate by changing the approach-avoidance predispositions to communicate interculturally.

The final component of ICC competence—skill—reflects the needed behaviors to interact appropriately and effectively with members of different cultures. Research has discovered several behaviors that are positively associated with ICC competence: being mindful (Gudykunst, 1992), intercultural adroitness (Chen & Starosta, 1996), interaction involvement (Cegala, 1984), recognition of nonverbal messages (Anderson, 1994), appropriate self-disclosure (Li, 1999), behavioral flexibility (Bochner & Kelly, 1974), interaction management (Wiemann, 1977), identity maintenance (Ting-Toomey, 1994), uncertainty reduction strategies (Sanders, Wiseman, & Matz, 1991), appropriate display of respect (Ruben, 1976), immediacy skills (Benson, 1978), ability to establish interpersonal relationships (Hammer, 1987), and expressing clarity and face support (Kim, 1993). These behaviors reflect the ability to communicate in an adaptive, flexible, and supportive manner.

CONCLUSION

This chapter has attempted to explore some of the issues involved in theorizing and researching ICC competence. A researcher must make a number of decisions about the choice of a topic, its conceptualization, metatheoretical orientations, substantive theories explaining the concept, and methodological decisions regarding the actual investigation of the concept. It is hoped that this essay will assist the researcher in making these decisions carefully and mindfully. With constructive research, productive findings and recommendations should result, thereby improving the communication and relations among the members of the cultures of our global village.

REFERENCES

Abe, H., & Wiseman, R. L. (1983). A cross-cultural confirmation of the dimensions of intercultural effectiveness. *International Journal of Intercultural Relations, 7,* 53-67.

Adler, P. S. (1975). Beyond cultural identity: Reflections on cultural and multicultural man. In L. Samovar & R. Porter (Eds.), *Intercultural communication: A reader* (2nd ed., pp. 362-378). Belmont, CA: Wadsworth.

Allen, R. R., & Wood, B. S. (1978). Beyond reading and writing to communication competence. *Communication Education, 27,* 286-292.

Anderson, J. W. (1994). A comparison of Arab and American conceptions of "effective" persuasion. In L. Samovar & R. Porter (Eds.), *Intercultural communication: A reader* (7th ed., pp. 104-113). Belmont, CA: Wadsworth.

Benson, P. G. (1978). Measuring cross-cultural adjustment: The problem of criteria. *International Journal of Intercultural Relations, 2,* 21-37.

Berger, C. R. (1977). The covering law perspective as a theoretical basis for the study of human communication. *Communication Quarterly, 25,* 7-18.

Berger, C. R. (1979). Beyond initial interactions. In H. Giles & R. St. Clair (Eds.), *Language and social psychology* (pp. 122-144). Oxford, UK: Basil Blackwell.

Bochner, A. P., & Kelly, C. W. (1974). Interpersonal competence: Rationale, philosophy, and implementation of a conceptual framework. *Speech Teacher, 23,* 279-301.

Bond, M. H. (1988). Finding universal dimensions of individual variation in multicultural studies of values: The Rokeach and Chinese value surveys. *Journal of Personality and Social Psychology, 55,* 1009-1015.

Bourhis, R. Y., Moïse, L. C., Perreault, S., & Senécal, S. (1997). Towards an interactive acculturation model: A social psychological approach. *International Journal of Psychology, 32,* 369-386.

Bradford, L., Allen, M., & Beisser, K. (2000). An evaluation and meta-analysis of intercultural communication competence research. *World Communication, 29,* 28-51.

Bradford, L., Kane, K. A., & Meyers, R. A. (1996, November). *Using focus group interviews to investigate Latino expectations of communication competence.* Paper presented at the annual meeting of the Speech Communication Association, San Diego, CA.

Braithwaite, D. O. (1991). Viewing persons with disabilities as a culture. In L. Samovar & R. Porter (Eds.), *Intercultural communication: A reader* (6th ed., pp. 136-142). Belmont, CA: Wadsworth.

Brislin, R. W. (1981). *Cross-cultural encounters: Face-to-face interaction.* Elmsford, NY: Pergamon.

Brown, P., & Levinson, S. (1978). Universals in language usage: Politeness phenomena. In E. Goody (Ed.), *Questions and politeness: Strategies in social interaction* (pp. 56-289). Cambridge, UK: Cambridge University Press.

Cargile, A. C., & Giles, H. (1996). Intercultural communication training: Review, critique, and a new theoretical framework. In B. Burleson (Ed.), *Communication yearbook 19* (pp. 385-423). Thousand Oaks, CA: Sage.

Cegala, D. J. (1984). Affective and cognitive manifestations of interaction involvement during unstructured and competitive interactions. *Communication Monographs, 51,* 320-338.

Chen, G. M., & Starosta, W. J. (1996). Intercultural communication competence: A synthesis. In B. Burleson (Ed.), *Communication yearbook 19* (pp. 353-383). Thousand Oaks, CA: Sage.

Chen, G. M., & Starosta, W. J. (1997). A review of the concept of intercultural sensitivity. *Human Communication, 1,* 1-16.

Chen, G. M., & Starosta, W. J. (1998). A review of the concept of intercultural awareness. *Human Communication, 2,* 27-54.

Chen, G. M., & Starosta, W. J. (2000). The development and validation of the intercultural sensitivity scale. *Human Communication, 3,* 2-14.

Chen, G. M., & Tan, L. (1995, April). *A theory of intercultural sensitivity.* Paper presented at the annual meeting of the Eastern Communication Association, Philadelphia.

Coker, D. A., & Burgoon, J. K. (1987). Trait versus state: A comparison of dispositional and situation measures of interpersonal communication competence. *Western Journal of Speech Communication, 47,* 364-379.

Collier, M. J. (1988). A comparison of conversations among and between domestic culture groups: How intra- and intercultural competencies vary. *Communication Quarterly, 36,* 122-144.

Collier, M. J. (1989). Cultural and intercultural communication competence: Current approaches and directions for future research. *International Journal of Intercultural Relations, 13,* 287-302.

Collier, M. J. (1996). Communication competence problematics in ethnic friendships. *Communication Monographs, 63,* 314-336.

Collier, M. J., & Thomas, M. (1988). Identity in intercultural communication: An interpretive perspective. In Y. Y. Kim & W. B. Gudykunst (Eds.), *Theories in intercultural communication* (pp. 99-120). Newbury Park, CA: Sage.

Cupach, W. R., & Imahori, T. T. (1993). Identity management theory: Communication competence in intercultural episodes and relationships. In R. L. Wiseman & J. Koester (Eds.), *Intercultural communication competence* (pp. 112-131). Newbury Park, CA: Sage.

Cushman, D., & Whiting, G. C. (1972). An approach to communication theory: Toward consensus on rules. *Journal of Communication, 22,* 217-238.

Dean, O., & Popp, G. E. (1990). Intercultural communication effectiveness as perceived by American managers in Saudi Arabia and French managers in the U.S. *International Journal of Intercultural Relations, 14,* 405-424.

Fox, S. A., & Giles, H. (1993). Accommodating intergenerational contact: A critique and theoretical model. *Journal of Aging Studies, 7,* 423-451.

Gao, G., & Gudykunst, W. B. (1990). Uncertainty, anxiety, and adaptation. *International Journal of Intercultural Relations, 14,* 301-317.

Gao, G., Schmidt, K. L., & Gudykunst, W. B. (1994). Strength of ethnic identity and perceptions of ethnolinguistic vitality among Mexican Americans. *Hispanic Journal of Behavioral Sciences, 16,* 332-341.

Gardner, G. H. (1962). Cross-cultural communication. *Journal of Social Psychology, 58,* 241-256.

Geertz, C. (1973). *The interpretation of cultures.* New York: Basic Books.

Getter, H., & Nowinski, J. K. (1981). A free response test of interpersonal effectiveness. *Journal of Personality Assessment, 45,* 301-308.

Giles, H. (Ed.). (1977). *Language, ethnicity, and intergroup communication.* London: Academic Press.

Giles, H., Mulac, A., Bradac, J., & Johnson, P. (1987). Speech accommodation theory. In M. McLaughlin (Ed.), *Communication yearbook 10* (pp. 13-48). Newbury Park, CA: Sage.

Goffman, E. (1967). *Interaction ritual: Essays on face to face behavior.* Garden City, NY: Anchor.

Gudykunst, W. B. (1992). Being perceived as a competent communicator. In W. B. Gudykunst & Y. Y. Kim (Eds.), *Readings on communicating with strangers* (pp. 382-392). New York: McGraw-Hill.

Gudykunst, W. B. (1993). Toward a theory of effective interpersonal and intergroup communication: An anxiety/uncertainty management (AUM) perspective. In R. L. Wiseman & J. Koester (Eds.), *Intercultural communication competence* (pp. 33-71). Newbury Park, CA: Sage.

Gudykunst, W. B. (1995). Anxiety/uncertainty management (AUM) theory: Current status. In R. L. Wiseman (Ed.), *Intercultural communication theory* (pp. 8-58). Thousand Oaks, CA: Sage.

Gudykunst, W. B. (1998). *Bridging differences: Effective intergroup communication* (3rd ed.). Thousand Oaks, CA: Sage.

Gudykunst, W. B., & Hammer, M. R. (1984). Comment on Abe & Wiseman: Dimensions of intercultural effectiveness—Culture specific or culture general. *International Journal of Intercultural Relations, 8,* 1-10.

Gudykunst, W. B., & Hammer, M. R. (1988). Strangers and hosts: An uncertainty reduction based theory of intercultural adaptation. In Y. Y. Kim & W. B. Gudykunst (Eds.), *Cross-cultural adaptation: Current approaches* (pp. 106-139). Newbury Park, CA: Sage.

Gudykunst, W. B., & Lim, T. S. (1986). A perspective for the study of intergroup communication. In W. Gudykunst (Ed.), *Intergroup communication* (pp. 1-10). London: Edward Arnold.

Gudykunst, W. B., & Shapiro, R. B. (1996). Communication in everyday interpersonal and intergroup encounters. *International Journal of Intercultural Relations, 20,* 19-46.

Gudykunst, W. B., Wiseman, R. L., & Hammer, M. R. (1977). Determinants of a sojourner's attitudinal satisfaction: A path model. In B. Ruben (Ed.), *Communication yearbook 1* (pp. 415-425). New Brunswick, NJ: Transaction.

Gudykunst, W. B., Yang, S. M., & Nishida, T. (1987). Cultural differences in self-consciousness and unself-consciousness. *Communication Research, 14,* 7-36.

Guthrie, G. M., & Zektick, I. N. (1967). Predicting performance in the Peace Corps. *Journal of Social Psychology, 71,* 11-21.

Hammer, M. R. (1984). Communication workshop on participants' intercultural communication competence: An exploratory study. *Communication Quarterly, 32,* 252-262.

Hammer, M. R. (1987). Behavioral dimensions of intercultural effectiveness: A replication and extension. *International Journal of Intercultural Relations, 11,* 65-88.

Hammer, M. R., Gudykunst, W. B., & Wiseman, R. L. (1978). Dimensions of intercultural effectiveness: An exploratory study. *International Journal of Intercultural Relations, 2,* 382-392.

Hammer, M. R., Nishida, H., & Wiseman, R. L. (1996). The influence of situational prototype on dimensions of intercultural communication competence. *Journal of Cross-Cultural Psychology, 27,* 267-282.

Hammer, M. R., Wiseman, R. L., Rasmussen, J., & Bruschke, J. (1998). A test of anxiety/uncertainty management theory: The intercultural adaptation context. *Communication Quarterly, 46,* 309-326.

Harré, R., & Secord, P. F. (1972). *The explanation of social behaviour.* Oxford, UK: Basil Blackwell.

Harris, J. G. (1975). Identification of cross-cultural talent: The empirical approach of the Peace Corps. *Topics in Culture Learning, 3,* 66-78.

Harris, J. G. (1977). Identification of cross-cultural talent: The empirical approach of the Peace Corps. In R. Brislin (Ed.), *Culture learning: Concepts, applications, and research* (pp. 182-194). Honolulu, HI: East-West Center.

Hawes, L. C. (1977). Alternative theoretical bases: Toward a presuppositional critique. *Communication Quarterly, 25*, 63-68.

Herek, G. M. (1991). Stigma, prejudice, and violence against lesbians and gay men. In J. Gonsiorek & J. Weinrich (Eds.), *Homosexuality: Research implications for public policy* (pp. 60-80). Newbury Park, CA: Sage.

Herek, G. M., & Giles, H. (2000, June). *New directions in intercultural communication competence: The process model.* Paper presented at the annual meeting of the International Communication Association, Acapulco, Mexico.

Hofstede, G. (1980). *Culture's consequences: International differences in work-related values.* Beverly Hills, CA: Sage.

Hoselitz, B. F. (1954). Problems of adapting and communicating modern techniques to less developed areas. *Economic Development and Cultural Change, 2*, 249-268.

Hwang, J. C., Chase, L. J., & Arden-Ogle, E. (1985, May). *Communication competence across three cultures: In search of similarity.* Paper presented at the annual meeting of the International Communication Association, Honolulu, HI.

Infante, D. A., Rancer, A. S., & Womack, D. F. (1997). *Building communication theory* (3rd ed.). Prospect Heights, IL: Waveland.

Jacobson, N. S., & Moore, D. (1981). Spouses as observers of the events in their relationship. *Journal of Consulting and Clinical Psychology, 49*, 269-277.

Kealey, D. J. (1989). A study of cross-cultural effectiveness: Theoretical issues, practical applications. *International Journal of Intercultural Relations, 13*, 397-428.

Kim, M. S. (1993). Culture-based interactive constraints in explaining intercultural strategic competence. In R. L. Wiseman & J. Koester (Eds.), *Intercultural communication competence* (pp. 132-152). Newbury Park, CA: Sage.

Kim, Y. (1995). Cross-cultural adaptation: An integrative theory. In R. L. Wiseman (Ed.), *Intercultural communication theory* (pp. 170-193). Thousand Oaks, CA: Sage.

Kim, Y. (2001). *Becoming intercultural.* Newbury Park, CA: Sage.

Koester, J., & Olebe, M. (1988). The behavioral assessment scale for intercultural communication effectiveness. *International Journal of Intercultural Relations, 12*, 233-246.

Kowner, R., & Wiseman, R. L. (2000, June). *Cultural patterns of status-related behavior: Japanese and American perceptions of behavior in asymmetric dyadic interaction.* Paper presented at the annual meeting of the International Communication Association, Acapulco, Mexico.

Landis, D., & Brislin, R. W. (Eds.). (1983). *Handbook of intercultural training* (3 vols.). New York: Pergamon.

Langer, E. (1989). *Mindfulness.* Reading, MA: Addison-Wesley.

Lee, L. (1979). Is social competence independent of cultural context? *American Psychologist, 34*, 795-796.

Li, H. Z. (1999). Grounding and information communication in intercultural and intracultural dyadic discourse. *Discourse Processes, 28*, 195-215.

Lieberson, S. (1985). *Making it count: The improvement of research and theory.* Berkeley: University of California Press.

Lonner, W. J. (1980). The search for psychological universals. In H. C. Triandis & W. W. Lambert (Eds.), *Handbook of cross-cultural psychology* (Vol. 1, pp. 143-204). Boston: Allyn & Bacon.

Lustig, M. W., & Koester, J. (1999). *Intercultural competence: Interpersonal communication across cultures* (3rd ed.). New York: Longman.

Lustig, M. W., & Spitzberg, B. H. (1993). Methodological issues in the study of intercultural communication competence. In R. L. Wiseman & J. Koester (Eds.), *Intercultural communication competence* (pp. 153-167). Newbury Park, CA: Sage.

Markus, H., & Kitayama, S. (1991). Culture and self. *Psychological Review, 98*, 224-253.

Martin, J. N. (Ed.). (1989). Intercultural communication competence [Special issue]. *International Journal of Intercultural Relations, 13*(3).

Martin, J. N. (1993). Intercultural communication competence: A review. In R. L. Wiseman & J. Koester (Eds.), *Intercultural communication competence* (pp. 16-32). Newbury Park, CA: Sage.

Martin, J. N., & Hammer, M. R. (1989). Behavioral categories of intercultural communication competence: Everyday communicators' perceptions. *International Journal of Intercultural Relations, 13,* 303-332.

Milhouse, V. H. (1993). The applicability of interpersonal communication competence to the intercultural communication context. In R. L. Wiseman & J. Koester (Eds.), *Intercultural communication competence* (pp. 184-203). Newbury Park, CA: Sage.

Monge, P. R. (1977). The systems perspective as a theoretical basis for the study of human communication. *Communication Quarterly, 25,* 19-29.

Morreale, S. P., Spitzberg, B. H., & Barge, J. K. (2001). *Human communication: Motivation, knowledge, and skills.* Belmont, CA: Wadsworth/ Thomson Learning.

Neuliep, J. W., & McCroskey, J. C. (1997). The development of intercultural and interethnic communication apprehension scales. *Communication Research Reports, 14,* 385-398.

Nishida, H. (1985). Japanese intercultural communication competence and cross-cultural adjustment. *International Journal of Intercultural Relations, 9,* 247-269.

Nishida, H., Hammer, M. R., & Wiseman, R. L. (1998). Cognitive differences between Japanese and Americans in their perceptions of difficult social situations. *Journal of Cross-Cultural Psychology, 29,* 499-524.

Oetzel, J., Ting-Toomey, S., Masumoto, T., Yokochi, Y., Pan, X., Takai, J., & Wilcox, R. (2000, June). *Face and facework in conflict: A cross-cultural comparison of China, Germany, Japan, and the United States.* Paper presented at the annual meeting of the International Communication Association, Acapulco, Mexico.

Parks, M. R. (1976, November). *Communication competence.* Paper presented at the annual meeting of the Speech Communication Association, San Francisco.

Pearce, W. B. (1977). Metatheoretical concerns in communication. *Communication Quarterly, 25,* 3-6.

Pearce, W. B., & Cronen, V. (1980). *Communication, action, and meaning.* New York: Praeger.

Pruegger, V. J., & Rogers, T. B. (1993). Development of a scale to measure cross-cultural sensitivity in the Canadian context. *Canadian Journal of Behavioural Science, 25,* 615-621.

Randolph, G., Landis, D., & Tzeng, O. (1977). The effects of time and practice upon culture assimilator training. *International Journal of Intercultural Relations, 1,* 105-119.

Rogers, E. M. (1983). *Diffusion of innovations* (3rd ed.). New York: Free Press.

Ruben, B. D. (1976). Assessing communication competency for intercultural adaptation. *Group and Organization Studies, 2,* 470-479.

Ruben, B. D., & Kealey, D. (1979). Behavioral assessment of communication competency and the prediction of cross-cultural adaptation. *International Journal of Intercultural Relations, 3,* 15-48.

Rubin, M., & Hewstone, M. (1998). Social identity theory's self-esteem hypothesis. *Personality and Social Psychology Review, 2,* 40-62.

Sanders, J. A., & Wiseman, R. L. (1993). Uncertainty reduction among ethnicities in the United States. *Intercultural Communication Studies, 3*(1), 28-44.

Sanders, J. A., Wiseman, R. L., & Matz, S. I. (1991). Uncertainty reduction in acquaintance relationships in Ghana and the United States. In S. Ting-Toomey & F. Korzenny (Eds.), *Cross-cultural perspectives on interpersonal communication* (pp. 79-98). Newbury Park, CA: Sage.

Shearer, A. (1984). *Disability: Whose handicap?* Oxford, UK: Basil Blackwell.

Simmel, G. (1950). The stranger. In K. Wolff (Ed. & Trans.), *The sociology of Georg Simmel* (pp. 402-408). New York: Free Press. (Original work published 1908)

Smith, M. B. (1966). Explorations in competence: A study of Peace Corps teachers in Ghana. *American Psychologist, 21,* 525-556.

Snyder, M. (1987). *Public appearances, private realities.* New York: Friedman.

Spitzberg, B. H. (1988). Communication competence: Measures of perceived effectiveness. In C. Tardy (Ed.), *A handbook for the study of human communication* (pp. 67-105). Norwood, NJ: Ablex.

Spitzberg, B. H. (2000). A model of intercultural communication competence. In L. Samovar & R. Porter (Eds.), *Intercultural communication: A reader* (9th ed., pp. 375-387). Belmont, CA: Wadsworth.

Spitzberg, B. H., & Cupach, W. R. (1984). *Interpersonal communication competence.* Beverly Hills, CA: Sage.

Spitzberg, B. H., & Cupach, W. R. (1989). *Handbook of interpersonal competence research.* New York: Springer-Verlag.

Spitzberg, B. H., & Kube, T. (1988, November). *Progress and pitfalls in conceptualizing and researching intercultural communication competence.* Paper presented at the annual meeting of the Speech Communication Association, New Orleans, LA.

Stening, S. W. (1979). Problems in cross-cultural contact: A literature review. *International Journal of Intercultural Relations, 3,* 269-313.

Tannen, D. (1990). *You just don't understand: Women and men in conversation.* New York: Ballantine.

Ting-Toomey, S. (1988). Intercultural conflicts: A face-negotiation theory. In Y. Y. Kim & W. B. Gudykunst (Eds.), *Theories in intercultural communication* (pp. 213-238). Newbury Park, CA: Sage.

Ting-Toomey, S. (1994). Managing conflict in intimate intercultural relationships. In D. Cahn (Ed.), *Intimate conflict in personal relationships.* Hillsdale, NJ: Lawrence Erlbaum.

Ting-Toomey, S., & Kurogi, A. (1998). Facework competence in intercultural conflict: An updated face-negotiation theory. *International Journal of Intercultural Relations, 22,* 187-226.

Triandis, H. C. (1977). Subjective culture and interpersonal relations across cultures. *Annals of the New York Academy of Sciences, 285,* 418-434.

Triandis, H. C. (1995). *Individualism-collectivism.* Boulder, CO: Westview.

Wiemann, J. M. (1977). Explication and test of a model of communicative competence. *Human Communication Research, 3,* 195-213.

Wiseman, R. L., & Abe, H. (1984). Finding and explaining differences: A reply to Gudykunst & Hammer. *International Journal of Intercultural Relations, 8,* 11-16.

Wiseman, R. L., & Abe, H. (1985). Cognitive complexity and perceptions of intercultural effectiveness in American-Japanese dyads. In M. McLaughlin (Ed.), *Communication yearbook 9* (pp. 456-479). Beverly Hills, CA: Sage.

Wiseman, R. L., Emry, R., & Morgan, D. (1987). A normative analysis of the intercultural communication between nondisabled and disabled persons. *World Communication Journal, 16,* 137-155.

Wiseman, R. L., Hammer, M., & Nishida, N. (1989). Predictors of intercultural communication competence. *International Journal of Intercultural Relations, 13,* 349-370.

Wiseman, R. L., & Koester, J. (Eds.). (1993). *Intercultural communication competence.* Newbury Park, CA: Sage.

11

Identity and Intergroup Communication

JESSICA ABRAMS
JOAN O'CONNOR
HOWARD GILES
University of California, Santa Barbara

Communication scholars have recognized the importance of identity in intercultural research (Collier & Thomas, 1988; Lustig & Koester, 2000) and have articulated it in several different ways. Among others, scholars have differentiated between racial identity, based largely on physical characteristics (Martin, 1997), and cultural identity, the extent to which individuals hold their larger culture to be important (Ting-Toomey et al., 2000). Ethnic identity has been described as "a set of ideas about one's own ethnic group membership, including self-identification and knowledge about ethnic culture (traditions, customs, values, and behaviors), and feelings about belonging to a particular ethnic group" (Martin & Nakayama, 1997, p. 74). Consistent with an "intergroup" approach (see Giles & Coupland, 1991), this latter definition is our preferred conceptual stance because we contend ethnic identity is likely to be salient, given that group distinctions are often evoked when engaging in intercultural communication. Little attention has been directed toward the processual nature of the relationship between identity and communication. Our goal is to explicate its transactional and intergroup characteristics.

Scholars have offered various perspectives on studying identity. The social psychological emphasizes that it is created, in part, by the self and, in part, by group membership and acknowledges "persistent sharing of some kind of essential character with others" (Erikson, 1959, p. 109). Social identity theory (SIT) proposes that an individual's self-concept is composed of both *social* and *personal* identities (Tajfel & Turner, 1986).

AUTHORS' NOTE: We wish to acknowledge the constructive comments of William Gudykunst on a previous draft of this chapter.

Personal identity refers to an individual's unique characteristics, irrespective of cultural or social group, and social identity is defined as one's knowledge of membership in certain social groups and the social meanings attached to the group. The central tenet of SIT is that the groups with which individuals identify (and there usually are a myriad of them) determine their social identities. Age, gender, profession, nationality, region, religion, and so forth all serve as different social identities and have their own cultural components of shared values, habits, and history. For example, many African Americans, who strongly identify with their ethnicity, will likely view themselves as "belonging" to "their" group.

Research, generally, conceptualizes identity as a multidimensional concept. For example, Kashima, Kashima, and Hardie (2000) distinguished two dimensions: self-typicality (perceived typicality of the self as an ingroup member) and group identification (the affective-evaluative response to ingroup membership). This distinction may be particularly important when considering ethnic identity. Phinney (1992) argues that the behavioral component of ethnic identity involves the degree to which individuals engage, and are competent, in the activities associated with their ethnic groups. These activities can include, but are not limited to, eating ethnic foods, engaging in ethnic behavioral patterns, speaking and writing the languages of the ethnic group, sharing networks with ethnic group members, and demonstrating common communication styles (Gudykunst, 2001; Gudykunst, Sodetani, & Sonoda, 1987). Although individuals may define themselves as a member of a certain ethnic group, they may not perceive themselves as being a "typical" member of it. Other individuals may both highly identify with their ethnic identity and perceive themselves as typical. Either way, these conceptions of identity may

manifest themselves communicatively in differing ways.

For example, recent research suggests that one way ethnic identity is communicated is via conflict patterns. In their investigation of the impact of ethnic identity on conflict styles, Ting-Toomey et al. (2000) reveal individuals with a strong ethnic identity use integrating conflict styles (i.e., a high concern for both self and others during negotiation), whereas individuals with a weak ethnic identity use neglecting (tactfulness and consideration of others' feelings conveyed through the use of obligation and avoidance in conflict) and third-party (using a third party to deal with conflict issues) conflict styles. The authors argue that because the larger U.S. culture tends to engage in a low-context mode of conflict patterns, individuals who strongly identify with the larger U.S. culture will directly negotiate conflict. More specifically, they found that Asian Americans with a weak cultural identity use avoiding more than other ethnic groups, whereas Latino Americans with a weak cultural identity use neglecting more than other ethnic groups.

THE INFLUENCE OF IDENTITY ON COMMUNICATION BEHAVIORS

A communication perspective emphasizes that the self does not create identities alone; instead, they are co-created through communication with others (Martin & Nakayama, 1997). The central tenet is that identities emerge when messages are exchanged between persons (see Table 11.1). In this way, Collier (1997) argues that ethnic identities are negotiated, reinforced, and challenged through communication, and she describes how the respective "properties" of ethnic identity are enacted and developed through communication. One of these, she argues, is that identities are enacted in interpersonal

Table 11.1 Identity as Communication

	Convergence ◄————————————————————————————► Divergence				
Nonverbal behavior	Ingroup rejection Assimilation	Positive allocation bias Smiling, gaze, gestures Time		Outgroup rejection Ethnophaulisms Negative allocation bias Symbols	Crowd behavior Conflict Physical boundaries
Language	Outgroup language with nativelike pronunciation Language acquisition	Outgroup language with features of ingroup pronunciation Topic choice Code switching Language intensity	Ingroup language with slow speech rate Conversation interruptions Conversation turn taking Sarcasm, hostility, disagreement	Ingroup language with normal speech rate Non-language acquisition Labels	Patronizing talk
Paralanguage	Accent, dialect, idioms, speech rate, pauses, utterance length, phonological variants can all be modified to signal convergence	Self-disclosure (quality and quantity) Language		Accent, dialect, idioms, speech rate, pauses, utterance length, phonological variants can all be modified to signal divergence	

NOTE: Please contact the chapter authors if interested in specific citations for exemplars in each cell.

contexts through *avowal* or *ascription* processes. Avowal is the self an individual portrays (i.e., saying, "This is who I am"), whereas ascription is the process by which others attribute identities to an individual (e.g., through stereotypes). The avowal and ascription processes acknowledge that identity is shaped by our own and by others' communicated views of us. Identities are also expressed through *core symbols, norms,* and *labels* (Collier, 1997). The Mexican flag, the yarmulke, Kwanza, and the adjective Japanese American are examples of how ethnic pride is communicated via norms, symbols, and labels. The property of ethnic identities being dynamic and context related (Martin, 1997) underscores that they are emphasized depending on whom we are communicating with and the topic of conversation.

Although Collier (1997) intended that the properties of ethnic identities she articulated would help build models of ethnic identity and communication, theorists have been slow to articulate the symbiotic and transactional relationship. The processes whereby individuals construct and reconstruct their identity through communication is often absent in intercultural theorizing, despite prominent intercultural theories including, explicitly or implicitly, the roles of identity in intercultural communication (see Wiseman, 1995). Gudykunst (1995) argues that the management of anxiety and uncertainty is fundamental to effective communication, with identity influencing uncertainty and anxiety but not being directly related to effective communication. This is an assertion we would question given the growing body of evidence linking identity to particular communication styles.

Similarly, cross-cultural adaptation theory (Kim, 1995) describes the process and structure in which individuals adapt to a new and unfamiliar culture. Although the three primary assumptions underlying the theory discuss the complex and dynamic process of adaptation and highlight the importance communication plays in one's social environment, identity is ostensibly absent in the theory. Although one could argue it is "identity" that is undergoing transformation in adapting to new environments, the interplay of how it may be negotiated is neglected. Instead, Kim (1995) contends that an "intercultural identity" emerges as a result of the intercultural transformation.

Face-negotiation theory addresses how issues of face are negotiated in cross-cultural conflict. Ting-Toomey (1988) proposes that conflict is an identity-bound concept in which the *faces* or *situated identities* of the interactants are called into question, particularly with persons from individualistic and collectivistic cultures having different situated identities. In turn, these different face concerns will lead to different conflict styles. In her continual attention to intercultural theorizing, Ting-Toomey (1993) directly pursues the issue of identity and intercultural communication competence. According to her, effective identity negotiation refers to the "smooth coordination between interactants concerning salient identity issues, and the process of engaging in responsive identity confirmation and positive identity enhancement" (Ting-Toomey, 1993, p. 73) and, as such, requires an individual to draw on a wide range of cognitive, affective, and behavioral resources to deal with intercultural situations. Although communicative resourcefulness highlights the importance of identity in intercultural interactions, we might challenge the assumption of the theory. That is, in many intercultural interactions, individuals may not be overly concerned with having smooth interaction but rather may take bold measures to highlight their distinct ethnic identities. Communication, of course, is crucial in underscoring ethnic identity.

Identity management theory (IMT) also seeks to understand and explain communication competence in intercultural interactions. Cupach and Imahori (1993) argue that although intercultural interactions involve those with different social identities, the universal desire to maintain face (own and other's) will propel them to forge a more interpersonal relationship. In essence, intercultural interlocutors become interculturally competent as a new enmeshed relational identity emerges for them. Similar to communicative resourcefulness, IMT focuses on the achievement of effortless interaction. Most notably, it assumes that interactants eventually reach a point where identities can, in fact, be enmeshed—a stance we contend to be overly optimistic.

Intercultural theorizing has yielded important insight into intercultural dynamics. Even so, little understanding of the fundamental relationship between communication and identity has been offered. The same limitations of intercultural theory also plague models of identity development (Collier, 1997; Martin & Nakayama, 1997). Contrary to the view that one is simply born into an ethnic identity, most scholars endorse the notion that it develops over time and is created, in part, by the self becoming aware of its own ethnic group as well as through communication with other group members. Although identity development models acknowledge that ethnic identity is negotiated, most of these stage models culminate in some type of identity resolution or achievement that results in an uncharacteristically finite appraisal. Both intercultural theory and models of identity development neglect to address two important issues: the role communication plays in the formation of ethnic identity, and its negotiative character. Hence, identity is more peripheral to the theoretical boundaries of intercultural communication, and current positions treat it as a static input-output variable, not something dynamic that is constantly being reconstructed (Brewer, 1999; Deaux, 1996).

Although some theories discussed above feature *intergroup* communication, they attempt to understand intercultural interactions primarily as interpersonal encounters. Intergroup communication scholars argue that there is much to be gained by combining the social-psychological and communication perspectives and that such a synergy can better elucidate the transactional relationship between communication and identity.

In particular, communication accommodation theory (CAT) maintains that language and speech (as well as other communicative markers, such as dress, house, artifacts, tattoos, festivals, marches, etc.) are important elements of personal and social identity. CAT explains the process of how identity may influence communication behaviors in that individuals are motivated to accommodate (move toward or away from others) our use of language, nonverbal behavior, and paralanguage in different ways to achieve a desired level of social distance between the self and our interacting partners. The degree to which the communicator feels positive or negative about their identity may be manifested through communication behavior, and CAT theorists propose many types of accommodation, convergent and divergent strategies being the most fundamental. Convergence is a strategy whereby individuals adapt their communicative behavior to become more similar to their interlocutor, particularly those they identify with and admire (Giles & Noels, 1997). Divergence refers to the way in which speakers accentuate communicative differences between themselves and others.

Based on assumptions of SIT, CAT maintains that individuals categorize the social world according to groups and derive a part of their identity and self-esteem (social identity) from groups to which they belong. Assuming people are motivated to maintain self-esteem (see Aberson, Healy, & Romero, 2000), CAT proposes they will tend to communicatively differentiate their own group from other groups (providing they are content with their membership in that group), sometimes just on the basis of perceiving cues of the other's outgroup membership. In sum, the central premise of CAT is that individuals will assert their identity through their communication patterns. For example, individuals may wish to communicate identity solidarity with their partner by convergence or, conversely, by divergence in order to distinguish one's identity. Identity may be communicated (as continuous variables) several ways, with respect to subordinate and dominant groups, some of which are summarized in Table 11.1.

Thus far, we have articulated how identity is communicated, but less clear is what determines convergence or divergence. Intergroup encounters do not occur in a vacuum, and when interactants come together from different cultures there is often a history of relations that may include rivalry, conflict, social inequity, and prejudice (Hewstone & Brown,

1986). It stands to reason that majority and subordinate groups will communicate their identity in different ways. For example, when an encounter is defined (consciously or unconsciously) as "intergroup" by participants, the accommodative norm is for the subordinate group to converge toward the dominant group (rather than vice versa). We turn now to consider the reality that intergroup encounters are often characterized by social stratification based on demography, power, and status inequalities.

IDENTITY IS SUBJECTIVE

Most conceptualizations of identity include some assignment to a socially derived category, which exists and accrues meaning only through opposition to other social categories with contrasting features (Giles, Bourhis, & Taylor, 1977); as those contrasting features change, so does one's identity. Given its contextual nature, social identity cannot be discussed meaningfully without contemplating social comparison processes. A review of identity theories (Leets, Giles, & Clément, 1996) demonstrates that conceptualizations of identity have become increasingly subjective and contextual, moving from identity as a result of group affiliation (e.g., SIT) to identity as situated in social relationships (symbolic interactionism) to identity as entirely context dependent (constructivism) to identity as entirely interactive. According to SIT (Tajfel & Turner, 1986), to assess social identity one engages in social comparison, but only with those groups whose relative positions in society provide diagnostic information. Put another way, identity guides social comparison at the same time that social comparison refines and reinforces one's self-concept. Identity, therefore, is both subjective and processual and seen as a dialectical

interplay between objectivity and subjectivity. Therefore, discussions of identity reasonably situate the person within the individual's social-psychological world, accounting for such subjective assessments as the pride of group membership (ingroup identification), the extent to which the community is a viable group (vitality), and the group's ability to take on characteristics of a dominant group (social boundaries). Ethnolinguistic identity theory (ELIT; e.g., Giles & Johnson, 1981) was, arguably, among the first intergroup communication theories to acknowledge the importance of the sociopsychological climate in which intergroup relations occur. It predicts that if an individual perceives high ingroup identification, cognitive alternatives to ingroup status, strong group vitality, and hard, closed boundaries, intergroup differentiation will occur. It is within this framework that we discuss subjective perceptions of identity and offer propositions for intergroup encounters that could generate future research.

Members of socially derived groups exhibit varying levels of ingroup dependency and solidarity; both of these subjective assessments are not limited to intragroup qualities, however. Group members also make ingroup-outgroup distinctions according to such construals as the ratio of perceived ingroup-outgroup differences (Oakes, Haslam, & Turner, 1994). Indeed, current operationalizations of identity fall along both intra- and intergroup subjective dimensions—attraction to group, depersonalization, perceived self-group interdependency, and intergroup competition (Jackson, 1999). In a study of minority groups in a multigroup setting, it was found that social identity has quite different effects on intergroup bias depending on which subjective dimensions of identity are taken into account. An "open" social identity is composed of ingroup attraction, compatible intergroup goals, positive appraisals by other groups, satisfaction with status quo, and self-reliance and was found to be inversely related to ingroup bias. A "threatened" identity, however, composed of ingroup attraction, self-group interdependency, and intergroup competition, predicted higher levels of intergroup bias and perceived group interdependency (Jackson & Smith, 1999).

Regarding dominant groups, although research has shown that strong anti-outgroup views are often held by strongly identified whites, dominant group identity need not be inevitably divisive. Increasing the centrality of the group to one's identity can have a positive impact on intergroup relations. For example, white students who think a lot about being white, and about what they have in common with other white students, were found to demonstrate fewer negative views of conflict about, and report more positive interactions with, various groups of color and support multicultural policies. It is suspected that centrality prompted reflections on power and privilege in critical ways that transformed identities (Gurin, Peng, Lopez, & Nagda, 1999). These findings demonstrate that although much still needs to be learned about social identity for minority and majority group members, the very act of ingroup identification is subjective with varying implications for intergroup relations, as proposed in the following:

Proposition 1a. Individuals who are highly dependent on their group, consider it central to their being, feel high solidarity for it, and possess a threatened social identity are likely to perceive intergroup encounters in intergroup terms.

Proposition 1b. Individuals who are not dependent on their group, do not consider it central to their being, feel little solidarity for it, and possess an open social identity

are not likely to perceive intergroup encounters in intergroup terms.

As ELIT makes clear, broad, societal forces also impact the subjective experience of identity. The types of sociopsychological processes operating between groups in contact will differ according to whether the groups have high, medium, or low vitality. Vitality, composed of status, demography, and institutional support factors, is both an inherently objective and subjective concept (Harwood, Giles, & Bourhis, 1994). For example, the signing of a treaty is an objective occurrence that is open to subjective interpretations, which correspond to group memberships. As we shall see, those subjective, group-based interpretations may be as—or more—important to intergroup relations than objective differences. Explicitly or implicitly, researchers are using the subjective dimensions of vitality proposed by Giles and colleagues, demonstrating differences in intergroup bias as predicted by group status, size, and power. For example, Jackson (1999) found support for the phenomenon of "the few, the proud" in that participants expressed the most ingroup attraction when the group was small and of high status. In addition, Gurin et al. (1999) found a power differential in that dominant group identity is associated with negative intergroup perceptions, attitudes, and behaviors, and subordinate group identity is associated with positive perceptions of intergroup relations.

Language is another status component of vitality that is increasingly recognized for its subjective qualities and seen less as a static reflection of power than as an "active coplayer in the exercise of power" (Reid & Ng, 1999, p. 120). Although it is true that low-status speakers tend to use powerless forms of language, language can also *create* power as in the case of females who may use low-power language to gain a turn when among males only to establish conversational control. Perhaps it is this strategic use of language that best presents its subjective nature. Reid and Ng (1999) explain that Aborigines cast themselves as "original Australians" in an effort to highlight a need for reparations while also appealing to a superordinate mainstream identity. However, the government response implicitly categorized Aborigines as simply Australians, thereby rejecting their status as a legitimate special interest group. Meanwhile, a study by Tong, Hong, Lee, and Chiu (1999) demonstrated that evaluative reactions to bilingual code switching appear to be governed by norms regarding ingroup-outgroup behavior. When a Hong Kong speaker converged to the official language of the mainland, self-identifying "Hongkongers" evaluated the speaker less favorably than did those who claimed a genuine "Chinese" identity. In addition, the Chinese-identity respondents judged the Hong Kong speaker more favorably when he converged to the mainland language than when he maintained a Hong Kong dialect. Whether the goal is to depoliticize power, as in Australia, or to maintain distinctiveness via language evaluations, as in Hong Kong, language attitudes expressed by dominant and subordinate groups both reflect intergroup relations and shape them, thereby underscoring the dialectical qualities of identity components such as language.

> *Proposition 2a.* Groups high in vitality will be more likely to express ingroup attraction and negative intergroup perceptions, and they will be more likely to use language strategically to achieve or maintain a positive and distinct social identity.
>
> *Proposition 2b.* Groups low in vitality will be less likely to express ingroup attraction and negative intergroup perceptions, and

they will be less likely to use language strategically to achieve or maintain a positive and distinct social identity.

It is also critical to assess groups' sociohistorical status, but here, too, perceptions of history are subject to group-based interpretations. In a study of the Maori (Polynesian origins) and Paheka (European origins) in New Zealand, both Maori and Paheka agreed that the Treaty of Waitangi was the most important event in New Zealand history, but only the Maori (the subordinate group) demonstrated ingroup favoritism in their judgments of the treaty (Liu, Wilson, McClure, & Higgins, 1999).

Inevitably, political climates change and research shows that identities change accordingly. For evidence of this, we turn to a variety of studies conducted in Hong Kong during the transition from British to Chinese rule. Brewer (1999) found that the change of sociopolitical context was less problematic for Hongkongers, who see themselves as possessing independent Hong Kong (regional) and Chinese (ethnic) identities, than for the "Hong Kong-Chinese," who see their ethnic identity as nested within their regional identity. Thus, a corresponding shift in self-labeling from *Hong Kong-Chinese* to either *Hongkonger* or *Chinese* is interpreted as an identity conflict for those who saw their regional and ethnic identities as intertwined in a context that now fosters distinctiveness between the two. Similarly, Fu, Lee, Chiu, and Hong (1999) found that the referential meaning of Hongkonger changed when the immediate sociopolitical context changed. When the context called for an essay regarding the Beijing government's policies, "primarily Hongkongers" and "primarily Chinese" demonstrated an intergroup orientation. However, that intergroup orientation was not evident when these same two groups were called on to write about protecting Chinese territory from an external aggressor. In other words, when that referential meaning is made salient, Hongkongers may differentiate from those from the mainland. However, *Hongkonger* may also refer to a subordinate identity nestled within a Chinese entity that, upon activation, may prompt differentiation from those not ethnic Chinese.

Therefore, when the immediate context changes, the frame of reference changes accordingly, and so will referential meanings of identity. Taken together, these findings tell us that not only are perceptions of history subject to group-based interpretations, but efforts at optimal distinctiveness are subject to a shifting political climate, with corresponding shifts in ethnic identity. All of which is further evidence of Liu et al.'s (1999) contention that history can be both a unifying and divisive mechanism for social identity and that the social context should not be treated like a "black box"—something largely outside the scope of intergroup theory.

> *Proposition 3.* Group-based efforts at vitality and positive distinctiveness will prompt interpretations of history and shifts in identity consistent with the sociohistorical and sociopolitical context.

ELIT contends that another predictor of intergroup bias is the perception of hard, closed group boundaries. We return to Hong Kong to illustrate this process. Indeed, the very method by which individuals make social comparisons in a changing sociopolitical context appears linked to their implicit theories about human character, interpreted herein as subjective assessments of the boundaries of human nature. Hong, Chiu, Yeung, and Tong (1999) found that those who believe that character is a fixed attribute ("entity theorists") used trait-based dimensions in social

comparison to achieve group distinctiveness. Such fixed-attribute thinking suggests that entity theorists perceive human nature as having hard and closed intergroup boundaries. In this framework, it makes sense that entity-Hongkongers relied more on economic wealth as a frame of reference than did entity-Chinese, because such a trait-based dimension provided Hongkongers with optimal distinctiveness in their social comparisons. By contrast, "incremental theorists," who subscribe to the view that human attributes and character are malleable, did not display a systematic relationship between their social identity and the weight given to trait-based comparisons. This finding may suggest that incremental theorists perceive human nature as having permeable boundaries. Given the fluid aspect of human nature, therefore, trait-based dimensions do not allow for optimal distinctiveness in social comparisons and, most important, do not mesh with incremental theorists' subjective views of human nature. Therefore:

> *Proposition 4a.* The perception of hard, closed boundaries contributes to trait-based intergroup distinctions consistent with cultural values and optimally suited for positive distinctiveness.

> *Proposition 4b.* The perception of permeable boundaries is not associated with trait-based intergroup distinctions that conflict with an implicit theory of human nature as malleable and thus are not optimally suited for positive distinctiveness.

This recent intergroup literature reiterates the value of SIT and ELIT in understanding intergroup behavior as well as the ongoing need to frame identity as a concept that is highly variable and subject to the active construction of the individual. In sum, these propositions tell us that because identity is neither fixed nor merely reflective of a given context but rather influenced *by* it, it is logical to surmise that identity is a vibrant phenomenon subject to societal, situational, and communicative forces; just as identity prompts communication, so too does communication create and alter identity.

THE INFLUENCE OF COMMUNICATION ON IDENTITY

Recognizing that identity is not only objective but also subjective, we have stressed that rather than perceiving it as static, identity is continually negotiated. This final section is devoted to furthering our understanding of the transactional relationship between communication and identity. Although identity influences communication, the latter can be critical to identity construction. In their discussion of language, power, and intergroup relations, Reid and Ng (1999) demonstrate that identity is enacted via a communication process that is contextual. For instance, they found that it is the *ability* to take a conversational turn on the floor, not the very language style adopted, that leads to perceptions of higher influence. This suggests that the very root of identity can be found in the process of interaction and should be understood from a contextual perspective.

Given the influence of the immediate context, the relevant state of the individual's "power mosaic" is not so much the community at large but the *communication network* that defines the individual's interpersonal context and identity referents (Leets et al., 1996, p. 135). The empirical challenges of testing it notwithstanding, Hecht (e.g., Hecht & Baldwin, 1998) in his development of a "communication theory of identity" agrees that the individual's speech community serves to create, expand, preserve, validate, and perpetuate language and identity. However, that

community must not be divorced from its own origins but instead must remain tied to ancestral, cultural, and linguistic roots. Ebonics and Spanglish, which emanate from and reinforce African and Hispanic cultural goals of linguistic collectivity and separatism, respectively, can be seen as supporting this notion.

The influence of communication on ethnic identity, however, is often overlooked given the focus on individual processing, which fails to address the creation of shared meanings among group members. Indeed, group consensus is either taken for granted or ignored. Only recently have models of social categorization recognized that consensus "is not simply an automatic outcome of intrapsychic processes, but rather results from processes of debate among group members—albeit framed by social cognitive factors" (Sani & Reicher, 1999, p. 280). Recognizing that people who share a salient self-categorization may debate core dimensions of their common social identity, Sani and Reicher (1999) examined the split in the Church of England that took place as a result of the ordination of women. They hypothesized that the anti-ordination group would perceive the inclusion of women clergy as contradicting the very essence of the group's identity, such that consensus with pro-ordination church members would be blocked and differences nonnegotiable. Indeed, debate between the "pros" and "antis" on an identity-relevant matter was significant enough that people perceived they could not be members of the same group, and a schism resulted. Communication created identity.

Communication, in the form of labels, also shapes identity, each in its own way (Tanno, 1994). Think of the various labels that represent a Hispanic identity. *Spanish* designates ancestral origin, *Mexican American* describes a dual cultural background, *Latina* represents historical connectedness to others of Spanish descent, and *Chicana* suggests a political perspective. Because no label exists outside of its

Table 11.2 Communicating Identity

	Nonverbal Behavior	Language	Paralanguage
Positive social identity	Crowd behavior Conflict Physical boundaries Outgroup rejection Ethnophaulisms Negative allocation bias Symbols	Patronizing speech Ingroup language with normal speech rate Non-language acquisition Labels	Accent, dialect, idioms, speech rate, pauses, utterance length, phonological variants can all be modified to signal positive social identity
Moderate social identity	Smiling, gaze, gestures Time	Ingroup language with slow speech rate Conversation interruptions Conversation turn taking Sarcasm, hostility, disagreement Code switching Language intensity Topic choice	Accent, dialect, idioms, speech rate, pauses, utterance length, phonological variants can all be modified to signal moderate social identity Laughter
Negative social identity	Ingroup rejection Positive allocation bias Assimilation	Outgroup language with native-like pronunciation Outgroup language with features of ingroup pronunciation Language acquisition	Information density Self-disclosure

relational meaning, these and other ethnic labels construct relational meaning within communication episodes. Just as we may communicate our identities to others, they are also very much tied to the way that others represent our interests, and when created identities are incongruent, they must be renegotiated (Martin & Nakayama, 1997).

In an explicit attempt to bring awareness to the experiences of older women, Paoletti (1998) examined the construction of older women's identities in Perugia, Italy, who took part in the European Older Women's Project.

Her analysis shows how they resisted age-group memberships. Aware that the label *old* is value laden, rejection of it is particularly evident in the women's discussion of their group name. The moniker chosen, the Italian Association of Active/Older Women, is an indication that these elderly women wished to communicate a more positive identity.

We turn (and, in one case, return) to two theories that further our understanding of communication-identity linkages. Social dominance theory (SDT), a macro explanation of the human predisposition toward group-based social hierarchies, *implicitly* (albeit far from explicitly) places communication squarely in the middle of its framework in the form of legitimizing myths (Sidanius & Pratto, 1999). The theory begins with group status, sex/gender, socialization, and temperament, which are seen as contributing to a social dominance orientation. That orientation then leads to the communication of legitimizing myths, which have a reciprocal relationship with individual and institutional discrimination, behavior, and group-based social hierarchy. Therefore, group-based inequality is created and re-created through the language of legitimizing myths that provide moral and intellectual justification for social hierarchies. Hierarchy-enhancing myths include ideologies such as racism, manifest destiny, and internal attributions for being poor, and hierarchy-attenuating myths include ideologies such as feminism, liberation theology, and themes in the American Declaration of Independence. An assumption of SDT is that conflict between hierarchy-enhancing and hierarchy-attenuating forces yields a relatively stable social system that always entails some sort of group-based hierarchical arrangement. As much as legitimizing myths (e.g., the U.S. meritocracy) contribute to dominance and subordination, communication can be seen as creating social identities and the tension between opposing myths as maintaining them. SDT does not explicitly address how a social dominance orientation may be a product of communication, making only minimal references to socialization processes of education and stigmatization.

CAT affords insight, also perhaps implicitly, into the transactional relationship between communication and identity. In addition to demonstrating how identity influences communication, acts of convergence and divergence (see Table 11.2) communicate the strength of group identity in intergroup en-

counters (positive, moderate, and negative). Accordingly, divergence or convergence is largely driven by group identity, and these very social actions communicate how individuals feel about their group identities. In an effort to promote their distinctiveness, those whose groups have a positive social identity are more likely to diverge in intergroup encounters in an effort to demonstrate their distinctiveness.

Keeping in mind that communication may entail nonverbal, language, and paralanguage components, group members may use a myriad of communicative expressions. A most extreme form of groups communicating their positive identity is crowd behavior (protesting, pushing, shouting). This act of divergent communication implies group members feel strongly about their group membership, such that they are willing to engage in physical confrontation (Drury & Reicher, 1999). Similarly, subordinate and dominant groups may use *ethnophaulisms* (ethnic slurs) when referring to outgroups in an attempt to differentiate their group and communicate a positive social identity (Mullen, Rozell, & Johnson, 2000). Conversely, subordinate groups who have a negative social identity are likely to converge to the dominant group (Giles & Johnson, 1981). Positive allocation bias, discrimination against outgroups when the outcomes involve the allocation of positive resources (e.g., money or praise), is a form of ingroup bias that communicates negative group identity for the outgroup (Jackson, 1999).

Acquiring the outgroup's language can also communicate negative social identity. Moreover, ingroup members who attempt to maintain a positive group identity through language may have disdain for ingroup members who adopt the outgroup language. When Hogg, D'Agata, and Abrams (1989) investigated the perceptions of ingroup members speaking the dominant outgroup's language, they found that the more people identified with their cultural ingroup, the more likely they were to have negative feelings toward fellow ingroupers who spoke the dominant group's language. Adjustments in accent, dialect, idioms, and speech rate may function in the same fashion. Groups may accentuate their accent in order to positively distinguish their group membership, whereas outgroups who have a negative social identity may attenuate their accent or dialect in an effort to appear similar to the dominant group (Burt, 1998). These examples all lend support to the notion that accommodation is a primary form of identity expression.

Regardless of the actual communicative act, accommodation is fundamental to identity construction. However, consistent with our claim of identity being subjective, individuals' accommodation will vary as a function of ingroup identity and group vitality (Giles & Coupland, 1991). Even so, as group members (be they subordinate or dominant) accommodate their communication, they continue to influence, shape, create, and re-create their identity. The scope of accommodation, though, can be broadened to include a *rhetorical* element. That is, literal dialogue, argument, and debate are also critical to identity. SIT theorists have placed heavy emphasis on socially shared perceptions among group members. Potential intragroup dynamics are often ignored or similarity among group members is taken for granted (see Oakes et al., 1994). Yet, as Sani and Reicher (1999) explain, "by excluding the rhetorical dimension, we exclude the possibility that group members may differ even on core issues such as whether a given stance supports, subverts, or is irrelevant to the essence of group identity" (p. 296). In their analysis of the split in the Church of England mentioned above, these authors highlight the significance of the rhetorical

element in communicating identity. Clearly, members of the Church of England had different conceptions of church identity, including that which produced a schism between members. These findings highlight the serious attention that must be paid to the rhetorical process in which groups engage.

CONCLUSION

Our goal has been to introduce and detail the transactional relationship between communication and identity. To do so, we have drawn on the social-psychological and communication literatures. Moreover, our strong theoretical underpinning provides insights into both identity and communication. The theories reviewed provide an extensive view of different levels and dimensions of identity. Similarly, we were able to demonstrate a multitude of communicative expressions. Communication does not refer just to language. Instead, actions, rules, behavior, discrimination, and labels are all communicative. Above all, we encourage those who are interested in the relationship between communication and identity to not only include "objective" notions of identity in their own research and theorizing but also consider the "subjective" aspect of identity. All this cannot be understood without consideration of context, history, and status between the conversants. If we can stress anything (see Figure 11.1), it is that identity and communication are mutually reinforcing.

REFERENCES

Aberson, C. L., Healy, M., & Romero, V. (2000). Ingroup bias and self-esteem: A meta-analysis. *Personality and Social Psychology Review, 4,* 157-173.

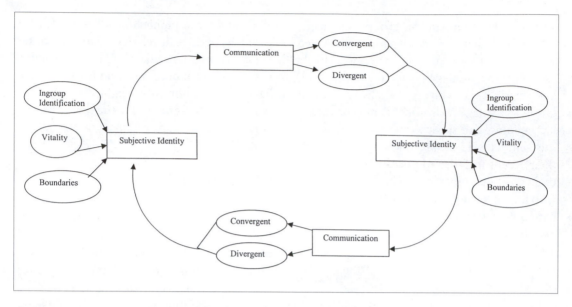

Figure 11.1.   Transactional Nature of Communication and Identity

Brewer, M. (1999). Multiple identities and identity transition: Implications for Hong Kong. *International Journal of Intercultural Relations, 23,* 187-197.

Burt, S. M. (1998). Monolingual children in a bilingual situation: Protest, accommodation, and linguistic creativity. *Multilingua, 17,* 361-378.

Collier, M. J. (1997). Cultural identity and intercultural communication. In L. A. Samovar & R. E. Porter (Eds.), *Intercultural communication: A reader* (pp. 36-44). San Francisco: Wadsworth.

Collier, M. J., & Thomas, M. (1988). Cultural identity in inter-cultural communication: An interpretive perspective. In Y. Y. Kim & W. B. Gudykunst (Eds.), *Theories in intercultural communication* (pp. 94-120). Newbury Park, CA: Sage.

Cupach, W., & Imahori, T. (1993). Identity management theory: Communication competence in intercultural episodes and relationships. In R. L. Wiseman & J. Koester (Eds.), *Intercultural communication competence* (pp. 112-131). Newbury Park, CA: Sage.

Deaux, K. (1996). Social identification. In E. T. Higgins & A. W. Kruglanski (Eds.), *Social psy-*

chology: Handbook of basic principles (pp. 777-798). New York: Guilford.

Drury, J., & Reicher, S. (1999). The intergroup dynamics of collective empowerment: Substantiating the social identity model of crowd behavior. *Group Processes & Intergroup Relations, 2,* 381-402.

Erikson, E. (1959). *Identity and the life cycle: Selected papers by Erik H. Erikson.* Psychological issues 1. New York: International Universities Press.

Fu, H.-Y., Lee, S.-L., Chiu, C.-Y., & Hong, Y.-Y. (1999). Setting the frame of mind for social identity. *International Journal of Intercultural Relations, 23,* 199-214.

Giles, H., Bourhis, R. Y., & Taylor, D. M. (1977). Towards a theory of language in ethnic group relations. In H. Giles (Ed.), *Language, ethnicity and intergroup relations* (pp. 307-343). London: Academic Press.

Giles, H., & Coupland, N. (1991). *Language: Contexts and consequences.* Milton Keynes, UK: Open University Press.

Giles, H., & Johnson, P. (1981). The role of language in ethnic group relations. In J. Turner & H. Giles (Eds.), *Intergroup behavior* (pp. 199-243). Oxford, UK: Basil Blackwell.

Giles, H., & Noels, K. A. (1997). Communication accommodation in intercultural encounters. In J. N. Martin, T. K. Nakayama, & L. A. Flores (Eds.), *Readings in cultural contexts* (pp. 139-149). Mountain View, CA: Mayfield.

Gudykunst, W. B. (1995). Anxiety/uncertainty management (AUM) theory: Current status. In R. L. Wiseman (Ed.), *Intercultural communication theory* (pp. 8-58). Thousand Oaks, CA: Sage.

Gudykunst, W. B. (2001). *Asian American ethnicity and communication.* Thousand Oaks, CA: Sage.

Gudykunst, W. B., Sodetani, L., & Sonoda, K. (1987). Uncertainty reduction in Japanese American/Caucasian relationships in Hawaii. *Western Journal of Speech Communication, 51,* 256-278.

Gurin, P., Peng, T., Lopez, G., & Nagda, B. A. (1999). Context, identity, and intergroup relations. In D. A. Prentice & D. T. Miller (Eds.), *Cultural divides: Understanding and overcoming group conflict* (pp. 133-170). New York: Russell Sage Foundation.

Harwood, J., Giles, H., & Bourhis, R. Y. (1994). The genesis of vitality: Historical and discoursal dimensions. *International Journal of the Sociology of Language, 108,* 167-206.

Hecht, M. L., & Baldwin, J. R. (1998). Layers and holograms. In M. L. Hecht (Ed.), *Communicating prejudice* (pp. 57-86). Thousand Oaks, CA: Sage.

Hewstone, M., & Brown, R. (1986). Contact is not enough: An intergroup perspective on the "contact hypothesis." In M. Hewstone & R. Brown (Eds.), *Contact and conflict in intergroup encounters* (pp. 1-44). London: Basil Blackwell.

Hogg, M. A., D'Agata, P., & Abrams, D. (1989). Ethnolinguistic betrayal and speaker evaluations among Italian Australians. *Genetic, Social, and General Psychology Monographs, 115,* 153-181.

Hong, Y.-Y., Chiu, C.-Y., Yeung, G., & Tong, Y.-Y. (1999). Social comparison during political transition: Interaction of entity versus incremental beliefs and social identities. *International Journal of Intercultural Relations, 23,* 257-279.

Jackson, J. W. (1999). How variations in social structure affect different types of intergroup bias and different dimensions of social identity in a multi-intergroup setting. *Group Processes & Intergroup Relations, 2,* 145-173.

Jackson, J. W., & Smith, E. R. (1999). Conceptualizing social identity: A new framework and evidence for the impact of different dimensions. *Personality and Social Psychology Bulletin, 25,* 120-135.

Kashima, E. S., Kashima, Y., & Hardie, E. A. (2000). Self-typicality and group identification: Evidence for their separateness. *Group Processes & Intergroup Relations, 3,* 97-110.

Kim, Y. Y. (1995). Cross-cultural adaptation: An integrative theory. In R. L. Wiseman (Ed.), *Intercultural communication theory* (pp. 170-193). Thousand Oaks, CA: Sage.

Leets, L., Giles, H., & Clément, R. (1996). Explicating ethnicity in theory and communication research. *Multilingua, 15,* 115-147.

Liu, J. H., Wilson, M. S., McClure, J., & Higgins, T. R. (1999). Social identity and the perception of history: cultural representations of Aotearoa/New Zealand. *European Journal of Social Psychology, 29,* 1021-1047.

Lustig, M. W., & Koester, J. (Eds.). (2000). *Among us: Essays on identity, belonging, and intercultural competence.* New York: Longman.

Martin, J. N. (1997). Understanding whiteness in the United States. In L. A. Samovar & R. E. Porter (Eds.), *Intercultural communication: A reader* (pp. 54-63). San Francisco: Wadsworth.

Martin, J. N., & Nakayama, T. K. (1997). *Intercultural communication in contexts.* Mountain View, CA: Mayfield.

Mullen, B., Rozell, D., & Johnson, C. (2000). Ethnophaulisms for ethnic immigrant groups: Cognitive representation of "the minority" and "the foreigner." *Group Processes & Intergroup Relations, 3,* 5-24.

Oakes, P. J., Haslam, A., & Turner, J. C. (1994). *Stereotyping and social reality.* Oxford, UK: Basil Blackwell.

Paoletti, I. (1998). *Being an older woman: A study in the social production of identity.* Mahwah, NJ: Lawrence Erlbaum.

Phinney, J. S. (1992). The multiple group ethnic identity measure. *Journal of Adolescent Research, 7,* 156-176.

Reid, S. A., & Ng, S. H. (1999). Language, power, and intergroup relations. *Journal of Social Issues, 55,* 119-139.

Sani, F., & Reicher, S. (1999). Identity, argument and schism: Two longitudinal studies of the split in the Church of England over the ordination of women in priesthood. *Group Processes & Intergroup Relations, 2,* 279-300.

Sidanius, J., & Pratto, F. (1999). *Social dominance: An intergroup theory of social hierarchy and oppression.* Cambridge, UK: Cambridge University Press.

Tajfel, H., & Turner, J. C. (1986). The social identity theory of intergroup relations. In S. Worchel & W. Austin (Eds.), *The social psychology of intergroup relations* (pp. 33-47). Monterey, CA: Brooks/Cole.

Tanno, D. (1994). Names, narratives, and the evolution of ethnic identity. In A. Gonzalez, M. Houston, & V. Chen (Eds.), *Our voices: Essays in ethnicity, culture, and communication* (pp. 30-33). Los Angeles: Roxbury.

Ting-Toomey, S. (1988). Intercultural conflicts: A face-negotiation theory. In Y. Y. Kim & W. B. Gudykunst (Eds.), *Theories in intercultural communication* (pp. 213-238). Newbury Park, CA: Sage.

Ting-Toomey, S. (1993). Communicative resourcefulness: An identity negotiation perspective. In R. L. Wiseman & J. Koester (Eds.), *Intercultural communication competence* (pp. 72-111). Newbury Park, CA: Sage.

Ting-Toomey, S., Yee-Jung, K., Shapiro, R., Garcia, W., Wright, T., & Oetzel, J. (2000). Ethnic/cultural identity salience and conflict styles in four U.S. ethnic groups. *International Journal of Intercultural Relations, 24,* 47-82.

Tong, Y.-Y., Hong, Y.-Y., Lee, S.-L., & Chiu, C.-Y. (1999). Language use as a carrier of social identity. *International Journal of Intercultural Relations, 23,* 281-296.

Wiseman, R. L. (Ed.). (1995). *Intercultural communication theory.* Thousand Oaks, CA: Sage.

12

Communication in Intercultural Relationships

LING CHEN
Hong Kong Baptist University

Research on intercultural relationship communication is still in its infancy, with limited studies on intercultural communication in interpersonal relationships such as intercultural marriage, dating, and friendship. Interest in intercultural marriages arises mainly from a practical need to understand marriages between partners of different cultural backgrounds as a social phenomenon. Research on other intercultural relationships including friendship grows out of interests in intercultural communication as a whole: Relationships are a context in which intercultural communication occurs. Despite an absence of systematic inquiry, issues have emerged that are essential to communication in intercultural relationships. Whereas many issues are the same as those in relationships in general, such as intimacy and privacy, some have greater salience or impact, such as dealing with differences and social perception of the intercultural relationship.

In this chapter, I discuss communication in intercultural relationships in two parts. In the first, I review the literature on relational processes in intercultural relationships. In the second section, I propose a dialectical approach to the study of intercultural relationships. Informed by the dialectical perspective to relational communication (Baxter & Montgomery, 1997), I discuss the peculiarity of dialects in intercultural relationships and explore directions for communication studies. As cultural difference between relationship partners necessarily sets intercultural relationships apart from intracultural ones, the discussion starts with a brief review of underlying cultural influences on relational communication.

RELATIONAL PROCESSES IN INTERCULTURAL COMMUNICATION

Cross-Cultural Variability

Culture here refers to cultures or cultural groups of all levels (national, ethnic, gender, age, etc.). Views on and the practice of interpersonal relationships vary across cultures, often along conceptual dimensions such as individualism and collectivism (see Gudykunst & Lee, Chapter 2 in this volume). Cross-cultural studies have identified cultural influence on several aspects of communication in intercultural relationships.

Social penetration. Social penetration occurs with increase of self-disclosure, in topic variety and intimacy of information, and thus, the development of relationship intimacy. Culture's influence on relational communication is most evident in self-disclosure. Scholars (G. Chen, 1995; Ting-Toomey, 1991) have reported that, in a same relationship type, members of cultures or cultural groups high in individualism (e.g., United States, France, Anglo-Americans) tend to self-disclose more than those from low individualistic cultures (e.g., Japan, China, Asian Americans). This difference may reflect culturally stipulated intimacy of relationships by type; for example, Japanese perceive romantic relationships as less intimate than Americans (Gudykunst & Nishida, 1986). Also, because self-disclosure is a form of direct communication preferred by individualistic cultures, members of individualistic cultures would self-disclose more.

Uncertainty management. The work of Gudykunst and associates has informed us much about cultural differences in this area. Members of collectivistic cultures reportedly feel more uncertain interacting with out-groups than with ingroups, whereas members of individualistic cultures reported no distinction. In managing uncertainty, for example, Japanese have more attribution confidence interacting with ingroup friends than do Americans. Consistent to their orientation toward group or individual, cultures differ in the type of information sought in initial interactions (i.e., group- vs. personal-based backgrounds, respectively) and in the effect of communication frequency on uncertainty reduction, found for individualistic cultures only (see Gudykunst, 1989, for an overview).

Ingroup versus outgroup communication. Cultures higher in collectivism are found to make greater ingroup-outgroup distinctions, as is consistent with the concept of collectivism. In a cross-cultural study of perceptions of interaction, Gudykunst, Yoon, and Nishida (1987) found that members of cultures higher in collectivism differentiated ingroups and outgroups more in their perceptions of the synchronization, personalization, and difficulties of interaction with others. American respondents made the least distinction, followed by Japanese and Korean respondents, respectively. Similarly, Gudykunst et al. (1992) reported that Chinese samples differentiated between ingroup and outgroup members in self-disclosure, whereas no ingroup-outgroup differentiation was found for the Australian and U.S. samples.

Relationship Development

Cultural differences assert influences on intercultural communicators from the very start and throughout the process of relationship development.

Initial interaction. Initial interaction is often crucial if a relationship is to continue and even more so for intercultural relationships, for the initial social penetration proves more difficult in these relationships (Lee & Boster, 1991). Studies (e.g., L. Chen, 1995, 1997) have suggested that intercultural communicators in initial interaction are less perceptive and less responsive than intracultural communicators, and they may need explicit message input and adaptive verbal strategies to increase interaction involvement and facilitate interaction. Similarly, topic sharing is positively associated with the perception of intercultural accommodation and interaction involvement (Chen & Celaga, 1994). Appropriate communicative strategies leading to perceived accommodation and proper involvement may facilitate intercultural interaction beyond the initial encounter.

Relationship formation. What starts an intercultural relationship represents an old scholarly interest that relates indirectly to communication. Studies have examined dating, or romantic, relationships for reasons, attributes of individuals, and contextual circumstances for entering a personal relationship across cultural boundaries. There is much similarity regarding reasons of relationship formation in intercultural and intracultural relationships. Studies (e.g., Gurung & Duong, 1999; Kouri & Lasswell, 1993; Lampe, 1982; Shibazaki & Brennan, 1998) have found that same- and interethnic dating couple members entered relationships for similar reasons. They formed a dating relationship because of personal liking for each other or perceived common interests and goals, and they also reported similar levels of relationship intimacy, commitment, and relationship satisfaction. With respect to reasons for relationship formation, therefore, intercultural relationships appear to be more similar to intracultural relationships than different.

As for personal attributes of individuals likely to be involved in intercultural romantic relationships, both individual and social characteristics of groups that influence individuals on an aggregate level have been investigated. Greater strength of ethnic identity and personal preference for intercultural contact are found to facilitate formation of intercultural romantic relationships (e.g., Nguyen, 1998; Parsonson, 1987; Shibazaki & Brennan, 1998). Educational level and socioeconomic status of individuals also predict likelihood of such a relationship (e.g., Mills, Daly, Longmore, & Kilbride, 1995; Sung, 1990; Tucker & Mitchell-Kernan, 1995). Sex and ethnicity (e.g., Clark-Ibanez, 1999; Fujino, 1997), on the other hand, seem to interact with the factor of social dominance and status: Members of the dominant group, compared with nondominant group members, are less likely to enter intercultural relationships. (See the section on status.) In the case of immigrants, the higher their degree of acculturation, the more likely they are to form intercultural relationships (Hanassab & Tidwell, 1998; Hwang, Saenz, & Aguirre, 1997; Nguyen, 1998). In addition, diversity of friendship circles, individual comfort level, and social stereotypes of the opposite sex in various cultural groups are found to have influences on the initiation of intercultural dating or romantic relationships (Chan, 1990; Clark-Ibanez, 1999). Contextual factors such as propinquity, group size, and sex ratio have been found to exert strong structural constraints on marriage partner choices (Anderson & Saenz, 1994; Fujino, 1997; Hwang et al., 1997). The same is true for the social status of the group (Back, 1993; Blau, 1994; Collier & Bornman, 1999; Hoffman & Schwarzwald, 1987). Diversity of parents' friends and family attitudes toward intercultural dating or marriage facilitate or discourage these relationships (Clark-Ibanez, 1999; Mills et al., 1995).

Perceived similarity. An important factor in intercultural relationship formation, romantic or nonromantic, is perceived similarity, based on the perspective of similarity-attraction. Studies typically report perceived similarity associating with the likelihood of intercultural interaction (Grant, 1993; Osbeck, Moghaddam, & Perreault, 1997; cf. McDermott, 1991). Many studies also focus on specific aspects of similarity. Obot (1988) shows that African Americans perceive persons with similar values as more attractive and rated them more positively on nonaffective traits than they did targets with dissimilar values. Simard (1981) reports language and attitude similarity as important for French- and English-speaking ethnic groups in Canada in their interethnic interactions, more so than factors such as comparability in occupation or social class. Collier and Bornman (1999) note that for interethnic friendship in South Africa, perceived group dissimilarity in what is considered acceptable, appropriate behaviors toward a friend greatly discourages formation of intercultural friendship. Lee and Gudykunst (in press) report that perceived similarity in communication styles predicted attraction between European and non-European Americans. This suggests that similarities in cultural and sociological backgrounds play a role mainly during the orientation and exploratory affective stage of relationship formation (Gareis, 1995, 1999; Kouri & Lasswell, 1993). A few studies further suggest perceived similarity between intercultural partners as a function of communication that takes place (e.g., Horenczyk & Bekerman, 1997; Hubbert, Gudykunst, & Guerrero, 1999). From a communication perspective, it seems that the relationship between similarity and intercultural relationship formation is an interactive one: Greater perceived similarity fa-

cilitates a communicative relationship; interactions, once started, may lead to perception of greater similarity or convergence of partners' behavior, or both.

Relationship sustenance and progression. Once a relationship is formed, how partners manage to develop and maintain the relationship is the focus of interest. Investigating North American-Japanese relationships, Gudykunst and associates have examined personal accounts of individuals on their relationships. For opposite-sex romantic relationships (Gudykunst, Gao, Sudweeks, Ting-Toomey, & Nishida, 1991), they generalized themes of typicality, communication competence, similarity, and involvement and reported that the presence, form, and interconnections among themes and subthemes varied by the type of relationship. For example, cultural dissimilarities were not mentioned frequently as affecting the relationship in acquaintance relationships but were noted as important in the romantic relationships. Personal accounts of female intercultural relationships (Sudweeks, Gudykunst, Ting-Toomey, & Nishida, 1990) revealed four similar themes: communication competence, similarity, involvement, and turning points. The presence, form, and interconnections among the relational themes varied across intimacy levels. For example, in low-intimacy relationships, cultural differences were used to explain lack of intimacy, whereas when intimacy of relationship is high, cultural differences are mentioned without judgment or as a positive factor. The study also found that the subthemes of cultural similarity, language/cultural knowledge, and accommodation emerged more frequently in these relationships than in those between same-culture members. Overall, both studies found that intimacy of relationship is associated with empathy expressed and mutual accommodation between the partners.

Of mixed marriages, Rohrlich (1988) notes the visible movement from problem-oriented studies to adjustment analysis. The problem of intercultural marriage typically was identified as arising from social prejudice and an inability to deal with cultural and gender role expectation differences or demands for rapid acculturation (Breger & Hill, 1998; Crohn, 1998). Alternatively, personal narratives of intercultural couples are studied for a view from inside the mixed marriage. Johnson and Warren (1994) reported that in sharp contrast to many outsiders who understand mixed marriages solely in the large sociocultural context, to couples in the mixed marriage the relationship is primarily personal affairs between individuals. The couples' accounts of development, sustenance, and maintenance of their long-term relationships revealed it as a process of mutual adjustment and learning where its "mixed" character matters more to others around them. They pointed out that "relationships within all marriages are at times difficult and trying. But not always more so because they are 'mixed.' Happiness, loving and sharing are equally attributes of marriage. No less so because they are 'mixed' " (Johnson & Warren, 1994, p. 12). On the other hand, relationship matters for intercultural couples tend to become more complicated as a result of their being mixed and, thus, different. For this reason, commitment, tolerance of differences, and the ability to go against family and/or society are more critical for success of the relationship (e.g., Chan & Wethington, 1998; McGuire, 1992).

Uncertainty management. Cognitive uncertainty that individuals experience directly inputs into their relationship development. Communication is the only means of uncertainty management, which, in turn, is necessary for communication to proceed. Intercultural communicators reportedly perceive their partners to be less similar to themselves as compared with intracultural partners (Gudykunst, 1983; Lee & Boster, 1991). They also report less confidence in making attributions about their interaction partner and less interpersonal attraction. More directly, intercultural communicators report greater uncertainty and less positive expectations than those in intracultural interactions (Gudykunst & Shapiro, 1996). Greater anxiety is related with greater uncertainty. The more communicators are uncertain, the more they feel apprehensive about communicating in intercultural encounters (Neuliep & Ryan, 1998). The uncertainty and anxiety, however, decrease as interaction continues over time (Hubbert et al., 1999). In established intercultural relationships, uncertainty is reduced with the increase of intimacy level in the relationship as well as across relationship types (Gudykunst, 1985; Gudykunst, Nishida, & Chua, 1986).

Self-disclosure. Little has been done regarding this important topic in intercultural relationship. A few intercultural studies have reported findings in support of social penetration theory. Generally, communicators in initial intercultural encounters are likely to have higher levels of self-disclosure than in first meetings with a stranger from the same culture (e.g., Gudykunst & Nishida, 1984). The greater amount of self-disclosure, however, is simply due to greater unfamiliarity between communicating partners and, thus, remains superficial, for participants in initial intercultural interaction rarely request intimate information (Lee & Boster, 1991). In existing intercultural relationships, social penetration corresponds with the intimacy level of the relationship type and is comparable to similar intracultural relationships (Gudykunst, 1985; Gudykunst et al., 1986). Social penetration deepens as an intercultural relationship progresses from the initial encounter to acquaintance and to friendship. Frequency and intimacy of self-disclosure increase after the initial foundation for the relationship has been established (Gudykunst,

Nishida, & Chua, 1987; Hubbert et al., 1999). This positive relationship between self-disclosure and relationship intimacy has prompted Rohrlich (1988) to suggest a creative use of self-disclosure: Intercultural couples consciously self-disclose perceived aspects of differences in each other to increase understanding and preempt possible problems related to the difference. Where expectations and role perceptions are immediately different, awareness and discussion of how spouses see themselves would enable partners to match impression with perceived self-image of their spouse.

Communication Processes

Intercultural relationship communication by default involves intercultural issues such as stereotypes and cultural identity.

Differences and stereotypes. Individuals in intercultural relationships encounter differences at two levels. They face cultural differences between them and learn to interact in spite of the difference. They also face the fact that their relationships are different from what is common in society and, thus, tend to be stereotyped. Relationship partners deal with the first type of difference through communication of mutual respect and acceptance. There must be perceived respect for or willingness to accept differences and overcome stereotypes (e.g., Collier, 1996; Collier & Bornman, 1999; Hecht, Ribeau, & Sedano, 1990). Respect and acceptance are expressed in everyday mundane exchanges, such as requests for more information or expressed curiosity to learn about the other, and contribute positively to establishment of an intercultural friendship (e.g., Chen, Isa, & Sakai, 1996; Collier & Bowker, 1994; Hecht, Larkey, & Johnson, 1992). Social stereotypes about intercultural romantic relationships are

dealt with by seeking or building social networks for support (e.g., Johnson & Warren, 1994; Spickard, 1989).

Cultural identity. Cultural or ethnic identity has a dynamic role in intercultural relationships. Individuals with strong and insecure cultural identification tend not to interact cross-culturally and, consequently, have no or few intercultural relationships of any type. Individuals with strong and secure or those with weak cultural identification are more likely to enter an intercultural relationship. This applies to sojourners, immigrants, and ethnic groups alike (e.g., Hanassab & Tidwell, 1998; Nguyen, 1998; Strom, 1988). This pattern is shown in intercultural dating of individuals at different stages of ethnic identity transformation. Those at stages characterized by security in or rejection of ethnic identity are more likely to date outside of their ethnic group than those at stages with insecure or strong ethnic identity (Chung, 1990). An explanation is that individuals with strong ethnic identity tend to perceive potential outgroup dating partners with greater social distance and less trust and receptivity (Chung & Ting-Toomey, 1999).

As communicators, members of major ethnic groups in the United States and South Africa have described rules for *ethnic identity enactment* as important for intercultural friendship (Collier, 1996; Collier & Bornman, 1999). Ethnic identity enactment rules vary between groups. Latino and Asian Americans abide by respect, exchanging ideas, and learning more about the other's cultural background; expressing understanding and appreciating culture are rules for African Americans; showing respect for other cultures, for Anglo Americans. For all South African ethnic groups, identity rules include explaining differences and learning from one another. In spite of the variety in identity rules, violation of these rules is perceived by all to be inappropriate to the intercultural friendship.

Cultural identity is dynamic in many other ways. Communicators report awareness of a gradual shift from cultural identity to individual identity as an intercultural relationship develops. This is reflected in topics of conversation, perceptions of closeness, and reported conscious observations of this movement of identity (Hubbert et al., 1999). From a different perspective, Larkey and Hecht (1995) examined African American and European American interethnic interactions and found ethnic identity to be negatively related to interethnic communication satisfaction in less intimate relationships and no significant relationship to interethnic communication with friends. Cultural identity is present but not salient in a closer relationship or in a more intimate stage of a relationship. It is also argued that in actual interactions, different facets or levels of the cultural identity (national, ethnic, gender, age, etc.) may alternately emerge into salience depending on the circumstances and nature of the interaction, which must be negotiated and managed in communication (Collier, 1996).

Social power and status. Dominance defined as social power and status is often communicated unequivocally in intercultural relationships. Status-based differentiation in psychological aspects is observable and expressed in communication. In intergroup interactions, members of nondominant groups, blacks and females, were reportedly perceived as more homogenized with less individuality than members of dominant groups, whites and males (Cabecinhas & Amancio, 1999). The perception of similarity-attraction is reportedly stronger when the target is a member of a nondominant group than when it is a dominant group member (Osbeck et al.,

1997), reflecting a stereotypical belief that members of minority groups "keep to themselves" and "won't mix" (Back, 1993). Studies have also shown that members of the dominant group are more likely to assume their cultural rules to be the norms and standard, expecting everyone to conform to these rules (Collier & Bornman, 1999; Collier & Bowker, 1994).

Research has indicated social status equality to be a positive predictor of interethnic marriages between Mexican Americans and white Americans (Anderson & Saenz, 1994). Nondominant groups/cultures are relatively more receptive to this unconventional marital form, especially when the outgroup partner is from a dominant cultural group (Sung, 1990; Tuch, Sigelman, & MacDonald, 1999), a fact that members of nondominant groups/cultures are also more aware of. Overall, social perceptions of an intercultural relationship vary in degrees of disapproval based on the ethnicity, gender, and status combination of partners involved (Mills et al., 1995). Social judgment and attribution of intercultural relationships are more negative when directed at partners from nondominant groups (Breger & Hill, 1998).

Social perceptions and social support. By and large, intercultural relationships or marriages are perceived negatively across cultural and ethnic groups (e.g., Agranat & Titov, 1994; Bizman, 1987; Levkovitch, 1990), although there is evidence of increased tolerance among the U.S. population ("Race Relations," 1991; Tuch et al., 1999). The more intimate relationships are perceived more negatively than are the less intimate ones (Garcia & Rivera, 1999). People consider love as significantly more important in ethnically heterogeneous marriages than in homogeneous ones, but rate homogeneous couples as more compatible (Bizman, 1987). As a result, intercultural couples have reported significantly more external problems with parents, extended family members, relatives, friends, and the community (e.g., Graham, Moeai, & Shizuru, 1985; Nguyen, 1998; Rosenblatt, Karis, & Powell, 1995). There are usually greater assimilation pressures on a spouse, usually the wife, toward accepting the culture of the other spouse (Breger & Hill, 1998; Graham et al., 1985). These findings indicate that for an intercultural marriage to succeed it demands considerably more sacrifice, patience, and commitment.

Social perceptions of intercultural relationships are directly reflected in the social support to partners in such relationships that may "make or break the relationship" (Spickard, 1989). Social support operates at every stage of relational development contributing substantially to the growth, maintenance, or dissolution of a relationship. The support or lack of it is communicated in various messages that comment or give advice on some general or specific aspects of the relationship or on its development, often by explicitly or implicitly comparing the relationship with community expectations or other relationships in the community (Payne, 1998). A salient perception of individuals in interethnic relationships is reportedly a lack of support from the general public (Chan & Wethington, 1998; Rosenblatt et al., 1995), so much so that Shibazaki and Brennan (1998) in discussing their study on interethnic dating offer the suggestion that "the trouble with inter-racial relationships is not race, it's racism" (p. 254). Social support in intercultural relationships is so important that intercultural couples often seek communities or form their own social networks where they may find support (Gaines & Ickes, 1997; Johnson & Warren, 1994).

Commitment and attachment. Of special importance to the sustenance of intercultural

relationships is commitment to the relationship, when relationship partners talk about their differences, share experiences, and express mutual support in the face of adversity (Johnson & Warren, 1994; McGuire, 1992; Rosenblatt et al., 1995). Haas and Stafford (1998) in their study on gay men and lesbians in committed relationships note that being "out" as a couple to one's social networks is a means of strengthening the relationship against social stigma. The practice may well apply to other intercultural relationships encountering social disapproval. Presentation of themselves in public as a unit communicates the relationship partners' commitment to the relationship, not only to the community but also to each other, hence the positive effect on the relationship.

On the other hand, commitment also affects communication in the relationship. Gaines and colleagues (Gaines et al., 1999; Gaines et al., 1997) investigated interethnic couples for the association between relationship attachment and response to marital conflict situations. Securely attached relationship partners reportedly displayed greater accommodative tendencies. Securely, compared to insecurely, attached individuals consistently produced lower level of destructive or relationship-threatening responses (e.g., exit and neglect), whereas insecure attachment was a positive correlate of destructive responses.

A DIALECTICAL APPROACH

A dialectical approach explicates social phenomena with a small set of conceptual assumptions about contradiction (Baxter & Montgomery, 1997). It holds that contradictions, known as dialectics, are inherent to social life and change is the norm (Mao, 1965): Amid dialectics people constantly act and are acted upon to manage the tension. This perspective provides a meta-theoretical framework for a systematic understanding of communication in intercultural relationships. Integrating the literature reviewed above, this section discusses the dialectics in intercultural communication most relevant to personal relationships and examines the interplay of intercultural and relationship dialectics. The discussion serves to organize the scattered research on intercultural relationships and explores directions for future research.

Interpersonal Relationship Dialectics

Relationship partners experience from the very start various internal and external contradictions (Werner & Baxter, 1994). Interpersonal communication scholars have identified six dialectics that are internal or external to the relationship surrounding the interrelated matters of information sharing, interdependence, and variability (Baxter, 1988, 1993; Baxter & Montgomery, 1997; Rawlins, 1992). Information sharing bears on the contradictions of openness-closeness within and revelation-nonrevelation outside the relationship, about how much relationship partners share information about each other, and about how much they share relationship information with others in their social networks and with the society at large. Autonomy-connection and separation-integration are internal and external contradictions relating to interdependence. These dialectics involve the extent to which relationship partners give up individuality to bond into an entity and participate in interaction with others in the community or focus on the relationship interaction. Relationship variability underlies the internal predictability-novelty and external conventionality-uniqueness contradictions. The dialectics are about how partners interact with and relate to each other in predictable ways without losing interest and

contribute to stability as well as change of their culture and society.

Intercultural Communication Dialectics

Among the contradictions salient in intercultural communication (Martin & Nakayama, 1999), the dialectics of difference-similarity, individual-culture, and personal-social are particularly relevant to intercultural relationships, which represent the fundamental contradictions in communication between individuals (internal), between individuals and the culture of their partners (external), and between individuals and their respective cultures (external). The dialectic of difference-similarity essentially defines intercultural interaction. Although communication is impossible without a minimal common ground, the need to communicate often results from differences in the first place. The contrast between communicators in their cultural upbringings is such that they often find it hard to keep a balance between meaning assignment attributed to the individual or to the culture, hence the individual-culture dialectic. Attention solely on the cultural risks stereotyping and losing sight of the person, whereas an emphasis on the individual overlooks cultural influences and cultural identification. The pull between the personal and the social arises out of the relationship between individuals and society. It is individuals who communicate, but the capacity in which individuals communicate always represents a social role. Even the private communication between two individuals occurs between two individual social members and with social impact.

Dialectics in Intercultural Relationships

In intercultural relationships, intercultural dialectics juxtapose relational dialectics.

Arising from the fundamental human needs of information sharing, interdependence, and variability (Bochner, 1984), the latter contradictions underlie every facet of a relationship. Manifestation of dialectics takes on myriad forms in concrete conditions and matters, which may be internal or external to a relationship. Regardless, both are important to the survival of the relationship as an entity with a social standing.

Openness-closeness: Internal information sharing. Internally, due to the dialectic of difference-similarity, intercultural relationship partners' self-disclosure or routine communication may look rather different from that in similar intracultural relationships regarding the kind of information exchanged. Although self-disclosure varies with the relationship type, information on many taken-for-granted aspects of life, redundant in intracultural relationships, may take on considerable importance for partners in any intercultural relationships (Rohrlich, 1988). On the other hand, disclosure may affect partners' mutual perceptions where it matters, in cultural identity and stereotypes (Braithwaite, 1991). To communicate with consideration of both idiosyncratic wants of the partners and the cultural identification each wishes acknowledged is evident of the individual-culture dialectic at work.

The interplay of openness-closeness and difference-similarity dialectics underlies the management of uncertainty/anxiety and perceived similarity, which decreases or increases over time in a relationship (Hubbert et al., 1999). We may learn how it occurs by identifying the kind of information exchanged and the pace of exchange in various relationship contexts. Similarly, the two dialectics may play out in partners' efforts to deal with differences and stereotypes. When intercultural friends express respect for or acceptance of differences between them and willingness to learn

more about each other (Chen et al., 1996), what they want to learn about the other and how they communicate respect and acceptance will inform us of their experience of the dialectics.

Revelation-nonrevelation: External information sharing. Externally, there may be pressure for relationship partners to make known the nature of their intercultural relationship. Here the contradiction of personal-social also bears on the situation. The social dimension of a relationship is highlighted when others in the community and social networks want to know how to react to the relationship or interact with relationship partners. In contrast, possible consequences of the revelation, such as negative social perception and social sanction (Bizman, 1987), may give rise to greater desires on the part of the partners to have control of the information about their relationship as a personal affair. On the other hand, revelation is necessary to gain needed social support. To explore the interplay of revelation-nonrevelation and personal-social, selection of information to reveal by relationship partners and selection of certain others as receivers of the information are worthy topics. As outsiders tend to make attributions about motivations of individuals in intercultural relationships (Shibata, 1998) and predictions about the future of such relationships (Payne, 1998), also relevant is the information that others are interested in about a relationship and the partners involved.

Autonomy-connection: Internal management of interdependence. This dialectic operates in relationship partners' attempts to connect with each other. The simultaneous presence of the similarity-difference contradiction may necessitate particular efforts and greater connection desires on the part of intercultural partners for the relationship to form and be sustained (Shibazaki & Brennan, 1998). By the same token, commitment of partners to their relationships may take on greater importance in maintenance and development of a relationship. Connection desires and commitment enable partners to redefine what is similar and what is different between them on the basis of the relevance of their cultures to their personal lives to mitigate the dialectical tensions (Aguilera, 1992).

The intersection of individual-culture and autonomy-connection contradictions in intercultural relationships underlies the issue of cultural identity. Partners relate to each other as individuals who are at the same time cultural members. Whether the pull is toward or away from the end of cultures of those involved decides whether relationship partners move toward or against autonomy. The individual-culture tension is found in daily communication between relationship partners in, for example, their negotiation on acceptable behaviors between them. The outcome depends on whether each attributes certain behaviors to culture or to a personality trait. Greater tolerance is exercised when the other's behavior is perceived as culture specific; the same perception of self-behavior is a ground for its legitimacy (Romano, 1997). For an intercultural relationship to form and be sustained, a baseline is mutual respect of cultural identity (Gudykunst et al., 1991; Sudweeks et al., 1990).

A three-way interplay of similarity-difference, individual-culture, and autonomy-connection dialectics in a relationship conceivably also influences the strength of cultural identities of individual partners and, thus, the relationship. Attention on a specific aspect of cultural difference between the partners, for example, may bring new appreciation of their own cultures and a reinforced, more secure cultural identity. Specific outcome always depends on actual substantiation of the dialectics involved.

Separation-integration: External management of interdependence. Externally, intercultural relationship partners face a double bind created by the interaction of separation-integration and similarity-difference dialectics. Relationships of any type, just as individuals in a relationship, are by default part of a culture (Baxter & Montgomery, 1996). Conventional forces in the culture require a relationship to be included to receive support and protection. At the same time, the same forces tend to become barriers to easily integrating an intercultural relationship, because of its differences from other relationships. To mediate between the opposing ends of the contradiction, relationship partners often take the initiative to select or even establish their own community and social networks. They may move to another location—even another country—or consciously socialize with others of similar experience or similar views on the relationship (Johnson & Warren, 1994). Studies on these networking activities would inform us of the manner in which the above dialectics transpire in intercultural relationships. On the other hand, albeit a much harder and slower process, relationship partners' political and social interactions with the society at large may facilitate redefinition of similarity and difference in terms of race, class, and culture. Aguilera (1992) has contended that the extent to which interracial marriage is practiced in a society is a good indicator of harmonious racial relations. Social acceptance and endorsement of intercultural relationships are a sign of social change. Change in a society's view on similarity and difference will affect the way in which intercultural relationships are positioned in the integration-separation dialectic.

Managing interdependence also involves the personal-social dialectic, as relationship partners may have very different views than the society at large regarding the nature of their relationship. That social perceptions of intercultural relationships tend to be negative is manifestation of forces pushing for separation and for a social view of personal relationships (Rosenblatt et al., 1995). Countermoves on the part of the relationship partners include public expression and proclamation of commitment to the relationship. In this sense, formation of alternative social networks, as does disassociation from unsympathetic families or intimacy display in public, functions to reclaim the private and independent dimension of a relationship. Relationship partners are holding onto their right to personal decisions without separating from society, thus unfolding the dynamics of interdependence.

Predictability-novelty: Internal variability. Internally, disparity in partners' cultural backgrounds brings to an intercultural relationship more novelty and less predictability. Novelty, therefore, is a marked characteristic of this type of relationship, a conventional wisdom substantiated by extensive support from the research. However, the dialectic of predictability-novelty may play out rather differently with the contradictions of individual-culture and similarity-difference also in the game. On one hand, as a relationship progresses, each developmental stage, with different priorities and foci of attention, brings anew issues thought to have been long resolved (Romano, 1997). Often it involves matters that the partners experience together for the first time and that have to do with cultural value orientations such as collectivism-individualism. Value orientations are internalized early in life in enculturation and hard to change, and they may surface as newly discovered differences that must now be renegotiated for a mutually agreeable solution. In the process, the partners may take another look at each other and at themselves. As they decide what is negotiable and what is not negotiable for the rela-

tionship, they also reevaluate what is cultural and what is individual about each other.

On the other hand, partners of a long-term intercultural relationship, such as marriage, have grown accustomed to each other and their cultural differences. At later stages of social penetration, they may be desensitized to the cultural side of each other and thus behave more like their counterparts in an intracultural relationship (Gaines & Ickes, 1997). In this case, partners may be less likely to detect certain belatedly surfaced cultural differences. Some may attribute these differences as being personal and respond with less tolerance, leading to severe marital difficulties. The scenario provides another explanation for the higher divorce rate among intercultural couples reported in some studies (Ho & Johnson, 1990). Cultural difference, however, is a never-exhausted resource. Conscious efforts to explore the resource may help keep relationships exciting and rewarding. Unfortunately, we currently know very little about this aspect of intercultural relationships.

Conventionality-uniqueness: External variability. In any given community, desire for stability and convention tend to outweigh desire for change in normal circumstances. Social perceptions, as a reflection of the conventionality-uniqueness mechanism, are generally negative toward intercultural relationships (Breger & Hill, 1998). The very form of intercultural relationship presents a deviation, a challenge to the convention. For intercultural relationship partners choosing to remain integrated despite social bias, several options are available in the pull between conventionality and uniqueness. With simultaneous presence of the dialectic of similarity-difference, the partners may deny their uniqueness and prove that their relationship lies within the parameter of and is not a deviation from social norms. Or they may own up to their unconventionality and persuade others that variety in the social fabrics is beneficial and valuable. A more difficult alternative is to evoke the personal-social dialectic and convince others that the relationship is private in nature with no impact on society.

The above options are conceptualizations of a new direction for research. We may examine the verbal and nonverbal communication strategies and practices people employ for external persuasion to manage the tension of each or a combination of the three dialectics. We may investigate how the relationship partners experience each or a combination of these dialectics (Haas & Stafford, 1998). Also, we may study how intercultural relationships are conceptualized in the minds of those who are involved in one, and how they perceive these contradictions. A better understanding of intercultural relationship and social change can be gained by looking at how relationship partners relate to society under different social conditions.

The manifestation of the conventionality-uniqueness dialectic is also seen in the role of social power and status in intercultural relationships. Whereas some scholars consider the states of privilege and disadvantage as a separate dialectical force (Martin & Nakayama, 1999), it can be subsumed under that of conventionality-uniqueness. Given the prevalence of hierarchical structure in most societies today, inequality of social status represents a specific aspect of conventions. There is a general acceptance of social hierarchy and a general bias for social power; cultural differences in this respect are a matter of degree, not of kind. The conventional force in this sense is one against the lower status and against the different. Thus, juxtaposition of conventionality-uniqueness and similar-difference contradictions, along with the working of personal-social contradiction, transpires in social perceptions and attitudes related to group status of individuals in the relationship.

CONCLUSION

An intercultural relationship is by nature both interpersonal and intercultural. The interface between the individual and the relationship, on one hand, and the relationship and the culture, on the other, has brought great complexity to communication in intercultural relationships. A dialectical approach offers a coherent understanding of the intricacies in such relationships. In this light, perceived similarity, uncertainty, cultural identity, social support, social status, and so on are all manifestations of dialectical forces. The corollary of dialectics is change, the inevitable and the constant in each and every aspect of social life (Mao, 1965). Every shift of a particular dialectic in the relationship will trigger other shifts, thereby developing the relationship. It is clear, then, that the dialectical perspective is compatible with the developmental perspective of intercultural relationships, albeit with different emphasis: The former focuses on the dialectical operations underlying relationship development, whereas the latter focuses on the relationship progression as a result or condition of dialectics (Gudykunst, Ting-Toomey, Sudweeks, & Steward, 1995). Last, a distinction in research is needed between insider and outsider perspectives (Gaines & Ickes, 1997), as two parties may not perceive or understand a relationship in similar ways. Although both are valid and informative, a tension exists between the two. Therein lies the essence of the dialectical approach, the ever-present struggle between polar forces and never a definite win one way or another: Neither diversity nor separation nor any one side of a contradiction can be the ultimate end state (Blau, 1994). All must be considered for a systematic understanding of the phenomena of intercultural relationships.

REFERENCES

Agranat, A. B., & Titov, V. N. (1994). Osobennosti demograficheskikh ustanovok moskovskikh as-siriytsev: Traditsiya i sovremennaya situatsiya [Demographic features of Moscow's Assyrians: Tradition and the current situation]. *Sotsiologicheskie Issledovaniya, 21,* 59-63.

Aguilera, R. V. (1992). Marriage between black and white people. *Revista Espanola de Investigaciones Sociologicas, 60,* 47-61.

Anderson, R. N., & Saenz, R. (1994). Structural determinants of Mexican American intermarriage, 1975-1980. *Social Science Quarterly, 75,* 414-430.

Back, L. (1993). Race, identity and nation within an adolescent community in south London. *New Community, 19,* 217-233.

Baxter, L. A. (1988). A dialectical perspective of communication strategies in relationship development. In S. Duck (Ed.), *Handbook of personal relationships* (pp. 257-273). New York: John Wiley.

Baxter, L. A. (1993). The social side of personal relationships: A dialectical perspective. In S. Duck (Ed.), *Social context and relationships: Understanding relationship processes* (Vol. 3, pp. 139-169). Newbury Park, CA: Sage.

Baxter, L. A., & Montgomery, B. M. (1996). *Relating: Dialogues & dialectics.* New York: Guilford.

Baxter, L. A., & Montgomery, B. M. (1997). Rethinking communication in personal relationships from a dialectical perspective. In S. Duck (Ed.), *Handbook of personal relationships* (pp. 325-349). New York: John Wiley.

Bizman, A. (1987). Perceived causes and compatibility of interethnic marriage: An attributional analysis. *International Journal of Intercultural Relations, 11,* 387-399.

Blau, P. M. (1994). *The paradox of multiculturalism.* Unpublished manuscript, University of North Carolina at Chapel Hill, Department of Sociology.

Bochner, A. P. (1984). The functions of communication in interpersonal bonding. In C. Arnold & J. Bowers (Eds.), *Handbook of rhetorical and communication theory* (pp. 544-621). Boston: Allyn & Bacon.

Braithwaite, D. O. (1991). Just how much did that wheelchair cost? Management of privacy boundaries by persons with disabilities. *Western Journal of Speech Communication, 55,* 254-274.

Breger, R., & Hill, R. (Eds.). (1998). *Cross-cultural marriage: Identity and choice.* New York: Berg.

Cabecinhas, R., & Amancio, L. (1999). Asymmetries in the perception of other as a function of social position and context. *Schweizerische Zeitschrift fuer Psychologie Revue Suisse de Psychologie* [Swiss Journal of Psychology], *58,* 40-50.

Chan, A. Y., & Wethington, E. (1998). Factors promoting marital resilience among interracial couples. In H. I. McCubbin, E. A Thompson, A. I. Thompson, & J. E. Fromer (Eds.), *Resiliency in Native American and immigrant families* (pp. 71-87). Thousand Oaks, CA: Sage.

Chan, M. (1990, December 19). Gentlemen prefer Asians: Why some Anglos are only attracted to Asian women. *The Rafu Shimpo, 1,* 4.

Chen, G. (1995). Differences in self-disclosure patterns among Americans versus Chinese. *Journal of Cross-Cultural Psychology, 26,* 84-91.

Chen, L. (1995). Interaction involvement and patterns of topical talk: A comparison of intercultural and intracultural dyads. *International Journal of Intercultural Relations, 19,* 463-482.

Chen, L. (1997). Verbal adaptive strategies in U.S. American dyadic conversations with U.S. American or East-Asian partners. *Communication Monographs, 64,* 1-22.

Chen, L., & Cegala, D. J. (1994). Topic management, shared knowledge and accommodation: A study of communication adaptability. *Research on Language and Social Interaction, 27,* 389-417.

Chen, L., Isa, M., & Sakai, J. (1996, November). *Our communication with North Americans: A study of intercultural experience of Japanese visiting students.* Paper presented at the annual conference of the Speech Communication Association, San Diego, CA.

Chung, L. (1990). *Analysis of cultural identity and stereotypes as factors influencing interethnic dating*. Unpublished manuscript, California State University, Fullerton, Department of Speech Communication.

Chung, L. C., & Ting-Toomey, S. (1999). Ethnic identity and relational expectations among Asian Americans. *Communication Research Reports, 16*, 157-166.

Clark-Ibanez, M. K. (1999). *Gender, race and friendships: Structural and social factors leading to the likelihood of inter-ethnic dating*. Unpublished manuscript, American Sociological Association.

Collier, M. J. (1996). Communication competence problematics in ethnic friendships. *Communication Monographs, 63*, 314-336.

Collier, M. J., & Bornman, E. (1999). Core symbols in South African intercultural friendships. *International Journal of Intercultural Relations, 23*, 133-156.

Collier, M. J., & Bowker, J. (1994, November). *U.S. American women in intercultural friendships*. Paper presented at the annual conference of the Speech Communication Association, New Orleans, LA.

Crohn, J. (1998). Intercultural couples. In M. McGoldrick (Ed.), *Re-visioning family therapy: Race, culture, and gender in clinical practice* (pp. 295-308). New York: Guilford.

Fujino, D. C. (1997). The rates, patterns and reasons for forming heterosexual interracial dating relationships among Asian Americans. *Journal of Social and Personal Relationships, 14*, 809-828.

Gaines, S. O., Jr., Granrose, C. S., Rios, D. I., Garcia, B. F., Youn, M. S. P., Farris, K. R., & Bledsoe, K. L. (1999). Patterns of attachment and responses to accommodative dilemmas among interethnic/interracial couples. *Journal of Social and Personal Relationships, 16*, 275-285.

Gaines, S. O., Jr., & Ickes, W. (1997). Perspectives on interracial relationships. In S. Duck (Ed.), *Handbook of personal relationships* (pp. 121-145). Chichester, UK: Wiley.

Gaines, S. O., Jr., Reis, H. T., Summers, S., Rusbult, C. E., Cox, C. L., Wexler, M. O., Marelich, W. D., & Kurland, G. J. (1997). Impact of attachment style on reactions to accommodative dilemmas in close relationships. *Personal Relationships, 4*, 93-113.

Garcia, S. D., & Rivera, S. M. (1999). Perceptions of Hispanic and African-American couples at the friendship or engagement stage of a relationship. *Journal of Social and Personal Relationships, 16*, 65-86.

Gareis, E. (1995). *Intercultural friendship: A qualitative study*. Lanham, MD: University Press of America.

Gareis, E. (1999). Adult friendship: Examples of intercultural patterns. In M. E. Roloff (Ed.), *Communication yearbook 22* (pp. 431-468). Thousand Oaks, CA: Sage.

Graham, M. A., Moeai, J., & Shizuru, L. S. (1985). Intercultural marriages: An intrareligious perspective. *International Journal of Intercultural Relations, 9*, 427-434.

Grant, P. R. (1993). Reactions to intergroup similarity: Examination of the similarity-differentiation and the similarity-attraction hypotheses. *Canadian Journal of Behavioral Science, 25*, 28-44.

Gudykunst, W. B. (1983). Similarities and differences in perceptions of initial intracultural and intercultural encounters. *Southern Speech Communication Journal, 49*, 49-65.

Gudykunst, W. B. (1985). A model of uncertainty reduction in intercultural encounters. *Journal of Language and Social Psychology, 4*, 79-98.

Gudykunst, W. B. (1989). Culture and development of interpersonal relationships. In J. Anderson (Ed.), *Communication yearbook 12* (pp. 315-354). Newbury Park, CA: Sage.

Gudykunst, W. B., Gao, G., Schmidt, K. L., Nishida, T., Bond, M. H., Leung, K., Wang, G., & Barraclough, R. A. (1992). The influence of individualism-collectivism, self-monitoring, and predicted outcome value on communication in ingroup and outgroup relationships. *Journal of Cross-Cultural Psychology, 23*, 196-213.

Gudykunst, W. B., Gao, G., Sudweeks, S., Ting-Toomey, S., & Nishida, T. (1991). Themes in opposite sex, Japanese-North American relationships. In S. Ting-Toomey & F. Korzenny (Eds.), *Cross-cultural interpersonal communication* (pp. 230-258). Newbury Park, CA: Sage.

Gudykunst, W. B., & Nishida, T. (1984). Individual and cultural influences on uncertainty reduction. *Communication Monographs, 51,* 23-36.

Gudykunst, W. B., & Nishida, T. (1986). The influence of cultural variability on perceptions of communication behavior associated with relationship terms. *Human Communication Research, 13,* 147-166.

Gudykunst, W. B., Nishida, T., & Chua, E. (1986). Uncertainty reduction in Japanese-North American dyads. *Communication Research Reports, 3,* 39-46.

Gudykunst, W. B., Nishida, T., & Chua, E. (1987). Perceptions of social penetration in Japanese-North American dyads. *International Journal of Intercultural Relations, 11,* 171-191.

Gudykunst, W. B., & Shapiro, R. B. (1996). Communication in everyday interpersonal and intergroup encounters. *International Journal of Intercultural Relations, 20,* 19-45.

Gudykunst, W. B., Ting-Toomey, S., Sudweeks, S., & Stewart, L. (1995). *Building bridges: Skills for a changing world.* Boston: Houghton Mifflin.

Gudykunst, W. B., Yoon, Y.-C., & Nishida, T. (1987). The influence of individualism-collectivism on perceptions of communication in ingroup and outgroup relationships. *Communication Monographs, 54,* 295-306.

Gurung, R. A. R., & Duong, T. (1999). Mixing and matching: Assessing the concomitants of mixed-ethnic relationships. *Journal of Social and Personal Relationships, 16,* 639-657.

Haas, S. M., & Stafford, L. (1998). An initial examination of maintenance behaviors in gay and lesbian relationships. *Journal of Social and Personal Relationships, 15,* 846-855.

Hanassab, S., & Tidwell, R. (1998). Intramarriage and intermarriage: Young Iranians in Los Angeles. *International Journal of Intercultural Relations, 22,* 395-408.

Hecht, M. L., Larkey, L. K., & Johnson, J. N. (1992). African American and European American perceptions of problematic issues in interethnic communication effectiveness. *Human Communication Research, 19,* 209-236.

Hecht, M. L., Ribeau, S., & Sedano, N. V. (1990). A Mexican American perspective on interethnic communication. *International Journal of Intercultural Relations, 14,* 31-55.

Ho, F. C., & Johnson, R. C. (1990). Intra-ethnic and inter-ethnic marriage and divorce in Hawaii. *Social Biology, 37,* 44-51.

Hoffman, M., & Schwarzwald, J. (1987). Moderating effects of educational standing on inter-ethnic relations in the classroom. *International Journal of Intercultural Relations, 11,* 357-367.

Horenczyk, G., & Bekerman, Z. (1997). The effects of intercultural acquaintance and structured intergroup interaction on ingroup, outgroup, and reflected ingroup stereotypes. *International Journal of Intercultural Relations, 21,* 71-83.

Hubbert, K. N., Gudykunst, W. B., & Guerrero, S. L. (1999). Intergroup communication over time. *International Journal of Intercultural Relations, 23,* 13-46.

Hwang, S. S., Saenz, R., & Aguirre, B. E. (1997). Structural and assimilationist explanations of Asian American intermarriage. *Journal of Marriage and the Family, 59,* 758-772.

Johnson, W. R., & Warren, D. M. (Eds.). (1994). *Inside the mixed marriage: Accounts of changing attitudes, patterns, and perceptions of cross-cultural and interracial marriages.* Lanham, MD: University Press of America.

Kouri, K., & Lasswell, M. (1993). Black-white marriage. *Marriage and Family Review, 19,* 241-255.

Lampe, P. (1982). Interethnic dating: Reasons for and against. *International Journal of Intercultural Relations, 6,* 115-126.

Larkey, L. K., & Hecht, M. L. (1995). A comparative study of African American and European American ethnic identity. *International Journal of Intercultural Relations, 19,* 483-504.

Lee, H., & Boster, F. (1991). Social information for uncertainty reduction during initial interactions. In S. Ting-Toomey & F. Korzenny (Eds.), *Cross-cultural interpersonal communication* (pp. 189-112). Newbury Park, CA: Sage.

Lee, C. M., & Gudykunst, W. B. (in press). Attraction in initial interethnic interactions. *International Journal of Intercultural Relations.*

Levkovitch, V. P. (1990). Marital relationships in binational families. *Soviet Journal of Psychology, 11,* 26-37.

Mao, T. (1965). *On contradiction.* Beijing: Foreign Languages Press.

Martin, J. N., & Nakayama, T. K. (1999). Thinking dialectically about culture and communication. *Communication Theory, 9,* 1-25.

McDermott, S. T. (1991). The generalizability of the communication to attraction relationship to intercultural communication: Repulsion or attraction? In J. A. Anderson (Ed.), *Communication yearbook 14* (pp. 492-497). Newbury Park, CA: Sage.

McGuire, W. M. (1992). Key influences in interracial mate selection. *Dissertation Abstracts International, 53,* DA 9300188.

Mills, J. K., Daly, J., Longmore, A., & Kilbride, G. (1995). A note on family acceptance involving interracial friendships and romantic relationships. *Journal of Psychology, 129,* 349-351.

Neuliep, J. W., & Ryan, D. J. (1998). The influence of intercultural communication apprehension and sociocommunicative orientation during initial cross-cultural interaction. *Communication Quarterly, 46,* 88-99.

Nguyen, L. T. (1998). To date or not to date a Vietnamese: Perceptions and expectations of Vietnamese American college students. *Amerasia Journal, 24*(1), 143-169.

Obot, I. S. (1988). Value systems and cross-cultural contact: The effect of perceived similarity and stability on social evaluations. *International Journal of Intercultural Relations, 12,* 363-379.

Osbeck, L. M., Moghaddam, F. M., & Perreault, S. (1997). Similarity and attraction among majority and minority groups in a multicultural context. *International Journal of Intercultural Relations, 21,* 113-123.

Parsonson, K. (1987). Intermarriage. *Journal of Cross-Cultural Psychology, 18,* 363-371.

Payne, M. (1998). Waiting for lightning to strike: Social support of interracial couples. In J. N. Martin, T. K. Nakayama, & L. A. Flores (Eds.), *Readings in cultural contexts* (pp. 379-387). Mountain View, CA: Mayfield.

Race relations responses to General Social Survey. (1991, January 9). National Opinion Research Center. *Los Angeles Times,* p. A15.

Rawlins, W. K. (1992). *Friendship matters.* New York: Aldine de Gruyter.

Rohrlich, B. F. (1988). Dual-culture marriage and communication. *International Journal of Intercultural Relations, 12,* 35-44.

Romano, D. (1997). *Intercultural marriage: Promises and pitfalls* (2nd ed.). Yarmouth, ME: Intercultural Press.

Rosenblatt, P. C., Karis, T. A., & Powell, R. D. (1995). *Multiracial couples: Black and white voices.* Thousand Oaks, CA: Sage.

Shibata, Y. (1998). Crossing racialized boundaries: Intermarriage between "Africans" and "Indians" in contemporary Guyana. In R. Breger & R. Hill (Eds.), *Cross-cultural marriage: Identity and choice* (pp. 83-100). New York: Berg.

Shibazaki, K., & Brennan, K. A. (1998). When birds of different feathers flock together: A preliminary comparison of intra-ethnic and inter-ethnic dating relationships. *Journal of Social and Personal Relationships, 15,* 248-256.

Simard, L. M. (1981). Cross-cultural interaction: Potential invisible barriers. *Journal of Social Psychology, 113,* 171-192.

Spickard, P. (1989). *Mixed blood: Intermarriage and ethnic identity in twentieth-century America.* Madison: University of Wisconsin Press.

Strom, W. O. (1988). Cross-cultural friendships on the university campus: Testing the functional and identity validation models. *Dissertation Abstracts International, 49,* 3204A.

Sudweeks, S., Gudykunst, W. B., Ting-Toomey, S., & Nishida, T. (1990). Developmental themes in Japanese-North American interpersonal relationships. *International Journal of Intercultural Relations, 14,* 207-233.

Sung, B. L. (1990). Chinese American intermarriage. *Journal of Comparative Family Studies, 21,* 337-352.

Ting-Toomey, S. (1991). Intimacy expression in three cultures. *International Journal of Intercultural Relations, 15,* 29-46.

Tuch, S. A., Sigelman, L., & MacDonald, J. A. (1999). Race relations and American youth,

1976-1995. *Public Opinion Quarterly, 63,* 109-148.

Tucker, M., & Mitchell-Kernan, C. (1995). Social structure and psychological correlates of interethnic dating. *Journal of Social and Personal Relationships, 12,* 341-361.

Werner, C. M., & Baxter, L. (1994). Temporal qualities of relationships: Organismic, transactional and dialectical view. In M. L. Knappy & G. R. Miller (Eds.), *Handbook of interpersonal communication* (2nd ed., pp. 323-379). Thousand Oaks, CA: Sage.

13

Adapting to an Unfamiliar Culture
An Interdisciplinary Overview

YOUNG YUN KIM
University of Oklahoma

The swirling interface between cultures spins off new problems that require new learning and new solutions. This global transformation compels us to stretch the limits of our usual ways of thinking. At the forefront of this reality are countless people who are on the move across cultural boundaries—millions of immigrants, refugees, and other long-term resettlers who seek a better life. Others relocate temporarily for a narrower set of purposes—artists, musicians, writers, business people, construction workers, nurses, doctors, Peace Corps volunteers, students, professors, researchers, diplomats and other government employees, military personnel, missionaries, and journalists.

Academic efforts to understand and explain the cross-cultural adaptation phenomenon have been extensive across social science disciplines. The complex nature of the phenomenon manifests itself in the variety of existing conceptions and research approaches, making

it difficult for individual investigators to gain a clear picture of the body of knowledge accumulated over the decades. Although the field has benefited from rich information and insights, it suffers from disconnectedness. Broadly, the existing approaches can be grouped into two broad categories: group level and individual level. *Group-level studies* have traditionally been common among anthropologists for more than 60 years. During the 1930s, the Social Science Research Council appointed the Subcommittee on Acculturation composed of three anthropologists—Redfield, Linton, and Herskovits—and charged it with the task of defining the parameters for this inquiry in cultural anthropology. The term *acculturation* was formally adopted as the concept representing the new area of study dealing with "those phenomena which result when *groups* of individuals have different cultures and come into first-hand contact with subsequent changes in the

243

original pattern of either or both *groups*" (Redfield, Linton, & Herskovits, 1936, p. 149, italics added). By viewing acculturation as a group phenomenon, anthropological studies traditionally observed the dynamics of change in "primitive" cultures (e.g., Herskovits, 1958), the presence of kin, friends, and ethnic community organizations in supporting immigrants' adaptation (e.g., Eames & Schwab, 1964). Paralleling the anthropological studies of cultural groups are sociological studies that have focused on issues pertaining to *stratification,* that is, the hierarchical classification of the members of society based on the unequal distribution of resources, power, and prestige (e.g., Parrillo, 1966). Many sociological studies have investigated minority-majority relations in which minority groups are structurally integrated into the political, social, and economic systems of the society at large (e.g., Marrett & Leggon, 1982).

Comparatively, studies in psychology and communication have dealt primarily with the intrapersonal-interpersonal phenomenon of individual newcomers in an unfamiliar environment. These *individual-level studies* are aimed at understanding and explaining the experiences of individuals who (1) have had a primary socialization in one culture and find themselves in a different and unfamiliar culture, (2) are at least minimally dependent on the host environment for meeting personal and social needs, and (3) are at least minimally engaged in firsthand contact and communication with that environment. Given these conditions, efforts have been made recently to include in this domain members of ethnic minority groups such as African Americans and American Indians who face pressure to adapt from the dominant sociocultural milieu in the United States (e.g., Kim, Lujan, & Dixon, 1998). The present essay offers an overview of these individual-level studies that investigate cross-cultural adaptation focusing on the experiences of immigrants, refugees, and other long-term resettlers, as well as temporary sojourners and native-born ethnic minorities.

KEY TERMS AND DEFINITIONS

A variety of terms have been used to refer to what is essentially the same process immigrants and sojourners go through in an unfamiliar culture. The term *assimilation* (or *amalgamation*) has often been employed to emphasize acceptance and internalization of the host culture by the individual. The term *acculturation* has been defined as the process by which individuals acquire some (but not all) aspects of the host culture. In a more limited sense, *coping* and *adjustment* have been employed to refer to psychological responses to cross-cultural challenges, whereas *integration* has been defined as social participation in the host environment. The terminological usage becomes more complex when we consider the variations in operational definitions (or indicators) of each of these terms.

The term *adaptation* is employed here to refer to the dynamic process by which individuals, upon relocating to an unfamiliar cultural environment, establish (or reestablish) and maintain a relatively stable, reciprocal, and functional relationship with the environment. At the core of this definition is the goal of achieving an overall person-environment "fit" for maximization of one's social life chances. Adaptation, thus, is an activity that is "almost always a compromise, a vector in the internal structure of culture and the external pressure of environment" (Sahlins, 1964, p. 136). Placed at the intersection of the person and the environment, adaptation is essentially a communication process that occurs as long as the individual remains in contact with the environment. This communication-based definition enables us to move beyond the conven-

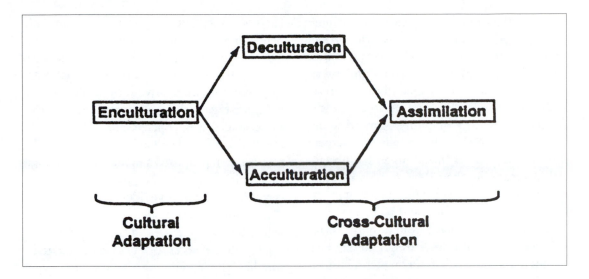

Figure 13.1. Relationships Among Terms Associated With Cross-Cultural Adaptation

tional linear-reductionist-causal assumption underlying almost all of the existing investigations in the field of cross-cultural adaptation and encourages us to examine the phenomenon in its totality—all of an individual's personal and social experiences vis-à-vis the host environment.

In this interactive and inclusive conception, the term *cross-cultural adaptation* serves as a "superordinate category" (White, 1976, p. 18) under which other commonly used terms can be subsumed. First, cross-cultural adaptation is a phenomenon that occurs subsequent to the process of childhood *enculturation* (or socialization) of individuals into recognizable members of a given cultural community. Second, all individuals entering a new and unfamiliar culture undergo some degree of new cultural learning, that is, the acquisition of the native cultural practices in wide-ranging areas, particularly in areas of direct relevance to the daily functioning of the resettlers—from attire and food habits to behavioral norms and cultural values. The resocialization activities are the very essence of acculturation, consistent with the definition

offered by Marden and Meyer (1968): "the change in individuals whose primary learning has been in one culture and who take over traits from another culture" (p. 36). Acculturation, however, is not a process in which new cultural elements are simply added to prior internal conditions. As new learning occurs, *deculturation* (or unlearning) of some of the old cultural habits has to occur, at least in the sense that new responses are adopted in situations that previously would have evoked old ones. The act of acquiring something new is inevitably the "losing" of something old in much the same way as "being someone requires the forfeiture of being someone else" (Thayer, 1975, p. 240). As the interplay of acculturation and deculturation continues, newcomers undergo an internal transformation in the direction of *assimilation,* a state of the highest degree of acculturation and deculturation theoretically possible (cf. Montalvo, 1991; van Oudenhoven & Eisses, 1998). (See Figure 13.1.)

Studies focusing on historical change in immigrant communities have demonstrated the acculturative, deculturative, and assimilative trends within and across generations. Gupta (1975), for example, reported that Asian Indian immigrants to the United States with originally vegetarian food habits underwent significant changes over time toward increasingly nonvegetarian habits. A study by the American Jewish Committee showed a significant increase in the members' merging into non-Jewish organizations and a substantial decrease in their Jewish identification (Zweigenhalf, 1979-1980). Likewise, Triandis, Kashima, Shimada, and Villareal (1986) and Suro (1998) have found both acculturative and deculturative trends among Hispanics in the United States: Long-term Hispanics showed diminished Hispanic "cultural scripts" in their judgments and increased social interactions with non-Hispanics.

LONG-TERM AND SHORT-TERM ADAPTATION

Division has existed between studies of immigrants and refugees living in a new culture more or less permanently and those of short-term adaptation of temporary sojourners. These two groups of studies have been carried out largely independent of each other with few cross-citations. The apparent divergence between the research foci of long-term and short-term adaptation studies is clearly due to the relative isolation in which such studies have been carried out over the years.

On the one hand, *long-term adaptation* has been investigated over the past several decades mainly in social psychology and, more recently, in communication. These studies employed anthropological and sociological concepts such as acculturation, assimilation, and marginality to analyze individual adaptation experiences. Taft (1957) identified concepts such as attitudes, frames of reference, social motivation, ego involvement, beliefs, reference groups, role expectations, and role behavior as key aspects of immigrants' assimilation in the new culture. Based on these variables, Taft delineated seven stages of assimilation, moving progressively from the cultural learning stage to the congruence stage. Each of these stages was conceptualized in two dimensions, internal and external. Berry (1970, 1980, 1990) proposed a model of psychological acculturation based on two questions concerning the subjective identity orientation: "Are [ethnic] cultural identity and customs of value to be retained?" and "Are positive relations with the larger society of value and to be sought?" By combining the response types (yes, no) to these two questions, Berry and associates identify four modes of adaptation: "integration" (yes, yes), "assimilation" (no, yes), "separation" (yes, no), and "marginality" (no, no). A modified version of this model has been presented by Bourhis, Moïse, Perreault, and Senécal (1997), replacing "marginality" with "anomie" and "individualism."

The substantial history of academic interest in long-term adaptation of immigrants and ethnic communities has been followed by studies of *short-term adaptation*. Studies of temporary sojourners began increasing in number during the 1960s, stimulated by the beginning of the Peace Corps movement, the increase in international student exchange programs, and multinational trade during the postwar reconstruction period. Companies found that their overseas operations were being hampered because their staff members were not effective in coping with unfamiliar social and business practices. Military personnel and experts engaged in technical assistance experienced similar problems. Accordingly, short-term adaptation studies have been predominantly influenced by practical (and less theoretical) concerns of "easing" the temporary but often bewildering transition into a new environment. Extensive writings in this area describe the psychological difficulties in encountering unfamiliar environmental demands during the overseas sojourn (e.g., Ward, Okura, Kennedy, & Kojima, 1998). Many studies have focused on "culture shock" (Oberg, 1960) or various physical and psychological responses and strategies of sojourners in an unfamiliar culture (e.g., Hansel, 1993; Ward & Kennedy, 1994; Wilson, 1993).

Despite these two disparate research traditions, there are common experiences of cross-cultural adaptation shared by everyone crossing cultures, long term or short term. Everyone is challenged by the unfamiliar milieu to engage in at least some degree of new cultural learning and modification in old cultural habits. Kim's (1988, 1995, 2001) theory, discussed later in this chapter, suggests a way to understand the commonalities in both short-term and long-term adaptation and place them in a broader explanatory system. It does so by focusing not on the length of time but on multitudes of other adaptation-facilitating (or adaptation-impeding) factors of individual predisposition, the new environment, and communication activities linking the person and the environment. The assumption here is that even though the adaptation process plays out in time and, thus, is correlated with the individual's cumulative change, what really contributes to this change is not the length of time itself but the individual's communicative interface with the new environment.

ADAPTATION-AS-PROBLEM AND ADAPTATION-AS-LEARNING/GROWTH

In both short-term and long-term adaptation studies, the main emphasis has been on the problematic nature of cross-cultural experience. Most investigators have tended to view

adaptation experiences mainly in terms of difficulties they present, justifying their studies as scientific efforts to find ways to help ease such predicaments. This *problem-oriented view* of cross-cultural adaptation is most apparent in studies of culture shock that almost exclusively focus on individual sojourners' frustration reactions to their new environment (Anderson, 1994) or lack of such reactions measured in various physical and psychological indicators (Ady, 1995). Taft (1977), for instance, identified a number of common reactions to cultural dislocation: (1) "cultural fatigue" as manifested by irritability, insomnia, and other psychosomatic disorders; (2) a sense of loss arising from being uprooted from one's familiar surroundings; (3) rejection by the individual of members of the new society; and (4) a feeling of impotence stemming from being unable to deal with an unfamiliar environment (see also Furnham & Bochner, 1986; Torbiörn, 1988). Bennett (1977) expanded the meaning of this term and regarded it as part of the general "transition shock," a natural consequence of individuals' inability to interact with the new environment effectively. According to Bennett, transition shock occurs when individuals encounter "the loss of a partner in death or divorce; change of life-style related to passages; loss of a familiar frame of reference in an intercultural encounter; or, change of values associated with rapid social innovation" (p. 45). Zaharna (1989) added to the discussion of culture shock the notion of "self-shock," emphasizing "the double-binding challenge of identity" (p. 501). Concern for the problematic nature of cross-cultural adaptation has been a force behind many long-term adaptation studies of immigrants, as well. Early studies (e.g., Stonequist, 1937) examined the strain of isolation called "marginality." Many subsequent studies have analyzed "acculturative stress" (e.g., Mishra,

Sinha, & Berry, 1996) and mental health-related clinical issues (e.g., Dyal & Dyal, 1981; Westmeyer, Vang, & Neider, 1986).

On the other hand, many other investigators have emphasized the *learning and growth-facilitating* nature of the adaptation process. Adler (1975) explained that the culture shock experience should be viewed in a broader context of transition shock, a phenomenon that leads to profound learning, growth, and self-awareness. Likewise, Ruben (1983) questioned the problem-oriented perspective in his discussion of a study of Canadian technical advisers and their spouses on two-year assignments in Kenya (Ruben & Kealey, 1979). In this study, the intensity and directionality of culture shock were found to be unrelated to patterns of psychological adjustment at the end of the first year in the alien land. Of particular importance is the finding that in some instances, the magnitude of culture shock was positively related to the individuals' social and professional effectiveness within the new environment. Based on this finding, Ruben (1983) suggested that culture shock experiences might, in fact, be responsible for (rather than impeding) their adaptation. Adler (1975) echoed this point when he stated that culture shock is a transitional learning experience reflecting a "movement from a state of low self- and cultural awareness to a state of high self- and cultural awareness" (p. 15).

The learning and growth-facilitating function of culture shock has been indirectly supported by other sojourner studies that attempted to describe the stages of the adaptation process. Oberg (1979), for instance, described four stages: (1) a "honeymoon" stage characterized by fascination, elation, and optimism; (2) a stage of hostility and emotionally stereotyped attitudes toward the host society and increased association with fellow sojourners; (3) a recovery stage characterized by increased language knowledge and ability to get

around in the new cultural environment; and (4) a final stage in which adjustment is about as complete as possible, anxiety is largely gone, and new customs are accepted and enjoyed. Many other investigators have documented evidence for what is commonly called a "U-curve hypothesis" (e.g., Furnham, 1988; Ward et al., 1998). According to this model, sojourners typically begin their cross-cultural adaptation process with optimism and elation in the host culture, followed by the subsequent dip or "trough" in satisfaction and a recovery. The U-curve hypothesis has been further extended to the "W-curve" (e.g., Gullahorn & Gullahorn, 1963; Trifonovitch, 1977) by adding the "reentry shock" or "reverse culture shock" (Gaw, 2000) after returning home (see Figure 13.2).

This learning/growth perspective has been frequently validated by findings in studies of long-term adaptation of immigrants. Nagata (1969) demonstrated a trend toward increasing levels of the social and cultural integration of Japanese Americans across three successive generations. Many others have documented a cumulative-progressive adaptation process that is generally upward-moving and linear (e.g., Kim, 1977, 1989; van Oudenhoven & Eisses, 1998). Based on cross-sectional comparisons according to the length of residence, these studies showed an incremental trend of psychological and social adaptation. An effort to refine the cumulative-progressive description further has been made in Kim's (1988, 1995, 2001) process model depicting the "stress-adaptation-growth dynamic" (see Figure 13.3). The three-pronged model highlights the dialectic of stress and adaptation that, together, bring about a gradual psychological movement. This process follows a pattern that juxtaposes novelty and confirmation, attachment and detachment, progression and regression, integration and disintegration, construction and destruction. Large and sudden changes are described as occurring

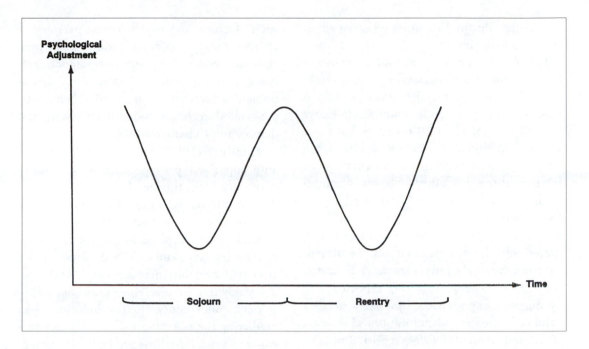

Figure 13.2.   The U-Curve and W-Curve Adaptation of Sojourners

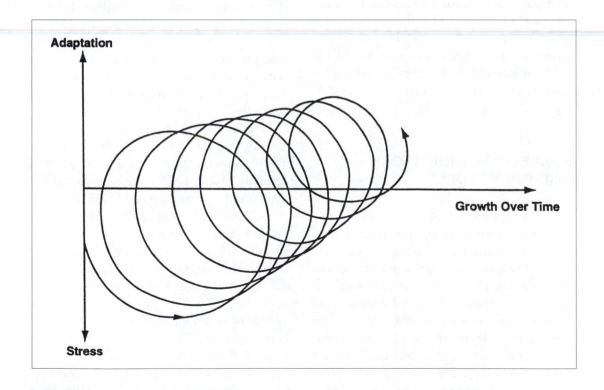

Figure 13.3.   The Stress-Adaptation-Growth Dynamic: Kim's (1988, 1995, 2001) Process Model

more often during the initial phase of exposure to a new culture.

Research data offer some indirect evidence for stressful experiences laying the groundwork for subsequent adaptation growth. A study of Canadian technical advisers in Kenya (Ruben & Kealey, 1979) revealed that those who would ultimately be the most effective in adapting to a new culture underwent the most intense culture shock during the transition period. Rivera-Sinclair (1997) reported a positive association between the psychological orientation of Cuban Americans to be integrated into the American culture (biculturalism) and the level of stress (anxiety). In Australia, Gebart-Eaglemont (1994) reported that immigrants experienced less stress as they achieved greater acculturation. Likewise, Ward and Kennedy (1994) reported notable psychological stress in those international students in Singapore who attempted to integrate in Singaporean society, whereas Gil, Vega, and Dimas (1994) found that foreign-born Hispanic teenagers who were undergoing the cross-cultural adaptation process had higher levels of stress than their American-born bicultural counterparts (see also Redmond & Bunyi, 1993; Steen, 1998).

ADAPTATION INDICATORS AND PREDICTORS

In searching for generalizable patterns of the adaptation process, many investigators have proposed models that are designed to identify (1) key features of adaptation as indicators of differing adaptation levels of individuals or (2) factors (commonly called independent variables, explanatory variables, or predictors) that facilitate or impede the adaptation process. Often, investigators have not distinguished these two different conceptual underpinnings, thereby creating ambiguity and confusion. The existing models include

such factors as psychological/personality characteristics, communication behaviors/ skills (especially language competence/preference), interpersonal relationship development/preference, mass media behaviors, job-related technical skill/effectiveness, and demographic characteristics.

Weinstock (1964), for example, focused on an occupational prestige scale in the country of origin and the transferability of skills in predicting differential rates of acculturation in the country where one settles. A psychologically based explanation, for example, is offered by Gudykunst (1995) based on his anxiety/uncertainty management (AUM) theory. Gudykunst applies three core concepts—anxiety, uncertainty, and mindfulness—to predicting the adaptation levels of sojourners who cross individualistic and collectivistic cultural boundaries (see also Gao & Gudykunst, 1990). Others such as Barona and Miller (1994) and Kim (1977) focused on the complexity of sojourners' perception of Americans. Similarly, Szalay and Inn (1988) examined the convergence of "subjective meaning systems" of Puerto Ricans in New York toward those of Anglo-Americans. Other investigators have examined changing patterns of cultural identity employing terms such as *bicultural identity* (Boekestijn, 1988; Dasgupta, 1983; Kanno, 2000), *multicultural man [woman]* (Adler, 1982), *cultural hybrid* (Park, 1939), and *intercultural identity* (Kim, 1988, 1995, 2000; Kim et al., 1998). Among other psychological factors assessed in various studies are self-image, self-esteem, morale, social isolation/belonging, (dis)satisfaction, and locus of control (e.g., Shah, 1991; Vega, Kolody, & Valle, 1987; Ying & Liese, 1991; Yum, 1986). In addition, Epstein, Botvin, Dusenberry, Diaz, and Kerner (1996) defined and assessed cross-cultural adaptation in terms of linguistic acculturation, whereas others assessed patterns of interpersonal relationships involving individuals of the host and ethnic

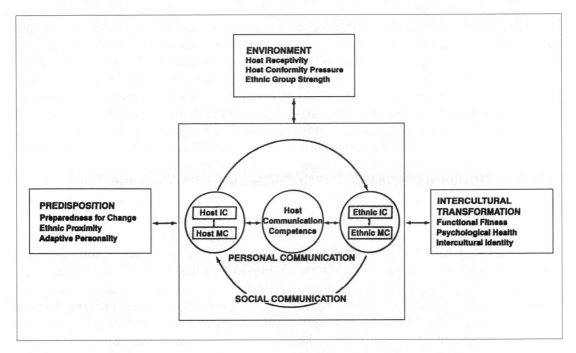

Figure 13.4. Factors Influencing Cross-Cultural Adaptation: Kim's (1988, 1995, 2000) Structural Model
SOURCE: Used with permission of the author.
NOTE: IC = interpersonal communication, MC = mass communication.

communities (e.g., Yum, 1983) and mass media behavior (e.g., Kim, 1980; Stilling, 1997).

Yet others have assessed a more broadly based set of factors in assessing or predicting adaptation. Hawes and Kealey (1981) assessed behavioral variables including interpersonal skills, cultural identity, and realistic pre-departure expectation as the best predictors of "overseas effectiveness." Others included an even wider range of factors—from demographic factors (e.g., age and sex) and factors of communication competence (e.g., knowledge of the host language, motivation for adaptation, and positive attitude toward the host environment) to factors of social integration (e.g., interpersonal relationships with the natives and with coethnics). Dawson, Crano, and Burgoon (1996) included multiple acculturation measures from background/demographic ("where raised" and "genera-

tion"), psychological ("self-identity" and "mother's identity"), and social indicators ("language spoken," "associate with now," "friends 6-18 years," "TV," and "movies"). In explaining acculturative stress, Berry and Kim (1987) identified several groups of factors: (1) the nature of the host society, (2) the type of adapting group, (3) the type of adaptation being experienced (integration, assimilation, separation, or marginalization), (4) demographic factors, (5) psychological factors, and (6) social characteristics of individual immigrants. Similar multilevel indexes have also been used by Jasinskaja-Lahti and Liebkind (2000) and DiPrete and Forristal (1994), among others.

Incorporating many of these and related concepts, Kim (1988, 1995, 2001) has proposed an integrative communication-based multidimensional model (see Figure 13.4). Defining adaptation as neither an independent variable nor a dependent variable but as the entirety of the phenomenon itself, six dimensions of factors and their interdependent relationships are identified by Kim as a systemic template for explaining the differential rates (or speeds) at which the adaptation process unfolds over time. At the core of this structural model is *host communication competence,* which serves as the engine of the adaptation process. Inseparably linked with host communication competence are activities of host social communication and ethnic social communication (interpersonal and mass communication). Also identified in this model are three conditions of the host environment (host receptivity, host conformity pressure, and ethnic group strength), as well as factors of the individual's *predisposition* (preparedness for the life in the host environment, the degree of the individual's ethnic proximity to the dominant ethnicity of the host environment, and the degree of openness, strength, and positivity of the individual's personality. Together, these dimensions of factors are explained in this theory as facilitating or impeding one's *intercultural transformation* embodied in his or her functional fitness, psychological health, and intercultural identity development.

IDEOLOGY: ASSIMILATIONISM AND PLURALISM

An additional important consideration that investigators in this field need to give attention to is the largely implicit underlying value premises with respect to cross-cultural adaptation. In the social scientific tradition, almost all of the studies examined in this chapter are predicated on the assumption that cross-cultural adaptation is a natural phenomenon

and that successful adaptation is a desirable goal. Most theories, of both short- and long-term adaptation, have been framed in such a way that the models and research findings would help ease the transition and facilitate the eventual functioning in the new environment. The common premise underlying these traditional approaches that affirm the adaptation phenomenon and recognize it as something desirable has been seen by some scholars as reflecting "assimilationist" or "melting-pot" social ideology.

Indeed, the conception of adaptation as ultimately leading to assimilation or cultural convergence has been questioned since the 1960s when the "new ethnicity" movement began, prompted by the civil rights movement in the United States. In their early sociological analysis, Glazer and Moynihan (1963) noted, "The point about the melting pot is that it did not happen" (p. 290). The previously described Berry's (1980, 1990) model of psychological acculturation further reflects a pluralistic ideological perspective. Pluralistic models such as these share a common emphasis on the significance of an individual's acceptance (or rejection) of the host culture and of his or her own cultural heritage. As such, these models project an implicit image of cross-cultural adaptation as a matter of conscious (or unconscious) choice, not necessity, by individuals and groups depending on the sense of group identity they hold in relation to the dominant group in the receiving society.

The trend toward pluralistic conceptions of cross-cultural adaptation has been further spurred by recent works by "critical" or "post-modern-postimperial" scholars who challenge the social scientific approaches examined in this chapter. These analysts question the legitimacy of some of the traditional theoretical accounts for their inherent "flaw" of reflecting and serving to reproduce the status quo of the dominant cultural ideology within and across cultures, ethnic/racial groups, and genders. Based on interviews with 10 Asian Indian immigrant women in the United States, for example, Hedge (1998) characterized the experiences of these women in such terms as "displacement" and "struggle" of having to deal with the "contradictions" between their internal identity and external "world in which hegemonic structures systematically marginalize certain types of difference" (p. 36). Critical analysts have tended to focus almost exclusively on the inherently stressful or problematic aspects of cross-cultural adaptation, firmly rooted in their idea that cultural identity is or should be inherently unchangeable or nonnegotiable (e.g., Moon, 1998; Tsuda, 1986; Young, 1996). The overriding concern for them appears to be preservation of cultural identity and the costs of having to adapt to a new culture that are regarded as placing immigrants or ethnic minorities in the position of "victims" in the face of "cultural oppression." This depiction of adaptation is in sharp contrast with, for instance, the stress-adaptation-growth dynamic in Kim's theory described earlier.

One must take caution, however, in denying either the assimilative or the pluralistic tendencies of immigrants or ethnic minorities. Few individuals in an unfamiliar environment can completely escape adaptation as long as they remain in, and are functionally dependent on, the mainstream culture. Conversely, few can attain a complete assimilation no matter how hard or long they try. Regardless of differing ideological views, ample evidence exists to demonstrate that individuals of minority cultural backgrounds do undergo change over time and across generations. Some form of new learning, accommodation, internalization, and convergence occurs among those who remain, willingly or not, in

some degree of communicative interaction with the host environment, as has been amply theorized about and empirically documented.

CONCLUSION

The phenomenon of cross-cultural adaptation continues to draw strong research interests across social sciences. The present chapter has been an effort to present a broad, interdisciplinary "mapping" of the field that remains far from being cohesive. The various disciplinary or individual researcher interests and ideological perspectives have led to the unwarrantedly dichotomous distinction drawn between long-term and short-term adaptation, between adaptation-as-problem and adaptation-as-learning/growth, between the many models and indexes, and between the ideological perspectives of assimilationism and pluralism. At the same time, we now have a number of broadly based multifaceted models that serve as possible avenues for continuing conceptual integration and theoretical development in the field—a task that is essential to achieving a more complete and realistic understanding of what happens, and how it happens, to individuals in an unfamiliar cultural milieu.

REFERENCES

Adler, P. (1975). The transition experience: An alternative view of culture shock. *Journal of Humanistic Psychology, 15*(4), 13-23.

Adler, P. (1982). Beyond cultural identity: Reflections on cultural and multicultural man. In L. Samover & R. Porter (Eds.), *Intercultural communication: A reader* (3rd ed., pp. 389-408). Belmont, CA: Wadsworth.

Ady, J. C. (1995). Toward a differential demand model of sojourner adjustment. In R. L. Wiseman (Ed.), *Intercultural communication theory* (pp. 92-114). Thousand Oaks, CA: Sage.

Anderson, L. (1994). A new look at an old construct: Cross-cultural adaptation. *International Journal of Intercultural Relations, 18*(3), 293-328.

Barona, A., & Miller, J. (1994). Short acculturation scale for Hispanic youth: A preliminary report. *Hispanic Journal of Behavioral Sciences, 16,* 155-162.

Bennett, J. (1977). Transition shock: Putting culture shock in perspective. In N. Jain (Ed.), *International intercultural communication annual* (Vol. 4, pp. 45-52). Falls Church, VA: Speech Communication Association.

Berry, J. (1970). Marginality, stress & ethnic identification in an acculturated aboriginal community. *Journal of Cross-Cultural Psychology, 1,* 239-252.

Berry, J. (1980). Acculturation as varieties of adaptation. In A. Padilla (Ed.), *Acculturation: Theory, models and some new findings* (pp. 9-25). Washington, DC: Westview.

Berry, J. (1990). Psychology of acculturation: Understanding individuals moving between cultures. In R. Brislin (Ed.), *Applied cross-cultural psychology* (pp. 232-253). Newbury Park, CA: Sage.

Berry, J., & Kim, U. (1987). Acculturation and mental health. In P. Dasen, J. Berry, & N. Sartorius (Eds.), *Health and cross-cultural psychology* (pp. 207-236). Newbury Park, CA: Sage.

Boekestijn, C. (1988). Intercultural migration and the development of personal identity: The dilemma between identity maintenance and cultural adaptation. *International Journal of Intercultural Relations, 12*(2), 83-105.

Bourhis, R. Y., Moïse, L. C., Perreault, S., & Senécal, S. (1997). Towards an interactive acculturation model: A social psychological approach. *International Journal of Psychology, 32,* 369-386.

Dasgupta, S. (1983). *Indian immigrants: The evolution of an ethnic group.* Unpublished doctoral dissertation, University of Delaware, Newark.

Dawson, E., Crano, W., & Burgoon, M. (1996). Refining the meaning and measurement of acculturation: Revising a novel methodological approach. *International Journal of Intercultural Relations, 20*(1), 97-114.

DiPrete, T., & Forristal, J. (1994). Multilevel models: Methods and substance. *Annual Review of Sociology, 20,* 331-357.

Dyal, J., & Dyal, R. (1981). Acculturation, stress and coping. *International Journal of Intercultural Relations, 5*(4), 301-328.

Eames, E., & Schwab, W. (1964). Urban migration in India and Africa. *Human Organization, 23,* 24-27.

Epstein, J., Botvin, J., Dusenberry, L., Diaz, T., & Kerner, T. (1996). Validation of an acculturation measure for Hispanic adolescents. *Psychological Reports, 79,* 1075-1079.

Furnham, A. (1988). The adjustment of sojourners. In Y. Y. Kim & W. B. Gudykunst (Eds.), *Cross-cultural adaptation: Current approaches* (pp. 42-61). Newbury Park, CA: Sage.

Furnham, A., & Bochner, S. (1986). *Culture shock: Psychological reactions to unfamiliar environments.* New York: Routledge.

Gao, G., & Gudykunst, W. (1990). Uncertainty, anxiety, and adaptation. *International Journal of Intercultural Relations, 14*(3), 301-317.

Gaw, K. (2000). Reverse culture shock in students returning from overseas. *International Journal of Intercultural Relations, 24*(1), 83-104.

Gebart-Eaglemont, J. (1994, July). *Acculturation and stress in immigrants: A path analysis.* Paper presented at the fifth International Conference on Language and Social Psychology, Brisbane, Australia.

Gil, A., Vega, W., & Dimas, J. (1994). Acculturative stress and personal adjustment among Hispanic adolescent boys. *Journal of Community Psychology, 22,* 43-54.

Glazer, N., & Moynihan, D. (1963). *Beyond the melting pot.* Cambridge: MIT Press.

Gudykunst, W. B. (1995). Uncertainty/anxiety management (AUM) theory: Current status. In R. L. Wiseman (Ed.), *Intercultural communication theory* (pp. 8-58). Thousand Oaks, CA: Sage.

Gullahorn, J., & Gullahorn, J. (1963). An extension of the U-curve hypothesis. *Journal of Social Issues, 19*(3), 33-47.

Gupta, S. (1975). Changes in the food habits of Asian Indians in the U.S. *Sociology and Social Research, 60*(1), 87-99.

Hansel, B. (1993). *An investigation of the re-entry adjustment of Indians who studied in the U.S.A.* (Occasional Papers in Intercultural Learning No. 17). New York: AFS Center for the Study of Intercultural Learning.

Hawes, F., & Kealey, D. (1981). An empirical study of Canadian technical assistance. *International Journal of Intercultural Relations, 5*(3), 239-258.

Hedge, R. (1998). Swinging the trapeze: The negotiation of identity among Asian Indian immigrant women in the United States. In D. Tanno & A. Gonzalez (Eds.), *Communication and identity across cultures* (pp. 34-55). Thousand Oaks, CA: Sage.

Herskovits, M. (1958). *Acculturation: The study of culture contact.* Gloucester, MA: Peter Smith.

Jasinskaja-Lahti, I., & Liebkind, K. (2000). Predictors of the actual degree of acculturation of Russian-speaking immigrant adolescents in Finland. *International Journal of Intercultural Relations, 24*(4), 503-518.

Kanno, Y. (2000). Kikokushijo as bicultural. *International Journal of Intercultural Relations, 24* (3), 361-382.

Kim, J. (1980). Explaining acculturation in a communication framework: An empirical test. *Communication Monographs, 47*(3), 155-179.

Kim, Y. Y. (1977). Communication patterns of foreign immigrants in the process of acculturation. *Human Communication Research, 4,* 66-77.

Kim, Y. Y. (1988). *Communication and cross-cultural adaptation: An integrative theory.* Clevedon, Avon, UK: Multilingual Matters.

Kim, Y. Y. (1989). Personal, social, and economic adaptation: The case of 1975-1979 arrivals in Illinois. In D. Haines (Ed.), *Refugees as immigrants: Survey research on Cambodians, Laotians, and Vietnamese in America* (pp. 86-104). Totowa, NJ: Rowman & Littlefield.

Kim, Y. Y. (1995). Cross-cultural adaptation: An integrative theory. In R. L. Wiseman (Ed.), *Intercultural communication theory* (pp. 170-193). Thousand Oaks, CA: Sage.

Kim, Y. Y. (2001). *Becoming intercultural: An integrative theory of communication and cross-cultural adaptation.* Thousand Oaks, CA: Sage.

Kim, Y. Y., Lujan, P., & Dixon, L. (1998). "I can walk both ways": Identity integration of American Indians in Oklahoma. *Human Communication Research, 25,* 252-274.

Marden, C., & Meyer, G. (1968). *Minorities in America* (3rd ed.). New York: Van Nostrand Reinhold.

Marrett, C., & Leggon, C. (Eds.). (1982). *Research in race and ethnic relations* (Vol. 3). Greenwich, CT: JAI.

Mishra, R., Sinha, D., & Berry, J. (1996). *Ecology, acculturation and psychological adaptation.* Thousand Oaks, CA: Sage.

Montalvo, F. (1991). Phenotyping, acculturation, and biracial assimilation of Mexican Americans. In M. Sotomayor (Ed.), *Empowering Hispanic families: A critical issue for the '90s* (pp. 97-119). Milwaukee, WI: Family Service America.

Moon, D. (1998). Performed identities: Passing as an inter/cultural discourse. In J. Martin, T. Nakayama, & L. Flores (Eds.), *Readings in cultural contexts* (pp. 322-330). Mountain View, CA: Mayfield.

Nagata, G. (1969). *A statistical approach to the study of acculturation of an ethnic group based on communication oriented variables: The case of Japanese Americans in Chicago.* Unpublished doctoral dissertation, University of Illinois, Urbana-Champaign.

Oberg, K. (1960). Cultural shock: Adjustment to new cultural environments. *Practical Anthropology, 7,* 170-179.

Oberg, K. (1979). Culture shock and the problem of adjustment in new cultural environments. In E. Smith & L. Luce (Eds.), *Toward internationalism: Readings in cross-cultural communication* (pp. 43-45). Rowley, MA: Newbury.

Park, R. (1939). Reflections on communication and culture. *American Journal of Sociology, 44,* 191-205.

Parrillo, V. (1966). *Strangers to these shores: Race and ethnic relations in the United States.* Boston: Houghton Mifflin.

Redfield, R., Linton, R., & Herskovits, M. (1936). Outline for the study of acculturation. *American Anthropologist, 38,* 149-152.

Redmond, M. V., & Bunyi, J. M. (1993). The relationship of intercultural communication competence with stress and the handling of stress as reported by international students. *International Journal of Intercultural Relations, 17*(3), 235-354.

Rivera-Sinclair, E. (1997). Acculturation/biculturalism and its relationship to adjustment in Cuban-Americans. *International Journal of Intercultural Relations, 21*(3), 379391.

Ruben, B. (1983). A system-theoretic view. In W. Gudykunst (Ed.), *International and intercultural communication annual: Intercultural communication theory* (Vol. 12, pp. 131-145). Beverly Hills, CA: Sage.

Ruben, B., & Kealey, D. (1979). Behavioral assessment of communication competency and the prediction of cross-cultural adaptation. *International Journal of Intercultural Relations, 3*(1), 15-27.

Sahlins, M. (1964). Culture and environment: The study of cultural ecology. In S. Tax (Ed.), *Horizons of anthropology* (pp. 132-147). Chicago: Aldine.

Shah, H. (1991). Communication and cross-cultural adaptation patterns among Asian Indians. *International Journal of Intercultural Relations, 15*(3), 311-321.

Steen, S. (1998). *"I've become a bicultural entity": The cultural adaptation processes of USM students abroad.* Paper presented at the annual convention of the Southern States Communication Association, San Antonio, TX.

Stilling, E. (1997). The electronic melting pot hypothesis: The cultivation of acculturation among Hispanics through television viewing. *Howard Journal of Communications, 8,* 77-100.

Stonequist, E. (1937). *The marginal man.* New York: Scribner's.

Stonequist, E. (1964). The marginal man: A study in personality and culture conflict. In E. Burgess & D. Bogue (Eds.), *Contributions to urban sociology* (pp. 327-345). Chicago: University of Chicago Press.

Suro, R. (1998). *Strangers among us: How Latino immigration is transforming America.* New York: Knopf.

Szalay, L., & Inn, A. (1988). Cross-cultural adaptation and diversity: Hispanic Americans. In Y. Y.

Kim & W. B. Gudykunst (Eds.), *Cross-cultural adaptation: Current approaches* (pp. 212-232). Newbury Park, CA: Sage.

Taft, R. (1957). A psychological model for the study of social assimilation. *Human Relations, 10*(2), 141-156.

Taft, R. (1977). Coping with unfamiliar cultures. In N. Warren (Ed.), *Studies in cross-cultural psychology* (Vol. 1, pp. 121-153). London: Academic Press.

Thayer, L. (1975). Knowledge, order, and communication. In B. Ruben & J. Y. Kim (Eds.), *General systems theory and human communication* (pp. 237-245). Rochelle Park, NJ: Hayden.

Torbiörn, I. (1988). Culture barriers as a social psychological construct: An empirical validation. In Y. Y. Kim & W. B. Gudykunst (Eds.), *Cross-cultural adaptation: Current approaches* (pp. 168-190). Newbury Park, CA: Sage.

Triandis, H., Kashima, Y., Shimada, E., & Villareal, M. (1986). Acculturation indices as a means of confirming cultural differences. *International Journal of Psychology, 21,* 43-70.

Trifonovitch, G. (1977). Culture learning/culture teaching. *Educational Perspectives, 16*(4), 18-22.

Tsuda, Y. (1986). *Language inequality and distortion in intercultural communication: A critical theory approach.* Amsterdam: John Benjamins.

van Oudenhoven, J., & Eisses, A. (1998). Integration and assimilation of Moroccan immigrants in Israel and the Netherlands. *International Journal of Intercultural Relations, 22*(3), 293-307.

Vega, W., Kolody, B., & Valle, V. (1987). Migration and mental health: An empirical test of depression risk factors among immigrant Mexican women. *International Migration Review, 21*(3), 512-530.

Ward, C., & Kennedy, A. (1994). Acculturation strategies, psychological adjustment, and sociocultural competence during cross-cultural transitions. *International Journal of Intercultural Relations, 18,* 329-343.

Ward, C., & Okura, Y., Kennedy, A., & Kojima, T. (1998). The U-curve on trial: A longitudinal study of psychological and sociocultural adjustment during cross-cultural transition. *International Journal of Intercultural Relations, 22*(3), 277-291.

Weinstock, S. (1964). Some factors that retard or accelerate the rate of acculturation. *Human Relations, 17*(4), 321-340.

White, R. (1976). Strategies of adaptation: An attempt at systemic description. In R. Moos (Ed.), *Human adaptation: Coping with life crises* (pp. 17-32). Lexington, MA: D. C. Heath.

Westmeyer, J., Vang, T., & Neider, J. (1986). Migration and mental health among H'mong refugees. *Pacific/Asian American Mental Health Research Center Review, 5*(3/4), 25-29.

Wilson, A. H. (1993). A cross-national perspective on reentry of high school exchange students. *International Journal of Intercultural Relations, 17*, 465-492.

Ying, Y., & Liese, L. (1991). Emotional well-being of Taiwan students in the U.S.: An examination of pre- to post-arrival differential. *International Journal of Intercultural Relations, 15*(3), 345-366.

Young, R. (1996). *Intercultural communication: Pragmatics, genealogy, deconstruction.* Philadelphia: Multilingual Matters.

Yum, J. (1983). Social network patterns of five ethnic groups in Hawaii. In R. Bostrom (Ed.), *Communication yearbook 7* (pp. 574-591). New Brunswick, NJ: Transaction.

Yum, J. (1986). Locus of control and communication patterns of immigrants. In Y. Y. Kim (Ed.), *Interethnic communication: Current research* (pp. 191-211). Beverly Hills, CA: Sage.

Zaharna, R. (1989). Self-shock: The double-binding challenge of identity. *International Journal of Intercultural Relations, 13*(4), 501-525.

Zweigenhalf, R. (1979-1980). American Jews: In or out of the upper class? *Insurgent Sociologist, 9*, 24-37.

14

Issues in Intercultural Communication Research

GEORGE A. BARNETT
State University of New York at Buffalo

MEIHUA LEE
Tamkang University, Taipei

Perhaps the greatest issue facing inter-cultural communication research is differentiating *intercultural* communication from the related research areas of international communication, international or comparative media studies, and cross-cultural research. Intercultural communication involves the exchange of cultural information between two groups of people with significantly different cultures. The focus of international communication is on the exchange of messages between nation-states (Barnett, 1999). International media studies are concerned primarily with the mass media, either print (international journalism) or electronic, generally comparing national media infrastructures and policies and their implications for the society in which they are embedded (Hudson, 1997). Cross-cultural re-search concentrates on the comparison of cultural groups and the implications of these differences for the process of communication (Gudykunst, Chapter 9 in this volume).

This chapter begins by defining intercultural communication. It then presents a structural model of intercultural communication that clarifies where the exchange of cultural information occurs so that we will know where to observe this phenomenon. Thus, the goal of this discussion will be to focus the attention of communication scholars on the central process of intercultural communication rather than on related areas. In doing so, the difficulties of intercultural communication research are exposed. These problems are discussed in detail in the final portion of the chapter, which focuses on the neglected role of the media in intercultural communication.

INTERCULTURAL COMMUNICATION

Intercultural communication is the exchange of cultural information between two groups of people with significantly different cultures. Although this definition is clearly circular, it can be clarified by specifying the meaning of its critical concepts. *Communication* may be defined as the process by which information is exchanged among two or more social systems (Barnett, 1997). These systems are embedded within a suprasystem, the environment that contextually bounds this process. In addition, this information exchange is purposeful. It has the goal of reducing the uncertainty in the systems' future behavior (Berger & Calabrese, 1975) or developing a shared understanding among the interactants (Rogers & Kincaid, 1981). In other words, intercultural communication should focus on the exchange of information among two or more cultural systems embedded within a common environment that results in the reduction of uncertainty about the future behavior of the other system through an increase in understanding of the other social group (Gudykunst, 1995; Gudykunst, Yang, & Nishida, 1985).

In the past, scholars have limited its study to the individual level. However, intercultural communication occurs on many levels (Smith, 1999), such as via mediated communication. Individuals' uncertainty about other cultures that they will never visit is reduced by reading or seeing films and videos about other cultures and by listening to recordings produced by members of other cultural groups. International organizations working throughout the globe link disconnected cultures, helping interactants understand the similarities and

differences among the groups. In the future, interpersonal communication will be increasingly computer mediated. Technologies such as the World Wide Web will continue to serve as channels to bring together people of diverse cultural backgrounds (Barnett, Chon, & Rosen, 2000).

Culture simply can be described as a "historically created system of explicit and implicit designs for living, which tends to be shared by all or specially designated members of a group at a specific point in time" (Kluckhohn & Kelly, 1945, p. 98).

Culture consists of the habits and tendencies to act in certain ways, but not the actions themselves. It is the language patterns, values, attitudes, beliefs, customs, and thought patterning. Goodenough (1964) defines culture not as things or behavior but rather as "the forms of things that people have in mind, their models for perceiving, relating, and otherwise interpreting them" (p. 36). Triandis, Vassiliou, Vassiliou, Tanaka, and Shanmugan (1972) label the values, feelings, and meanings as they are expressed in a society's language as subjective culture. Geertz (1973) treats culture as an ordered system of meanings and symbols, in which social interaction takes place and develops:

> [Culture is] an historically transmitted pattern of meaning embodied in symbols, a system of inherited conceptions expressed in symbolic form by means of which men [and women] communicate, perpetuate and develop their knowledge about and attitudes toward life. (p. 89)

Culture is a socially shared activity, and therefore, a property of a group rather than an individual (Nieberg, 1973). It is normative and may be best represented by the average or other measure of central tendency of the group mind (Durkheim, 1938). It does not derive from the internal conditions of the individual mind, but rather, from society's social conventions. Durkheim (1953) calls these shared cognitions "collective representations" (pp. 25-26). Collective representations do not derive from individual minds but from the association of minds. In forming the collective, each contributes his or her part, but private sentiments do not become social except by combination in association with others. The result is exterior to the individual. Each individual contains a part, but the whole is found in no one. Thus, to understand culture one must take the aggregate into consideration.

Collective representations are formed during the process of social interaction. As members of social groups communicate, they negotiate the shared meanings of symbols. As such, culture is an emergent property of the communication of society's members (Giddens, 1979; Poole, 1994). Communication as a shared symbolic process creates, gives rise, and sustains the collective group consciousness (Bormann, 1983). On the other hand, culture determines how group members communicate. The meanings that are attributed to verbal symbols and nonverbal behaviors are determined by the society as a whole. They represent cultural knowledge (D'Andrade, 1984). Culture may be taken to be a consensus about the meanings of symbols, verbal and nonverbal, held by the members of a community. This consensus is necessary for encoding and decoding messages. Without general agreement about the meaning of symbols and other communication rules, social interaction would be impossible.

As new members are socialized into groups, they acquire its culture. Individuals exchanging symbols, stimuli that are culturally defined with recognized conventions of meaning, make this process possible. Individuals are transformed into group members as a result of their interactions with other members of the group. It is through common social activities that they learn the meanings of the group's symbols and the generalized set of attitudes, values, and beliefs common to members of a social group. In the context of intercultural communication, the process of adults raised in one cultural system becoming members of another, learning the new group's culture is known as *acculturation* and has been investigated by Kim (1988, 1989).

To summarize, culture is a property of a group. It is a group's shared collective meaning system through which the group's collective values, attitudes, beliefs, customs, and thoughts are understood. It is an emergent property of the members' social interaction and a determinant of how group members communicate. The meanings that are attributed to verbal symbols and nonverbal behaviors are determined by the society as a whole. Culture may be taken to be a consensus about the meanings of symbols, verbal and nonverbal, held by the members of a community. Without general agreement about the meaning of symbols, intragroup interaction would be impossible.

Intercultural communication is thus the exchange of symbolic information between well-defined groups with significantly different cultures.[1] It is theoretically interesting because distinct groups may have idiosyncratic systems of meaning. As a result, the exchange of information is more difficult. The process itself is full of uncertainty. Individuals involved in the process often must negotiate the meaning for the exchanged symbols. Intercultural interaction has the greater potential for misunderstanding. The process of social interaction need not lead to the reduction in uncertainty about the interactants' future behavior. It may lead only to greater uncertainty, frustration, anxiety, and conflict. To avoid these adverse consequences, social scientists have examined the differences between groups in their behavior and the interpretations of symbols (Rogers, 1999). The goal of this research is to facilitate practitioners engaged in

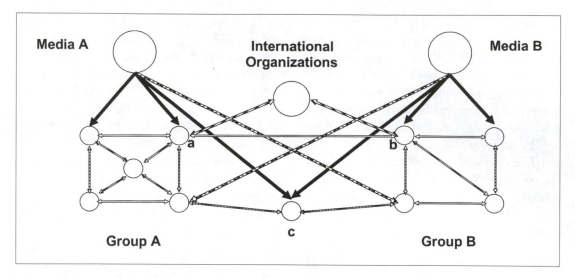

Figure 14.1. Structural Model of Intercultural Communication

process of communicating with individuals from other groups. One consequence of this research has been confusion about the boundaries of intercultural and cross-cultural communication.

A STRUCTURAL MODEL OF INTERCULTURAL COMMUNICATION

To help clarify the process of intercultural communication, one must answer the question, Where does it take place? An examination of Figure 14.1 may help. It represents the process of intercultural communication. It shows a sociogram of a communication network composed of two interacting groups, each with its own culture. Individuals or other information sources are represented as circles and the communication flows as lines. Arrows indicate the direction of information flows. This system is composed of two groups, A and B, with porous boundaries. Communication *within* the groups is relatively dense, whereas communication *between* the groups is sparse (Yum, 1988). Yum and Wang (1983, p. 296)

find support for this position based on data from Hawaii, where there was little inter-ethnic communication and what links there were occurred between the minority groups (Koreans, Filipinos, and Samoans) and the host ethnic groups (Japanese and Caucasians).

Spanning the cultural boundary is a link between individuals *a,* who is member of Group A, and *b,* a member of Group B. In network analysis terms, *a* and *b* are referred to as group members with a *bridge link* that connects them to the other group. These links tend to be weaker and less frequent, and they deal with a narrower range of topics than do intragroup links (Granovetter, 1973; Yum, 1988). These individuals may be sojourners (Gudykunst & Kim, 1997), individuals who travel to the physical environment of the other group for tourism, educational (Barnett & Wu, 1995), business (Barnett, Salisbury, Kim, & Langhorne, 1999; Salisbury & Barnett, 1999), military (Kim, 1998), or diplomatic (Kim & Barnett, 2000) reasons. These interactions have been facilitated by recent innovations in telecommunications and transportation. Individuals *a* and *b* may also be immigrants, individuals moving relatively permanently to the other group's physical environment but residing in a location composed primarily of members of their native group (Barnett, Rosen, & Chon, 2000; Massey et al., 1993; Smith, 1999). Through *a* and *b,* information about the other group is communicated to the group of which they are a member. This cultural information reduces the uncertainty about the other group. In other words, *a* and *b* serve as gatekeepers about information that facilitates the understanding of the other group.

Individual *c* is a member of neither group. He or she is a *liaison* connecting both groups. As such, *c* is not bound by membership in one particular culture. Most likely, *c* is a product of a multicultural marriage and, generally, is bilingual (Barnett, 1996). Because he or she has the capacity to function in more than one culture effectively, *c* serves as a facilitator for contacts between cultural groups. Individual *c* is what Park (1928) called a "marginal man [woman]" and Adler (1982) labeled a "multicultural man [woman]." Intercultural persons develop a "third culture" perspective (Ellingsworth, 1977; Gudykunst, Wiseman, & Hammer, 1977), which enables them to interpret and evaluate intercultural encounters more accurately. Through *c,* information about cultures *A* and *B* are passed on to the members of the other group.

Intercultural communication concerns the linkages between Groups *A* and *B* that involve individuals *a, b,* and *c.* These links also include the mass media (Korzenny, Ting-Toomey, & Schiff, 1992; Ware & Dupagne, 1994) because cultural information that reduces the uncertainty about Groups *A* and *B* is communicated via the mass media, either print (Kim & Barnett, 1996) or broadcast media (Varis, 1984). In this model, it is represented as Media *A,* the media expressing the culture of Group *A,* and Media *B,* the media expressing Group *B*'s culture. Typically, they are expressed in the unique language of each group. For example, American media are primarily in English. There may be only a few infrequently used paths from Media *A* to Group *B* or Media *B* to Group *A.* This is the case with non-English-language media in the United States, although Western media are widely distributed throughout the world (Nordenstreng & Varis, 1974). Media *A* are more strongly connected to individual *b.* The strength of Media *B*'s connections to person *a* is also stronger. Individual *c* receives both media sources. Barnett, Oliveira, and Johnson (1989) report that bilinguals (*a, b* and *c*) use the mass media in both of their languages that may emanate from more than one different group (*A* and *B*). This provides cultural information to reduce the uncertainty about these groups.

Also connecting the cultural groups in the model are international organizations that are not part of either Group *A* or *B* but rather are part of global society transcending any individual cultural group (Boli & Thomas, 1997; Meyer, Boli, Thomas, & Ramirez, 1997). These may be international governmental organizations (IGOs) such as the United Nations or the World Bank whose members are the nations of the world, nongovernmental issue-based organizations (international nongovernmental organizations; INGOs) such as Amnesty International and Greenpeace (Boli & Thomas, 1997; Jacobson, 1979); or transnational corporations (Monge & Fulk, 1999; Waters, 1995). These organizations bring people from different cultural groups together in a common forum where they interact and develop a greater understanding of one another.

Historically, these linkages among different cultural groups have increased, resulting in *globalization*—the process of strengthening the worldwide social relations that link distant localities in such a way that local events are shaped by circumstances at other places in the world (Giddens, 1990). That is, events occurring at one place reduce the uncertainty of the future behavior of groups at another location. The increase in transborder (intergroup) communication (A and B now have more and stronger links than those only between *a* and *b*) has led to the rapid global diffusion of values, ideas, opinions, and technologies, that is, the underlying components of culture. Transborder communication has opened cultural boundaries and created a global community with an increasingly homogeneous culture, particularly regarding political, economic, educational, and scientific activities (Beyer, 1994; Robertson, 1992).

Giddens (1990) argues that globalization is an inherent part of modernization. One consequence of modernization is the increase in time-space distanciation that renders physical distance less of a barrier to intergroup communication. This is due in part to innovations in telecommunications and transportation. Globalization stretches the boundaries of social interaction such that the connections among different social contexts or nations become networked across the globe. Thus, the communication among only two groups as presented in Figure 15.1 may be generalized to all the separate nations of the world.

Various forms of the structural model, also known as the network model, have been used to investigate intercultural (Smith, 1999; Weimann, 1989; Yum, 1984, 1988) and intergroup (Kim, 1986) communication.[2] Yum (1984) examined the applicability of the network model to the study of five areas of intercultural communication (cultural diversity, diffusion of innovations, rural-urban migration, acculturation of immigrants, and ethnicity) and concluded that

> intercultural communication is a process that involves the construction of new networks, and/or the restructuring or augmentation of existing networks. From this perspective, intercultural communication is a process of creating and

maintaining cultural boundaries, or bridging the boundaries between diverse cultural groups. (p. 96)

Weimann (1983) studied interethnic networks in Israel. Using "small world" techniques, he found a tendency toward the selective activation of personal networks according to ethnic similarity. The study examined the links and individuals activated, revealing the gatekeepers, the individuals (*a* and *b*) who serve as the bridges of contact between the ethnic groups (Groups A and B) and the links (the *a-b* bridge link) used to serve the crossing. Most participants preferred to forward messages to a person of the same ethnic group, and when crossing ethnic boundaries, the participants delayed spanning the two groups until the last steps of the chain, until it was unavoidable.

Yum and Wang (1983) examined interethnic communication and friendship networks among five ethnic groups (Koreans, Filipinos, Samoans, Japanese, and Caucasians) in Hawaii and the relation between these network ties and stereotyping. They found that interethnic communication had a significant positive relationship with the degree of favorableness in the evaluation of the other ethnic group.

Kim (1986) proposes three theorems about the relationship between an individual's personal network and intercultural communication competence: (1) The greater the ethnolinguistic heterogeneity of an individual's personal network, the greater the ego's overall outgroup (intercultural) communication competence; (2) the greater the centrality of an outgroup member in a personal network, the greater his or her outgroup communication competence; and (3) the stronger an ego's ties with outgroup members, the greater the outgroup communication competence.

Smith (1999) proposes seven propositions relating social networks and intercultural communication: (1) Intercultural identity strategies are discernible with social network structures; (2) culturally influenced perceptions shape the function and experienced nature of social networks; (3) as sociostructural heterogeneity increases, the probability of acculturation increases; (4) rate of change in an intercultural social network is a dynamic function dependent on the stage of integration with the host community; (5) structural constraints will affect the size of intercultural networks, in turn affecting the adjustment process; (6) as density increases, the provision of diverse resources with the net decreases, thereby affecting socialization/acculturation; and (7) intercultural networks will be less dense, with more radial ties in cultures reflecting a contextual-based relationship norm than those found in cultures reflecting a personal-based relationship norm.

Weimann (1982) found that individuals who occupy the bridge roles between groups tend to be peripheral (less integrated) in their own groups. The reason is that dense groups regulate intergroup flows and the existence of bridges because their members' resources are used to maintain intragroup ties (Yum, 1984). As a result, individuals strongly connected within a group tend not to be bridges. Thus, individuals with links to other groups are marginal in their groups.

The personal networks of individuals *a, b,* and *c* tend to be radial, whereas the other members of Groups *A* and *B* have denser, interlocking networks (Smith, 1999; Yum, 1988). In a radial network, the people an individual interacts with do not interact with one another. Interlocking groups tend to be culturally homogeneous, whereas radial networks tend to be heterogeneous. Also, intercultural networks are less likely to be multiplexed than intracultural ones (Yum, 1988). That is, the content of intercultural relations tends to be limited to a single topic, whereas intracultural communication may cover many subjects. Finally, intercultural links tend to be less transitive. Less information is passed on to other group members from *a* and *b* (Yum, 1988).

Culturally, individuals *a* and *b* also would be marginal. If we think of culture as being normally distributed about a central tendency, then those individuals with links to another group with a different culture would be located on the tails of their group's distribution. As Rogers (1999) says, an individual, "relatively free of such links in his or her system, can more easily deviate from the norms of the system" (p. 61). Individuals' external orientation frees them from the norms and expectations of their group and sets them apart from the others. They perceive their culture differently and are freer to consider ideas from other cultural systems. Thus, they would not be representative of their culture, at least on the dimensions activated by communication with other groups. The marginality of individuals who have bridge links raises the issue of validity of intercultural communication research. Because of their intergroup tie, these individuals may not be representative of the culture that they represent.

Massey and associates (Massey, 1988; Massey et al., 1993; Massey & Espana, 1987) reviewed the literature on the role of social and communication networks in the process of international migration and concluded that network formation is probably the most important mechanism supporting international migration. Networks dramatically lower the cost of movement and information, thereby increasing the benefits of emigration and focusing it on specific destinations. Once migration takes place, adjustment to a foreign culture is substantially less difficult if there are social contacts from the home culture present in the new location.

Although not directly related to intercultural communication, there has been considerable communication research that has examined international information flows using the structural model as its theoretical foundation. Barnett and associates have examined international telecommunications (Barnett, 1999, 2001; Barnett & Choi, 1995; Barnett, Jacobson, Choi, & SunMiller, 1996; Barnett & Salisbury, 1996; Choi & Ahn, 1996), trade (artifactual communication) (Barnett et al., 1999; Choi & Ahn, 1996), monetary flow (Salisbury & Barnett, 1999), news flow (Kim & Barnett, 1996), student exchanges (Barnett & Wu, 1995), air traffic (Barnett, 1996; Choi & Ahn, 1996), mail (Choi, 1993), migration (Barnett, Rosen, & Chon, 2000), and scientific citations (Barnett, Chon, & Rosen, 2000; Schott, 1993).

So where does intercultural communication take place? Typically, it occurs at the boundaries of social systems, where different ethnolinguistic groups come into contact (Yum, 1984). Often this takes place at national frontiers, for example at the U.S.-Mexican border. Also, intercultural communication occurs at ports of entry, such as New York. Typically, this would be seaports or international airports. Destinations for international tourism, such as Niagara Falls, are excellent places to observe intercultural communication. As higher education becomes increasingly international (Barnett & Wu, 1995), the university setting provides an environment for intercultural communication. Scientific conferences bring together individuals from different cultural groups (Schott, 1993). International business, the military stationed in foreign countries, and diplomatic activities provide additional contexts where intercultural communication occurs.

Intercultural communication occurs frequently in *world cities,* urban areas that serve as the command and control centers for the global economy (Smith & Timberlake, 2001). Examples include New York, London, and Tokyo. The international business center is the economic engine of the city in the global informational society (Castells, 1994). By focusing on spatially defined urban areas with prominent roles in the international economy, one can directly observe intercultural communication. It is in these settings where individuals from different societies come together to manage the global economy. In addition, unskilled labor migrates to world cities to service the corporate elite, taking jobs perceived as unsuitable to the native workforce and thus producing a rich multicultural environment ideal for the investigation of intercultural communication (Massey et al., 1993).

As noted above, in the past intercultural communication has focused on the individual. It also occurs via mass media and computer-mediated technologies and through international organizations. In the section that follows, the role of the mass media in intercultural communication will be discussed in detail.

ON STUDYING GLOBALIZATION AND INTERCULTURAL MASS MEDIA-MEDIATED EFFECTS

Although there had been a tendency to exclude the mass media from intercultural research, this chapter emphasizes their importance to provide a clear picture of intercultural processes. This section argues that with the developments in communication technologies and the globalization of the economy, most intercultural experiences are mediated rather than face-to-face. Being the catalyst for globalization, the mass media and communication technologies compress time and space (Giddens, 1990; Robertson, 1990). As a result, McLuhan's (1966) notion of the global village has become a reality.

Conceptualization Problems
in Intercultural Research

Johnson and Tuttle (1989) described the theoretical problems of context in intercultural research. Two important problems are that the majority of the past research was quantitative and conducted by Western researchers. They run the risk of wrongly interpreting the process of communication and the variables that determine the outcomes of these activities. Hofstede's (1980) work on multinational organizations in particular points to a number of problems in generalizing research from one society to another. Moreover, when studying transnational and domestic corporations in North America and Asia, researchers found that the symbols used by members to describe their organizational cultures vary in both their denotative and connotative meanings (Lee, 2000; Lee & Barnett, 1997).

Context is a crucial concern for intercultural research. It includes economic, political, educational, and religious factors (Parsons, 1968), as well as the family and the media, society's level of technology, and society's infrastructure. Knowledge of the factors influencing the process of intercultural interaction is important to correctly specify the relationships among intercultural variables.

According to Johnson and Tuttle (1989, p. 469), researchers should conduct preliminary qualitative studies and/or extensive pretests, cast the net more widely for relevant source materials, and engage in collaborative research with members of the culture that is the focus of the research. Moreover, they should be flexible in the research design by employing multiple strategies for collecting data. Collaboration with a member of the host culture can substantially aid the research process by interpreting the results in the context of the host culture. Last but not least, often an outsider is needed to point to the taken-for-granted assumptions of a culture (p. 479), be-

cause we do not know if differences in the results are attributable to methodological or cultural differences.

Many scholars have criticized cross-cultural studies for their lack of explanatory power (Singelis & Brown, 1995). One major criticism is the use of culture as a "catch-all" variable to explain any and all observed differences between national or ethnic groups. The use of culture as a post hoc explanation of observed differences does little to help us understand the underlying predictors of behavior and may be misleading at times (Singelis & Brown, 1995, p. 354).

Globalization and
Intercultural Communication

Kim (2000) identifies five main themes in intercultural communication: (1) intrapersonal processes in intercultural communication, (2) intercultural communication competence, (3) adaptation to a new culture, (4) cultural identity in intercultural contexts, and (5) power inequality in intercultural relations. Integral to the domain of intercultural communication are the subdomains *cultural communication,* which focuses on understanding a particular cultural or subcultural community, and *cross-cultural communication,* which compares two or more cultural or subcultural communities. Cultural and cross-cultural communication studies have been a vital part of the theorizing and researching activities in the area. However, it is generally agreed that the domain excludes studies of mass media and other technological forms of communication. Also excluded is *development communication,* which addresses issues associated with modernization and sociocultural change in traditional societies.

Mediated communication among cultural systems is a pivotal form of intercultural communication. The mass media and information technologies play an important role in compressing time and space, shortening the distance between peoples. Take television as an example. Throughout the world, many countries depend heavily on imported television programming, primarily from the United States, Western Europe, or Japan. Most are entertainment and sports programs (Frederick, 1993, p. 69). Since the early 1980s, along with the emergence of a genuinely global commercial media market, the newly developing global media system has been dominated by three or four dozen large, transnational corporations, with fewer than 10 mostly U.S.-based conglomerates towering over the global market (Herman & McChesney, 1997). During the 1990s, the shift to digital transmission of all forms of data has increased at an accelerated pace. This shift has redefined the music industry and will eventually overtake film, radio, and television production and distribution (p. 106).

Globalization has been a focus of intercultural communication research since the late 1980s (Hamelink, 1990), pervading academic, commercial, and political discourse. To trace its history, global challenges are caused by such phenomena as global warming. Today, McLuhan's global village has become reality. Media technologies such as the Internet, satellites, and optical fiber have made the world a smaller place. The word *global* generally has a positive ring. It connotes values such as one world, coming together, familiarity, and sharing. Because the use of the concept of global as a descriptive term lacks precision and relevance, it would be more useful to apply the concept of globalization processes (Hamelink, 1990, p. 382).

Barnett (2001) describes the current structure of international telecommunication based on its patterns of use and how it has changed since the late 1970s, demonstrating that globalization is taking place. He discusses the implications of these patterns for the development of a universal culture. Universal culture will be the result of all forms of communication including mediated cultural information exchanged among various cultural groups. He states,

> Over the last two decades, the frequency of interaction among the nations of the world has increased steadily. While there is regionalization due to physical and cultural (linguistic) barriers, today, the world consists of a single integrated network of nations centered about North America and Western Europe. One potential consequence of globalization is the cultural homogenization or the convergence of the indigenous cultures of the world into a universal culture (Barnett & Kincaid, 1983; Kincaid et al., 1983; Rogers & Kincaid, 1981). Universal culture would converge on the point proportional to the number of messages input into the system by each of the individual nation-states. That is, it would form around the culture of those societies that are most central in the world's communication system. Today, that would be the United States and Western Europe. (p. 1650)

Further justification for the study of mediated communication comes from a meta-analysis of mass media-mediated effects of U.S. television on foreign audiences. Ware and Dupagne (1994) concluded that there is

> support for the uniform effects thesis of such perspectives as media imperialism, cultural dependency, and cultivation. Though the effect size is small, the number of studies (averaging null results) necessary to void this relationship is quite large (232). This tolerance level suggests that it would be unlikely to find enough unpublished or uncollected studies to change the results to nonsignificant levels. In addition, there were no significant differences between effect sizes for studies using different sampling procedures, performed in countries of different developmental status, or using respondents of differ-

ent ages, thus suggesting that less developed countries and children are no more "at risk" than developed countries and older respondents, respectively. (p. 953)

Varan (1998) writes,

The attempt to understand the transcultural impact associated with television has largely been framed by two metaphors. One asserts that media systems act as vehicles for cultural imperialism. The other explores how audience "readings" of media "texts" help shape social realities. (p. 58)

He explores four processes associated with the transcultural impact of television. First is cultural abrasion, the friction between contrasting values in a cultural context and a foreign media agent. Second is cultural deflation, whereby the least consolidated facets within a culture are most vulnerable to foreign influence. Third is cultural deposition, in which foreign beliefs, practices, and artifacts supplement a cultural landscape providing cross-cultural fertilization, and fourth is cultural saltation, where social practices may be appropriate in communication systems in response to the perceived threat of a foreign media agent. Thus, there is a need for further research on the role of the media in intercultural processes.

CONCLUSIONS

Previous research from all over the world suggests the ongoing process of globalization, the increase of linkages among the world's unique cultural groups. Foreign media occupy an important place in people's viewing habits (Kenny, 1998), in spite of the use of media to foster national identity and interethnic solidarity. European and Asian audiences seem to have preferences for trans-

national (American) media content. The globalization-localization dialectic suggests that globalization involves the linking of their own locales to the wider world and localization incorporates trends of globalization. As a result, cultures could be developing hybrid characteristics (Lemish, 1998; Pieterse, 1995). Over time, with information exchange among people from different cultural groups, one potential consequence of globalization is cultural homogenization, the convergence of the indigenous cultures of the world into a universal culture.

More systematic studies should be carried out to assess the role of mass media in changing perceptions and values of foreign audiences, and their role in cultivation processes (Holaday, Xiaoming, & Hong, 1998). Specifically, research should be conducted on audiences from areas with political, economic, social, and contextual diversity. Studies should examine the relationships between audiences' foreign media exposure and their values and cultural identities.

To study the cultural transformations due to intercultural communication, qualitative and quantitative analyses should be applied to audiences in a variety of contexts. Context is a pervasive and multifaceted construct that deserves more consideration. Most current intercultural theories treat it as an indeterminate catch-all for whatever is left unspecified by the theory. The relevant dimensions of context should be identified and investigated while conducting intercultural research. For example, past research has shown that the context—formal or informal, public or private interpersonal relations and the physical setting—of the interaction determines the specific language a bilingual speaks (Barnett et al., 1989). The media represent one such context. While testing the influences of imported cultural content, research should also examine the aspects of culture that may cause individual-level differences. Because cultural and individual dimensions are not iso-morphic, researchers should employ measures of subjective culture to place groups on partic-ular dimensions, which predict individual dif-ferences in intercultural mediated research (Singelis & Brown, 1995).

In summary, this chapter identified the ma-jor issue facing intercultural communication: its definition as a unique subject separate from cross-cultural and international communica-tion and international mass media. It defined in detail intercultural communication and presented a structural model of intercultural communication demonstrating how mediated communication could be placed under its ru-bric. The final section justified the inclusion of intercultural media effects as an intercultural communication process.

NOTES

1. Groups' cultures may be considered signifi-cantly different in the statistical sense. Opera-tionally, Barnett (1988) describes the procedures for the precise measurement of culture consistent with the theoretical orientation presented in this chapter. Lee and Barnett (1997) provide an exam-ple of their application to determine if two cultures are significantly different.

2. For a technical introduction to network anal-ysis, see Rogers and Kincaid (1981) or Wasserman and Faust (1994). Smith (1999) provides a detailed discussion of the technical terms and their mathe-matical operationalizations to intercultural com-munication.

REFERENCES

Adler, P. S. (1982). Beyond cultural identity: Re-flections on cultural and multicultural man. In L. Samovar & R. Porter (Eds.), *Intercultural communication: A reader* (3rd ed.). Belmont, CA: Wadsworth.

Barnett, G. A. (1988). Communication and organi-zational culture. In G. M. Goldhaber & G. A. Barnett (Eds.), *Handbook of organizational communication* (pp. 101-130), Norwood, NJ: Ablex.

Barnett, G. A. (1996). Multilingualism and trans-portation/telecommunication. In H. Goebl, P. H. Nelde, Z. Stary, & W. Wolck (Eds.), *Hand-book on contact linguistics: An international handbook of contemporary research* (Vol. 1, pp. 431-438). Berlin: Walter De Gruyter.

Barnett, G. A. (1997). Organizational communica-tion systems: The traditional view. In G. A. Barnett & L. Thayer (Eds.), *Organization ↔ communication: Emerging perspectives: Vol. 5, The renaissance in systems thinking* (pp. 1-46). Greenwich, CT: Ablex.

Barnett, G. A. (1999). The social structure of inter-national telecommunications. In H. Sawhney & G. A. Barnett (Eds.), *Progress in communication sciences: Advances in telecommunications* (Vol. 15, pp. 151-186). Greenwich, CT: Ablex.

Barnett, G. A. (2001). A longitudinal analysis of the international telecommunications network: 1978-1996. *American Behavioral Scientist, 44* (10), 1638-1655.

Barnett, G. A., & Choi, Y. (1995). Physical distance and language as determinants of the interna-tional telecommunication network. *Interna-tional Political Science Review, 16,* 249-265.

Barnett, G. A., Chon, B. S., & Rosen, D. (2000, August). *International communication in cyber-space.* Paper presented at the International Geo-graphical Union, Kwangju, Korea.

Barnett, G. A., Jacobson, T. L., Choi, Y., & Sun-Miller, S. L. (1996). An examination of the inter-national telecommunication network. *Journal of International Communication, 3,* 19-43.

Barnett, G. A., & Kincaid, D. L. (1983). Cultural convergence: A mathematical theory. In W. B. Gudykunst (Ed.), *Intercultural communication theory: Current perspectives* (International and Intercultural Communication Annual, Vol. 7, pp. 171-194). Beverly Hills, CA: Sage.

Barnett, G. A., Oliveira, O. S., & Johnson, J. D. (1989). Multilingual language use and television exposure and preferences: The case of Belize. *Communication Quarterly, 37,* 248-261.

Barnett, G. A., Rosen, D., & Chon, B. S. (2000, April). *A network analysis of international migration.* Paper presented at the Sunbelt Social Networks Conference, Vancouver, British Columbia.

Barnett, G. A., & Salisbury, J. G. T. (1996). Communication and globalization: A longitudinal analysis of the international telecommunication network. *Journal of World-Systems Research, 2*(16), 1-17.

Barnett, G. A., Salisbury, J. G. T., Kim, C., & Langhorne, A. (1999). Globalization and international communication networks: An examination of monetary, telecommunications, and trade networks. *Journal of International Communication, 6*(2), 7-49.

Barnett, G. A., & Wu, Y. (1995). The international student exchange network: 1970 and 1989. *Higher Education, 30,* 353-368.

Berger, C. R., & Calabrese, R. J. (1975). Some exploration in initial interactions and beyond. *Human Communication Research, 1,* 99-112.

Beyer, P. (1994). *Religion and globalization.* London: Sage.

Boli, J., & Thomas, G. M. (1997). World culture in the world polity: A century of international nongovernmental organization. *American Sociological Review, 62,* 171-190.

Bormann, E. G. (1983). Symbolic convergence: Organizational communication and culture. In L. L. Putnam & M. E. Pacanowsky (Eds.), *Communication and organizations: An interpretive approach* (pp. 99-122). Beverly Hills, CA: Sage.

Castells, M. (1994). European cities, the information society, and the global economy. *New Left Review, 204,* 18-32.

Choi, Y. (1993). *Global networks in communication, transportation, and trade.* Unpublished doctoral dissertation, State University of New York at Buffalo.

Choi, Y., & Ahn, M. (1996). Telecommunication, transportation, and trade networks of 15 European countries. *Gazette, 58,* 81-106.

D'Andrade, R. G. (1984). Cultural meaning systems. In R. A. Shweder & R. A. LeVine (Eds.), *Cultural theory: Essays on mind, self, and emotion* (pp. 88-119). Cambridge, UK: Cambridge University Press.

Durkheim, É. (1938). *The rules of sociological method* (2nd ed., S. A. Sulovay & J. H. Mueller, Trans., G. C. Catlin, Ed.). Glencoe, IL: Free Press.

Durkheim, É. (1953). *Sociology of philosophy* (D. F. Pocock, Ed.). Glencoe, IL: Free Press.

Ellingsworth, H. (1977). Conceptualizing intercultural communication. In B. Ruben (Ed.), *Communication yearbook 1* (pp. 99-106). New Brunswick, NJ: Transaction.

Frederick, H. H. (1993). *Global communication and international relations.* Belmont, CA: Wadsworth.

Geertz, C. (1973). *The interpretation of cultures.* New York: Basic Books.

Giddens, A. (1979). *Central problem in social theory.* Berkeley: University of California Press.

Giddens, A. (1990). *The consequences of modernity.* Stanford, CA: Stanford University Press.

Goodenough, W. H. (1964). Cultural anthropology and linguistics. In D. Hymes (Ed.), *Language in culture and society* (pp. 36-39). New York: Harper & Row.

Granovetter, M. (1973). The strength of weak ties. *American Journal of Sociology, 73,* 1361-1380.

Gudykunst, W. B. (1995). Anxiety/uncertainty management (AUM) theory: Current status. In R. L. Wiseman (Ed.), *Intercultural communication theory* (pp. 8-58). Thousand Oaks, CA: Sage.

Gudykunst, W. B., & Kim, Y. Y. (1997). *Communicating with strangers: An approach to intercultural communication* (3rd ed.). New York: McGraw-Hill.

Gudykunst, W. B., Wiseman, R. L., & Hammer, M. (1977). Determinants of a sojourner's attitudinal satisfaction. In B. Ruben (Ed.), *Communication yearbook 1* (pp. 415-426). New Brunswick, NJ: Transaction.

Gudykunst, W. B., Yang, S., & Nishida, T. (1985). A cross-cultural test of uncertainty reduction theory. *Human Communication Research, 11,* 407-454.

Hamelink, C. J. (1990). Globalism and national sovereignty. In K. Nordenstreng & H. I. Schiller (Eds.), *Beyond national sovereignty: International communication in the 1990s* (pp. 371-393). Norwood, NJ: Ablex.

Herman, E. S., & McChesney, R. W. (1997). *The global media.* London: Cassell.

Hofstede, G. (1980). *Culture's consequences: International differences in work-related values.* Beverly Hills, CA: Sage.

Holaday, D., Xiaoming, H., & Hong, L. T. (1998). Television an identity in Singapore: The Chinese majority. *Media Asia, 25*(2), 78-87.

Hudson, H. E. (1997). *Global connections: International telecommunications infrastructure and policy.* New York: John Wiley.

Jacobson, H. K. (1979). *Networks and interdependence: International organizations and the global political system.* New York: Knopf.

Johnson, J. D., & Tuttle, F. (1989). Problems in intercultural research. In M. K. Asante & W. B. Gudykunst (Eds.), *Handbook of international and intercultural communication* (pp. 461-483). Newbury Park, CA: Sage.

Kenny, J. F. (1998). Peripheral vision: A perspective on foreign and urban-center television from rural Philippines. *Gazette, 60*(4), 281-303.

Kim, C. (1998, July). *The changing structures of global arms trade 1987-1994: A network analysis on major conventional weapons trade.* Paper presented at a meeting of the International Communication Association, Jerusalem, Israel.

Kim, K., & Barnett, G. A. (1996). The determinants of international news flow: A network analysis. *Communication Research, 23,* 323-352.

Kim, K., & Barnett, G. A. (2000). The structure of the international telecommunications regime in transition: A network analysis of international organizations. *International Interactions, 26,* 91-127.

Kim, Y. Y. (1986). Understanding the social content of intergroup communication: A personal network approach. In W. Gudykunst (Ed.), *Intergroup communications* (pp. 86-95). London: Edward Arnold.

Kim, Y. Y. (1988). *Communication and cross-cultural adaptation: An integrative approach.* Avon, UK: Multilingual Matters.

Kim, Y. Y. (1989). Intercultural adaptation. In M. K. Asante & W. B. Gudykunst (Eds.), *Handbook of international and intercultural communication* (pp. 275-294). Newbury Park, CA: Sage.

Kim, Y. Y. (2000). Mapping the domain of intercultural communication: An overview. In W. B. Gudykunst (Ed.), *Communication yearbook 24.* Thousand Oaks, CA: Sage.

Kincaid, D. L., Yum, J. O., Woelfel, J., & Barnett, G. A. (1983). The cultural convergence of Korean immigrants in Hawaii: An empirical test of a mathematical theory. *Quality and Quantity, 18,* 59-78.

Kluckhohn, C., & Kelly, W. H. (1945). The concept of culture. In R. Linton (Ed.), *The science of man in the world crisis* (pp. 78-106). New York: Columbia University Press.

Korzenny, F., Ting-Toomey, S., & Schiff, E. (1992). *Mass media effects across cultures.* Newbury Park, CA: Sage.

Lee, M. (2000). On studying organizational cultures and management styles of transnational corporations in Taiwan. *Mass Communication Research, 63,* 163-199.

Lee, M., & Barnett, G. A. (1997). A symbols and meaning approach to the organizational cultures of banks in the United States, Japan, and Taiwan. *Communication Research, 24,* 394-412.

Lemish, D. (1998). Global culture in practice: A look at children and adolescents in Denmark, France and Israel. *European Journal of Communication, 13*(4), 539-556.7

Massey, D. S. (1988). Economic development and international migration in comparative perspective. *Population and Development Review, 14,* 383-413.

Massey, D. S., Arango, J., Hugo, G., Kouaouci, A., Pellegrino, A., & Taylor, J. E. (1993). Theories of international migration: A review and appraisal. *Population and Development Review, 19*(3), 431-466.

Massey, D. S., & Espana, F. G. (1987). The social process of international migration. *Science, 237,* 733-738.

McLuhan, H. M. (1966). *Understanding media: The extension of man.* New York: Beacon.

Meyer, J. W., Boli, J., Thomas, G. M., & Ramirez, F. O. (1997). World society and the nation-state. *American Journal of Sociology, 103*(1), 144-181.

Monge, P. R., & Fulk, J. (1999). Communication technology for global network organizations. In G. DeSanctis & J. Fulk (Eds.), *Shaping organizational form: Communication, connection, and* community (pp. 71-100). Thousand Oaks, CA: Sage.

Nieberg, H. L. (1973). *Cultural storm: Politics and the ritual order.* New York: St. Martin's.

Nordenstreng, K., & Varis, T. (1974). *Television traffic—A one-way street?* (Reports and Papers on Mass Communication No. 70). Paris: UNESCO.

Park, R. E. (1928). Human migration and the marginal man. *American Journal of Sociology, 33,* 881-893.

Parsons, T. (1968). *The structure of social action.* New York: Free Press.

Pieterse, J. N. (1995). Globalization as hybridization. In M. Featherstone, S. Lash, & R. Robertson (Eds.), *Global modernities* (pp. 45-68). Thousand Oaks, CA: Sage.

Poole, M. S. (1994). The structuring of organizational climates. In L. Thayer & G. A. Barnett (Eds.), *Organization ↔ communication: Emerging perspectives: Vol. 4. The renaissance in systems thinking* (pp. 74-113). Greenwich, CT: Ablex.

Robertson, R. (1990). Mapping the global condition: Globalization as the central concept. *Theory, Culture & Society, 7,* 15-30.

Robertson, R. (1992). *Globalization: Social theory and global culture.* Newbury Park, CA: Sage.

Rogers, E. M. (1999). Georg Simmel's concept of the stranger in intercultural communication research. *Communication Theory, 9,* 58-74.

Rogers, E. M., & Kincaid, D. L. (1981). *Communication networks: Toward a new paradigm for research.* New York: Free Press.

Salisbury, J. G. T., & Barnett, G. A. (1999). A network analysis of international monetary flows. *The Information Society, 15,* 1-19.

Schott, T. (1993). World science: Globalization of institutions and participation. *Science, Technology & Human Values, 18,* 196-208.

Singelis, T. M., & Brown, W. J. (1995). Culture, self, and collectivist communication: Linking culture to individual behavior. *Human Communication Research, 21,* 354-389.

Smith, D. A., & Timberlake, M. F. (2001). World city networks and hierarchies, 1977-1997: An empirical analysis of global air travel links.

American Behavioral Scientist, 44(10), 1656-1678.

Smith, L. R. (1999). Intercultural network theory: A cross-paradigmatic approach to acculturation. *International Journal of Intercultural Relations, 23,* 629-658.

Triandis, H. C., Vassiliou, V., Vassiliou, G., Tanaka, Y., & Shanmugan, A. V. (1972). *The analysis of subjective culture.* New York: John Wiley.

Varan, D. (1998). The cultural erosion metaphor and the transcultural impact of media systems. *Journal of Communication, 48(2),* 58-85.

Varis, T. (1984). International flow of television programs. *Journal of Communication, 34(1),* 143-152.

Ware, W., & Dupagne, M. (1994). Effects of U.S. television programs on foreign audiences: A meta-analysis. *Journalism Quarterly, 71,* 947-959.

Wasserman, S., & Faust, K. (1994). *Social network analysis: Methods and applications.* Cambridge, UK: Cambridge University Press.

Waters, M. (1995). *Globalization.* London and New York: Routledge.

Weimann, G. (1982). On the importance of marginality: One more step into the two-step flow of communication. *American Sociological Review, 47,* 764-773.

Weimann, G. (1983). The not-so-small world: Ethnicity and acquaintance networks in Israel. *Social Networks, 5,* 245-267.

Weimann, G. (1989). Social networks and communication. In M. K. Asante & W. B. Gudykunst (Eds.), *Handbook of international and intercultural communication* (pp. 186-203). Newbury Park, CA: Sage.

Yum, J. O. (1984). Network analysis. In W. B. Gudykunst & Y. Y. Kim (Eds.), *Methods for intercultural communication research* (pp. 95-116). Beverly Hills, CA: Sage.

Yum, J. O. (1988). Network theory in intercultural communication. In Y. Y. Kim & W. B. Gudykunst (Eds.), *Theories in intercultural communication* (pp. 239-258). Newbury Park, CA: Sage.

Yum, J. O., & Wang, G. (1983). Interethnic perception and the communication behavior among five ethnic groups in Hawaii. *International Journal of Intercultural Relations, 7,* 285-308.

Author Index

Subject Index

About the Editor

William B. Gudykunst is Professor of Speech Communication and a faculty member in Asian American Studies at California State University, Fullerton. He is author of *Bridging Differences* and *Asian American Ethnicity and Communication,* as well as coauthor of *Culture and Interpersonal Communication, Communicating with Strangers,* and *Bridging Japanese/North American Differences,* among others. He has edited or coedited numerous books including *Communication in Japan and the United States, Theories of Intercultural Communication,* and *Communication in Personal Relationships Across Cultures. Communicating with Strangers* and *Culture and Interpersonal Communication* received the Outstanding Book Award from the International and Intercultural Division of the Speech Communication Association. He is a past editor of the *International and Intercultural Communication Annual* and *Communication Yearbook,* and a Fellow of the International Communication Association.

About the Contributors

Jessica Abrams is a doctoral student in communication at the University of California, Santa Barbara. She studies intergroup communication and has a particular interest in understanding how intergroup identity affects communication.

Peter A. Andersen, Professor of Communication at San Diego State University, was the recipient of the Outstanding Faculty award from the Alumni Association for 2000. He is author of three books—*The Handbook of Communication and Emotion*; *Nonverbal Communication, Forms and Functions*; and *Close Encounters: Communication in Interpersonal Relationships*—and more than 100 book chapters and journal articles. He was recognized in 2000 as one of the 100 most prolific scholars in the history of the communication field. He has served as president of the Western Communication Association and editor of the *Western Journal of Communication*.

George A. Barnett is Professor in the School of Information Studies at the State University of New York at Buffalo. He is editor of *Progress in Communication Sciences*. He has authored numerous articles on mass, organizational, political, and international/intercultural communication, as well as the diffusion of communication technologies. His current research examines the international flow of information and its role in the process of globalization.

Ling Chen is Associate Professor of Communication Studies at Hong Kong Baptist University. Her research interests include intercultural communication, Chinese communication, organizational communication, and language and social interaction. Her work has been published in journals such as *Communication Monographs, International Journal of Intercultural Relations, Communication Research,* and *Management Communication Quarterly.*

Jung-Wook Choi received B.A. degrees from Dong-Eui University in Korea and San Francisco State University. Currently, she is an M.A. student in sociology at San Jose State University.

Brenda Franklin is an M.A. student at San Francisco State University. She plans to pursue a Ph.D. in clinical-community psychology and develop prevention and intervention programs for at-risk youth. Her current research interests include culture and emotion, and particularly the role of experienced emotion in stereotype formation.

Howard Giles is Professor of Communication at the University of California, Santa Barbara. His research interests encompass an array of intercultural and intergroup arenas, with a current focus on intergenerational communication patterns around the Pacific Rim and police-citizen encounters. He is a Fellow and past president of the International Communication Association.

Michael L. Hecht is Professor and head of the Department of Speech Communication at Pennsylvania State University. He has written on topics such as communicating prejudice, interethnic communication, communication and identity, nonverbal communication, interpersonal communication, and adolescent relationships and drug use. He has a decade-long project to study adolescent drug resistance strategies and develop culturally appropriate adolescent drug abuse prevention curriculum. He teaches courses on ethnicity and communication, research methodology, interpersonal relationships, nonverbal communication, and communication theory.

Gregory Hoobler is a doctoral student and University Distinguished Fellow at Michigan State University specializing in international conflict. He received his MA degree from San Diego State University and has taught and published in the areas of international conflict negotiation and diplomacy, intercultural communication, leadership and group communication, and nonverbal communication.

Young Yun Kim is Professor of Communication at the University of Oklahoma. Her research has been aimed primarily at explaining the role of communication in the cross-cultural adaptation process. She has conducted research in the United States among Asians, Hispanics, American Indians, and European Americans. She has published over 60 journal articles and book chapters, and has

authored or edited 11 books including *Interethnic Communication* (1986), *Communication and Cross-Cultural Adaptation* (1988), *Becoming Intercultural: An Integrative Theory of Communication and Cross-Cultural Adaptation* (2001), and *Communicating with Strangers* (4th ed., 2003, with W. Gudykunst). She is a Fellow of the International Communication Association.

Carmen M. Lee is a doctoral student in communication at the University of California, Santa Barbara. Her research interests focus on intercultural communication, especially intercultural attraction. She has presented papers at regional and international conferences and published articles in the *Journal of Family Communication* and *International Journal of Intercultural Relations*.

Meihua Lee is Associate Professor of Mass Communication at Tamkang University in Taipei. Her research interests include the impact of the American media and interpersonal contacts on the Chinese culture of Taiwan.

Tae-Seop Lim is Professor at the School of Media and Communication Studies, Kwangwoon University. His research interests include intercultural communication, language and social interaction, interpersonal communication, and speech communication.

David Matsumoto is Professor of Psychology and Director of the Culture and Emotion Research Laboratory at San Francisco State University. His research focuses on emotion, human interaction, and culture. He is author of about 250 works on culture and emotion, including original research articles, paper presentations, books, book chapters, videos, and assessment instruments. He has made invited addresses to professional and scientific groups in the United States and internationally.

Joan O'Connor is a doctoral candidate in communication at the University of California, Santa Barbara. Her research interests focus on issues of identity, self-disclosure, and social stigma. Current projects address assault disclosure among adult and adolescent women and the willingness to report sexual violence to public agencies.

John G. Oetzel is Associate Professor in the Department of Communication and Journalism at the University of New Mexico. His research interests include understanding the influence of cultural diversity in work groups and organizational communication, particularly conflict communication. His publications have appeared in journals such as *Human Communication Research, International Journal of Intercultural Relations,* and *Management Communication Quarterly.* He is coauthor of *Managing Intercultural Conflicts Effectively* (with Stella Ting-Toomey, 2001).

Gerry Philipsen is Professor and Chair of the Department of Speech Communication at the University of Washington. His research interests are cultural communication, ethnographic methods in communication research, American cultures, the discourse of social difference, and group decision making.

David Rogers is an M.A. student in psychology at San Francisco State University. His current interests embody cross-cultural issues and emotion. In the future, he plans to investigate humor and laughter from a cultural perspective.

Maya Smallwood is an M.A. candidate in communication theory at Pennsylvania State University. She was awarded a Ford Foundation Pre-Doctoral Fellowship in 1998. Her areas of interest include the communication of cultural identities, interethnic relations in

organizations, philosophy of communication, and nonverbal communication.

Cookie White Stephan is a professor emeritus of sociology at New Mexico State University. Her major research focus is on intergroup relations. She has conducted studies of intercultural relations in Japan, Costa Rica, Russia, and Morocco. With Walter Stephan, she is author of *Improving Intergroup Relations* (2002) and *Intergroup Relations in Multicultural Education Programs* (in press); with L. R. Renfro and W. G. Stephan, "The Evaluation of Multicultural Education Programs: Techniques and a Meta-Analysis," in J. A. Banks & C. A. M. Banks (Eds.), *Handbook of Research on Multicultural Education* (2nd ed., in press); and is a contributor to a forthcoming special issue of the *Journal of Social Issues: On Improving Arab-Jewish Relations in Israel: Theory and Practice in Coexistence Education Programs.*

Walter G. Stephan is Professor of Psychology at New Mexico State University. He has published articles on attribution processes, cognition and affect, intergroup relations, and intercultural relations. He wrote *Reducing Prejudice and Stereotyping in the Schools* (1998) and is coauthor with Cookie Stephan of *Improving Intergroup Relations* (2002).

Haruyo Tatani is a facilitator in intercultural communication for corporations and public institutions in Japan and the United States. Her research interests focus on intercultural adaptability potential.

Stella Ting-Toomey is Professor of Speech Communication at California State University, Fullerton. She is author or editor of 13 books, most recently, *Communicating Across Cultures* (1999), *Communicating Effectively With the Chinese* (coauthored, 1998), and *Managing Intercultural Conflict Effectively* (coauthored, 2002). Her research interests focus on testing face-negotiation theory and identity negotiation theory. She has held major leadership roles in international communication associations and has served on numerous editorial boards.

Richard L. Wiseman is Professor of Speech Communication at California State University, Fullerton. His areas of expertise are intercultural communication, nonverbal communication, persuasion, and instructional communication. He has published more than 50 articles in these areas in professional journals. He also has served as the editor of the *International and Intercultural Communication Annual.* He has served as an officer in several professional associations and is currently Chair of the Intercultural and Development Division of the International Communication Association.

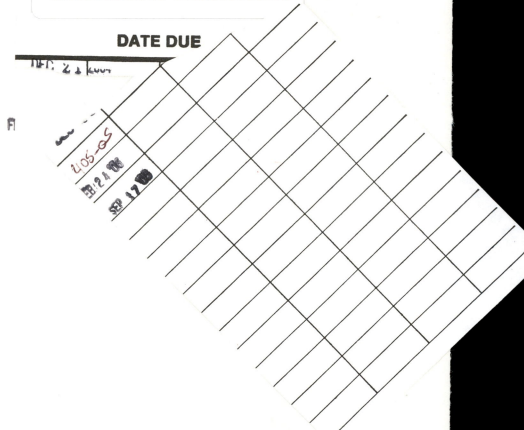